In the Shadow of El Tajín

CONFLUENCIAS

Series Editors

Susie S. Porter
University of Utah

María L. O. Muñoz
Susquehanna University

Diana Montaño
Washington University in St. Louis

IN THE SHADOW OF EL TAJÍN

The Political Economy of
Archaeology in Modern Mexico

Sam Holley-Kline

University of Nebraska Press ◆ Lincoln

Acknowledgments for the use of previously published material appear on page xvii, which constitutes an extension of the copyright page.

The University of Nebraska Press is part of a land-grant institution with campuses and programs on the past, present, and future homelands of the Pawnee, Ponca, Otoe-Missouria, Omaha, Dakota, Lakota, Kaw, Cheyenne, and Arapaho Peoples, as well as those of the relocated Ho-Chunk, Sac and Fox, and Iowa Peoples.

∞

For customers in the EU with safety/GPSR concerns, contact:
gpsr@mare-nostrum.co.uk
Mare Nostrum Group BV
Mauritskade 21D
1091 GC Amsterdam
The Netherlands

Library of Congress Control Number: 2025002765

Designed and set in Adobe Jenson Pro by L. Welch.

Contents

Illustrations

Tables

Preface

In 1952 American anthropologist Isabel Kelly published a short article for *Mexican Life* titled "In the Shadow of El Tajín." Kelly used this visual metaphor to contrast the "cluster of thirty-odd homes" comprising the Indigenous Totonac community of El Tajín, "all but hidden by the dense green vegetation of the tropical rainforest," with the well-known Pyramid of the Niches and the town of Papantla.[1] Kelly was right that the fame of the archaeological site overshadowed the experiences of the Totonac residents of El Tajín. Yet that overshadowing was not a coincidence. It was a legacy of disciplinary knowledge production and state heritage management, both of which elevated a particular period of the pre-Hispanic past over all other regional histories. Overlooked were the histories and concerns of the inhabitants of those households. This book is about them.

Gregory Younging suggests that following the Indigenous communities at the center of a work "means declaring your limitations as an arbiter of language: explain the choices and thought that inform the words on the page."[2] When referring to those who reckon their descent from the cultures that predate the coming of the Spaniards, I use "Indigenous," as an adjective and capitalized.[3] While still derived from colonial efforts to deal with difference, "Indigenous" at least avoids the racialized category of "Indian," which is often pejorative in Mexico. When possible, I use more specific self-designations. I use "Totonac" as the most direct English translation of *totonaca* or *totonaco*, which is the most common way that the residents of El Tajín and the surrounding communities refer to their Indigenous identities (though *tutunakú*, a Totonac-language self-description, is also gaining currency).

The most common terms used to refer to Indigenous cultures before 1492—pre-Columbian, pre-contact, pre-Hispanic, precolonial—are unsatisfactory, insofar as they locate the existence of these cultures with reference to the colonial period: "A by-product of relentless boundary maintenance, the 'pre' does not constitute a historical era.... It is a narrative space auto-populated by features that define temporal Otherness for the self-consciously modern observer."[4] Nevertheless, I use pre-Hispanic for its frequent use in Mexican law and scholarly literature, and precolonial more generally to emphasize the existence of non-Spanish colonial efforts in Mexican and Totonac territories. I also use the term "Mesoamerican," which has the advantage of defining the cultures in question without explicit reference to the colonial period. However, the term is not neutral: scholars have critiqued the frequent association of Mesoamerica with "ancient Mexico," tying deep and diverse Indigenous pasts to a modern state.[5]

Other terms will be best left untranslated. The employees of Mexico's federal Instituto Nacional de Antropología e Historia charged with maintaining and protecting archaeological sites are nowadays called *custodios*. In the past, they have been called *conserjes, vigilantes, peones,* and *guardianes,* among others. This work is wide-ranging: custodios are caretakers, landscapers, civil servants, guards, customer service professionals, educators, and sentinels. Consistently translating the term into English—as custodian or guard, for instance—would narrow this breadth and evoke associations not otherwise associated with their labor. Following recent scholarship on the Porfirian Inspectorate of Monuments, I also use *conserje*. Along similar lines, many of those interviewed for this study identified themselves as *de campo*, or working as *campesinos*. This term broadly refers to subsistence cultivation with access to land, and it is often translated as "peasant." This English-language term, however, recalls long-running scholarly debates on the topic and carries complex connotations today, not all of which are positive.[6] I thus leave the term untranslated. Another term refers to the expert Indigenous interlocutors who shared their time and experiences with me. In Native American and Indigenous studies and adjacent fields, these people are often called Elders.[7] In this book, I use the term *abuelo*. Most often translated as "grandfather" or "grandparent," Totonac residents of the communities around El Tajín use *abuelo* as a term of respectful address for older generations and to emphasize specific genealogical relationships. I leave the term untranslated to evoke these overlapping associations.

This book stems from research conducted for a doctorate in anthropology. I followed both the conventions of the field and the procedures I submitted for the Stanford University Institutional Review Board (28865) in anonymizing my interviews. I do not know that I would do the same today. As Margot

Weiss has observed, "Normative forms of writing . . . [may] reproduce an extractive mode of knowledge production by refusing to acknowledge our interlocutors as cotheorizers, even (ironically) when this is precisely what we are writing against."[8] Naming, citation, and acknowledgment are ways of recognizing experts and expertise, as I discuss in the introduction. However, because I conducted these interviews under conditions of anonymity, I use pseudonyms for specific interviewees. All translations from Spanish are mine unless otherwise noted.

Acknowledgments

> El secreto, por lo demás, no vale lo que valen los caminos que me
> condujeron a él. Esos caminos hay que andarlos.
>
> —Jorge Luis Borges, "El etnógrafo," *Elogio de la sombra*

What became this project began during an undergraduate semester abroad
in 2011. At DePauw University, Alejandro Puga encouraged my interest in all
things Mexico, figured out my interest in archaeology before I did, and invited
me to participate in my first field research. Rebecca Upton introduced me to
theorizing and anthropology. Angela Castañeda taught me the ethnographic
methods that I used throughout graduate school and beyond. I owe a special
thanks to Rob Kruger in Xalapa for supporting my interest in Mesoamerican archaeology during that semester abroad and since. I also owe a debt of
gratitude to Maggie Morgan-Smith, who accepted me for three field seasons
on the Bolonchen Regional Archaeological Project. My understanding of
archaeological practice owes much to my participation on that project, to the
collegiality of Ken Seligson, Evan Parker, and Tomás Gallareta Cervera, and
to the support of project directors George Bey III, the late William Ringle,
and Tomás Gallareta Negrón.

My debts in Mexico are too many to list, but I can try. S. Jeffrey K. Wilk-
erson, Victoria Chenaut, the late Álvaro Brizuela Absalón, Daniel Nahmad
Molinari, Patricia Castillo Peña, María Guadalupe Espinoza Rodríguez,
Arturo Pascual Soto, Andrés Curti Díaz, José Luis Rodríguez Badillo, Ser-
gio Rivera Nasser, the late Rocio Aguilera Madero, and the late Víctor Poo
Echaniz generously shared their time, perspectives, and expertise on the Gulf
Coast, past and present. Jesús Eduardo Medina Gutiérrez assisted me with
laborious transcriptions of interviews and payroll documents. I was fortunate
to meet other scholars of El Tajín and the Totonac region while in the field.
Conversations with Luis Cabrera Rodríguez, Mónica Salas Landa, Montserrat

Rebollo Cruz, Svenja Schöneich, Amilcar Vargas, Jazmin Jaimes Reyes, Karla Beltrán Rosas, Erika María Méndez Martínez, and Francisco Javier López Vallejo continually enriched my perspectives. I was likewise fortunate to cross paths with Judith Álva Sánchez, Benjamin Blaisot, Lilia Bermúdez Rojas, Marilú Tognola, Ana Elba Casarín, Juan Ángel García González, Antonio Hernández Monfil, and Fernando Cruz Ticante in El Tajín; their friendships were integral to the success of this project at different points in the process. Despite changes in employment over the years, Jesús Trejo González and Elizeth Rivera Atzin remain steadfast friends.

This work would have been impossible without the support of archivists in Mexico City, Xalapa, Veracruz, and Dallas. I thank the late José Luis Ramírez, José Humberto Medina González, and Ana Torreblanca Muñoz of the INAH's Archivo Técnico; Fernando Sansores, Paola Pacheco, and Jonathan López of the Archivo Histórico Institucional del INAH; Armando Aguilar Ruiz of the Archivo Histórico del Centro INAH Veracruz; Gabriela Mota of the Fototeca Nacional; Brenda Marín of the Fototeca del Centro INAH Veracruz; Juan Eloy Rivera Velázquez of the Archivo General del Estado de Veracruz; and Azucena Espíndola of the Archivo Histórico de Petróleos Mexicanos. Terre Heydari, Anne Peterson, and Cindy Boeke of Southern Methodist University's DeGolyer Library made my research in the Isabel T. Kelly Ethnographic Archive a highlight of my research. During the COVID-19 pandemic, the online resources made available by HathiTrust, the Internet Archive, and El Colegio de México were invaluable; I thank these institutions for their work.

I was only able to develop these relationships thanks to the support offered by a variety of Mexican institutions. Juan Pablo Zebadúa Carbonell, then of the Universidad Veracruzana Intercultural Sede Totonacapan, provided a letter of affiliation for my initial fieldwork. With the support of Victoria Chenaut once again, the Centro de Investigaciones y Estudios Superiores en Antropología Social Unidad Golfo granted me an *estudiante huésped* position for my dissertation fieldwork. The late Pedro Francisco Sánchez Nava signed multiple permissions on behalf of the Coordinación Nacional de Arqueología, and Baltazar Brito Guardarrama on behalf of the Biblioteca Nacional de Antropología e Historia. As successive directors of El Tajín, Adolfo Vergara Mejía, Rogelio Rivero Chong, Jesús Trejo González, and the late Olaf-Jaime Riverón all welcomed me to Tajín with *todas las facilidades*. The H. Ayuntamiento of Papantla under Marcos González Romero and the H. Ayuntamiento of

Coatzintla under César Ulises García Vázquez both provided me with letters of recommendation that did much to facilitate my research in the region's communities. The (sub)agentes municipales of those same communities, too, allowed me to present at their assemblies, introduced me to potential interviewees, and welcomed me to the area more generally. Thank you especially to Gumersindo Morales of El Tajín, Marta García of San Antonio Ojital, Manuel Castaño of Nuevo Ojital, Camerino Simbrón of San Lorenzo Tajín, Donato Santes of Zapotal Santa Cruz, Rodrigo García of Lagunilla, Sergio Lorenzo García of Plan del Palmar, and Salvador Pérez of Plan de Hidalgo.

In the community of El Tajín, my debts are more dispersed; the support and friendship I have received for the past decade enriched my life far beyond this study. Primitivo Pérez de Luna and Carmela García Xochihua and their family—Lidia, Diana, Yazmina, Miriam, and Fabián—were among the first to welcome me to Tajín. Alma García Reyes provided a gracious living space, and her children—Arsenio, Alejandro, Héctor, Araceli, Magaly, and Filemón—treated me like family. Juan García Elías, Ireneo Méndez González, Epifania González Méndez, Francisco de León Pérez, Melitón Juárez García, Epifanio de León Méndez, Francisco García Xochihua, José Xochihua Ibarra, Eva Juárez Méndez, the late Maclovio Calderón Loreto, and their families were among those who always welcomed me to their houses. Outside of El Tajín, the late Agustín González Blas, Alejandrino García Méndez, José Luis González, Juan Salazar, Romualdo García de Luna, the late Valente Santes Méndez, and their families generously received me on multiple occasions in their respective communities.

At Stanford University, this project developed into a dissertation. Coursework laid the foundations: thank you especially to Paulla Ebron, Sharika Thiranagama, and Lochlann Jain for their teaching. Annalisa Bolin, Claudia Liuzza, Sabrina Papazian, Nathan Acebo, Misha Bykowski, Grace Alexandrino Ocaña, Paul Christians, Sam Maull, and Jasmine Reid were among those who provided friendship and solidarity. I could not have asked for a better dissertation committee. Ian Hodder, Miyako Inoue, and Rosemary Joyce dedicated time, effort, and expertise to my work. Lynn Meskell was, and remains, a model advisor: supportive, consistent, and ever generous with her feedback. I owe this book's particular orientation to the generosity of historians who shared sources and ideas with me at various stages of the project; thank you to Christina Bueno, Larissa Kennedy Kelly, Andrés Bustamante Agudelo, and Haydeé López Hernández.

At Florida State University, that dissertation developed into a book. Colleagues in the Department of History supported me at every stage of the writing process. Thank you to Suzanne Sinke, Robinson Herrera, and the late Edward Gray for their supportive mentorship. While at FSU, friends and colleagues near and far read chapter drafts for this book. Thanks to Kyle Olson, Trinidad Rico, Morgan V. Leathem, Dick Powis, María Fernanda Escallón, and Allison Mickel. Laura Heath-Stout and Maia Dedrick deserve special thanks for reading drafts of every section of this book and for their friendship during difficult times. Eben Levey invited me to present this manuscript in his graduate course; comments from Eben, along with Kent Kiser and Joshua Dunlap, aided me in completing a final round of revisions. Developmental editor Erin Martineau's feedback sharpened this study's argumentation and style, Erin Greb's illustrations markedly enhanced the presentation of visual material, and Kerin Tate's copyediting significantly improved the book's polish. From the University of Nebraska Press, I had the benefit of Bridget Barry's and Emily Casillas's supportive guidance throughout the process. I thank Lisa Pinley Covert and an anonymous reviewer for their thoughtful reader reports, as well as Susie Porter for her feedback on a revised manuscript draft.

In material terms, this book depended on a variety of funding sources and agencies for support: a Fulbright-García Robles (IIE) All-Disciplines Award to Mexico; the Stanford Archaeology Center and the Stanford Center for Latin American Studies; a Wenner-Gren Foundation for Anthropological Research Dissertation Fieldwork Grant; a Fulbright-Hays Doctoral Dissertation Research Abroad Fellowship; the Freeman-Spogli Institute; the Stanford University School of Humanities & Sciences; the Office of the Vice Provost for Graduate Education; the Program in History & Philosophy of Science at Stanford; and the Florida State University Department of History all supported my field-based research. The Stanford Institute for Research in the Social Sciences, the Stanford Humanities Center, the Florida State University Department of History, and the American Council of Learned Societies supported my writing at various stages.

Family, near and far, likewise supported my efforts. Thanks to my family, Rachel Holley, Dan Kline, and Jacob Holley-Kline, this project always seemed possible. Julianne and Tony Pederson hosted me in Dallas for three months, enriching both my research and family relationships. Kevin E. and Rachel O'Brien Kline, as well as Kay and Bob Wood, provided material and moral support throughout. Over the years, my biggest support has been Stephanie

Claire Wood. Our relationship evolved in tandem with this project. We met at DePauw around October 2010, shortly before that semester abroad. I submitted the final draft of this book fourteen years later, with our cats Syllabus, Merlot, and Hallie loafing about and our daughter, Rachel Kay Holley-Kline, nestled in the crook of my arm. This book is for them.

Portions of chapter 1 previously appeared in "Archaeology, Land Tenure, and Indigenous Dispossession in Mexico," *Journal of Social Archaeology* 22, no. 3 (2022): 255–76, https://doi.org/10.1177/14696053221112608. Copyright 2022 by Sam Holley-Kline. Reprinted by permission of Sage Publications.

Portions of chapter 2 previously appeared in "Nationalist Archaeology and Foreign Oil Exploration in El Tajín, Mexico, 1935–1940," *Archaeological Dialogues* 27, no. 1 (2020): 79–93, https://doi.org/10.1017/s1380203820000100. Copyright 2020 by Cambridge University Press. Reproduced with permission.

Portions of chapter 4 previously appeared in "Archaeology, Wage Labor, and Kinship in Rural Mexico, 1934–1974," *Ethnohistory* 69, no. 2 (2022): 197–221, https://doi.org/10.1215/00141801-9522189. Copyright 2022 by the American Society for Ethnohistory. All rights reserved. Republished by permission of the copyright holder and the publisher. www.dukeupress.edu.

In the Shadow of El Tajín

Introduction

The exchange of words and deeds between ourselves and others is inevitably charged by the political and economic inequalities that structure the world we all live in.

—Paul Sullivan, *Unfinished Conversations: Mayas and Foreigners Between Two Wars*

August 2019: The men heard the echoes of heavy machinery from somewhere to the north. Soon, El Tajín's *custodios* would be busy tending to the vacation-season tourists, but visitors had yet to arrive. A few custodios took the path winding around the outskirts of the site to the trails used by the Indigenous Totonac residents of San Antonio Ojital. Past the fields of corn and bananas, the custodios soon found the source of the racket. The moving backhoe's silhouette was clear against the morning sky, and it was entirely too close to the site. Everyone knew that there were pre-Hispanic mounds around here. Though located inside El Tajín's 1,221-hectare buffer zone, this particular parcel of land was private property. Clearly, the new owner's designs went beyond cultivation. The custodios observed, from a distance, and documented what they could.

Upon returning to El Tajín, the custodios would file a formal notification of the presumed destruction to the site authorities. The authorities, a local branch (or subdirectorate) of the federal Instituto Nacional de Antropología e Historia (INAH), hold legal responsibility for safeguarding Mexico's pre-Hispanic material culture and architecture. The site's archaeologist would intervene on behalf of the state and suspend the work until an archaeological study could be carried out to verify that the construction would not affect any pre-Hispanic materials. His predecessors had regularly done the same, halting the building of local commercial establishments, residences, and infrastructural projects so that site authorities could fulfill their mandate of protecting Mexico's pre-Hispanic heritage.

A scandal developed over the course of the following month. Contrary to expectations and normative responsibilities, the archaeologist did not suspend the work. Stories circulated that those now clearing the newly purchased parcel carried rifles. With insecurity a fact of daily life in this part of rural Veracruz, the legal authority to suspend work that threatened the pre-Hispanic past seemed ineffectual. Residents of San Antonio Ojital complained bitterly to the local press: archaeologists seemed to always intervene to stop the unauthorized drilling of artesian wells and the construction of roads, but this property owner could all but level his ten-hectare parcel? The site custodios continued to denounce the apparent destruction to the local press and to the INAH's state office, the Centro INAH Veracruz (CIV). Memos and cosigned letters flew from El Tajín to the CIV and the INAH in Mexico City as the custodios continued with their local media campaign. How could this destruction have been allowed to continue?

Accusations continued as regional and national press agencies picked up on the local news stories: "Destruction of Archaeological Vestiges Continues in El Tajín," "Destruction of Cultural Heritage Denounced in El Tajín," "Dialogue between INAH and Custodios of El Tajín Broken."[1] A high-ranking archaeologist from the Centro INAH Veracruz traveled to the municipality of Papantla, inspected the site, and formally suspended the work; the INAH's director-general visited the parcel; and an army detachment arrived for a two-week stay, complete with regular patrols and drone surveys. A series of federal agencies opened investigations. INAH archaeologists sought to determine the extent of the damages, while officials posited that the destruction was linked to organized crime. The custodios charged that the INAH had simply failed in its responsibility to protect the site, and any proposed links with criminal organizations were excuses for negligence. By the end of August a memorandum from the site custodios made it to the hands of President Andrés Manuel López Obrador. In his daily press conference, he referenced the event and commented that "those who damage archaeological sites should be punished, [the sites] are cultural heritage [and] first-rate history for which we must care."[2] In the following few months, the unauthorized work stopped, the investigations continued, and tensions between custodios, the INAH, Totonac residents, and the authorities returned to their normal simmer.

The events of August 2019 were not unique in degree or kind, in El Tajín or elsewhere in Mexico. If anything, they were resolved relatively peacefully. The same could not be said of a 2019 conflict in Monte Albán, in which members of the community of Santa Cruz Xoxocotlán attempted to dislodge alleged squatters who claimed ownership of parcels inside the site's boundaries. At least one person died in the ensuing conflict.[3] Nor could this be said of the infamous Chinkultic massacre, when state and federal police killed six Maya residents occupying the eponymous archaeological site in 2008.[4] In the past few decades, Guatemala, Honduras, Colombia, Peru, Ecuador, and Brazil, among others, have seen conflict involving Indigenous or Afrodescendant communities and the operations of archaeology.[5] Yet the peaceful resolution of the incident discussed above belied a longer history of contestation. The legal responsibilities of the Mexican state and the relative fame of El Tajín, a UNESCO World Heritage Site and federal Zona de Monumentos Arque-ológicos, primed such conflicts for broader visibility.

One line of conflict was local, concerning the proper disposition of land and resources in a rural, largely Indigenous municipality.[6] Totonac communi-ties have lived around El Tajín since well before the Aztec-Spanish War of 1519–21, while state-led projects fundamentally changed the region's patterns of production and exchange during the late nineteenth and early twentieth centuries. Successive research projects, and efforts to administer the site, involved restrictions of land use that communities like San Antonio Ojital had vociferously protested since the 1890s. By the 2000s these restrictions meant that, for communities inside the buffer zone, something as simple as adding a room to one's house required going to an archaeologist with plans and paperwork. But where were those requirements for someone wealthy enough to buy ten hectares and hire heavy equipment to clear it, residents wondered? Why were residents' rights to their dwellings, land, and farms a source of constant friction with the INAH administration, here represented by an ever-shifting configuration of social scientists based in El Tajín?

A second set of conflicts was institutional, involving the inner workings of the INAH. Often described as a governmental monopoly on archaeology, the institution's broad objectives have been consistent since its 1939 founding: to "research, conserve, and disseminate the nation's archaeological, anthropo-logical, historical, and paleontological heritage to strengthen the identity and memory of the society that possesses it."[7] Those groups mentioned above—the custodios, the site subdirectorate, the Centro INAH Veracruz, and the INAH's

Mexico City offices—all formed part of this institution, working toward the aforementioned goal. In the day-to-day life at site, they were known by their respective place-names, with the broader INAH affiliation assumed: Tajín, Veracruz, México. But every turn of events brought these actors to cross purposes: the custodios criticized Tajín and sought to involve Veracruz, Veracruz leveraged its authority with Mexico City, and Mexico City either responded slowly but decisively, or sought to cover up Tajín's inaction (depending on one's perspective). The roots of these two lines of conflict lie in a complex series of relationships between diverse political-economic processes and the Totonac communities of north Veracruz.

In this book I aim to study archaeology less as a means of knowledge production and more as a mechanism of resource distribution that interacts with diverse sociohistorical processes—like transformations in land tenure, the development of export economies, and systems of labor—to shape possibilities for making a living in modern Mexico. As I will argue, the situated understandings of Indigenous interlocutors demonstrate how commonplace understandings of "archaeological site" tend to downplay the broader relationships of labor, production, and exchange that residents recognize as both significant to local history and necessary for understanding "the ways in which archaeology works in the world."[8]

The Political Economy of Archaeology in Historical Perspective

"Archaeology is what archaeologists do."[9] In Mexico, state archaeologists have historically worked not just in the study of the past through material remains but also in what is now called heritage management, involving the conservation, curation, management, and administration of archaeological materials and places in the present.[10] The result is "a craft industry financed by the Mexican state and justified by the joint aim of recuperating national glory and attracting mass tourism," focusing especially on the reconstruction of pre-Hispanic architecture.[11] Geographic specificity complements this practical breadth: archaeologists trained in Mexico tend to focus their research on Mesoamerica, and on delimited areas called sites.[12] What does it mean to call a place an "archaeological site"? Denis Byrne observes that archaeologists tend to "regard the archaeological record for any one period of the past as part of a landscape that belongs *in* that period and *to* that period" while "local peoples tend to absorb 'archaeological' traces into the lived reality of contemporary lives."[13]

The term "archaeological site" links the material remains of the past and the scientific study thereof to a location. This location is distinct from its surroundings in that it is archaeological, a place of the past. Yet not all pasts are created equal: "The bigger the material mass, the more easily it entraps us."[14] The name Chichén Itzá is more likely to evoke the iconic Castillo pyramid than the pre-Hispanic periphery or the "trees selectively left standing, discarded stones, paths, weeds, tourist stands, rest areas, waste disposal sites, and boundary-marking roads" that also form part of the modern "site."[15] Nor are all forms of studying the past created equal. Discussing "Maya archaeology" is more likely to conjure images of the monumental pre-Hispanic past than the nineteenth-century Caste War heritage of interest to many contemporary Maya people in Yucatán, even though both periods left material remains that have been studied archaeologically.[16] In the Mexican context, the relationship between these time periods is legally defined. Current heritage legislation defines archaeological monuments as "movable and immovable property that is a product of the cultures existing prior to the establishment of Hispanic culture in the national territory."[17] Legally, an archaeological site is pre-Hispanic. More recent works are, by definition, historical. The "archaeological site" label thus provides a location for conflicts like those discussed above, but continually redirects attention to the distant past, to particular ways of understanding history, and away from the products of more recent histories—including the broader political economy of archaeology.[18]

In this book, I use the descriptor "political economy of archaeology" in two overlapping but distinct senses. First, in a usage familiar to history and anthropology, I approach the archaeological site and its environs to understand the tendencies "governing the production and exchange of the material means of subsistence."[19] This emphasis avoids an artificial distinction between the discipline and its diverse political, social, and economic contexts, drawing attention to how the "imbrication of archaeology with global capitalism plays out in the crosscurrents of social class and economic fortunes or instability."[20] In this view, processes like changes in land tenure, the development of the oil industry, and the decline in vanilla production are relevant to archaeological concerns like the drawing of site boundaries, the machinery used for reconstruction, and site security—and vice versa. Second, I explore archaeology's "political economy of knowledge," seeking "to analyze the economic strategies and material mechanisms that operate behind discourses," after Silvia Rivera Cusicanqui.[21] Redirecting attention from the discursive politics of interpreting and appropriating the past, I focus on "circumstances associated with getting a living and the structures of power that shape and constrain activity" in archaeology.[22] I explore how campesinos working as wage laborers, unionized site guards, and expert heritage managers relate to archaeology not just as a knowledge-production enterprise, but as a job.

Thinking about the political economy of archaeology is a way of relating archaeology to its varied historical contexts, understanding the discipline according to those who make a living from it. In so doing I call attention to "the linkages between seemingly unrelated spheres and events," what Lynn Meskell has called the "hyperconnectivity" of cultural heritage.[23] Following this line of thinking enables me to put studies of archaeology and cultural heritage in dialogue with the well-developed historiography of political change and economic development in Mexico, here represented by studies by Victoria Chenaut, Michael Ducey, Emilio Kourí, and others. I seek to provide a productive contrast to approaches in archaeology that focus on changing interpretations of the past, the contributions of key scholars, and state appropriations of history.

The specificity of this perspective can be illustrated by contrast with other historiographies of archaeology and Mexico, especially those that focus on nationalism, looting, and tourism. Mexico is a foundational example of the concept of nationalist archaeology, and for good reason.[24] Since the Mexican Revolution of 1910, the Mexican state has employed archaeology for "the means it provides to exalt a nationalistic pride in their country," as "part of national integration and the formation of historical awareness."[25] As Ignacio Bernal wrote in his canonical history of the discipline, "The state is concerned not so much with the increase of knowledge as with the creation, by excavating and restoring suitable ruins, foci of national pride, of a greater feeling of continuity with the people's own past."[26] Works like Bernal's, Haydeé López Hernández argues, served "to establish an (invented) tradition that held the power of armed struggle, the management of the new nation (rejecting the Porfiriato) and of the scientific vanguard of the period."[27] Recent historiography questions the degree of rupture that came with the revolutionary generation.

Studies of Porfirian archaeology have demonstrated how the state passed laws, funded institutions, and rewrote national history to furnish evidence of a civilized pre-Hispanic past whose legacies were preserved by a modern state, on par with European appropriations of the ancient classical civilizations of Greece and Rome.[28] Despite later ideological changes, the state uses of the past key to the "Mexican School of Archaeology" or "Official Mexican Archaeology" are found in the dictatorship of Porfirio Díaz rather than in the revolutionary state that founded the INAH.[29] No study of archaeology in Mexico can exclude the state, and mine is no exception. However, Mónica Salas Landa rightfully cautions that centering elite imaginings of the pre-Hispanic past tends to overlook labor and practice.[30] In this book, the politics of archaeology are less about how the state leveraged archaeologists' interpretations than how archaeological practice mediated interactions between broader sociohistorical processes and Totonac communities.

Still, what I call the political economy of archaeology recalls two mainstays of research in the history and politics of archaeology in Mexico and further afield: looting and tourism. Classic research on looting drew archaeologists' attention to the scale and extent of data lost through illicit excavation.[31] Because archaeology depends on analyzing materials with documented stratigraphic context—an artifact's location relative to local layers of earth that can be correlated with different periods of time—failure to record context means a loss of data, constraining possibilities for interpretation. While most archaeologists decry looting as such, other research has sought to understand the motivations of "subsistence digging" and the socioeconomic factors involved in the production of artifacts as commodities.[32] Today, scholarship on looting explores the complex ethical dimensions of the informal excavations that produce artifacts for art markets and museums.[33] Debates around looting continue, as archaeologists are necessarily enmeshed with processes of valorization, though rarely with the power to effect substantial change in markets.[34] I occasionally heard, or read, accounts of looting and subsistence digging around El Tajín. Yet the evidence suggests that north Veracruz was not a hotspot for this kind of informal excavation.[35] I found little evidence to indicate that the political economy of subsistence digging played an important role in regional history.[36]

The same cannot be said of tourism. Advocates and critics alike agree on the tourism industry's mutually constitutive relationship with archaeology in Mexico.[37] Archaeologist José Luis Lorenzo emphasized the political and economic objectives of this relationship: "Outsiders must be shown the glories of a past and, in so doing . . . be induced to part with more foreign exchange."[38] Elsewhere in Mexico, the promotion of places like Pátzcuaro and San Miguel de Allende for tourism was key to nation-building and the propagation of postrevolution ideas of "Mexicanness."[39] As an economic development strategy, tourism increased in importance during the twentieth century, and its negative effects became increasingly clear.[40] M. Bianet Castellanos and Matilde Córdoba Azcárate have shown how tourism depends on a settler-colonial logic of Indigenous displacement and circumscribes prospects for the future in the Yucatán Peninsula.[41] As with the state, few would argue about the importance of tourism for the state promotion of archaeology in Mexico—or, for that matter, in El Tajín. This is especially the case for the communities nearest the archaeological site, which remain "stuck with tourism," working as guides, artisans, or vendors.[42] Yet rural Totonac communities vary in the extent of their involvement with tourism; a few are economically dependent on the industry, but most have no engagement whatsoever. I refer to tourist traffic when needed, but adopting a specific focus on this industry would have narrowed the scope of this study to just a few communities, in the service of a topic better addressed by those I cite here.

In choosing an entry point to the political economy of archaeology, I take a cue from the theory and practice of Indigenous archaeology. Authors like George Nicholas, Julie Hollowell, and Sonya Atalay argue that too often archaeology functions as "scientific colonialism," disqualifying traditional sources of knowledge while rewarding Western understandings of the past, material culture, and science itself.[43] Research "with, for, and by" Indigenous communities should attend to the pasts that members consider relevant, in the ways they consider most appropriate.[44] One key argument that emerges from this body of literature is that disciplinary concerns may not be shared by Indigenous, descendant, or proximate communities. Tsim D. Schneider and Katherine Hayes suggest that "decenter[ing] archaeology itself" serves decolonizing aims.[45] I thus limit my discussions of archaeologists' interpretations of El Tajín's pre-Hispanic past. Rather, I draw on archival research, ethnographic interviews, and close readings of secondary sources to revisit the constitutive silences of archaeology and to tell another story of landscape and labor in Papantla during the changing circumstances of the twentieth century. The relationships indicated by Totonac interlocutors center political-economic processes—related to changes in land tenure, the effects of oil exploration, the decline of the vanilla economy, and different forms of labor—each of which offers the opportunity to center Totonac assessments of history and the operations of archaeology alike.

Totonacapan

Totonacapan, most often defined as the area where the Totonac language is spoken, includes parts of the eastern Mexican states of Veracruz, Puebla, and Hidalgo.[46] Along with Tepehua, the Totonac language is a member of the Totonacan language family, whose relationships with other Mesoamerican relationships are enigmatic but deeply rooted.[47] As of 2020 some 252,012 people spoke Totonac, making it the eighth most spoken Indigenous language in Mexico.[48] The region's history attests to a long history of production, commerce, and migration.[49] In 1600 one Don Luis of Zacatlán told Friar Juan de Torquemada of Totonac history: like the ancestors of the Mexica, the Totonacs had migrated from Chicomoztoc, the Place of the Seven Caves. They arrived in Teotihuacan—where they built the famed Pyramids of the Sun and Moon—and moved to the mountains of the Sierra Madre Oriental, from which they dispersed toward the coast over generations.[50] At the eve of the Aztec-Spanish War, the region was populated largely by Totonac speakers, with long-running cultural ties to the Huastec region to the north and substantial Nahua influence.[51] Politically, the area was subject to the Aztec Triple Alliance, having been subjugated with the intention of collecting tribute during the reign of Moteuczoma II (1502–20).[52] When the Spaniards arrived in 1519, the invaders encountered the Totonac city and Aztec tributary province of Cempoala. The Totonacs became important allies for Cortés in his war against the Aztecs.[53]

The Spanish expedition's eventual victory proved disastrous for the Gulf Coast. During the first century after the arrival of the Spanish, novel diseases and colonial violence took upward of 95 percent of the population.[54] The "Relación de Hueytlalpa y su partido" of 1580 suggests a population as high as 60,000 for when Cortés arrived. At the time of writing, the population was perhaps 1,200.[55] Cempoala, whose precolonial population ranged from 10,500 to 20,000, had only eight families by 1609.[56] The population recovered only slowly, and according to pre-Hispanic patterns that remained durable throughout the colonial period. Residents were largely Totonac, living by their *milpas* (fields cultivated by slash-and-burn agriculture to produce crops like maize, beans, and chile), and dedicated to subsistence farming.

For much of the colonial period, Spanish colonization and evangelization were sparse. The region was devoid of the resources of interest to the colonizers and separated from the central highlands by the rugged Sierra Madre Oriental. In a 1610 visit, Bishop Alonso de la Mota y Escobar recorded only "five Spanish residents."[57] As he continued north to the Tuxpan River, the bishop also noted that Andrés de Tapia Sosa ran a fishery with the labor of enslaved Africans.[58] A set of admittedly poorly preserved baptismal records from 1698 provides a demographic portrait whose proportions remained consistent during the later colonial period: of 1,696 baptisms, 1,398 (82.4 percent) were "indios," 228 (13.4 percent) were "mulatos y otros," and 32 (1.8 percent) were "españoles," while the remaining 38 (2.2 percent) were mixed-race or, in one case, possibly foreign.[59] By 1743 the jurisdiction of Papantla had 1,543 Indigenous families and 215 Spanish and mixed-race families, while Afrodescendants may have composed as much as 12 percent of the population by the 1770s.[60]

Given Spanish disinterest and low population density, early-colonial Papantla lacked pressures on land and conflicts related to labor. However, political violence increased during the eighteenth century. This violence was often associated with the Bourbon Reforms, a series of policies that concentrated power and wealth in Spain, often at the cost of colonial subjects' well-being.[61] One of the key Bourbon policies that proved unacceptable to the Totonac residents of Papantla was the royal tobacco monopoly (1764), which outlawed the cultivation of a crop that had cultural and economic significance.[62] Such pressures led to armed uprisings in 1736, 1764–65, 1767, and 1787.[63] Ethnolinguistic identity did not determine participation in such events. Totonacs, Spaniards, and Afrodescendants joined different factions in accordance with local political and commercial interests.[64]

Amid the Bourbon Reforms, royal military official Diego Ruiz was searching for illegal tobacco plantations when, in 1785, he stumbled upon a structure later known as the Pyramid of the Niches in a "place called in the Totonac language, El Tajín."[65] The resulting publication in the *Gazeta de México* did not go unnoticed. In colonial New Spain, Mesoamerican antiquities served as evidence for a budding nationalism that defended early-colonial and Indigenous sources against northern European charges of barbarism, and advocated for the nativism that helped motivate the Wars for Independence (1810–21).[66] In this context, news of the so-called Pirámide de Papantla attracted visitors during and after the colonial period: the structure was mentioned by the likes of Alexander von Humboldt, Pedro José Márquez, and Carl Nebel, among others.[67]

Totonacs participated in Mexico's War for Independence and the ensuing conflicts with interpretations of liberal theory and practice that supported community autonomy.[68] Serafín Olarte frustrated royalist forces with guerilla warfare from his redoubt of Cuyuxquihui, and son Mariano Olarte led a successful federalist revolt that extended to parts of Puebla between 1836 and 1838.[69] The violence of nineteenth-century political conflicts and occasional epidemics took their toll, but demographic recovery and migrations from the Sierra de Puebla meant that the overall population continued to grow.[70] Writing in 1845, José M. Bausa calculated a figure of 6,682 residents for Papantla and its communities; one-third were said to be *de razón*.[71] During the century, European immigrants also joined this growing population. French colonists arrived south of the Totonac region beginning in 1833, while Italian migrants arrived in Papantla and settled on the coast between 1857 and 1880.[72]

Toward the end of the century, a series of related processes—liberal land reforms, oil prospecting, and a boom in vanilla cultivation, among others— transformed the region, while the discipline of archaeology became an increasingly professional pursuit anchored in the state control of the past. This book benefits from recent scholarship that seeks to understand these processes on their own terms, rather than as teleological culminations of earlier nineteenth-century processes or antecedents to the Mexican Revolution. Scholars like Casey Lurtz, Christina Bueno, and Miruna Achim have used this logic in discussing processes ranging from land tenure and export economies to archaeology for nation-building purposes and the growth of museum collections, showing the utility of organizing research according to emergent periodizations. Sharing this emphasis, my research remains firmly rooted in the regional scale, opting for conceptual breadth and geographic specificity across otherwise well-defined historiographic periods.

Modern Mexico: Politics, Economics, and Cultural Policy since c. 1880

A brief overview of the politics, economics, and cultural policies (regarding the use of the precolonial past and attitudes toward contemporary Indigenous communities) of modern Mexico will prove useful for understanding the more regional transitions I discuss in the rest of this study.[73] The story proper begins in the nineteenth century, whose "great thrust" involved "integrat[ing] the spaces of production and consumption through the transformations of exchange as well as landscape."[74] During the dictatorship of Porfirio Díaz (1876–1911), this "progress" was underwritten by efforts to achieve internal stability and strengthen the state via a complex combination of repression, concession, and co-option epitomized in well-known axioms of the day, *pan o palo* (bread or the cudgel) and *poca política, mucha administración* (less politicking, more administration). Economic policies generally focused on export-led development. By investing in infrastructure like railroads and ports, Díaz's government revitalized historically profitable commodities like silver, encouraged direct foreign investment in the nascent oil industry, and intensified production of relatively novel commodities like henequen, in response to broader trends of North Atlantic industrialization. Exports grew at the rate of 6.1 percent annually.[75]

Another plank of this state-building involved rewriting national history to locate the origins of the Porfirian state in the pre-Hispanic past. In 1884 one Leopoldo Batres proposed the creation of an inspector of monuments position to Porfirio Díaz.[76] Batres was appointed to the position the following year. The effective founding of the Inspectorate of Monuments as part of the Secretaría de Instrucción Pública y Bellas Artes created a lasting infrastructure—the state control of archaeology and presence of state personnel at archaeological sites—and generated conflicts with local communities and foreign researchers.[77] Through the Inspectorate and related institutions, the Díaz dictatorship invested unprecedented funding in archaeology, excavated sites like Teotihuacan and Mitla, collected artifacts in the National Museum, and advertised the nation's civilized antiquity at international expositions.[78] Contemporary Indigenous communities, by contrast, were considered fallen from their pre-Hispanic glory. What elites called the "Indian problem" held that, because of their differences in race, language, and lifeways, these communities were obstacles to liberal nation-building: "The ties linking the pre-Columbian and contemporary Indian had been severed, whether by Spanish abuse or an inadequate diet."[79] There was thus no necessary contradiction between Porfirian efforts to appropriate artifacts that were otherwise part of Indigenous landscapes, and ethnocidal drives to secure the all-too-autonomous Yaqui and Maya zones.

The dictatorship of Porfirio Díaz came to an end with what became the Mexican Revolution.[80] The state that emerged from the struggles of the 1920s and 1930s continues to challenge analysts for its synthesis of democratic and authoritarian practices. In Paul Gillingham's concise analysis it is best described as "a *dictablanda,* a punning neologism combining *dictadura,* dictatorship, with *blanda* (soft) in place of *dura* (hard) ... a complex blend of political monopoly fostered by election rigging, *no reelección,* and a broad governing coalition; a qualified level of cultural control, ranging from the nationalism of school programs to the censorship of the national newspapers; strategic payoffs from a mixed economy, access to which relied on the benevolence of governmental gatekeepers; and, in some times and some places, considerable violence."[81] The potential for violence was made abundantly clear in Mexico's Dirty War and in the 1968 massacre of student protestors in advance of the Mexico City Olympics.[82] Still, what became the singular Partido Revolucionario Institucional (PRI) governed Mexico from its 1929 founding as the Partido Nacional Revolucionario until its loss in the elections of 2000.

The functioning of the system was closely linked to the success of the economic policies in place during most of the twentieth century. Through the 1940s an emphasis on export-oriented growth gave way to import-substitution industrialization (ISI), which encouraged the development of domestic industry and markets through direct import controls, protective tariffs, state ownership of industries, and similar policy instruments.[83] The resulting period of "stabilizing development" or the "Mexican Miracle" saw the country's gross domestic product grow at an annual rate of 6.7 percent between 1956 and 1970.[84] The benefits were real and visible: "Society was transformed from an agrarian one into an urban, semi-industrial one in the midst of a demographic boom, the share of investment and manufacturing industries in total output soared, and the literacy rate and life expectancy jumped."[85] But they were also unequally distributed, dedicated to developing an urban middle class. As I will discuss, Papantla does not represent these tendencies.

Cultural policy between the 1920s and 1940s was directed toward the development of a *mestizo* nationalism that incorporated Mexico's Spanish and Indigenous heritages into national identity, ostensibly revaluing the Indigenous present in the face of Porfirian repression.[86] Revolutionary governments founded diverse state institutions like the Instituto Indigenista Interamericano (1940) and the Instituto Nacional Indigenista (1948) to support this ideology, called *indigenismo*.[87] The scattered agencies that attended the pre-Hispanic past were consolidated into the INAH under archetypal revolutionary president Lázaro Cárdenas (1934–40).[88] The INAH has historically functioned as a legal monopoly over the control of archaeology in Mexico.[89] Drawing on the older Porfirian emphasis on monumental sites, representative of pre-Hispanic urban centers, INAH archaeology is sometimes known as Official Mexican Archaeology.[90] This archaeology, which sought to make Mesoamerica into Ancient Mexico, materialized a glorious, pre-Hispanic past to legitimize the postrevolutionary state and attract foreign tourism, while researching and protecting archaeological sites and materials.[91] After the social unrest of the 1960s, critical anthropologists charged that indigenismo was a continuation of the colonial project that sought Indigenous subjugation in the form of assimilation, rather than violent oppression alone.[92] Toward the 1980s, indigenista institutions responded with efforts to facilitate language revitalization and self-determination through frameworks like participatory indigenismo.[93] These changes were felt more in governmental policy and social anthropology than archaeology, however.

The political-economic system began to falter in the early 1970s. Policymakers considered that populist social programs could address the social unrest of the 1960s, but ISI had depended on governmental support for industries that were neither cost-effective nor internationally competitive. Foreign debt and inflation quickly grew during the 1970s.[94] The discovery of massive oil deposits off the shores of Campeche promised to revitalize Mexico's economy, but declining oil prices of the early 1980s instead facilitated a debt crisis.[95] In order to demonstrate creditworthiness to the likes of the International Monetary Fund (IMF), reforms dubbed "shock treatments"—including the privatization of public companies, the lifting of price controls, the floating of the peso on the open market, and subsequent agreements to reduce the budget deficit—began under President Miguel de la Madrid Hurtado (1982–88).[96] Neoliberal reforms reached their maximum extent under the government of President Carlos Salinas de Gortari (1988–94). The combined reforms targeting "deregulation, privatization, trade liberalization, and exchange rate policy" initiated under de la Madrid expanded in scale and scope, affecting revolutionary mainstays like land reform, which ended in 1992.[97] The results of the reforms did not accrue evenly to all: "Between 1987 and 1994," Alexander Dawson notes, "Mexico welcomed twenty-one new billionaires, while the minimum wage lost 40 percent of its value."[98]

The country's politics remained anything but static, especially in the era of globalization. The PRI's elite underwent a "technocratic revolution," in which high-ranking officials started in politics thanks to education (rather than party loyalty), garnered experience in bureaucracy (rather than electoral politics), and legitimized their presence based on criteria of professional administration (rather than on the continuation of the institutionalized revolution).[99] A series of unfortunate events led to the neoliberal era beginning with a "lost decade." Notable crises included the 1985 Mexico City earthquake, the stolen presidential elections of 1988, and the Zapatista uprising of 1994. These were among the events that contributed to the 2000 election of the country's first opposition president, Vicente Fox Quesada, of the right-wing Partido de Acción Nacional.[100]

In Mexico's cultural sector, neoliberalism entailed a reworking of broader state-society relations.[101] Combined with hemispheric Indigenous activism and the end of the Cold War, discourses of multiculturalism gradually eroded indigenista assimilationist policies, though the state's recognition of ethnolinguistic plurality has not entailed political autonomy or the redressing of structural inequalities.[102] The nationalist framework for INAH archaeology remains resilient.[103] The current Federal Law on Archaeological, Artistic, and Historic Monuments and Zones of 1972 enshrined the legal objectives of heritage management, while the broader tendencies of deregulation, liberalization, and privatization generated new institutional actors in the cultural sector.[104] The disputed founding of a new federal secretary of culture in the mid-2010s was an outcome of this process.

From Mapping Trails to Ethnographic Archives

El Tajín is compelling for what it is not: a privileged site in nationalist imaginaries (à la Cochasquí, Ecuador, or the Olmec Region), a wellspring of foreign scholarship (like Chichén Itzá or Copán, Honduras), an international tourism destination (like Machu Picchu, Peru), or a key site for the history of archaeology (like Palenque or Teotihuacan).[105] A site documented since the colonial period, with a long history of Mexican research and of regional importance, El Tajín is deceptive in its apparent simplicity. "El Tajín" most often refers to the capital of a Classic Veracruz state that began during Mesoamerica's Early Classic era (c. 350 CE), expanded toward the end of the Classic period (c. 650 CE), and collapsed around 1200 CE, contemporary with polities like Tula, Xochicalco, and Cacaxtla-Xochitécatl.[106] Scholars associate El Tajín, a city of perhaps twenty thousand residents during its c. 1100 CE apogee, with intricate low-relief carvings, Mesoamerican ballgame iconography, and the use of architectural niches. Compared with other Mesoamerican centers, El Tajín remains enigmatic: researchers debate the existence of an Early Classic occupation and the ethnolinguistic affiliation of those who built the site.[107] For places like El Tajín, so often associated with pre-Hispanic urban centers, referring to "landscape," as I do in this book, draws attention to "what lies beyond the site, or the edge of excavation."[108] Terms like "archaeological landscape" help to decenter the site, while retaining it as a frame of reference.[109]

Landscapes like that of El Tajín do not just result from the succession of geological and archaeological strata but emerge "in a complex dynamic in which objects from a distant past continue to have an impact."[110]

Other ways of knowing the landscape and its histories map onto the material prevalence of the pre-Hispanic past. To understand these historical associations, I lived in the community of El Tajín for a total of twenty-eight months between 2012 and 2018, and spent another six months doing archival research in Mexico and the United States in 2017–19.[111] I began my research intending to study cultural heritage as practice, "a particular kind of social relationship among all kinds of users of a heritage site."[112] The site's administrative staff helped introduce me to the surrounding communities, especially the five communities brought inside the site boundaries by a 2001 presidential declaration: El Tajín, Zapotal Santa Cruz, San Lorenzo Tajín, San Antonio Ojital, and Ojital Nuevo.[113] Site custodios helped me to see that focusing exclusively on these communities was ultimately limiting; the boundary was a historically recent one. They suggested a different avenue of analysis: the local, historic pedestrian trails known as *caminos reales*. Following up on the topics that my interviewees discussed with reference to the caminos reales took me outside the site. As I introduced myself to local authorities and assemblies, my previous intention to emphasize heritage as practice at the site seemed restrictive: "It is not possible to parse out heritage from other issues, including matters pertaining to ancestral land, forced dislocation, landscape, power, oppression, and recent histories."[114] Topics like changing transportation patterns (especially the gravel roads constructed by the state-owned Petróleos Mexicanos, PEMEX) and cultivation trends (especially the decline in vanilla cultivation) assumed an importance that I had not heard in El Tajín, perhaps because I had been so focused on the archaeological site rather than the broader political-economic landscape.

Studying the caminos reales, the communities they passed, the histories they referenced, and the people who used them provided a useful way to reorient my work. As Chip Colwell has written, "Researchers have typically begun their investigations with a monumental site . . . and then moved outward to the nested social relations invariably formed around such sites, [presupposing] that archaeology is of distinctive significance."[115] In agreement with Colwell, I found this distinctive significance misleading. Framing my study with the caminos reales led me to argue for a locally relevant definition of the core study region, one that conformed to shared ideas of proximity and access.[116]

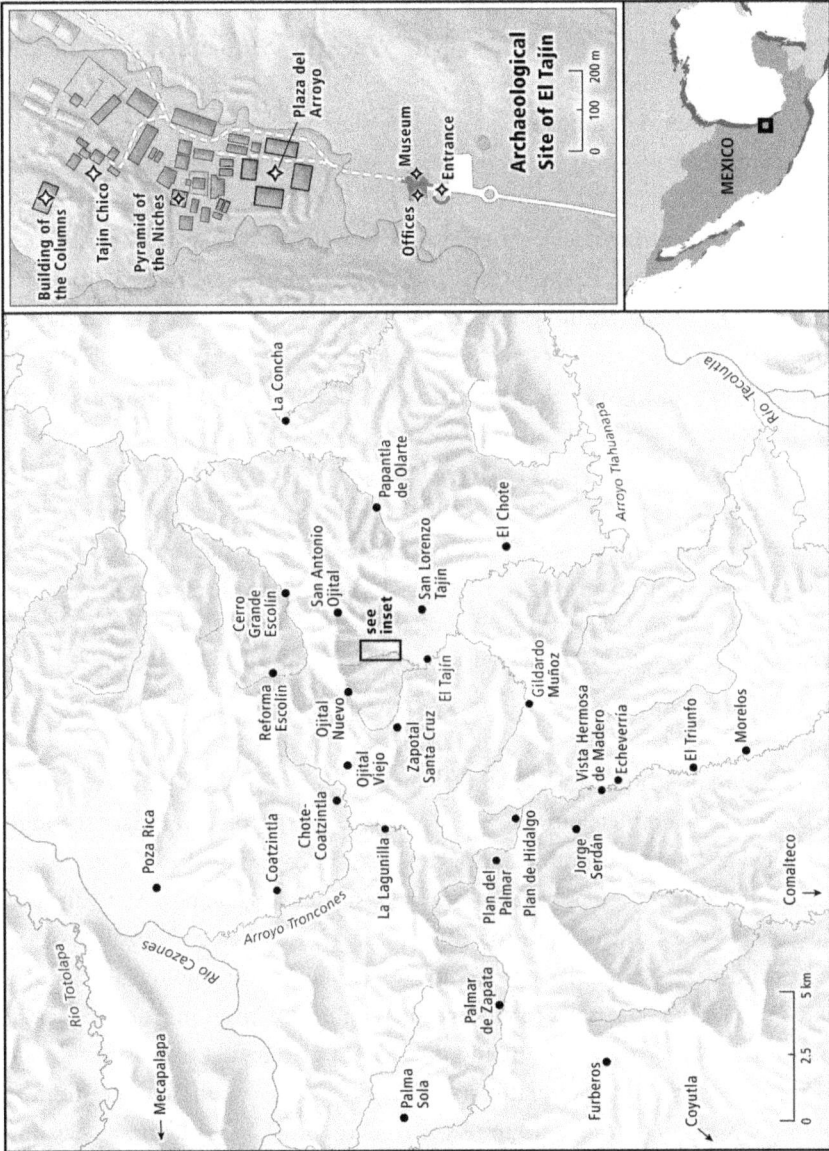

Inset (top left):
Archaeological
Site of El Tajín

Building of
the Columns

Tajín Chico

Pyramid of
the Niches

Plaza del
Arroyo

Museum

Entrance

Offices

0   100   200 m

Inset (top right):
MEXICO

Main map labels:
La Concha

Papantla
de Olarte

El Chote

Río Tecolutla

Arroyo Tlahuanapa

San Antonio
Ojital

San Lorenzo
Tajín

Cerro
Grande
Escolín

see
inset

Reforma
Escolín

Ojital
Nuevo

El Tajín

Gildardo
Muñoz

Zapotal
Santa Cruz

Ojital
Viejo

Vista Hermosa
de Madero

Echeverría

El Triunfo

Morelos

Poza Rica

Coatzintla

Chote-
Coatzintla

La Lagunilla

Plan del
Palmar

Plan de Hidalgo

Jorge
Serdán

Comalteco

Arroyo Troncones

Río Cazones

Río Totolapa

Mecapalapa

Palmar
de Zapata

Palma
Sola

Furberos

Coyutla

0   2.5   5 km

MAP I. The archaeological site of El Tajín, including the area open to the public and installations, relative to the communities within about a day's walk. Erin Greb Cartography.

This definition basically involved a network of communities that could be reached in about a day's walk during the middle of the twentieth century. The result of what Sabrina Papazian and I later called "heritage trekking" was an area of roughly one hundred square kilometers comprising approximately forty Totonac communities; I conducted interviews in twenty-three of them (see map 1).[117]

I took my interlocutors' references to the archives between 2017 and 2019, in Xalapa, Veracruz, Mexico City, and Dallas. The last of these is home to the Isabel T. Kelly Ethnographic Archive, housed at Southern Methodist University's DeGolyer Library.[118] Including material collected by Kelly during her 1947–48 and 1964 field seasons in El Tajín, this archive informs much of the book. American anthropologists of Kelly's generation tended to treat their interlocutors as objects of study, fitting for the colonial contexts in which many anthropologists practiced.[119] A context-free reading of the archival materials risks replicating the uneven power relations that rendered Indigenous peoples objects of research. Philip J. Deloria suggests that an ongoing challenge to historically Western scholarship is to "see Indigenous peoples as peoples—not as *objects* 'good to think with' or think about but as *intellectuals and historians* in their own right, good to think *with*, in partnerships borne out of respect."[120]

The kind of ethnography that Kelly practiced was positivist and empiricist in orientation, emphasizing the accurate collection of objective data through standardized methods. In Mexico, Kelly's research dovetailed with the broader indigenista orientation of contemporary Mexican anthropology. As an anthropologist of the Smithsonian Institution's Institute of Social Anthropology (ISA) and a teacher at Mexico's Escuela Nacional de Antropología e Historia (ENAH), Kelly's objectives in study of El Tajín were "to train students of the Escuela, both in the classroom and in the field; and to add to our knowledge of the native and rural populations of Mexico."[121] She conducted four months of fieldwork each in 1947 and 1948 with a team of ENAH students, including Ángel Palerm, José Luis Lorenzo, Roberto Williams, and María Cristina Álvarez at different times, along with a follow-up visit in 1964. The choice of El Tajín was purposeful: "It suggests an extension of the [INAH]'s interest in the ruins; and we can count on the moral support of the Instituto's three employees at the ruins."[122] With Ángel Palerm, Kelly published her results in a 1952 monograph, *The Tajín Totonac, Part I: History, Subsistence, Shelter, and Technology*, and in a few shorter articles. Funding difficulties following the closure of the ISA in 1952 prevented the completion of the second volume of *The Tajín Totonac*, which remains partially complete in Kelly's archive.

In reviewing Kelly's field notes, I find inspiration in Margaret Bruchac's use of "reverse ethnography," used to explore the dialogical interactions between U.S. anthropologists and Indigenous interlocutors during the twentieth century.[123] Kelly's notes are typewritten on five-by-eight-inch sheets and filed according to George Peter Murdock's *Outline of Cultural Materials*.[124] Each of these approximately 9,500 sheets registers the datum in question, as well as the interviewer, interviewee, date, and Murdock classification.[125] Because these notes link specific perspectives to individual residents of El Tajín, many now recognized as abuelos, I cite them by name when possible. These notes do not come unmediated: the circumstances of the interviews themselves are rarely clear, and the comments (rendered as "data") are isolated from their broader discursive contexts. Nevertheless, the act of naming and citing is a step toward acknowledging Kelly's interlocutors as experts in their own right.[126]

Research in Kelly's archives also offered opportunities for practical ethical engagement.[127] This orientation included facilitating access to primary sources and the iterative reporting of my research outcomes. In Kelly's archive I ran across undeveloped film and color slides from Kelly's fieldwork in El Tajín. The DeGolyer Library, especially Curator of Photographs Anne Peterson, and the Norwick Center for Digital Solutions, especially Assistant Director of Digital Collections Cindy Boeke, worked to digitize these materials. I was able to present these materials in El Tajín and via social media. I periodically cite the results of these encounters over the course of the book.

Outline of the Book

The first half of *In the Shadow of El Tajín* focuses on regional history, with an emphasis on political economy and the history of archaeology beyond site and disciplinary borders. Each of the three chapters traces a particular commodity relative to regional history and the practice of archaeology. Chapter 1 traces the complex relationships between archaeology and land tenure in El Tajín, following Totonac allegations of land dispossession made in 2016. Tracing these conflicts back to the liberal land reforms of the late nineteenth century, I argue that linking an idiom of patrimony with the views of space characteristic of private property provided residents a way of defending their lands against what they saw as archaeologists' incursions, while rendering the same lands vulnerable to other kinds of pressures that would result in eventual dispossession. Thus, by the 1990s archaeology functioned as a tool of land dispossession even without explicit intent or long-term planning on the state's part.

Chapter 2 follows another line of analysis opened by the spatialization of a private property regime, situating the history of oil exploration in regional context. It focuses on a series of key moments in the regional history of oil—the 1860s, the 1930s, the 1960s, and the 2010s—to understand the close entanglements of archaeology and extractive industry, as well as their effects on regional infrastructure and local livelihoods. The chapter illustrates how an extractive industry supports the functioning of an archaeological site, and how the history of oil production has been one of cumulative pollution for many rural communities.

Chapter 3 begins with what interlocutors considered a key effect of oil development, the decline of vanilla cultivation. This chapter focuses on the twentieth-century history of vanilla in Papantla, a contrasting example of how archaeology mediated between local practices of cultivation and the functioning of the global vanilla industry. The vanilla trade consolidated an elite merchant class involved in El Tajín's investigation and management through the 1950s, while exposing rural Totonac cultivators to a kind of violence once considered uncharacteristic of twentieth-century Mexico.

The second half of the book takes political economy as a framework for understanding the day-to-day operations of archaeology, with a specific focus on labor. Chapter 4 covers the early history of Totonac labor in El Tajín and the work of wage laborers, documenting the exclusion of workers from accounts of the site over time. Rectifying this exclusion, I suggest, requires attending to the political economy of archaeological practice as a complement to more common emphases on interpretation and knowledge production. Analyzing payroll records, I argue that employment in archaeology offered a survival strategy and opportunities for socioeconomic mobility while playing into local social stratification by excluding certain residents from employment opportunities.

Chapter 5 continues the discussion of Indigenous labor in El Tajín by focusing on the unionized and tenured personnel referred to as custodios. Though absent from published scholarship as workers and Indigenous subjects, episodes like the one that began this book demonstrate their local visibility. This chapter addresses the question of visibility by attending to how these custodios understand the site and its history. This approach, grounded in local historicity, is organized by cohorts and according to categories like how one became a custodio and the nature of the work. This history is key for understanding the custodios' ability to mobilize and protect their livelihoods.

This combination of historiographic invisibility and local prominence contrasts with the subjects of chapter 6, El Tajín's professional managerial and administrative staff. As the legal authorities, educated experts, and authors of reports, the staff and its counterparts elsewhere are well represented in academic scholarship. Yet they are subject to a degree of precarity not shared by the custodios and are regularly unable to defend their interests in matters as fundamental as making a living. Tracing the history of local heritage management, I argue that the neoliberal reforms of the 1980s and their unexpected outcomes are responsible for experts' overdetermined precarity. The conclusion draws out the implications of the study, while discussing recent violence, the COVID-19 pandemic, and natural disasters in El Tajín.

Lands

Public Pyramids, Private Parcels

1

> There wasn't any other option. . . . Well, I didn't want to leave my
> *rancho*, I was born here, I feel right [*estoy hallado*], my work, and every-
> thing. But I had purchased this lot before and it was neglected. . . . I
> told my son "you go, that's why I bought it, for my children." "No," he
> said, "I'm not going to go alone, we'll go together." . . . I made myself go.
>
> —Ricardo

In February 2016 representatives of seventeen families from San Antonio
Ojital lodged a complaint with Mexico's National Human Rights Commission
(CNDH). San Antonio Ojital is a marginalized Totonac community in which
few residents have access to land for subsistence cultivation, the economic
livelihood for most of the region. It had not always been so. Located just to
the north of the archaeological site of El Tajín, the community is at the end
of the gravel road that takes tourists from El Tajín's site installations and
museum to the pyramids. In the past, residents held title to parcels of land
located near that road. The loss of those parcels was at the heart of the CNDH
complaint. "Currently," the document begins, "we are informed that our lands
are considered national patrimony."[1] Beginning in the 1990s "we were deceived
with incomplete and/or distorted information, [and] threatened that we
could be dispossessed, driven off, and have our lands stolen."[2] It alleges that
the federal government sought to take San Antonio Ojital's lands because
they were part of the archaeological site of El Tajín. In her study of Chichén
Itzá, Lisa Breglia describes the apparent contradiction of public monuments
and private lands as "monumental ambivalence."[3] For the complainants of San
Antonio Ojital, this ambivalence had been resolved through dispossession.

In broader perspective, the residents of San Antonio Ojital are far from
unique in understanding conservation as dispossession. Beginning in the
nineteenth-century United States of America, the combination of "eviction,

enclosure, erasure of history, and the invocation of *terra nullius*" became a model for national parks elsewhere in the world.[4] Elsewhere, the conservation of cultural heritage has meant eviction, gentrification, and relocation in urban areas from Rome to Jerusalem.[5] In Mexico the INAH gives an institutional face to this kind of dispossession. More than a few residents of San Antonio Ojital feared digging wells or expanding their houses, lest an archaeologist come, stop the work, and require a study. This outcome was contingent rather than necessary. As Emily Wakild has shown, for nature conservation in the 1930s, "instead of using the U.S. wilderness ideal to shape their parks, Mexicans promoted a concept of human integration with nature."[6] This was less the case for archaeological remains, considered national patrimony and administered by the state since the colonial period.[7]

This understanding of conservation as dispossession intersects with Mexico's history of land reform to produce conflict. Amid the Mexican Revolution, the Constitution of 1917 codified new land reform efforts. The reform granted usufruct rights to agrarian communities to redress unjust losses incurred during the nineteenth-century breakup of communal lands known as disentailment, or for reasons of economic necessity.[8] These rights, and these communities, are known as *ejidos*. Prior to the end of the reform in 1992, fully half of Mexico's land was dedicated to ejidos.[9] As many as 90 percent of nominally public archaeological sites are located on ejido lands.[10] The coexistence of the INAH's legal mandates and the practical impossibility of completely fulfilling them has resulted in "archaeological limbos," sites administered de jure by the INAH and de facto by third parties like ejidos, private organizations, and municipal governments.[11] As I discuss below, the communities around El Tajín are distinct in that they retained control of the land as private owners through the 1950s.

The case of San Antonio Ojital illustrates how long-ago liberal land reforms, changes in regional political economy, and the gradual development of archaeological research worked together to enable effective land dispossession. Tracing the materiality of borders illustrates how archaeologists and Totonac landowners adopted and reinforced a vision of space structured by a private property regime. This view of space, what I call a language of lots and parcels, treats the landscape as a grid: a set of evenly sized, individually owned, mutually exclusive, contiguous, and alienable parcels of land. This vision of space became hegemonic, "a common material and meaningful framework for living through, talking about, and acting upon social orders characterized by domination."[12] In other words, the language of lots and parcels itself rarely appears as the object of conflict. Rather, it served as a channel for making claims on El Tajín, according to competing uses of an idiom of "patrimony." The results of these claims tended to be pragmatic accommodations between archaeologists and landowners. However, these accommodations left Indigenous private property vulnerable to more direct state action—as the residents of San Antonio Ojital would later argue.

Because archaeology depends on access to land, the political economy of archaeology begins with land tenure. During the dictatorship of Porfirio Díaz, the materialization of private property yielded a perception of the landscape—a language of lots and parcels—that enabled archaeologists and landowners alike to make claims on El Tajín and its lands. Carving up the landscape in this way required people (surveyors, archaeologists, and landowners), plants (trees), objects (fences and signposts), and paperwork (laws, maps, and land titles).[13] The objective was to remake a landscape characterized by an uneven distribution of semi-evergreen tropical rainforest; Totonac-speaking subsistence cultivators living in a dispersed settlement pattern; rivers and creeks meandering through low, rolling hills; and standing pre-Hispanic architecture.

The archaeological perspective on which I draw requires questioning the materiality and unexpected recurrence of processes that appear to have finished long ago. In *The Dark Abyss of Time*, Laurent Olivier contemplates a hypothetical city to illustrate this concept. "The structures that date back to ancient times, the roads and buildings and the networks of fields—have long since disappeared.... And yet, these works of the past still exist in boundaries, orientations, contour, and mass. They still delimit the physical structure and organization of the space in the present."[14] Following this view, the making of private property does not stop with legal changes in land tenure. Focusing on the material means by which private property endured, I explore how the logic of property structured conflicts between archaeologists and Totonac residents long before 2016, and how negotiation ended in dispossession.

From *Pueblo* Lands to Private Property

In the territory that became the Cantón de Papantla (1857–1917), land was largely dedicated to subsistence agriculture. For much of the colonial period, perhaps half the jurisdiction's lands were held by *pueblos de indios*—administrative units capable of holding land and governed by elected councils to manage Indigenous affairs—and the other half were private estates, mostly dedicated to cattle ranching.[15] In practice, Totonac subsistence farmers moved, settled, and cultivated ostensibly private lands; estate owners were typically unable, or unwilling, to enforce their property rights.[16] Given the roughness of the terrain, low population density, and limited access to external markets, the archetypal colonial hacienda did not develop in Papantla.[17] For similar reasons, Totonac farmers tended not to lose access to land even after Independence, and the end of the pueblo de indios administration.[18] The communities now known as El Tajín and San Antonio Ojital, in all probability, were largely autonomous, managed their land communally, and were dedicated to the cultivation of subsistence crops like corn, beans, and chile. While these communities have no definitive founding dates, Tajín and "Hojital" are mentioned in an 1871 census.[19]

Over the course of the nineteenth century, liberal reformers sought to dismantle the communal land tenure regime. This process of disentailment sought to take real estate out of the hands of the Catholic Church and civil corporations (including Indigenous communities) through the survey, sale, and distribution of collective landholdings and legally unoccupied lands.[20] Liberal political thought considered that "if property . . . could be freed from corporate, monopolistic, or governmental restrictions, then individual initiative, a natural division of labor, and free exchange between individuals would flourish."[21] Disentailment was a full-scale social engineering project, intended to create a class of agrarian smallholders out of Indigenous communities whose agricultural practices were considered inefficient and irrational. Governor Juan de la Luz Enríquez discussed disentailment's multifaceted "benefits" in a telling 1889 report: "Politically, because with the planning survey, the jurisdictional limits of municipalities will be marked. . . . Socially, because, when every Indigenous person becomes a smallholder, the regeneration of the race will come easily and spontaneously, like has happened for the most cultured [cultos] countries after the old and odious attachment to the land was erased; economically, because the cadaster, its legitimate consequence, will reveal its public wealth and the beneficial spillover of taxes."[22] Efforts at liberalizing land tenure in Papantla met with little success until the expansion of vanilla cultivation during the latter half of the nineteenth century, which provided an economic impetus for the state to carry out disentailment with force.[23]

With the authoritarian methods characteristic of Porfirio Díaz's dictatorship, the state divided and subdivided communal lands between 1870 and

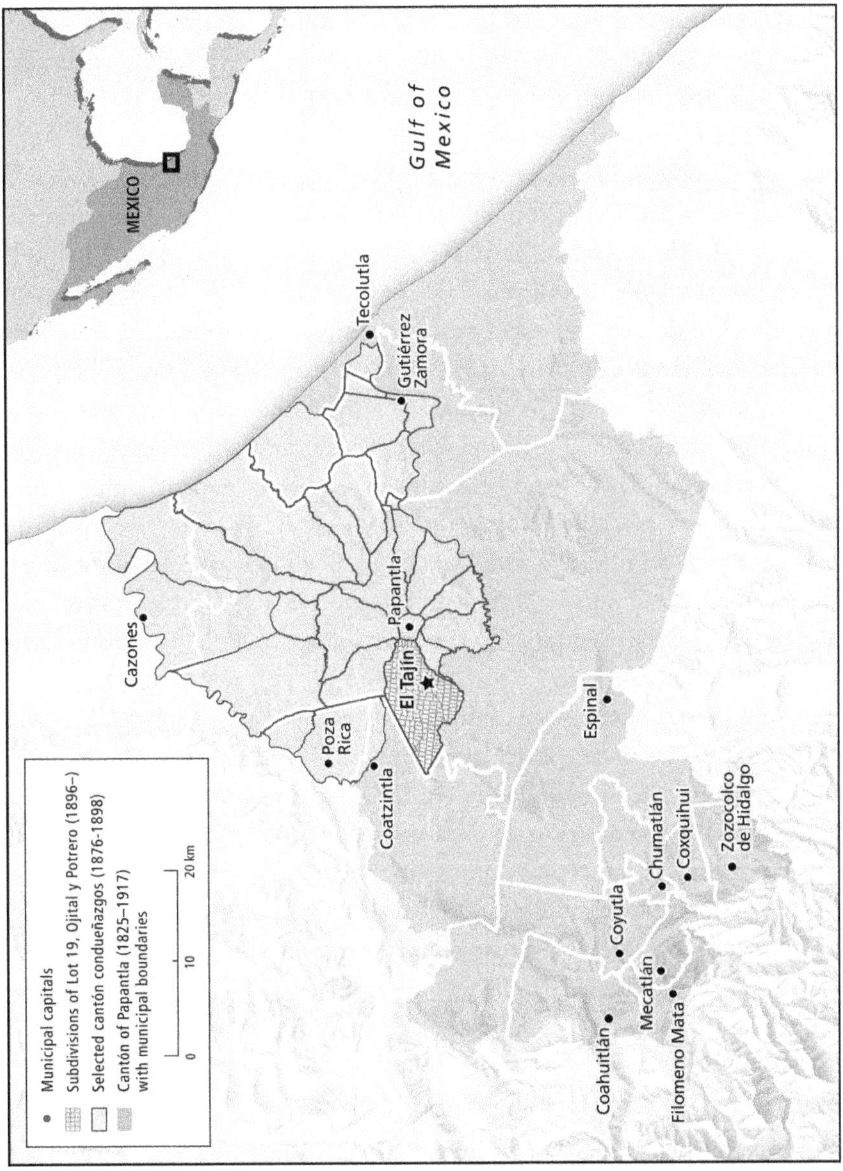
Municipal capitals
Subdivisions of Lot 19, Ojital y Potrero (1896–)
Selected cantón condueñazgos (1876-1898)
Cantón of Papantla (1825–1917)
with municipal boundaries
0
10
20 km
MEXICO
Gulf of
Mexico
Tecolutla
Gutiérrez
Zamora
Papantla
Cazones
El Tajín
Poza
Rica
Coatzintla
Espinal
Zozocolco
de Hidalgo
Chumatlán
Coxquihui
Coyutla
Mecatlán
Filomeno Mata
Coahuitlán

MAP 2. Papantla's condueñazgos relative to the broader cantón, a nineteenth-century second-level administrative division. Modern municipal boundaries are shown in white. For simplicity's sake, only the parcels of lot 19, Ojital y Potrero, are shown. Erin Greb Cartography.

1900 (see map 2). Initially, local resistance to the process resulted in the survey of large lots, governed as co-ownerships (*condueñazgos*, also known as *lotes grandes*). Condueñazgos were privately owned and managed by shareholders who, in theory, were the occupants of the old pueblo lands.[24] Though technically private, condueñazgos were subject to the same political pressures that led to the division of communal lands in the first place. Between these pressures and the expansion of the vanilla economy (see chapter 3), Papantla's condueñazgos were short-lived.[25] Their subsequent subdivision into parcels provoked at least two major armed uprisings from those who sought to maintain collective land ownership. In the territory later known as El Tajín, abuelo Santiago Simbrón recalled: "[My father] told me many times about when they divided up the lots, and when those from Polutla and other parts were in rebellion. Those from here were on the side of Papantla, on the side of the authorities, and in favor of the division. . . . My father was with the federal troops, and he said that they had killed many people; all of those who would not submit, were shot. In the end, the rebels were finished off, and the lots were handed out."[26] The factions involved did not break down along class or ethnic lines.[27]

While the rebellions were suppressed, surveying and subdividing the condueñazgos continued. After disentailment, Totonac political leaders and foreign merchants, elite rural families, Indigenous smallholders, and tenant and migrant workers made up the new socioeconomic landscape.[28] Legal disentailment was complete by 1900, and the extent of the region's social and economic change led Emilio Kourí to conclude that "by the time Mexico had a Revolution, Papantla had already finished one of its own."[29] It was just the beginning of conflict in El Tajín.

Disentailment in El Tajín

In 1878 what colonial travelers had called the Pirámide de Papantla became part of the 6,355-hectare condueñazgo of Ojital y Potrero (see map 3).[30] To carve out such lots, surveyors traced the boundaries of the communities they contained: in this case, Ojital and Potrero (the latter also called El Tajín).[31] The concept of enrollment, from science and technology studies, proves useful for understanding how state surveyors leveraged elements of the landscape to bring a private property regime into being.[32] Enrollment, the process by which different social and material actors are persuaded to accept particular roles in the context of broader negotiations, draws attention to how surveyors brought together paths that connected communities, creeks that flowed, hills that stood tall, survey crosses, and stone markers to materialize the boundaries necessary for a private property regime. By implication, one reason for the success of disentailment was that state surveyors enrolled such a diverse set of preexisting materials in the service of remaking the landscape. This provided a first means of materializing the state's liberal vision of landscape, "an immense grid of small properties."[33]

Survey crosses served to enroll landscape features as the boundaries for what became Ojital y Potrero. State surveyors appropriated the camino real that linked Papantla to the neighboring town of Coatzintla via the community of Escolin to form the northern boundary. Absent a suitable northwestern boundary, surveyors marked a straight line from the Coatzintla camino real to Cerro Laguna, which was also enrolled as the endpoint for the southwestern boundary. That straight line intersected Tlahuanapa Creek, which became the southern boundary. Snaking north, Tlahuanapa Creek met another camino real (likely the one that linked Papantla with the town of Espinal to the south) that became the southeastern boundary. The easternmost boundary of Ojital y Potrero was the western boundary of the city of Papantla.

The lote grande survey enrolled two caminos reales, Tlahuanapa Creek, and the Cerro Laguna. In so doing, it transformed them from walking paths, a popular fishing spot, and a notable hill, respectively, into the boundaries of the condueñazgo of Ojital y Potrero. The disentailment process thus also enrolled residents in the process of maintaining boundaries. Each time someone took the trail from El Tajín to Papantla, walked from Papantla to Coatzintla via Escolin, or participated in the regular communal labor that cleared these paths, they helped to maintain the boundaries of the new tract of land. This process appeared to be effective: a half century later, "the external boundaries of Ojital y Potrero [were] definitive and well known."[34]

The subsequent subdivision of Ojital y Potrero into individual parcels took the condueñazgo boundaries as a frame of reference. By 1896 the ex-condueñazgo of Ojital y Potrero consisted of 205 parcels of thirty-one hectares apiece, two half parcels for the town centers of Ojital and El Tajín, and a one-hectare boundary for the archaeological site (see below). The resulting allocation of land was not egalitarian, but neither did it result in immediate dispossession. At the conclusion of subdivision, approximately 79 percent of Ojital y Potrero was owned by its Totonac residents.[35] This process of subdivision reinforced the lot's external boundaries, even as the survey transformed

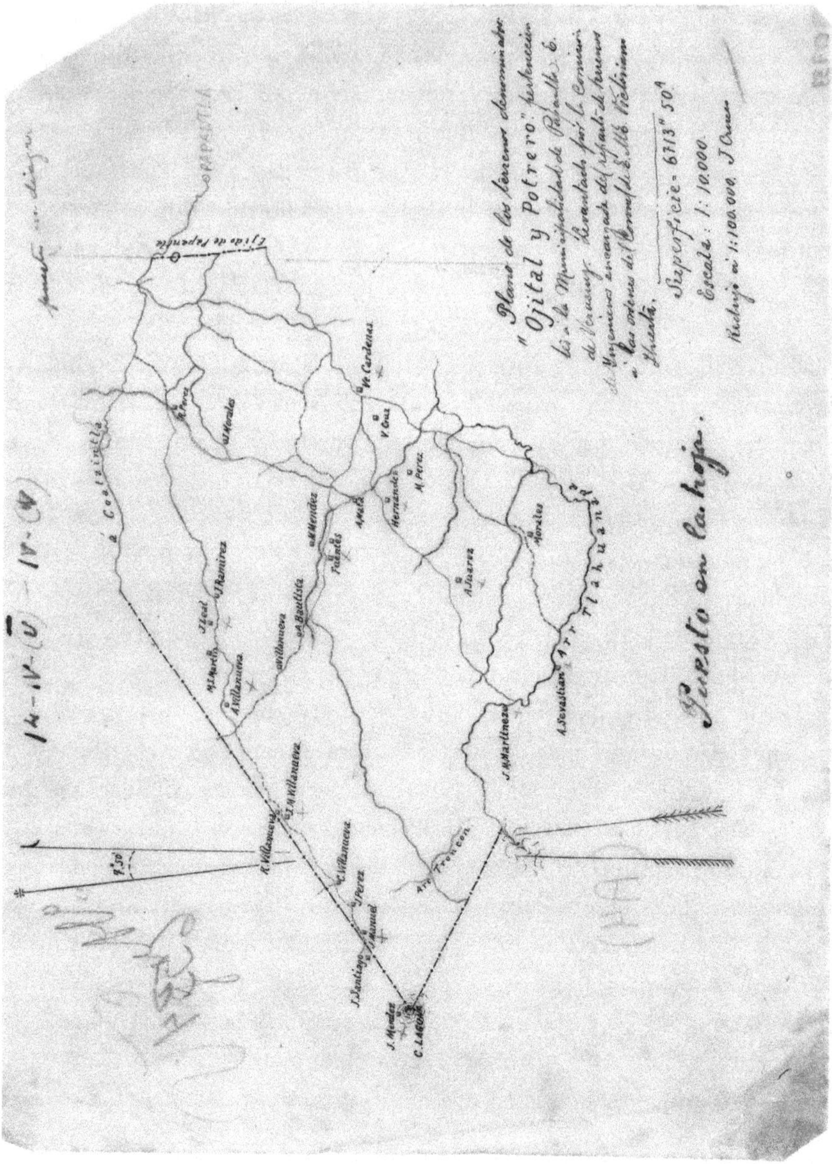

MAP 3. The condueñazgo of Ojital y Potrero, c. 1876. Mapoteca "Manuel Orozco y Berra" del Servicio de Información Agroalimentaria y Pesquera.

the tract's legal status (see map 4). Those "little signs with numbers on the sides of the path" that abuelo Modesto González recalled surveyors placing during subdivision have since been lost, but the maps persisted.[36] Maps, like map 4, provided another means of fixing, reproducing, and circulating the vision of space brought about by disentailment.

Evidence of disentailment's efficacy remains. Papantla's town hall holds a large-scale map of the municipality's lots and parcels. Modern land titles, too, retain the lot and parcel references laid down more than a century before. Between material boundaries and cadastral visualizations, disentailment established a vision of space with long-lasting effects in the region, and for the archaeological site of El Tajín.

As Álvaro Brizuela has documented, El Tajín became a part of Ojital y Potrero with the inscription of "a hectare in the place that the monument of El Ta[j]ín occupies."[37] This single line from a document then held in Papantla's Public Property Registry documents nothing less than the first mapping of the archaeological site of El Tajín. In that process, the structure acquired boundaries—a key step in making a ruin into a site. "Anyone who has done much fieldwork," archaeologists Robert Dunnell and William Dancey note, "is aware that distinguishing a site and setting its boundaries is an archaeological decision, not an observation."[38] Generally, these authors continue, this is a decision based on artifact density, in order to determine where to excavate. A certain density of potsherds on the surface makes one patch of land a promising place to excavate, and absence of the same may mark the edge of an archaeological site. This is a decision that someone has to make, according to professional judgment and criteria, rather than the kind of observation that involves recognizing that a potsherd is ceramic rather than lithic. In the case of El Tajín, the first person to make this decision was not an archaeologist but a government surveyor, one Ignacio Muñoz.[39]

During his work on the subdivision of Ojital y Potrero, Muñoz mapped a one-hectare boundary for the Pyramid of the Niches and recorded it in Papantla's Public Property Registry. This combination of pyramid and perimeter created a new territory: the archaeological site of El Tajín, located in the lot of Ojital y Potrero, in the jurisdiction of Papantla. The structure itself had theoretically been public property beforehand, but the lands "declared necessary for the care and conservation of the [monumental ruins]" were likewise public property after 1897.[40] However, the law provided no way to determine these boundaries. In the case of El Tajín, it was surveyors not

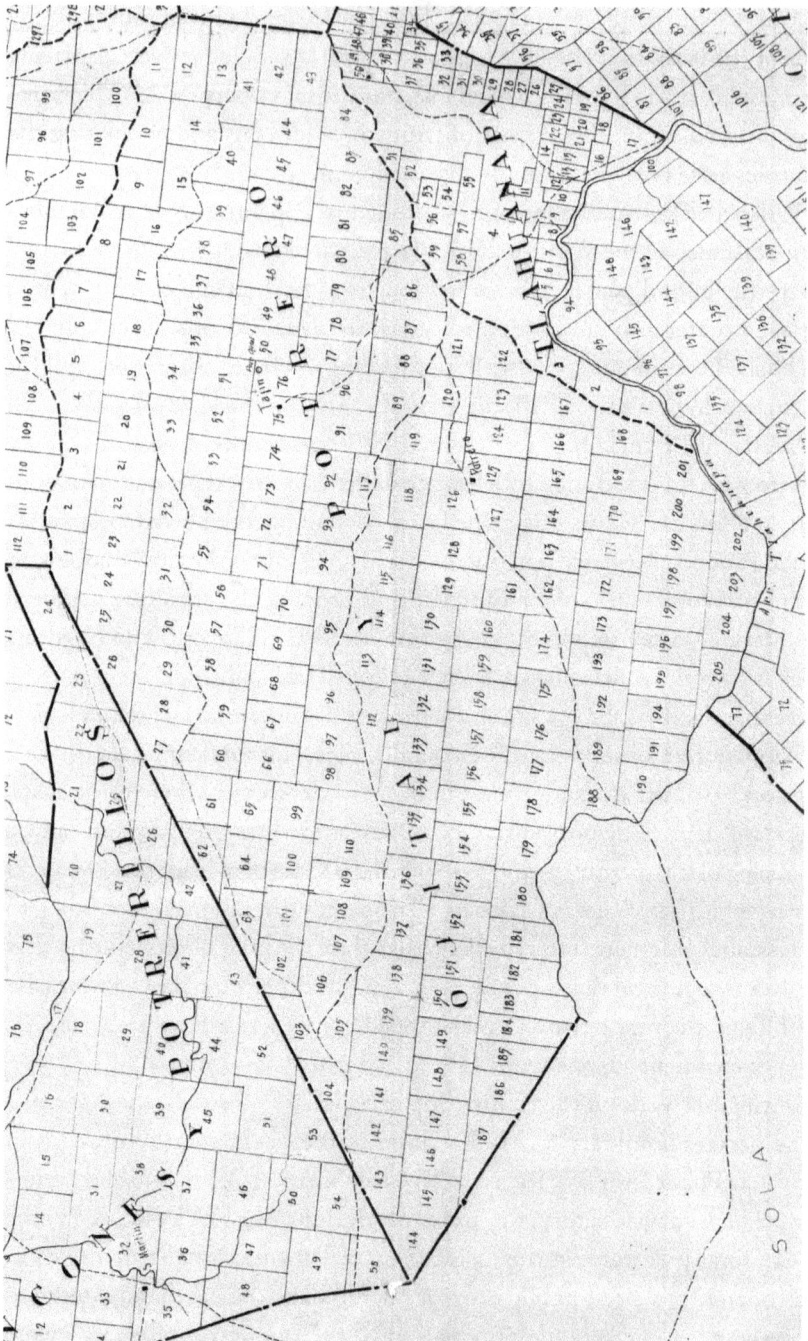

MAP 4. The ex-condueñazgo of Ojital y Potrero, divided into 205 parcels. Mapoteca "Manuel Orozco y Berra" del Servicio de Información Agroalimentaria y Pesquera.

otherwise associated with state archaeology that did the mapping. There are no apparent documentary traces of the criteria Muñoz used to set the boundary. Considering the contemporary volatility of private property rights in Papantla, I suspect that keeping the area as small as possible was the main consideration.[41] As of 1910 this boundary took the material form of a path or *brecha* between the pyramid, legally considered national property, and the privately held parcels.[42]

This boundary did not go unnoticed by the residents of El Tajín and San Antonio Ojital. A half century later, abuelo Lorenzo Xochihua remembered disentailment's role in uncovering the archaeological site. In conversation with José Luis Lorenzo, Xochihua recalled that his father's generation—born in the 1860s—had considered El Tajín as a series of small hills and a source of quality stone. But, Xochihua continued, "when they did the survey of the [community] because of the subdivision, the engineers who made the plan brought [the ruins] to light, this being the first news of them that we had."[43] A machete-cut path marking out a square hectare and duly registered in the Public Property Registry by a government surveyor plays a foundational role in constituting El Tajín as the ruins of a precolonial monument. The boundary also created the potential for a new kind of conflict, one that had not existed in the days when "few people lived [here]; they [farmed] wherever they wanted, without having to get anybody's permission to do so," as Modesto González and Lorenzo Xochihua recalled of the pre-disentailment era.[44] As in sites like Palenque, Mitla, and Teotihuacan, questions of land ownership came up against another Porfirian imperative: the control of the nation's pre-Hispanic past.[45]

The first registry of such a conflict appears just eight years after the subdivision of Ojital y Potrero. In 1904 conserje Leopoldo Armengual wrote to Inspector of Monuments Leopoldo Batres regarding a complaint that the guard had received while clearing the Pyramid of the Niches of vegetation. The owner of parcel 75, one Francisco García, approached Armengual and reminded the conserje to whom the land belonged, admonishing him to not cut down any of the trees on García's property. Armengual wrote to Batres for guidance, noting that the trees could damage the monument. Armengual's report features a simple sketch map: a rectangle with the numbers of the neighboring parcels on each side.[46] Batres's reply is not recorded. However, the structure of this conflict became familiar over the course of the century: government employees and private landholders making claims based on the protection of national patrimony and the use of private property, using a spatial language of lots and parcels.

Agustín García Vega and the Idiom of Patrimony, 1934–38

The Mexican Revolution ostensibly did away with the Porfirian discrimination against contemporary Indigenous communities. The revolutionary state supported Indigenous integration along modern, capitalist lines, reproducing a fundamentally racist logic of essential Indigenous deficiency.[47] At the scale of archaeological bureaucracy, Porfirian objectives, legal principles, and administrative structures endured.[48] Postrevolution conflicts in El Tajín echo the brief exchange between Batres, Armengual, and García. The state's efforts to clear vegetation beyond the Pyramid of the Niches prepared El Tajín for archaeological research and brought archaeologists into conflict with local landowners.

Agustín García Vega of the federal Departamento de Monumentos Prehispánicos began large-scale excavations in 1934, and his project continued over four field seasons, until 1938.[49] García Vega's success in stabilizing the Pyramid of the Niches, beset by precipitation, vegetation, and quarrying, was hardly a foregone conclusion.[50] Technical concerns were only the beginning. More than a few local landowners thought that this research was nothing less than an attack on local livelihoods. In 1935 a number of landowning families complained about the clearing of vegetation (*desmonte*). Identifying themselves as Indigenous Totonac agriculturalists, they wrote to then-president Lázaro Cárdenas. The Partido Nacional Revolucionario, which evidently received the correspondence, wrote to the Secretaría de Educación Pública (SEP) and requested clarification on what García Vega was doing and why.[51] The writers included the heirs of Francisco García—Jose María and Rosalía García (parcel 75)—as well as Fermina Rosas viuda de Jiménez (parcel 76), Marciano Juárez (parcel 52), and Agapito, Espiridion, and Francisco Juárez (parcel 51).[52] Each charged that García Vega had invaded their lands, cut down trees and crops that rightfully belonged to them, prevented them from planting, and ordered them to leave their lands. The account of the three Juárez brothers is particularly detailed:

> We are the owners of parcel number 51, belonging to lot number 17 [*sic*] called Ojital y Potrero of this municipality, there we work in agriculture and live with our families, [the parcel] is the only patrimony that our father left

us. . . . [García Vega] invaded our property, destroying a major part of the forest where we lost our vanilla plantations, in addition to around fifty trees of precious wood, including cedar, sapote, *chijol*, *frijolillo*, and *alzaprima*. . . . After not letting us plant on our land and demanding that we separate ourselves immediately from the place, he told us that said parcel is no longer ours, that it is now the Government's.[53]

Especially telling is the invocation of patrimony (*patrimonio*). "By using an idiom of patrimony to describe a given class of objects," Elizabeth Emma Ferry writes, "actors [make] claims about the ability of such objects to constitute a collectivity and to establish rights to use the objects and simultaneous obligations to maintain and transmit them to future generations."[54] The state's claims to the archaeological site as patrimony of the nation were well established, insofar as the legal ownership of archaeological monuments survived the revolution. However, the ambiguities of national patrimony belonging to the state and to the public opened the space for claims like these, countering the state's view of the monuments as exclusive and inalienable.[55]

The García, Jiménez, and Juárez families subvert the common trope of blaming Indigenous communities for the destruction of pre-Hispanic remains to justify archaeological intervention. They charged that the state was responsible for infringing on their private property rights to critique an overbearing archaeological project. To do so, the Juárez brothers invoke a notion of patrimony that grounds claims to resources in private property and the patrilineal inheritance thereof, derived from disentailment. Concluding their letter, they noted that their parcel "was allocated during the individual Reparto [subdivision] that was verified in 1896 and we possess the respective titles."[56] They were willing to have their parcel expropriated, if they were paid fairly, because "we are humble farmers. . . . We have no more patrimony than the land we work."[57] The contours of the conflict thus become clear: the land, crops, and lumber were rightfully family patrimony, backed by legally recognized private property rights, while the state's claims to the site as national patrimony were nothing less than infringement.

The SEP replied to these complaints by elaborating its claim on El Tajín, beginning with a patient discussion of El Tajín's archaeological importance: its architectural uniqueness, the Pyramid of the Niches' deterioration, and the recent discovery of the site's size. From there, the SEP argued that the desmonte was necessary to prevent the vegetation from damaging archaeological structures. Implicitly recognizing the legitimacy of private property rights in the site, the SEP noted that it was working to indemnify the landowners for their losses. Along similar lines, the SEP continued that the landowners had taken advantage of the desmonte to harvest the trees for valuable lumber.[58] This rhetoric affirms the legitimacy of local property-based claims but emphasizes the administration of archaeological patrimony as the state's property.[59]

The other Totonac landowners of Ojital y Potrero make similar claims. The uniformity in language, formatting, and the fact that all gave the same Papantla address to receive mail suggested that the petitioners worked together, and through an intermediary. However, they do not attempt to solicit an ejido for reasons of need, or a restitution of lands unjustly lost during the Porfiriato.[60] While they invoke indigeneity, the identification is a far cry from the claims to cultural rights that came about in the late twentieth century. Unfortunately, the archives do not hold the resolution to this conflict. Considering that archaeological research and local landownership both continued, it seems that the parties devised an arrangement by which archaeological research could continue with respect for local property rights and livelihoods.

Such pragmatic accommodations—case-by-case compromises that, built on past relationships, allowed the labor of landowners and archaeologists to continue—are certainly not unique to El Tajín.[61] Neither are they specific to archaeology: for the national parks of the period, state planners frequently negotiated with local communities for access to communal resources.[62] The conflicts intensified over time, but the expansion of the archaeological site was only a secondary cause. Rather, renewed pressures on land and local demographic growth made lands more valuable than ever. The vision of space set by disentailment, its boundaries, and its maps remained hegemonic, the idiom by which different actors contested the proper use of the archaeological landscape.

José García Payón, Tourism, and Cattle Ranching, 1939–77

There had long been hints that El Tajín extended well beyond the Pyramid of the Niches. Travelers noted the other mounds and carved sculptures in the vicinity. After García Vega's desmonte, El Tajín's size was undeniable. Likewise undeniable was that the old one-hectare boundary contained only a small portion of the precolonial city. The issue of how to grapple with archaeological research on private property was a recurrent issue for INAH archaeologist José García Payón, who oversaw the expansion of the site from a single fully excavated structure to ten over the course of his career.[63] The process began in earnest during the 1940s and 1950s. Land-use conflicts became flashpoints only in the 1960s and 1970s, thanks to changes in Papantla's broader political economy.

For the first few decades of García Payón's tenure, there is little documentary evidence for the kinds of conflicts that García Vega confronted. The potential was there. According to one manager's map in use during the late 1940s, the parcels surrounding the Pyramid of the Niches—parcels 35, 50–52, and 75–76—were part of the site, marked again by paths.[64] According to notes on a conversation between Isabel Kelly and Modesto González, only parcel 75 had "a part taken by the government, for the issue of the pyramid."[65] With the exception of parcel 76, the rest of these parcels remained in the hands of those families who had complained about García Vega back in 1935.[66] Archaeological research and conservation did not entail the same land-use restrictions that came about by the 1960s and 1970s.

More importantly, lands were abundant. During Kelly's fieldwork in 1947–48, fully 40 percent of Ojital y Potrero's 205 parcels were held by the same families to which they had been allocated in 1896. Of the 60 percent that were not, 86.9 percent were held by other residents of Ojital y Potrero.[67] In other words, 92 percent (189 parcels) of Ojital y Potrero was in local (likely Totonac) hands. It appears that the rate of local landownership actually increased between 1896 and 1947. This remains the most common local explanation for why Ojital y Potrero has no ejidos: for the abuelos, there was simply no need for land grants or restitution.[68] Kelly's contemporary observations noted the lack of local advocacy for land reform: "There is no sinarquismo and no agrarismo in Tajín."[69] Agrarian compression, in which "population growth intersected with land loss, declining wages, and insecure tenancies to produce widespread economic deterioration" was more characteristic of the 1960s than the 1890s.[70]

Between the 1940s and the 1970s the region experienced what Benjamín Ortiz Espejel called "a period of transition and articulation with the market," characterized by the expansion of commercial agriculture—coffee, oranges, and bananas—and cattle ranching.[71] Around El Tajín, the growth of the oil industry and the related development of transportation infrastructure played important roles in making cattle ranching profitable and generating agrarian compression. Though ranching had colonial antecedents, Papantla was not a great place for raising livestock. Precipitation was inconsistent, and the region was poorly integrated into national transportation networks.

Cattle had to be driven south to Veracruz, north to Tampico, or southwest to Teziutlán to board Mexico City–bound trains. The trip took a week or two, and the cattle lost weight (and therefore value) along the way. With the paving of new roads in the 1950s, however, Mexico City could be reached via automobile in about a day.[72] Cattle ranchers were quick to take advantage of the new infrastructure. Between 1947 and 1967, pasturelands in the Mexican tropics expanded at between two and three times the national average.[73] The coastal plains of Papantla were no exception. Pasturelands that comprised 57,712 hectares in 1950 expanded to 128,589 hectares in 1970, an increase of just over 120 percent delivered at the cost of the milpas and forests.[74] Land previously held by the Totonac families of Ojital y Potrero shifted to market-oriented cattle ranchers, typically from outside the region.[75]

At the same time, demographic growth made land all the more important, as parents sought to distribute lands among their children (see table 1).[76] The communities of Ojital y Potrero grew steadily over the twentieth century, and population density almost doubled between 1940 and 1970. Settlements that had been neighborhoods periodically became independent, electing their own officials and managing their own communal labor.

Kelly's observations made during return visits in 1964–65 attest to the scope of the transformations: "The old days, when every man was a maize farmer, now are past; before long, at the rate land is being sold, such agriculture will be out of the question for the Totonac. . . . Instead of fine farmers, with very respectable returns from their produce, they are becoming underprivileged members of the 'national' culture."[77] In short, pressures on land increased, availability dwindled, and families grew between 1940 and 1970.

If the expansion of cattle ranching brought agrarian compression for the Totonac farmers of Ojital y Potrero, the improved access created new demands on the archaeological site of El Tajín: the number of annual tourists grew from 927 in 1950 to 23,917 in 1965, an increase of nearly 2,500 percent (see appendix). Federal and state governments redoubled efforts to define the site's boundaries for management purposes, and with an eye toward expropriation. In 1964 the INAH commissioned surveyor Carlos López Mata for a survey of the site. His report emphasized the necessity of bringing the archaeological site and the parcels on which it sat into the same land tenure regime: "To regularize the legal situation, the boundary survey will be based on the smallest area that contains the largest possible number of archaeological monuments located to date."[78]

TABLE I. Population and density of Ojital y Potrero communities, 1871–2010

YEAR	EL TAJÍN	LAGUNILLA	ZAPOTAL SANTA CRUZ	SAN LORENZO TAJÍN	OJITAL VIEJO	SAN ANTONIO OJITAL	OJITAL NUEVO	TOTAL	RESIDENTS PER HECTARE
1871	247				317			564	0.09
1900	271				389			660	0.10
1910	441				793			1,234	0.19
1921	683				499			1,182	0.19
1930	839				630			1,469	0.23
1940	718				599	218		1,535	0.24
1950	980	347			314	267	207	2,115	0.33
1960	1,097	414			326	258	155	2,250	0.35
1970	1,209	573			418	312	244	2,756	0.43
1980	2,156	793			291	865	395	4,500	0.71
1990	1,352	632			484	353	432	3,253	0.51
2000	1,162	628	250	152	379	238	431	3,240	0.51
2010	1,363	668	446	185	473	193	484	3,812	0.60

Sources: 1871 data from *Memoria leída*, 30. 1900–2010 data from INEGI, Archivo Histórico de Localidades Geoestadísticas, AGEE Veracruz, AGEM 124-Papantla.

Comparing López Mata's map with its predecessors suggests that the site's boundaries came to conform to the boundaries of Ojital y Potrero's parcels, rather than the archaeological extent of the pre-Hispanic city. During the 1920s it was still possible to consider the Pyramid of the Niches an isolated construction, and the one-hectare boundary sufficient. This was much less the case by the late 1960s.[79] Nevertheless, the successive boundary surveys do not demonstrate a simple enlargement of the site's area, or more accurate coverage of the archaeological structures. Surveys conducted in the 1930s by García Vega and guard Erasmo Rodríguez resulted in irregular polygons, expanding into neighboring parcels; López Mata's survey of 1964 conforms to the already-established parcels and fractions. The hegemonic, material effects of disentailment remain visible in how the site's boundaries developed over the course of the twentieth century.

The expansion of cattle ranching, combined with this renewed emphasis on boundaries, intensified conflicts during the 1960s and 1970s. García Payón explained one such conflict in a 1973 letter to his INAH superiors:

> Perhaps because we have enlarged our field of action in the Zona Arqueológica of El Tajín ... or perhaps because the children of the families of Mariano [sic] Juárez and Agapito Juárez have grown; owners of parcels 51 and 52 which includes all of Tajín Chico, and parcel 7[5] which includes the Pyramid of the Niches and is property of Ms. Morales ... not a week passes that we do not have arguments and difficulties with [landowners] for the question of cultivation.... The property owners say that they pay their taxes for the lands that we have taken from them and they want to plant them.[80]

García Payón ends the same letter on a prodding note, commenting that the origins of the conflict, and the necessity of resolving them, were well known: the problem of private parcels and public pyramids.

García Payón's letter offers only a glimpse of the landowners' claims, and echoes of the invocation of patrimony some forty years before. The legitimate ownership of lots and parcels is backed up by paid property taxes. Once again, this conception of landscape is a channel for, rather than the object of, conflict. The landowners could have made their claims in other ways. Perhaps they could have evoked the pre-disentailment system of communal land tenure or attempted to solicit an ejido. But, given the previous efficacy of invoking patrimony with reference to private property rights, why should they have? García Payón, for his part, does not specifically contest the legality or justness of private land ownership in the archaeological site; he critiques land use. To negotiate with landowners, the archaeologist uses lots and parcels as his frame of reference, charting excavations and reconstructions not across a generic "landscape," and not across the specific spatial distribution of precolonial structures common in archaeology. Rather, García Payón had to contend with (and thus continually reinforce) a land tenure regime structured by contiguous, mutually exclusive, and individually owned plots of land on which there happened to be archaeological structures.

This problem of public pyramids and private parcels has a definite historical origin: Porfirian disentailment, rooted in the ideals of nineteenth-century liberalism. From a material point of view, disentailment had unexpected and long-lasting effects crucial to understanding these conflicts. Nearly eighty years after Muñoz made his maps, the language of lots and parcels remained a channel by which archaeologists and landowners used the idiom of patrimony to make claims on El Tajín. As we shall see, these claims eventually failed landowners.

Conservation as Dispossession, 1982–92

Agrarian compression remained the norm during the second half of the twentieth century. The community grew (see table 1) but few Totonac families owned the parcels once held by their parents and grandparents; if they had access to land, it was through informal agreements with neighbors and relatives.[81] By the late 1980s the number of landowners had declined to only twenty-three, and they owned four hundred total hectares because the original thirty-one-hectare parcels had been subdivided and sold piecemeal.[82] In other words, resident land ownership declined 93 percent between 1947 and 1989 (see table 2).[83]

Archaeology was no longer a question of García Payón's small-scale, seasonal excavations. The scale of Proyecto Tajín—a decade-long megaproject that eventually reconstructed twenty-four hectares of the archaeological site (see chapter 6)—further intensified conflicts with landowners.[84] Proyecto Tajín reconstructed three and a half times the number of pre-Hispanic buildings that García Payón did, in one-third of the time. While considering that the question of land tenure was "a very important aspect for the future of the site," project codirectors Jürgen Brüggemann of the INAH and Alfonso Medellín Zenil of the Universidad Veracruzana nevertheless relegated the topic to "the margins of the project" and "a question between the INAH's legal

TABLE 2. Resident landownership in Ojital y Potrero, 1896–2003

YEAR	HECTARES OWNED BY RESIDENTS	HECTARES OWNED BY NONLOCALS	PERCENTAGE OF RESIDENT LANDOWNERS
1896	5,022	1,333	79%
1947	5,859	496	92%
1989	400	5,955	6%
2003	380	5,975	6%

Sources: 1896 data from "Acta general de reparto de los terrenos del Lote No. 19 denominado 'Ojital y Potrero,' entre 205 condueños," AHPM, Fondo Expropriación, c. 1566, exp. 44050; Kourí, A Pueblo Divided; and "Tajín (property, inheritance)," ITKEA, s. 2, b. 42, fol. 330332. 1947 data from "Tajín (property, wealth, inheritance)," ITKEA, s. 2, b. 42, fol. 330232. 1989 data from Kasburg, Die Totonaken, 86–87. 2003 data from Nahmad Molinari and Rodríguez Martínez, "Informe del programa," 32–49, 68. Note that data for 1896 and 1947 were reported in parcels.

office and the State of Veracruz and not the responsibility of the professionals that work on the archaeological project."[85] However, residents of San Antonio Ojital well remember their disputes with Proyecto Tajín officials. The outcomes of these disputes demonstrate the extent to which past pragmatic accommodations ultimately depended on the hegemonic conception of land as property, rendering it vulnerable to dispossession.

Such was the topic of an interview with an abuela I will call María, in her house near the archaeological site. The matriarch of one of the families whose lands ended up in the hands of the state government, she lived on land to which she no longer had legal title. This process was the proximate cause for the 2016 CNDH complaint. María charged that, during Proyecto Tajín, government officials had come to see her, saying that if she did not sell her land, the armed forces would come and take it from her with no recompense, and no relocation. Better to sell, move, and take the money they give you, they told her. María described the discussions she had with her late husband. He "didn't want to sell, because it's the only place we have." She continued: "[My husband] said, 'Look, we don't want to sell our lands, because they're [private] properties and our father gave them to us, how are we going to sell?'" María's account, with the mentions of private property and inheritance, recalls earlier invocations of the idiom of patrimony.

María remembered what happened to her neighbors. She and her family were not the only landowners to experience what followed: "The mayor in

Papantla . . . he got lots of workers, plenty of them. They cut down all the vegetation [*monte*], all that's back there, they hacked away it with machetes, the vanilla beans, they cut down the vanilla vines, and [we] yelled at them 'stop working, don't do that, because [the land is] not sold' and from there things got bad." María and family figured that the incursion meant that their land was going to be seized one way or another. They decided to sell. The legal transaction that followed was not exactly a sale, though the landowners were compensated.[86] Recorded in the Public Property Registry as a donation, María explained the terms they had worked out with Proyecto Tajín officials: "We're going to pay you a little bit, but you're going to continue living here, like you've always lived . . . and if the workers arrive here to work, you can change [residence], where there is no [archaeological] stone you can construct more houses."[87] But those workers have yet to arrive. After 1994 María, along with four other families of the community of San Antonio Ojital, continued to live and work on the land whose titles were now held by the state government.

Such was the case for a total of 201 hectares spread across nine parcels. Of the seventeen landowners involved in this process, twelve "donated" the land and were compensated, four sold their plots, and only one—whose land became the site of the current site facilities and museum—was the subject of a formal expropriation.[88] Some families, like abuelo Ricardo, cited in this chapter's epigraph, accepted the payments and moved elsewhere. This process finished by the mid-1990s, and the state government became the owner of the parcels that composed the archaeological site that was open to the public. Once again, the boundaries of private property determined the extension of the archaeological site.

By the mid-1990s the archaeological site long administered by the INAH and the parcels previously owned by the Totonac residents of San Antonio Ojital were now under similar tenure regimes. The result was similar to what García Payón had experienced: pragmatic, case-by-case accommodations that permitted research to continue while allowing residents to keep farming. A key difference was that the language of lots and parcels that had allowed for María's predecessors to articulate a competing concept of patrimony now demonstrated the hegemonic nature of the property relation, and the extent to which the state controlled the terms of the exchange. As María's experience shows, local economic contexts and state priorities had changed, and older invocations were no longer successful.

Indeed, the 2016 CNDH complaint that opened this chapter failed precisely because the "donations" were duly recorded as such in the Public Property Registry. Nearly a century's worth of documentation cited here reveals repeated invocations of patrimony, referring to private property. But the idiom of patrimony in the context of Indigenous private property held no legal value for the CNDH. Long ago, the complainants had "acquired the properties in question by private title and in good faith, each of them obtaining the right to dispose of the real estate."[89] Past underpayment notwithstanding, the fact that the complainants had been paid at all demonstrated the legality of the overall process: "Contracts are perfected by mere consent, which means that the legal act is valid and effective from the moment of its creation."[90] The CNDH acknowledged the possibility of undue coercion. However, the statute of limitations that would have enabled the complainants to question the contracts had long since expired. Finally, the ethnolinguistic claims of the complainants of San Antonio Ojital had also failed. The protections offered to Indigenous property by the American Convention on Human Rights did not apply, because "the characteristic element of Indigenous communal property rights is that the exercise thereof corresponds to the community in its entirety."[91] The patrimonial value of the archaeological site was unquestioned, but Indigenous private property was an oxymoron.

The language of patrimony, backed up by the legal ownership of private property, had proven useful for the residents of El Tajín and San Antonio Ojital through the 1980s. The private property rights to land and its products that had once enabled Francisco García, the Juárez brothers, and their descendants to contest the state's claims—articulated by Leopoldo Armengual, Agustín García Vega, and José García Payón—had been rendered ineffective without the necessary legal backing, demonstrating the extent to which their earlier success had ultimately depended on the state's willingness to accept such claims. There had been no apparent top-down effort at dispossession, but that was the result. For the communities around El Tajín, the subsequent events of the 2000s were taken as proof positive that dispossession was not just an unexpected consequence, but the state's intent all along.

The Zona de Monumentos Arqueológicos El Tajín, 1999–Present

By the early 2000s El Tajín's economy had radically transformed. Few of its residents had access to the land necessary for subsistence cultivation. A contemporary study of the communities in Ojital y Potrero registered a com-

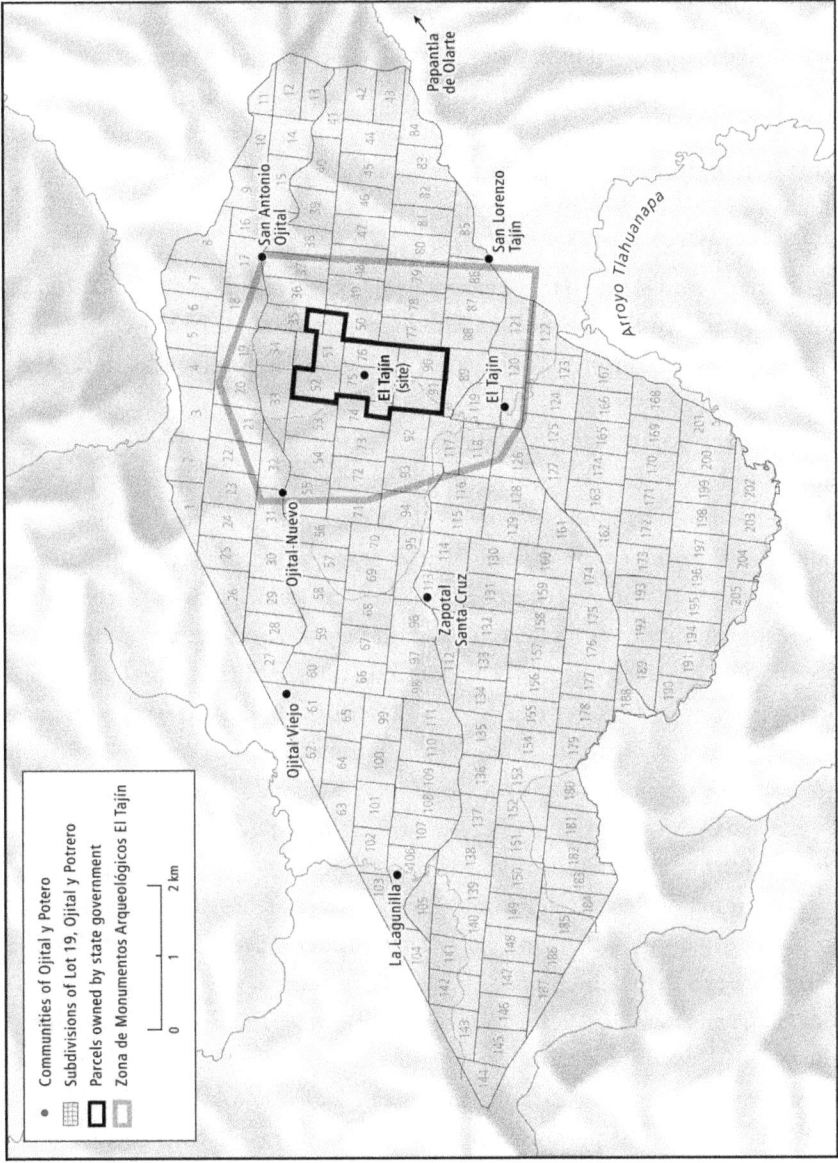

MAP 5. The communities and parcels of contemporary Ojital y Potrero, relative to the boundaries of the Zona de Monumentos Arqueológicos El Tajín. Erin Greb Cartography.

bined total of 380 hectares under local ownership (see table 2). Most of the archaeology conducted in El Tajín was for conservation purposes. Toward the end of the decade, the state government of Veracruz under Miguel Alemán Velasco (1998–2004) sought to develop the northern Veracruz region through tourism. One of the principal outcomes of the effort was the annual Cumbre Tajín event, held in March (see chapter 6). Ostensibly a promotion of Totonac cultural expression, the fact the event brought international musicians and a light-and-sound show to the archaeological site occasioned no small opposition from academics, civil society, and local communities.[92] The controversy caused renewed concern for the conservation of El Tajín, and a new set of boundaries (see map 5).

On March 30, 2001, the administration of President Vicente Fox Quesada declared El Tajín the Zona de Monumentos Arqueológicos El Tajín (ZMAET) with an area of 1,221.5688 hectares.[93] This declaration set forth a new set of boundaries in the shape of an irregular seven-sided figure, locally known as the *poligonal*, and a series of land-use restrictions that gave the INAH the responsibility to evaluate any constructions that involved the digging of foundations.[94] The poligonal was based on an unpublished archaeological survey that, as one former site director described to me, was "very well done in archaeological terms and very poorly done in political terms" because it ignored modern communities. Overnight, residents of the communities of El Tajín, San Antonio Ojital, San Lorenzo Tajín, Nuevo Ojital, and Zapotal Santa Cruz found themselves living within an archaeological monuments zone.

The timing of this declaration was a surprise: the available planning documents only note that "delimiting is a synonym for protecting" and cite the precedent of a 1976 delimitation.[95] Colleagues in the academy and communities alike considered Cumbre Tajín the main cause. The federal government, they argued, used the declaration to prevent the state government's tourism development plans from affecting the archaeological site. "When they bought the land for the Parque Temático and it was installed," one former local official told me, "[the federal government] said that the [state government] was going to invade everything and [the INAH] preferred to stop it there." To most residents, however, it looked like the state government built whatever it wanted inside the poligonal, like the event space known as the Parque Temático, while landowners had to solicit permission just to add a room to a house or drill a well.

In 2002 affected residents formed a Property Defense Committee when the INAH began to suspend unauthorized constructions in the community of El Tajín. The local authority cited above described the necessity of defense: "Why should I get permission? If I'm on my property, there are no mounds, there's nothing. . . . We too see where there are mounds, [and we ensure] that nobody goes to excavate, and nobody goes to destroy them." In April 2002 this committee worked through Senator Fidel Herrera Beltrán to request the suspension of the 2001 declaration, arguing that the poligonal was disrupting the livelihoods of the proximate communities, and that there had been no consultation done beforehand.[96] While the federal government did not change the declaration, the INAH carried out a series of applied studies to educate residents on the purpose and importance of the new measures.[97]

Currently, those who live inside the poligonal are required to seek permission from the INAH before beginning construction on their lands. An informational leaflet available to residents during the tenures of the past few site directors outlines the requirements: an INAH 017 form (one original and two copies), legal identification (two copies), a description of the work with the requisite technical specifications (two copies), an architectural plan (two copies), five photographs (originals and one copy), and the title or lease (two copies). After submitting these materials, a local INAH archaeologist would be dispatched to the construction site for evaluation and possible salvage excavation. From the perspectives of residents who have battled to maintain ever-shrinking pieces of the lands bequeathed to them by their parents and grandparents, such restrictions look like nothing less than proof of the state's intention to expropriate El Tajín. One former San Antonio Ojital resident who still owns property inside the poligonal put it succinctly: "We're inside [but the lands] aren't ours."

Conclusion

The definition of certain landscapes as "worthy of conservation" typically entails disqualifying certain uses of land, including private ownership, in favor of Western conservation procedures. To affect dispossession in the name of heritage conservation, it may not be necessary to recast inhabitants as interlopers—and police them accordingly—or to carry out "spatial cleansing" operations for development.[98] Following the political economy of archaeology suggests that neither long-term purpose nor intent is necessary to affect land dispossession.[99] In this case, the trajectories of disentailment (1876–96), state-led archaeological research (1892–2001), and agrarian compression (1950s–80s) intersected to create the conditions for dispossession. Yet residents' concerns about possible land expropriation are correct in their allocation of responsibility: disentailment, archaeological research, and the oil development that facilitated the expansion of cattle ranching all led back to the state, and its effects disproportionately affected the rural Totonac inhabitants of the region. The complainants of San Antonio Ojital, who declared that "it is unjust that we should be dispossessed, threatened, deceived, or have our lands stolen, simply because we are Indigenous," would likely agree.[100]

Underlying the private property regime and the eventual dispossession was a language of lots and parcels, grounded in the creation and visualization of material boundaries that persist today. This particular vision of space, and channel for land-use conflict, was one among many impacts of disentailment. The growth of the oil industry was another result. A chance encounter in Mexico's National Archives brought home this point. While looking for correspondence related to an old oil well drilled on the outskirts of El Tajín, I found myself dully looking through a bound set of documents related to drilling permissions. One document, a parcel plan, stood out because of how similar it looked to others of its kind—that is, boring.[101] The plan's heading located the land and its owners in a nested political geography: parcel-lot-municipality-state. The map consisted of a rectangle featuring the designation "N° 75" surrounded by the names of other owners and their parcels' numbers. The plot of land was represented by clear boundaries, mutually exclusive and interchangeable with others of its kind, and was empty of topography, vegetations, or dwellings. Representing the vision of space set out by nineteenth-century disentailment, this plan on folio 40 was all the more interesting for erasing the region's best-known archaeological structure: the Pyramid of the Niches.

I was tempted to read the erasure metaphorically, assuming that further research would reveal how rapacious capitalists had overridden the pre-Hispanic past. Unfortunately, it is not difficult to find case studies of archaeological sites destroyed by the operations of extractive industry. Even in El Tajín, recent excavations by Arturo Pascual Soto in the Building of the Columns Complex indicate the existence of historic oil infrastructure and the probable modification of archaeological structures.[102] The celebrated Olmec site of La Venta, Tabasco, is another example: excavated with the support of the state-owned oil company in 1955, important parts of the site were looted and built over shortly thereafter.[103]

Nevertheless, examining the relationships between the extraction of oil, the production of knowledge, and the management of the pre-Hispanic past yields unexpected results. There was conflict, especially in regard to land tenure. Here, too, the idiom of space naturalized by disentailment became a channel for oil companies and speculators to join the discussions between archaeologists and landowners. Yet there was also a surprising degree of intermittent but long-term cooperation, ranging from the material to the financial. The following chapter will explore the relationships between archaeology and oil extraction in El Tajín.

Oil

2

Practical Entanglements, Cumulative Contamination

> After the oil arrived, then there began to be the plague, polluted
> water everywhere, because they began to drill in the communities. . . .
> If you have water close, [an oil well] affects you, that's what they
> don't pay you for. They pay a bit, they're taking out [natural] gas or
> gasoline and you're not paid for that, that's why they say the poor are
> exploited, they're extracting on your own land but they don't pay you.
> Had you not realized that?
> —Valerio

The old oil well was a short hike from the trail that led to San Antonio
Ojital. The cement bases and platform were still visible, and the rusted blue
well casing bore the welded inscription "Ojital-1" with the date of its sealing:
August 28, 1939. The older residents of San Antonio Ojital and El Tajín knew
about Ojital-1. A few remembered how their parents had told them about
the oil workers' settlement and the school, or the unusual hanging bridges
that permitted access to the well. During the 1990s, site custodios recalled,
the casing had given off a foul odor. That smell, combined with the sounds
of dripping liquid that you could hear if you got close, made the custodios
concerned about the well's safety. Some recalled Petróleos Mexicanos coming
to El Tajín, resealing the well, and repainting the well casing. But the well
itself, and how anyone let it be drilled within just a hundred meters of the
Pyramid of the Niches, remained mysterious.

The history of the well was obscure, but its future looked clear. Before budget cuts eliminated his position in 2015, INAH anthropologist Jesús Trejo was
working on an ecotourism route with the Unión de Campesinos Ruta Turística
San Antonio Ojital.[1] The route would follow the trail that led from the
archaeological site to San Antonio Ojital. As described in the official reports,
the objectives of this community-managed project were to take advantage of

tourism in El Tajín, conserve local flora and fauna, and introduce "Totonac cultural expressions and practices into the range of tourist attractions, not as a return to the past, but an alternative, to develop indigenous knowledge."[2] This project—"Lankasipi," Totonac for "high hill"—slowly advanced between 2012 and 2017. The organization sought funding, support, and permissions from the municipal government, INAH, PEMEX, and the Comisión Nacional para el Desarrollo de Pueblos Indígenas. The Unión de Campesinos purchased and facilitated the donation of land to ensure easy passage via the trail, and to construct a restaurant in San Antonio Ojital. While Lankasipi was officially opened and is technically operating, organizational difficulties as of 2024 have prevented the ecotourism trail from becoming the alternative to informal commerce that residents and INAH anthropologists had hoped it would be.

The project's interpretations of the landscape recontextualized Ojital-1 and the remains of its installations.[3] The trail opens with a thematic section in which the guide and visitors ask permission to pass from Kiwigkolo, the Lord of the Monte, and stories of the Tajininis, mischievous sprites often blamed for the disappearance of household goods. The second section, titled "history of the oil industry," involves stops at Ojital-1 and a nearby masonry structure commonly identified as an oil company office (see figure 1).[4] The foundations of this building appear to be stone from the archaeological site, the dimensions of its bricks are atypical compared with the local standard, and one outward-facing brick is stamped with an Evens & Howard maker's mark.[5] In the photographic archives of the Centro INAH Veracruz, I was surprised to find pictures documenting the building's construction in 1941. The corresponding reports from José García Payón confirmed that the building was not an office but an unfinished field house, intended to form part of the archaeological site's installations.[6] Yet the common association of the infrastructure of archaeology with the oil well is not wrong. In the unfinished house, distinctions between state archaeology and the oil industry are literally immaterial, indistinguishable at the level of the things of which they were made.

I take this association as a starting point to trace the exchanges between the use of the pre-Hispanic past and the extraction of oil in the broader political economy of archaeology. To do so, I discuss four episodes in the history of oil development in northern Veracruz: small-scale, artisanal exploration (1869–1908); widespread industrialization (1908–40); the expansion of the nationalized industry (1940–70); and the results of declines, crises, and

FIG. 1. José García Payón's unfinished field house, 2012. Photograph by the author.

unconventional oil exploitation (1970–2020). I tie each of these tendencies to the practice of archaeology, and to rural Totonac livelihoods, in which extraction is an ongoing and cumulative process of contamination. A well that begins to produce salt water may be sealed and end its contribution to oil production but, as Poza Rica historian José Luis Rodríguez Badillo once admonished me, "A well never ceases to be active." The potential for further production, and pollution, is always present. Whether productive, sealed, or in ruins, oil infrastructure continues to affect the landscape.

Nationalist Archaeology and Foreign Oil Exploration

The parallels between archaeology and oil extraction predate the emergence of either as specific extractive practices. Colonization was not yet complete when the Spanish crown began establishing its claims to the pre-Hispanic past. A 1536 law regulated pre-Hispanic materials as "treasures," subject to royal authority.[7] As Grace Alexandrino Ocaña has observed, Francisco Álvarez de Toledo, Viceroy of Peru (1569–81), implemented legal reforms that brought antiquities and precious metals into the same legal framework.[8] The tendency to consider pre-Hispanic materials as national property administered by the state thus began with the Spanish crown.[9] The same was true of oil: the earliest efforts to extract oil in Mexico were governed by a late-colonial law that reserved "bitumen and juices of the earth" to the Crown and the Mexican state that succeeded it.[10] The Porfirian state's legal reforms adopted "an Anglo-American conception of property rights" to encourage oil development but without letting go of the nation's subsoil wealth.[11] The Porfirian nationalization of archaeological sites, embodied in the Law of Archaeological Monuments of 1897, thus appears in line with the state's view of the subsoil. The Constitution of 1917 made this understanding explicit: Article 27 vested "an original right of property over the lands and waters within the boundaries of the national territory" to the nation.[12] This became the legal basis for land reform and, eventually, the 1938 expropriation of the foreign-owned oil industry.[13] The expropriation "pulled archaeology into its later conceptualization and use, since archaeological remains . . . were found in the subsoil [and] considered property of the Nation, neither more nor less than the legal concept that constituted the essence of the expropriation decree."[14] Archaeology and oil became twin national patrimonies.[15]

Parallel disciplinary trajectories further link the study of the past and the search for oil. By the 1930s archaeology and petroleum geology had only recently become professional disciplines focused on the subsoil. Before the 1910s, archaeological methods in Mexico emphasized iconographic interpretation and collecting expeditions rather than excavation.[16] Only by the 1920s had professional petroleum geologists taken charge of oil exploration from the so-called practical men, whose authority was derived from experience and results rather than formal training.[17] Toward the 1940s both archaeology and oil production involved the site-specific, expert extraction of subsurface materials in the service of a metropolitan center that operated through state agencies.

These alignments influenced, but did not determine, how archaeology and oil operated on the ground. Rosemary Coombe and Melissa Baird describe such landscapes as "places of emergent agency at the intersection of industrial enterprise, transnational governmentalities, international norms, and local interests . . . in which natural heritage and sustainable development initiatives uneasily coexist with extractive industry and people who have cultural attachments to lands."[18] By the 1930s the grounds of this conflict in Mexico are clear. State-sponsored archaeology inherited the Porfirian state ownership of precolonial monuments, now redirected toward forging a mestizo national identity. Foreign oil companies, once lauded as an instrument of modernization, represented a "perverse, parasitic imperialism" in the aftermath of the

FIG. 2. Ojital-1 with associated infrastructure, c. 1938. The Pyramid of the Niches is visible at left, while the oil well can be seen at the end of the path to the right. Zona Arqueológica Tajín, 1939, Fondo Aerofotográfico Oblicuas, FAO_01_001565, Acervo Histórico, Fundación ICA.

revolution.[19] These foreign firms were famously expropriated in 1938, creating the state monopoly on oil production: Petróleos Mexicanos (PEMEX).

These events, and their legacies, shape how people understand the pre-expropriation era. I saw these understandings at work during public presentations of this research. On one such occasion, a PEMEX surveyor was in attendance. He was no stranger to Ojital-1, having been a member of the team that resealed the well in the 1990s. He recalled his shock at seeing the overgrown well so close to the archaeological site: "I'd say that it was criminal because we know beforehand that Porfirio Díaz made a deal with the United States to give them oil extraction concessions in exchange for the technology to construct trains and railroads, and the foreigners came to take it and to keep the oil." He continued: "I think that consciousness of our cultural and archaeological richness is [now] more marked in society . . . and how many things we've lost." In this account, the state's responsibilities to manage the nation's subsoil materials as patrimony include archaeological materials and oil. Photos like figure 2 provided the opportunity to reflect on the cultural materials lost because of the foreign drive for Mexico's subsurface riches—and, by implication, the fundamental linkages between oil production and archaeological research as part of the same nationalist project.

Rodríguez Badillo described this project to me as a *"patriotismo de cuidar"*: patriotism articulated through the care of the nation's twin patrimonies of oil and archaeological remains. In this view, the drilling of Ojital-1 is an example of the state's failure to protect the pre-Hispanic past, and of the greed of foreign capitalists. Yet Ojital-1 was not the first time that interests in archaeology and oil crossed paths in Papantla, and the resulting interactions were closer to mutual constitution than opposition.

Artisanal Exploration, 1869–1908

The early history of oil in Mexico was written in El Tajín's environs: names like Furberos, Palma Sola, and Poza Rica were hotspots for petroleum exploration beginning in the 1860s. The same geological formations that provided bitumen to the pre-Hispanic builders of El Tajín and their ancestral neighbors provided Mexico with petroleum.[20] Between the world's first oil boom—in Pennsylvania, 1859—and the apocalyptic Dos Bocas fire of 1908, Mexican petroleum went from regional curiosity to national economic priority.[21] Porfirian legal reforms soon sought to encourage foreign investment in the new commodity.[22] In Papantla this process developed according to local antecedents.

Scarcely a decade after the Pennsylvania oil boom, Papantla became "the setting of a key episode in the history of petroleum-related activity in the country," the founding of the Compañía Explotadora del Golfo Mexicano.[23] In 1869 American Lawrence W. O'Bannon and Scot Henry P. Manfred founded the company to exploit the surface seepages known as Caguas, Cougas, or Quhax, about twenty kilometers west of El Tajín. The Compañía Explotadora got a bank loan, purchased machinery in the United States, drilled a forty-meter well, and eventually produced between four and five barrels of oil daily.[24] The venture was unprofitable, however, and the company failed by 1872. In 1880 former company shareholder and local doctor Adolphus Autrey claimed the abandoned installations, mounting a small-scale kerosene refinery in Papantla.[25] Collecting surface seepages and transporting the petroleum from the tract now called La Constancia to Papantla via mule train, Autrey refined a total of four thousand gallons of kerosene for local sale.[26] Once the kerosene business proved unsustainable, Autrey moved to Tampico in 1892 and founded what became a national pharmaceutical supply chain.[27]

Correspondence from Autrey suggests that the linkages between archaeological research and oil extraction were material, setting the foundations for similar interactions during the twentieth century. In an 1892 letter, Autrey drew on contemporary scholarship to discuss the history of the region.[28] Humboldt's account of El Tajín from the *Political Essay on the Kingdom of New Spain* and "Indian tradition" provided evidence of the region's long history of human habitation. Etymology and landscape demonstrated the antiquity of Totonac uses of oil: "Cougas" is a Totonac word meaning "a kind of black oil or wax," while Autrey encountered "an old shaft, thoroughly walled up with rock" during his first explorations.[29] Well before the disciplinary consolidation of archaeology or petroleum geology, researching the past and finding oil went together: "Everywhere that the Company dug or broke the earth in any form in the vicinity of the [oil] springs, idols, broken pottery, &c., were constantly encountered, all of which goes to show that in this vicinity a past race had their place of abode."[30] Autrey's expertise proved valuable to El Tajín's occasional tourists.[31]

The troubling features of epistemic colonialism were likewise in place. After taking the trouble to note that "knowledge of the [seepages'] existence were known & guarded by the Totonaco Indians," Autrey declared that because "I was the first white man that ever made a track in that section of dense forest . . . I claim to be the modern discoverer of the Cougas oil."[32] Despite Autrey's admitted debt, Indigenous knowledge of petroleum is relegated to the nonmodern and simply does not count. Another section of this letter reads like an omen. Autrey recounted how "a lone peon Indian" was mining a tunnel when he encountered a slate formation about fifty feet in. When the worker cracked the stone face, oil came through.[33] He left the tunnel and dammed the mouth to avoid losing the oil, and returned the following day, candle in hand to investigate. "The poor Indian was fearfully burnt and I had a hard task to save his life," Autrey wrote.[34] The fire burned itself out after six hours. In Autrey's reckoning, the impacts of this event were that "no one could be induced to go into the tunnel to finish the work so nearly completed," but fortunately he was able to acquire quality oil by completing the dam and letting the oil flow.[35] What was a life-altering accident for an unnamed Indigenous worker was an impediment to oil extraction for Autrey. Oil taking precedence over Indigenous livelihoods became a pattern.

Autrey's efforts were not commercially successful, but they attracted attention: he was said to have won an award for the quality of his kerosene at the I Exposición Industrial de Querétaro in 1882.[36] In 1897 British entrepreneur Percy Norman Furber and lawyer Luis de la Barra got word that oil had been discovered in the Papantla region.[37] Following up on the lead took Furber to the massive Palma Sola estate, home to the tract once known as Caguas and La Constancia. Palma Sola was the property of Italian vanilla magnate Pedro Tremari, who expanded the estate in the aftermath of disentailment (see chapter 3).[38] In a 1906 report to prospective buyers, Theodore Gestefeld described Palma Sola as "as handsome a piece of property as can be found in the tropics, [in] that the climate and soil conditions are all that can be asked for an agricultural and cattle raising proposition," where vanilla, chicle, and tobacco were cultivated, though the infrastructural deficiencies were significant.[39] After meeting with Tremari, and following some legal wrangling, Furber purchased the former Caguas/La Constancia tract and founded the Oil Fields of Mexico Company in 1903.

The 2,500-hectare tract, soon renamed Furbero, was an early epicenter for oil development: it proved productive by 1904.[40] Furber's company also constructed a narrow-gauge railway, linking Furbero with the port of Cobos, near Tuxpan. This railway, later known as La Maquinita, spurred infrastructural development and remains an important symbol of industrial heritage for the region.[41] Furber was far from alone in his efforts to exploit this newly profitable resource; in 1907 he partnered with British engineer Weetman Pearson, whose Compañía Mexicana de Petróleo El Águila was one of the country's largest oil producers.[42] El Águila bought out Furber and the Oil Fields of Mexico Company in 1914, cementing corporate attention to the area later known as the Golden Lane (Faja de Oro) for its wealth.[43]

Industrialization, 1908–40

Gonzalo Bada Ramírez was six years old when the San Diego del Mar No. 3 well blew. Seventy years later, he recalled the morning of July 4, 1908. The uncontrolled blowout (also known as a gusher) accidentally ignited. A kilometer and a half away, residents of the municipality of Tantima fled. "We left running," Bada explained, "as far as we could, we went four or five kilometers to stop and see the smoke, and how the people were leaving, some on foot, others running, some half-shoeless, others didn't even have time to put on a shirt."[44] It was the kind of thing one remembered for the rest of their life, he added, not only for the magnitude of the disaster, but for its effects: "Ruin came to the region, we didn't have water to drink, the water became salty, the agricultural lands were spoiled, the livestock—everything was ruined."[45] The fire burned out after fifty-six days, overcoming all efforts to extinguish it.[46] After five years, Dos Bocas, so called for the twin craters left by the disaster, "was an awesome sight. It smelled and looked like I imagine hell might look and smell," American geologist Charles Hamilton wrote.[47]

For contemporary officials and foreign oil interests, Dos Bocas was less outright disaster than proof positive of Mexico's oil wealth, a symptom of the country's transition to modernity.[48] In its aftermath, artisanal exploration gave way to "savage industrialization": a large-scale production process characterized by short, geographically specific boom-and-bust cycles.[49] Between 1901 and 1921 Mexican oil production grew an astonishing 18,695 times.[50] Companies focused their efforts on the Huasteca—a region comprising parts of the states of Veracruz and Tamaulipas to the north, and San Luis Potosí to the northwest—where exploitation was most feasible. These sources provided much of the country's overall production through 1921. Despite a subsequent decline in production at the national scale, local oil exploitation continued to expand.[51] Near El Tajín, El Águila shifted production from Furbero and Palma Sola to Poza Rica. The transition was swift: in 1930 well Poza Rica-2 proved productive, and by 1936 the Poza Rica fields accounted for fully one-third of all Mexican oil production.[52] Two years later, the foreign-owned industry was expropriated to create Petróleos Mexicanos.

Indexing the results, local historian and oil worker Sinesio Capitanachi Luna later recounted the Poza Rica firsts that accompanied these developments: the first movie theater (1930); the first school and the first grocery store (1933); the first medical doctor and the first newspaper (1934); and the first car, bus, and airline (1936).[53] The traditional dispersed settlement pattern gave way to rapid urbanization, as the workers of Palma Sola were reassigned to Poza Rica in 1932.[54] Domestic and foreign workers now joined the Totonac residents of the municipality of Coatzintla, creating "a clear territorial segregation [that] made social differences explicit. Foreigners lived in canvas or wooden houses and enjoyed a recreational and social center, as well as their own dining halls; the [non-Indigenous] Mexican laborers lived in huts built by themselves with perishable materials, principally *tarro* [bamboo] and palm."[55] The Poza Rica zone thus became quite distinct from its neighbor, Papantla.

As the violence of the revolution declined, archaeologists and oil interests continued to cross paths. Petroleum geologist and archaeologist Walther Straub made the relationship clear: "Revolutionary conditions had, heretofore, made archaeological explorations in the Huasteca impossible, but with the opening up of the various oil fields opportunity came for scientific investigation."[56] Ojital y Potrero became a hotbed for both: between 1920 and 1938 some 727 contract operations related to land—sales, transfers, purchases, leases, and the like—were completed, and fully 95 percent (195 parcels) of the lot was affected in some way.[57] Among these operations was Concession 1308, to drill for oil in parcel 76, otherwise known as the archaeological site of El Tajín.[58] By early 1936 the American-owned Stanford y Compañía owned parcel 76 and held its drilling rights.[59] While these negotiations were in progress, the company set to surveying the parcel to plan drilling. It dispatched employees Luis Galvin Parker and Emilio Alvarez with a work crew—only to have their work suspended by conserje Erasmo Rodríguez, who notified his superiors accordingly.[60] The Departamento de Monumentos Prehispánicos contacted the federal Secretaría de la Economía Nacional; the company did the same. On December 23, 1935, Monumentos Prehispánicos directed Rodríguez to allow the survey to continue "under your supervision, caring that the clearing does not damage the monuments."[61] By New Year's Eve 1935, Monumentos Prehispánicos had granted the company permission to conduct a topographical survey, with the stipulation that "it should not execute any work in places where there are archaeological ruins of any class, advising for all drilling or preliminary work near the archaeological site."[62] The survey was evidently completed, and Monumentos Prehispánicos was duly notified.

In response to the notification, Monumentos Prehispánicos dispatched architect Luis R. Ruíz to inspect the proposed location of the well on January 8, 1936.[63] The Compañía Stanford contracted a plane to fly Ruíz over El Tajín before landing in the nearby airstrip in El Chote. From there, he accompanied company officials on horseback to inspect the well's proposed location relative to the pre-Hispanic structures.[64] Ruíz was a sympathetic observer. According to correspondence between company officials, Ruíz "insisted in the convenience of the Company to build an embankment or a terreplein on the road which leads to this well and right over the archaeological platforms which can be easily appreciated at simple sight."[65] Ruíz further sought to convince the skeptical Rodríguez that "the Company would do all in its power to prevent any harm to those platforms."[66] The following day, Ruíz wired Monumentos

Prehispánicos to say that "on the indicated point and around it there are no problems for drilling, authorize work."[67] Rodríguez halted the work once more, but by January 27, 1936, the Departamento del Petróleo had granted the drilling permit.[68] Construction proceeded accordingly.

What does it take to drill an oil well? Estimating that the well would be drilled to a depth of 2,100 meters, the company planned on using fifty-five tons of blast-furnace cement for the piping, another ninety-five tons for the drilling of the well, and concrete bases for the seventeen-ton Parkersburg Rig and Reel Company tower.[69] The extant oil infrastructure helped with logistics: one could transport goods from Cobos to the nearby oil camp of Poza Rica via the Maquinita.[70] From Poza Rica (also known as Kilómetro 52 for its place on the railroad), one could take the path to the well Poza Rica No. 8 and head down a Compañía Stanford–built embankment toward El Tajín and Papantla.[71] From there, construction began. After leveling the ground, workers installed the concrete bases used to support the drilling tower. The drilling tower, in turn, scaffolded the drill bit (used to dig) and the drill pipe (used to remove the resulting soil and crushed rock). With the tower mounted, the work crew began the drilling process, pausing to remove debris until the drill struck an oil-rich geological formation, or useless saltwater.[72] While the work of leveling the ground, building the reservoir, and constructing the first houses began in January 1936, drilling did not commence until November of that year.[73]

To the extent that both archaeology and oil exploration had similar infrastructural requirements, practical collaboration won out over ideological opposition. Government archaeologists and oil companies shared infrastructure, equipment, and expertise. As Ruíz put it, "The construction of the road . . . would take men of science and tourists to these places so that they will be better studied and known. . . . The cooperation and conciliation of archaeological and petroleum interests is easy to carry out with mutual benefit."[74] The task fell to Agustín García Vega, then in charge of excavations at the site. In July 1936 García Vega wrote that he had solicited aid from the Compañía Stanford and El Águila, and he had received 500 pesos for the construction of the road and fencing material to line it.[75]

The equipment used to drill and maintain an oil well likewise proved useful for the reconstruction of archaeological monuments. In the same report, García Vega noted, "I began the construction of a small post, a crane, rather, for which I counted with the help of the head of the camp of the Oil Company that is drilling in El Tajín, who gallantly facilitated me the necessary material: three two-inch tubes, one four-inch tube, a half-inch round iron and a U-shaped iron, and as well he permitted that part of the construction be carried out in his workshops, though most of said work was carried out in Papantla."[76] This crane, García Vega continued, enabled him to "raise two large stone slabs that constituted the cornice of the lowest group of niches on the central staircase of the Pyramid, as well as the reconstruction of seven niches of the lower body of the same Pyramid on the North side."[77] In a context of nationalist archaeology, one might expect that projects like road-building and monumental reconstruction were the exclusive purview of the state. On the ground, however, García Vega's ability to do his state-commissioned excavation and reconstruction materially depended on the operations of the Compañía Stanford's Ojital-1 well.

The sharing of expertise is visible in how archaeologists and oil companies evaluated the landscape. Each conducted topographical surveys, to understand the distribution of the pre-Hispanic structures, and to decide where to drill an oil well, respectively. The company's January 1936 well localization report records the proposed location of the well, the parcel boundaries, and possible roads, as well as archaeological mounds—numbered and ranked according to a four-tier system, based on size.[78] García Vega began his own survey in June 1937. According to Compañía Stanford engineer Juan B. La Riviere, García Vega was tasked with surveying the site to determine an area for expropriation. Other company officials were thus suspicious when the two met and compared notes. La Riviere clarified that García Vega "had given him the measurements only with the understanding that we would give the engineer a copy of our plan when it is prepared. . . . In other words, we are not helping the engineer in any way."[79] Corporate mistrust aside, the exchange of information demonstrated the commensurability of knowledge generated by archaeological research and oil extraction.

One result of the Compañía Stanford's topographic survey was the determination, numbering, and categorization of El Tajín's unexcavated pre-Hispanic structures, one of the objectives for which García Vega had been commissioned.[80] At the same time, one result of García Vega's mapping was the determination of the site's boundaries for the purposes of expropriation, which was never carried out (see chapter 1). Though antithetical to the company's interests, the determination resulted from exchanges between García Vega and La Riviere. While the company's objectives were clear—the development of Ojital-1 for oil production—they did not predetermine the company's interactions vis-à-vis state-sponsored archaeology in El Tajín.

Despite ideological opposition between foreign oil interests intent on profiting from Mexico's subsoil and a nationalist archaeology intent on preserving the same, examining infrastructure, equipment, and expertise demonstrates their practical entanglement. Still, this collaboration had its critics. Luis R. Ruíz was asked to resign when Secretaría de Educación Pública head (and former Veracruz governor) Gonzalo Vázquez Vela saw where Ruíz's approved well had been drilled.[81] Papantla French teacher and Monumentos Prehispánicos honorary inspector Luis André likewise wrote to the secretaría, noting that "the company . . . cut a road, more like a path . . . very closely, TOO CLOSE, to the famous pyramids of the archaeological site of El Tajín."[82]

After expropriation in 1938, PEMEX took over the operation of Ojital-1, and parcel 76 passed into the state company's hands. The well was sealed in August 1939, having reached a depth of 2,584.86 meters and having produced mostly salt water.[83] The workers and wooden houses (see figure 2, far right) were relocated to Poza Rica, where they were given plots of land in Colonia Argüelles. That neighborhood was renamed Colonia Tajín in commemoration of the fact that its first settlers had worked in El Tajín; it retains the name to this day. The workers' union chapter, Local 19, merged with Local 30, representing the workers of Poza Rica, in 1940.[84] The bricks used in the well installation stayed. García Payón took advantage of them to begin construction of a field house, the same that remains incomplete today.[85] By 1947, considering "this intrusive petroleum element," Isabel Kelly wrote that "little trace remains in Tajín. . . . The ruins of the old camp are effectively hidden by dense vegetation; and, culturally, the enterprise seems to have left surprisingly few scars. The Totonac, it is said, had little direct contact with the outsiders."[86]

By the 1940s the environmental effects of oil exploration were clear, as Myrna Santiago has shown: oil well and storage tank fires, pollution, habitat loss, and uncontrollable well blowouts were among its symptoms.[87] The Papantla region seems to have suffered less than its neighbors during this period. However, the human cost of environmental destruction became a salient feature of local historical memory in short order. This destruction has less to do with the predatory foreign firms than the operations of the nationalized oil industry.

PEMEX and Its Discontents, 1940–70

Between the 1920s and the 1940s Mexico's oil industry transitioned from an export-oriented sector characterized by the predominance of foreign capital to a state-owned industry supporting the country's growing internal market.[88] What Germán Vergara calls "the other revolution" saw oil become a key domestic energy source and an important economic sector.[89] Under Director-General Antonio J. Bermúdez (1946–58), PEMEX established itself as a vertically integrated and state-owned firm at the service of Mexico's economic development through import-substitution industrialization.[90] The enterprise thus expanded its exploration programs: in 1941–46 PEMEX drilled 39 exploratory wells; in 1947–52, 286; and in 1953–58, 590.[91] Papantla was not exempt from this trend. Celebrating the nineteenth anniversary of the expropriation in 1957, Bermúdez announced "the discovery, which could be the most productive of the last twenty-five years, of the San Andrés fields, located south of Papantla, Veracruz."[92] In conjunction with the prior 1949 discovery of the Presidente Alemán fields, the development of the San Andrés fields became a key driver for regional infrastructural change.

Compared with the literature generated around the expropriation, there has been little written on the likes of these fields. Yet their local impacts were substantial. Anthropologist Ramón Ramírez Melgarejo describes the work necessary to inaugurate a new oil field:

An oil well occupies an area of 15,000 m2. It is an embankment-like structure made up of a thick layer of gravel that ensures adequate foundations . . . used to install and support the drilling rig, unloading and moving all the piping and drilling and machinery. . . . Then there is the dam for the well waste; there, the "mud" [drilling fluid] is deposited, as well as the "chapopote" [oil] that drains away and the surface for the gas burner. . . . Once the oil gushes out, the valve is put in place and then connected to the pipe then to the pipeline and the battery, and from there it is sent to the refinery by pipeline. . . . The well in production can last for many years, but above there is only a wide gravel surface, and in the center, a valve and pipe branches.[93]

This process was repeated every time a new well was drilled. PEMEX's entry into the ejido of Emiliano Zapata and ex-hacienda of San Andrés entailed significant (and ongoing) changes to the social and physical environment.[94] A key effect was the 1957 paving of the road from Poza Rica to San Andrés, an extension of the Stanford embankment that once linked Poza Rica and Coatzintla. The paved road made the archaeological site accessible year-round, with a significant effect on tourist numbers. Between 1957 and 1959 the number of annual visitors more than doubled, from 4,935 to 16,333 (see appendix). The expansion of transportation infrastructure further accelerated PEMEX exploration in Papantla.[95]

By the 1950s and 1960s El Tajín was not the frontier of the 1930s. The INAH was well established as Mexico's federal heritage management agency, and García Payón now conducted regular field research at the site. In his role as a manager, García Payón frequently drew on the shared ideological objectives of postrevolutionary oil development and archaeological research to lobby for further support. His correspondence with Benito Coquet Lagunas, then secretary for President Adolfo Ruíz Cortines (1952–58), serves as an example. Discussing the possibility of PEMEX funding with Coquet, García Payón used the same logic he does in petitions for funds from the federal government. There is the inherent (and legally mandated) necessity of preserving the pre-Hispanic past: "The great economic problems of the Government and Petróleos Mexicanos do not escape me, but neither should we forget that we have a transcendental historical inheritance to save from destruction."[96] There is also the question of tourism: "We should not forget that El Tajín, in addition to being the principal archaeological center of the State of Veracruz . . . is [also] one of the most visited."[97] This funding was urgent for García Payón, because "during 1954 we did not receive even a cent of support [from INAH for Tajín]. . . . The only cooperation that I received was the sending of a ramshackle dump truck."[98] In this instance Coquet's mediation was successful: García Payón's 1954–55 field seasons were funded by a 60,000-peso donation from PEMEX.[99] However, despite García Payón's efforts, PEMEX did not become a consistent source for site funding.[100]

Alignment between the oil industry and archaeology facilitated other kinds of practical arrangements: in 1951 PEMEX's Poza Rica machine shops repaired García Payón's 1942 Chevrolet truck, an array of piping donated by PEMEX was listed in a 1963 inventory, and PEMEX provided access to water for the site by 1967.[101] Some of the more visible arrangements remain today, like the entrance bridge crossing the creek into the archaeological site; it was installed by PEMEX in 1951.[102] Though far from a disinterested observer, García Payón later reflected that "the relationships between Petróleos Mexicanos and the Instituto Nacional de Antropología e Historia in the archaeological site of

El Tajín have always been cordial, always modified by mutual respect and collaboration."[103]

Still, the relationships between archaeology and oil development were not always beneficial for the former. García Payón made the negative effects, as well as their causes, clear in a 1966 request to PEMEX authorities. Recalling 1963, he noted: "Before Petróleos Mexicanos drilled wells Alemán 105, 108, 115, and 118 . . . we had access to the sand and gravel necessary for our work and, moreover, a paved road from the highway to the entrance of the archaeological site. Currently we have access to none of this, the material from the wells covered the sand and gravel deposits, and the Petróleos Mexicanos trucks completely destroyed the road."[104] Mobilizing tourist statistics and an engineer's eye for detail, García Payón continued that the thirty-to-forty-centimeter-deep potholes that covered the first fifty or sixty meters of the entrance road discouraged tourists from entering. While no record of a reply is archived, García Payón reported in December that the road had been fixed.[105]

Equipment continued to circulate between archaeology and the oil industry. PEMEX cranes repositioned the monumental blocks of the South Ballcourt in 1954, and García Payón credited PEMEX's Manuel Contreras with the two-week loan of a crane and personnel, capable of moving up to thirty-five metric tons, in 1961.[106] This crane played a key role in the 1961–62 field season's recovery of the two central panels of the South Ballcourt, without which El Tajín's scriptural program would remain incomplete.[107] All iconographic analysis of El Tajín's famous low-relief panels is indebted to PEMEX. Still, García Payón hoped for more. His proposed fieldwork for the late 1960s included the possibility of soliciting photogrammetric measurements of the site from PEMEX, and the company loaned the archaeologist a helicopter for an hour and a half in December 1966.[108] The company proved similarly willing to provide a helicopter and surveying equipment to Paula and Ray Krotser for their Wenner-Gren Foundation for Anthropological Research–funded project in 1969.[109]

The nationalization of the oil industry did not change the commensurability of knowledge exchanged between archaeologists and oil company engineers. For example, in 1962 García Payón requested information on a topographical map that PEMEX engineers had produced around 1956 or 1957, "something I have been unable to do for lack of pecuniary elements."[110] He had regional-scale PEMEX maps—one remains in his archive today—but they did not have the level of detail necessary for his work.[111] This relationship worked both ways. When PEMEX requested information on the extension of the archaeological site in parcel 76, the company simply asked García Payón to signal the locations of archaeological material on its plan.[112] The topographic expertise shared by García Vega and La Riviere during the 1930s remained a common point of exchange.

One reason for this commensurability was that PEMEX's coordinate systems, inherited from its foreign predecessors, remained the local standard. The measurements for Carlos López Mata's 1964 survey (see chapter 1) were calculated based on PEMEX's local coordinate system.[113] A PEMEX marker on the Pyramid of the Niches established the reference point for Krotser and Krotser's topographic map of 1973.[114] Facilitated by the ideological alignment of the national oil industry (via PEMEX) and the national archaeology program (via INAH), the midcentury cooperation between oil extraction and archaeology built on the unexpected precedent of collaboration between foreign oil companies and nationalist archaeology. In so doing, this cooperation set the stage for similar interactions later in the century.

For the Totonac communities of the region, PEMEX operations caused concerns that had little to do with the pre-Hispanic past: land use, environmental contamination, and the risk of disaster were more pressing matters. A 1979 newspaper account cites Totonac authority and well-known abuelo Juan Simbrón Méndez, who linked "the exploitation that we've been in since the Spaniards arrived" to "those from Petróleos Mexicanos who come with tractors to take our lands."[115] Ejidos like El Remolino and Palmar Kilómetro 40 faulted PEMEX for declining water quality, as did San Antonio Ojital; communities like Reforma Escolin and El Tajín complained of nonpayment for use of their lands; and explosions in Sombrerete and El Remolino affected local families and PEMEX workers alike.[116] In some cases, PEMEX operations proved disastrous. Near El Tajín, a gas leak once took the lives of seven brothers and one mother.[117] A 1966 explosion in San Andrés, near Emiliano Zapata, killed ten.[118] Urban Poza Rica was hardly exempt: in 1950 a twenty-minute hydrogen sulfide leak left twenty-two residents dead and another 240 hospitalized.[119] However, confronting PEMEX proved challenging. The postrevolutionary state "tended to neutralize the complaints that arose locally against [PEMEX] through a rhetoric that put any discontent against the company as the work of traitors," as Ana Julia del Palacio Langer has argued.[120]

One particular example of contamination and resistance illustrates the wide-ranging and cumulative effects of oil exploitation, as well as residents' responses. Rodrigo is a well-known abuelo whose parents were from El Tajín. Having lived in a neighboring community since his youth, he was especially concerned about the environmental changes he had experienced, and what they meant for the future: declining crop yields, reduced biodiversity, and dependence on artificial fertilizer. During an interview on the patio of his house, Rodrigo explained how this environmental degradation could be traced to oil extraction—not the predatory foreign firms, but PEMEX: "I was maybe nine years old, it's been a while [mid-1960s]. From here past Miguel Hidalgo, which is Coatzintla . . . they began to drill . . . [and] an oil well blew out, on the hill. So, that field began to spout oil, it began to spout day and night, day and night, [PEMEX] didn't realize . . . it began to pollute the creek that passes through here . . . killing off the fish, the *acamaya*, killing off all kinds of fish, all the *acamaya*, well, all of it."[121] As in El Tajín, members of the community relied on such creeks, springs, and artesian wells for water.

Rodrigo recounted how residents attempted to make their urgent concerns known: "They went to protest and [PEMEX] didn't take them into consideration . . . and the oil just came, and came, and came. . . . It began to fill the water wells, to pollute . . . so the abuelos began to cover up [the spill] with earth. . . . [PEMEX] didn't pay attention. . . . Well, a few of the abuelos said 'look, they're not paying attention, we're going to do something,' and they put a lighter to it." That got the attention of the authorities. "*N'ombre*, it caught like you wouldn't believe, everyone ran. . . . The trees began to burn, the monte began to burn, it began and it kept burning, and it was then that [PEMEX] discovered it, because of the smoke. . . . They only took the protest into consideration when the oil burned." Rodrigo tied this blowout, its initial environmental impacts, and PEMEX's negligence of the same to the later effects of contamination:

From there the mud that they use for drilling began to spill out, it's a mud that looks like lime . . . all of that began to spill into the creeks. . . . Afterwards, all of this creek was contaminated, all the way to Troncones Creek. . . . That one, too, had very clear water, like it was from a spring, but there the pollution began, little by little, little by little, it killed off the fish and the animals. . . . We had problems with taking the water that came from the wells near the creek because when you'd dig, oil would come out . . . with colors and all that, it tasted like oil, like petroleum. . . . But that was how the contamination of everything began, the great disaster of how they began to contaminate, there wasn't water, and more drilling began to arrive.

Individual events like a childhood well fire thus blended into the continuing operations of an industry whose pollution contaminated local supplies of food and water.

Rodrigo was familiar with the longer history of oil exploration in the region. He recalled his parents' stories of how the equipment used to drill Ojital-1 was brought in via mule train, and the fame of Furbero and Palma Sola even beforehand. There had been wells back then, he noted, but they had not contaminated like the PEMEX wells. Rodrigo always returned to the lived effects of such events, still felt in the present. "The *tarro* or bamboo plants began to disappear. . . . All of this, where I am now, to where the creek passes—you can check it out in a few—that was a *terral*, but with really thick *tarros*. . . . They were on both sides [of the creek], there was shade, the water was clear, clear, you could get in and take a bath. . . . But the contamination began to do away with all that, it finished it off completely, so you protest here, you protest there, [and you get] nothing, nothing, even today." While the history of PEMEX's environmental effects in Veracruz remains to be written, residents like Rodrigo find themselves in agreement with scholars who have explored what Martín Checa-Artasu calls "the microgeography of hydrocarbon exploitation," the site-specific impacts of an industry otherwise associated with national development, sovereignty, and progress.[122] The effects of oil exploitation are cumulative and ongoing: the specificities of individual events blend into the long history of environmental degradation, defying straightforward periodizations.

Crisis, Hydraulic Fracturing, and LIDAR Mapping, 1970–2020

PEMEX faced numerous challenges in the 1960s and 1970s. Some were structural: as a mainstay of Mexico's postrevolution brand of economic nationalism and political sovereignty, the company was responsible for subsidizing consumption, providing employment, and funding governmental operations.[123] Demand for oil eventually outstripped supply: between 1960 and 1972 the former grew at an annual rate of almost 10 percent, and the latter at only 4.1 percent; Mexico became a net importer of crude oil in 1971.[124] However, the discovery of new sources in the southeastern states of Tabasco and Campeche (and their offshores) promised to revitalize production, and the 1973 oil embargo made Mexican oil a particularly attractive prospect for the United States.[125] The state thus prioritized oil production for export. The move promised to improve Mexico's economic position on the world stage, and to fund social services after the social upheavals of the 1960s. The Mexican economy was "petrolized" (*se petrolizó*) with almost 75 percent of exports and 38 percent of tax revenues coming from oil.[126] Yet international circumstances did not cooperate: declining oil prices of the early 1980s were among the factors that created the debt crisis of 1982, which also began Mexico's period of neoliberal reforms (see chapter 6). As with archaeology, debates over private-sector participation in Mexico's oil industry would become flashpoints of controversy throughout the 1990s and 2000s.[127]

In northern Veracruz, the rate of exploration declined during the 1970s and 1980s. Wells, productive and unproductive alike, cluttered the landscape (see map 6). The offshore Cantarell field in Campeche contributed between 37 percent and 57 percent of national production between the 1980s and 2007.[128] Cantarell's declining production after 2004 spurred the search for new oil, and renewed attention to older fields. Chief among these was the Paleocanal de Chicontepec. Related to the San Andrés fields, this geological formation had been announced to contain fully 42 percent of Mexico's oil reserves in 1978.[129] But the Paleocanal's geology made conventional exploration difficult. By 2006 the project to exploit these so-called unconventional sources was given the name Aceite Terciario del Golfo (ATG). As Margaret Cruz explains, "Because of the lack of rock porosity, the strategy was to drill as many wells as possible to extract the oil little by little over the entire area."[130] Despite massive investments and the expansion of drilling, most analysts agree that production has been modest.[131] The expanse of ATG's operations provoked concern about damage to the archaeological record. In this vein, INAH developed a joint effort with PEMEX titled the Furbero–Presidente Miguel Alemán–Remolino Project, after its constituent oil fields.

Recent reports for El Tajín's Management Plan considered that, given the ongoing ATG activities, "the participation of the para-state company Petróleos Mexicanos is indispensable in the regulation and planning of the monuments zone and its surroundings."[132] The terms of the Furbero–Presidente Miguel Alemán–Remolino Project's agreements similarly echo older relationships.[133] According to the legal agreement between the INAH and oilfield services provider P.G.S. Mexicana, the latter pays and administers funding for the project, including salaries, equipment, lodging, and transportation; the INAH, in addition to conducting the research, works with the company to avoid archaeological remains encountered during the seismic survey.[134] The project was successful, insofar as the research was carried out and published in the

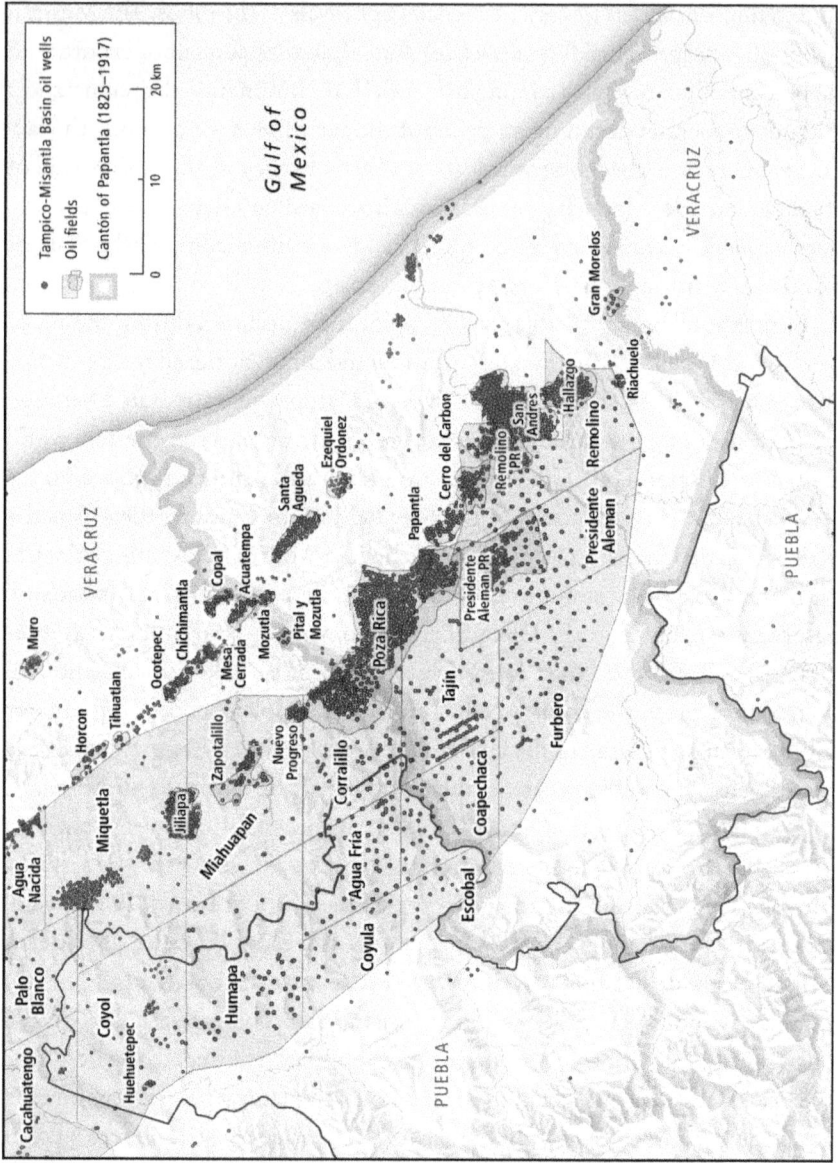

MAP 6. Southern extension of the Paleocanal de Chicontepec, including oil fields and wells. Erin Greb Cartography.

form of *Culturas del Golfo: Salvamento arqueológico y nuevas tecnologías*, jointly published by PEMEX's Exploración y Producción unit and the INAH.[135] The book documents the Geographic Information Systems (GIS) mappings of the area of study, including 126 archaeological sites, as well as LIDAR mapping of El Tajín's 1,221-hectare protected zone.[136] The contemporary commensurability of archaeological and oil knowledge, as well as the sharing of infrastructure and equipment, draws from a history of entanglement that extends back to the very beginnings of oil prospecting and archaeology in northern Veracruz.

However, much has changed in the half century since García Payón sought PEMEX funding, and even more since García Vega and the Compañía Stanford collaborated in El Tajín. Totonac residents like Rodrigo are well aware of the local effects of oil extraction, and the industry's contributions to greenhouse gas emissions are extensive and undeniable.[137] Increased drilling and the use of hydraulic fracturing (also known as fracking) has provoked controversy. Echoing Rodrigo's analysis, above, residents consider that PEMEX has not been responsive to the effects of contemporary drilling: contaminated water supplies, damage to crops, and infrastructural degradation affecting roads, bridges, and power lines.[138] The INAH's legal responsibilities for the protection of pre-Hispanic material culture require the participation of archaeologists in projects like ATG. As a result, however, the political economy of archaeology is also tied to the pollution whose effects are a semiregular topic on local news pages: "Artesian Wells Polluted in Emiliano Zapata," "Hydrocarbon Leak in Cerro Grande Escolin," "Papantla, Municipality Contaminated by PEMEX."[139]

Conclusion

At different moments in the histories of oil exploration and archaeology in north Veracruz, archaeology and extractive industry shared infrastructure, equipment, and expertise. These relationships were structural, ranging beyond the tenures of individual archaeologists, agencies, or companies. From the basic similarities of archaeological research and oil exploration during the nineteenth century to the formal agreements of the last decade, the complexity waxes (as during the drilling of Ojital-1) and wanes (as during the 1970s) but their interconnectedness in the political economy of archaeology is a constant. This topical concern, in dialogue with interlocutors like Rodrigo, facilitated a periodization that illustrates the long-running and cumulative territorial impacts of oil exploration in the region.

As I have highlighted, the expansion of oil drilling during the twentieth century affected far more than archaeology. Declining production forced residents to reckon with the decaying infrastructure and industrial ruins that now characterize former oil centers like Poza Rica and Emiliano Zapata. The ATG project has brought hopes for new labor opportunities while subjecting Totonac communities and ejidos to oil spills, water contamination, and other forms of pollution. In this sense, the Papantla region bears some similarity to the "ecology of oil" in the neighboring Huasteca during the early twentieth century.[140] But one key difference is that already by 1900, Papantla was associated with a major export that linked the region to markets in the United States and Europe: vanilla.

The vanilla orchid was on perceptive Honduran journalist Porfirio Hernández's mind when he passed through Papantla in 1937. He wrote that "the black flood of petroleum" was a "foreseeable threat" to the vanilla: "Two hours from here, the damned oil [*chapopote*] is about to erupt in a Compañía Sinclair well, next to El Tajín, the most vanilla-rich part of the district." When the chapopote would "fatally stain this rich and perfumed region of the Veracruz map," Hernández predicted that "the vanilla plantations will be abandoned, the abundant fields will pass to the hands of great petroleum speculators and cleanliness will disappear." "Not even the Devil would want that!" Hernández concluded.[141] Perhaps fortunately, Ojital-1 was unproductive. Vanilla did not disappear, but neither would it retain the fame and profitability that brought Hernández to Papantla. In the political economy of archaeology, vanilla represents a different degree and extent of entanglement with the discipline, one mediated through a local elite class that reaped disproportionate profit from the orchid's fruits while exposing Indigenous cultivators to risk and violence.

Vanilla

3

Violence and Temporality

> Just like now, there was a lot of thievery [*raterías*] because of the
> vanilla, because there was cash, there was everything, so the people
> that sold it would be accosted on the trail, in their houses. . . . When I
> was maybe five or six, my father was secretary, I tell you, and some-
> times a policeman, we'd be working in the milpa and just like that
> someone would come: "you know what? They killed so-and-so, we've
> got to go pick up the body," the next day, the same.
>
> —Juan

April 2013: While wandering around El Tajín, I decided to head up to Tajín
Chico. Vicente was working that day. Though only middle-aged—he started
working at the site in 1987—Vicente was a traditionalist: a fluent Totonac
speaker, he rolled his occasional cigars with dried tobacco leaves soaked in
local cane liquor, and was proud of the palm stars that adorned his altar
every Todos Santos.[1] "I'm going to show you something that I did," he said.
A former mason, Vicente had worked on Proyecto Tajín before starting as a
custodio. I had interviewed him about his history with the site a few weeks
before. Perhaps he was going to show me a building he had worked on? We
headed up to Building Y, a low, inconspicuous structure just on the edge of
the area open to the public.

I was surprised when he pointed out a green vine snaking up a tree: "I did
this," he repeated, with evident pride (see figure 3). This was vanilla, Vicente
explained. He had bought the cuttings from the community a few years ago
and planted them here. Vicente continued that it was important to preserve
the vanilla. The spice had been grown by the ton and exported abroad in the
past. Pollution from oil production had since damaged the vanilla, however,
and the bean pods were now short (he held his fingers about ten centimeters apart to illustrate) and twisted. It was important that the visitors see

FIG. 3. Vicente's vanilla in Tajín Chico, 2013. Photograph by the author.

the vanilla. They asked him about it while touring the site, but what if they lacked the time to visit a vanilla plantation (*vainillal*)? It was also important that I take pictures. I did as much, failing to find the words to diplomatically ask what, exactly, vanilla had to do with the site itself.

If Papantla is known for one thing, it is vanilla. The international origin of cultivated vanilla, Papantla is popularly known as the City That Perfumed the World. Given the relative expanse of scholarship on Papantla vanilla, researching the orchid in any depth seemed tangential to my fieldwork.[2] In contrast to the overgrown oil well (see chapter 2), vanilla seemed unconnected to the political economy of archaeology.

The following year, anthropologist Jesús Trejo introduced me to Rafael, in the nearby ejido of Plan de Hidalgo. El Tajín and Plan de Hidalgo historically maintained strong ties. Before the paving of PEMEX roads in the 1980s, Plan de Hidalgo residents had to pass through El Tajín to get to Papantla. Locally, the town is considered a bastion of lowland Totonac culture: most residents work in agriculture, assemblies are conducted in the Totonac language, and traditional dress is relatively common.[3] The interview with Rafael, which I had planned to use for mapping the region of study, took an unexpected turn when Rafael's wife, Antonia, joined us. In a freewheeling conversation that alternated between my gringo-accented Spanish, Jesús's diplomatic translations of my questions into more understandable Spanish, and Rafael's and Antonia's Totonac-language dialogue, the conversation soon turned to vanilla. Antonia recalled that if an unspecified but ominous "they" knew "that you plant that vanilla, *asu* . . . [if they see] that you're selling vanilla, 'that means you're rich,' they're going to say, they'll look for you in your house . . . and if they find you, they'll kill you, they'll come in, and the children, they'll kill them, if they shout, or someone, your wife, they'll kill her, and [if they don't kill them] they'll tie them all up here and they'll say 'where's your money?'" Rafael nodded along. Jesús was hardly surprised. When I mentioned the violence to him, Vicente, too, recalled its aftereffects. As a young man, he had seen the corpses of its victims, or the hanged bodies of the perpetrators, off the trails.

In the Totonac communities around El Tajín, vanilla evokes violence in ways that other regional commodities—oranges, corn husks, bananas, and even oil—do not. Unlike the kind of violence associated with contamination and oil production, this violence was visceral, personal, and physical.[4] Implied in Vicente's, Rafael's, and Antonia's references was a timeframe that located this violence roughly between the 1940s and the 1960s. In the triumphant narratives of the revolutionary generation, the mid-twentieth century was a period of modernization, social progress, and economic development: the so-called Mexican Miracle. More recent scholarship has shown that implied peace and stability was the exception rather than the rule.[5] Yet the violence to which my interlocutors referred was not directly linked to state violence or social movements.[6] Nor was it linked specifically to capitalist bosses like central Veracruz's Manuel Parra or Crispín Aguilar, or their union-head equivalents like Jaime J. Merino in Poza Rica.[7] The only constant seemed to be vanilla.

In contrast with the close, cumulative entanglements of oil production and the research and management of the pre-Hispanic past, vanilla's connections with the archaeological site are diffuse, mediated through other actors and forces. Focusing on the political economy of archaeology in this context leads me to suggest that while Mexico's pre-Hispanic past frequently plays into elite imaginings of the nation, much more remains to be written about the local politics of heritage. The presence of vanilla cultivation around the site and in the monte caused conflicts between landowners and custodios; merchant families made wealthy by vanilla were among the first employed to maintain the site; and their social and economic capital were used in other ways vis-à-vis El Tajín.

In what follows, I begin by discussing the history and political economy of vanilla production, including a division of labor between Totonac cultivation and mestizo or Euro-descendant curing and export. This division enabled relations of unequal dependence between cultivators and curers to develop, facilitating the kinds of violence discussed by my interlocutors. I then discuss the cultivation of vanilla, exploring how the particular temporality of the orchid's life cycle creates risk for cultivators. Along similar lines, I discuss the process of curing vanilla, exploring how the temporality of cultivation further exposed cultivators—but not curers—to violence. I argue that the temporality and the political economy of vanilla cultivation, taken together, enable an understanding of why the El Tajín landscape was one of danger and violence. In each of these sections, I draw connections between vanilla and the political economy of archaeology.

Violence and the History of the Vanilla Trade

Midcentury violence often came to the fore when discussing vanilla, in formal interviews and more casual conversation. Interlocutors spoke less of specific events than of a general context in which "there were killings" (*se mataba*). A representative statement comes from a 1983 profile of the community of Jorge Cerdán, west of El Tajín: "During [the 1940s], there were lots of thieves and bandits [*matones de gente*], they robbed gold money, rings, dishes, vanilla, clothing, and other things. In that time, the farmers had a lot of money, because their economy was mainly based on the cultivation of vanilla. . . . Because the robberies were ever more common in the dispersed houses, the victims decided to establish themselves in the town center to prevent more plunder."[8] Accounts like this mirror narratives that recount the depredations of cattle ranchers' hired thugs, feuds between musical groups, and local military operations. There is little space for such accounts in Papantla, where vanilla forms part of a nostalgic and tourist-oriented imaginary. The city takes advantage of its Pueblo Mágico status to promote itself as a traditional town, featuring well-conserved architecture and Totonac cultural practices.[9] In this imaginary, vanilla is chief among a series of other traditional products amenable to tourist consumption. This is fitting insofar as vanilla has historically been a cash crop. However, focusing on vanilla and the violence its cultivation entailed is a key but poorly understood aspect of the rural Totonac past.

In addition to the physical violence to which Rafael and others drew my attention, another form of violence emerges from the "consequences of the smooth functioning of our political and economic systems."[10] This systemic violence begins with the distinction between cultivators and curers, and the precarity to which the former have historically been subject, a "violence inherent to this 'normal' state of things."[11] A racialized division of labor—and the resulting inequality—stems from the colonial period and "a new set of economic relations born in the wake of an expanding export trade and dominated since its inception by *gente de razón*," Spaniards and mestizos based in Xalapa and the port of Veracruz.[12] The origins of this division of labor remain murky, but a few facts point to the early eighteenth century. By the 1740s rural Totonac cultivation was "the way it had always been done."[13] José Antonio Villa-Señor y Sánchez linked this cultivation to international commerce, saying that "fine and wild vanilla is grown in those mountains, bought by traders to be sent to Spain."[14] There were relatively few Spanish families in Papantla, and these were dedicated to commerce. It seems logical that these merchant families participated in the broader trade networks of the period via Xalapa, "the lynchpin of inland Atlantic trade for the Spanish."[15] For Totonac cultivators to profit, they would have had to work with these merchants. Questions of origins notwithstanding, these relations of production are constitutive of what became the Papantla vanilla industry.

The structural relations between cultivation and curing were, and remain, characterized by unequal dependency. Cultivators explained this to me by focusing on two factors: intermediaries and contracts. In some cases, cultivators would sell to intermediaries, who, through access to funds, transportation, and contacts, purchase green (raw) vanilla and resell it to specialized curers (*beneficiadores*) or curing firms known as houses (*casas*, for their origins in family production). Cultivators are mostly smallholders who produce green vanilla in limited quantities. They cannot compete with the intermediaries, who, with access to capital, are able to purchase vanilla from many cultivators and sell it in bulk to the curers. The latter benefit by purchasing at bulk prices. The intermediaries thus reap much of the profit from the sale of green vanilla.[16] The phrasing one cultivator used with me during fieldwork—"little by little this [system] made the cultivation process depend on the intermediates"— resonated with Alexander von Humboldt's nineteenth-century description of the system. The vanilla industry was "controlled by a few individuals referred to as *habilitadores*, because they advance money to the *cosecheros*, that is, to the Indians who perform the harvest and who thereby make themselves dependent upon the entrepreneurs. It is the latter who make nearly all the profit from this branch of Mexican industry."[17]

Along similar lines, contracts facilitate access to funds but also make cultivators dependent on curers. As I discuss below, cultivating vanilla requires commitments of time, money, and labor, years before the first harvest and the possibility of profit. Cultivators thus need funds in advance. In contracts designed for that end, intermediaries or curers advance funds to cultivators with agreements to sell certain quantities of vanilla at agreed-upon rates. For example, one 1924 contract specifies that the cultivator deliver 3,300 green vanilla bean pods, with an average weight of 1.84 kilograms per 100 beans, at a price of $120 per 1,000 beans.[18] In exchange, the buyer paid the cultivator the entirety of the contract's value at signing: $396. If the cultivator fell short in weight or quantity, they were responsible for paying back the value of the vanilla—but at the after-harvest market price, rather than the signing one. This after-harvest price would almost certainly be higher: Isabel Kelly recorded the October 1946 price for a kilogram of green vanilla as 6.50 pesos and the December 1946 price as 13.00 pesos.[19] In this example, using the 1946 prices and assuming constant weight, a shortfall of 300 beans would cost the cultivator $72—nearly one-fifth of the contract's value for less than one-tenth of the vanilla. Any shortfall in production, regardless of cause, was thus likely to cost cultivators.

Though unequal, continued participation in this system was beneficial for cultivators, as long as green vanilla remained reasonably profitable. But when profits declined, losses were often passed down to the cultivators.[20] A middle-aged Totonac carpenter recalled to me his fondness for the orchid and why he no longer cultivated it. Once, "I came to produce half a ton of [green] vanilla. My father and I had the orange grove, with vanilla . . . but obviously a price drop discourages you. You get discouraged. You get to Papantla with your load of vanilla and they tell you, 'you know what? Would you believe that the price dropped? Now it's at thirty pesos.'" What else was a cultivator to do but sell the vanilla cheap? The carpenter said that he would never again pollinate a vanilla blossom: "It's a slap in the face. [They tell you] the price dropped and that it's it. What can you do? Nothing. Just let your rage brew." The problem was a lack of direct access to export markets, a problem to which the well-connected curers were not historically subject.

These key features of the nineteenth-century political economy of vanilla remained resilient through the twentieth.[21] Mexican vanilla was produced largely in Papantla, cultivated by Totonacs and cured by Euro-descendants and mestizos; it retained importance in local economic terms; and its largest export market was the United States. However, because vanilla is primarily an export commodity, curers, cultivators, and intermediaries alike were subject to the broader forces of the international market, whose fluctuations came to affect production.

During the nineteenth and twentieth centuries, demand for vanilla grew as chemists and confectioners found new uses for the flavor. Cocoa powder and solid chocolate were nineteenth-century innovations that built on the precolonial use of vanilla as a flavoring for drinking chocolate. The ice cream industry became another important source of demand from the United States.[22] Thanks to advances in freezing and processing technology, production of ice cream grew from 4,000 gallons in 1859 to 144,073,000 gallons in 1919—a growth of 36,018 times in sixty years.[23] Partly as a result, the United States caught up to France as the most important market for Mexico's vanilla by the 1890s.[24] A 1938 issue of the *Revista del Comercio Exterior* reported that "the use of vanilla for ice cream flavoring, soft drinks, sweets and chocolates has become so popular in the United States that the imports of that product, which were 300,000 pounds in 1900, has grown every year, up to an annual average of 1,184,000 pounds during the 1932–36 period."[25] For Mexico, Papantla continued to be the key source for vanilla. A 1940 study provides an illustrative snapshot. Nationally, 4,701 hectares under cultivation produced 206,583 kilograms of cured vanilla; of that, 3,453 hectares (73 percent) and 153,037 kilograms (74 percent) came from the municipalities of the former Cantón of Papantla.[26]

However, as the gap between U.S. imports and Mexican production quoted above suggests, Mexico was not the only source for meeting this demand. Even by the 1860s, production in French colonies (Réunion and Madagascar) surpassed Mexico, driven by a combination of artificial fertilization, capitalist plantations, and the exploitation of enslaved Africans' labor.[27] European chemists also began to synthesize vanillin, a key component of vanilla's distinctive taste, first from conifer pulp (1874) and then from clove oil (1891).[28] A closer look at U.S. import statistics gives a sense of how vanilla demand grew, and supply shifted, during the twentieth century (see table 3).[29] Madagascar's production grew in absolute and relative terms, while Indonesia became an increasingly important supplier over the decades. Both Mexico and France (including the latter's colonial holdings) declined as sources of supply. By 1980 Mexico was not even included as a separate origin for U.S. vanilla imports.

TABLE 3. Pounds of vanilla imported into the United States by source and proportion, 1920–70

	MADAGASCAR	MEXICO	FRANCE	INDONESIA	OTHER	TOTAL
1920	27,229	274,221	898,419		39,842	1,239,711
	2.2%	22.1%	72.5%		3.2%	
1930		236,421	918,272	59,295	18,317	1,232,305
		19.2%	74.5%	4.8%	1.5%	
1940	493,992	370,987	390,813		54,062	1,309,854
	37.7%	28.3%	29.8%		4.1%	
1950	1,682,760	279,760	207,663	89,875	51,947	2,312,005
	72.8%	12.1%	9.0%	3.9%	2.2%	
1960	732,583	213,521	106,518	42,039	13,952	1,108,613
	66.1%	19.3%	9.6%	3.8%	1.3%	
1970	1,940,573	31,959	4,693	244,932	16,703	2,238,860
	86.7%	1.4%	0.2%	10.9%	0.7%	

Sources: 1920–40 data from U.S. Bureau of the Census, *Foreign Commerce and Navigation*. 1940–70 data from U.S. Bureau of the Census, *Imports of Merchandise*.

The notable decline in U.S. imports of Mexican vanilla after the 1960s was likely related to falling production (see figure 4).[30] A 1942 report gives an idea of the factors that affected local vanilla production: cyclones (1915), World War I–related staple-crop cultivation (1917), and droughts (1923, 1933).[31] Locally, the expansion of PEMEX activities in the region (see chapter 2), to which Vicente alluded, and a 1962 frost that affected the notoriously temperature-sensitive orchid were also blamed for declining cultivation.[32] Production did not recover until the 1990s, by which time many vainilleros had ceased planting.

A durable production process, unequal dependencies between cultivation and curing, and high value resulted in Totonac cultivators being exposed to violence during the mid-twentieth century. This violence specifically affected cultivators, especially during harvest and commercialization, rather than curers. The carpenter cited above explained it to me like this. Back in the days when his father had planted vanilla, "they had to care for their vainillales with shotgun at the shoulder during the night, because the bad guys [*gente mala*] like the darkness so that they won't be seen. So, these people came to get in to the vainillales and harvest without having done the work. Classic thievery

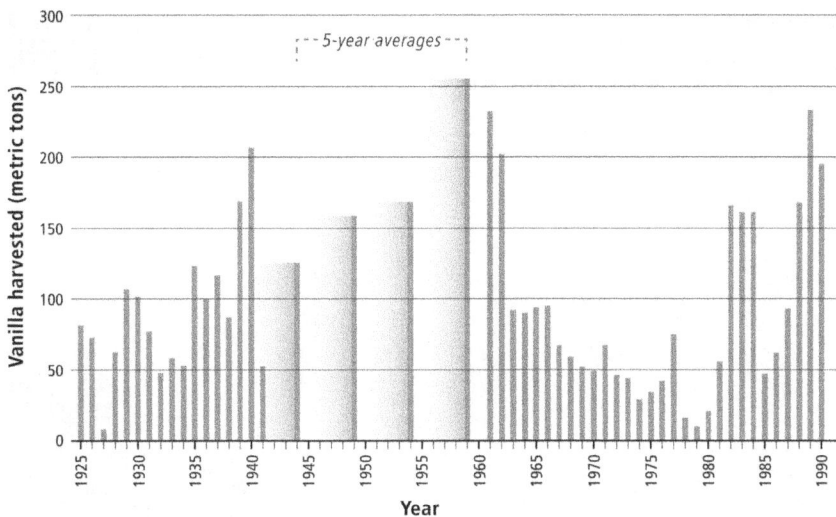

FIG. 4. Mexican vanilla production, 1925–90. Note that because vanilla is also grown in parts of Puebla and Oaxaca, production numbers are lower for Veracruz and for Papantla, specifically. Erin Greb Cartography.

[*ratero*]. But they were from here. . . . It was dangerous because the vanilla had value, and there were people who knew how to take advantage of that." This was a common fear during vanilla harvesting season. For unscrupulous residents or hired gunmen, the possibility of profit without actually having to cultivate the crop was an attractive option. As another farmer, now in his seventies, explained, "Those selling vanilla went to Papantla, but maybe it was those same [buyers] that sent [bandits], they knew that they'd bought vanilla from you, they'd pay you in Papantla but would make the trails dangerous, they'd wait for you and take your money." The vainillal and the trails used to take the product to market alike thus became dangerous.

Around El Tajín, this danger was further spatialized. Between the archaeological site and Papantla, a low hill called the Cerro de Trakgátlokg was an obligatory point of passage for several communities to the southwest of the municipal capital, like Plan de Hidalgo.[33] Traversing Trakgátlokg was the most direct way to Papantla, and generations of collective, intercommunal labor had lowered the trail to facilitate passage: up to three meters of earthen walls bordered the path (see figure 5).

At his house in Plan de Hidalgo, Rufino made the link between the landscape, vanilla, and violence: "It was dangerous there on Trakgátlokg, there, if

FIG. 5. Trail through the Cerro de Trakgátlokg, 2014. Road construction cut the hill in 2001, so the trail is no longer maintained. Photograph by the author.

you took your vanilla, they'd kill you or if not, they'd assault you; you'd go to sell your vanilla, and in the afternoon, they'd wait for you there, they'd take everything from you, and you couldn't hide because you can't go here or there, it's a gully . . . you have to go through there." A telling comment from Kelly, in correspondence with anthropologist George Foster, illustrates the association between vanilla and violence: "As I recall, this is 13 murders in the course of a year and a half—in a community whose total population is only a bit over 1,000. And we don't pretend to understand the current siege, for neither women nor vanilla seems involved."[34] By implication, the violence associated with vanilla (and with women) is common and understandable—in contrast with the violence Kelly describes, related to a series of local feuds. As I will discuss, vanilla's value-to-weight ratio, combined with the temporality of its care, made theft and banditry a particularly serious risk, and one to which cultivators were specifically exposed.

Unlike the cultivators, for whom green vanilla was a cash crop that supplemented subsistence agriculture, the curers translated profits from the international sale of cured vanilla into other sectors. Many invested in land.

Pedro Tremari was known for "rural and urban houses, forests of cedar and mahogany, [and] haciendas with cattle," including the 50,000-hectare Palma Sola estate.[35] Rodolfo Curti, whose family owned the 1,794-hectare estate of San Andrés, held a variety of political positions through the 1920s as "the leading man driving the political destinies of Papantla."[36] A 1903 newspaper profile of Bartolomeo Zardoni gives further examples of how elite curing families diversified their holdings: patriarch of "one of the most important exporting houses in Papantla . . . [Zardoni is] not just dedicated to the sale of vanilla, but also to other tropical products in Europe and the United States . . . [as well as] being an agent of the Bank of London and Mexico, of fire insurance companies, etc. etc."[37] After taking over his father's curing firm, Raúl del Cueto used his wealth to invest in shipping, radio, and banking concerns.[38] As I will discuss, this elite class took an interest in El Tajín.

As this overview suggests, one's experiences with vanilla depended fundamentally on their location within these relations of production: cultivation or curing. When discussing vanilla, interlocutors located violence not just in time (midcentury, when vanilla production was profitable) and space (as on the Cerro de Trakgátlokg) but according to different parts of the cultivation process. Attending to the specifics of this process also demonstrates the diverse ways that vanilla writ large plays into the political economy of archaeology in El Tajín.

Cultivating Vanilla

The orchid whose fruits are cured and processed to make vanilla products consists largely of two species: *Vanilla planifolia* (Mexican or Bourbon vanilla, cultivated in Papantla) and *Vanilla tahitensis* (Tahitian vanilla).[39] To understand how an orchid becomes a flavor, let us follow a hypothetical vanilla cultivator (vainillero) through the process. Since our vainillero is from Papantla, they will already know that the green, waxy vine cannot grow alone but must have a tree or support that it can climb (called a *tutor*). Vanilla is an epiphyte, meaning that it does not grow roots but instead depends on the water and nutrition from the decaying vegetation that collects around the bases of tutores. Between March and June the vainillero will "plant" a cut vanilla vine between fifty centimeters and one meter long in a bed of this natural fertilizer, incline it toward the tutor, and let the vine begin its climb. For this reason, vanilla is traditionally planted either in uncleared forest or in the fallow section of a milpa known as *acahual*.

The vainillero will have to wait three years before the orchid bears fruit. In the meantime, our vainillero may prune tutor branches, clear underbrush, and add fertilizer and water as necessary. They should ensure that the vanilla has the right proportion of sun, shade, moisture, and nutrients necessary to keep growing; that it does not have any fungus or insects; and that it is not subject to unnecessarily low temperatures.[40] After three years, their vanilla should begin to flower consistently, for another three to eight years. Had the vainillero lived during the eighteenth century, they would have simply waited for the vine to bear fruit; native stingless bees are presumed to fertilize the orchid in the wild.[41] Since the 1870s, and thanks to an enslaved Reunionese child by the name of Edmund Albius, vainilleros use small sticks to manually pollinate (*fecundar*) the orchid.[42] This is useful because the orchid blooms in the morning, and an individual blossom rarely remains open past the afternoon. If our vainillero has a family, they will be busy with *fecundación* most mornings between March and June. Between the dexterity necessary for pollination and the short timeframe for doing so, mechanizing vanilla cultivation is effectively impossible.

This pollination process means that certain kinds of labor are necessary to cultivate vanilla. Since the vainillero grew up in the trade, they have done this kind of work since childhood; they can fertilize around four flowers a minute. Depending on the abundance of blossoms, their relative locations, and the experience of the pollinator, the process may take as many as 300–600 days (lasting from around 6:00 a.m. to noon) of work per hectare.[43] By this point, our vainillero has invested time, money, and labor for three years before selling a single vanilla pod. If pollination is successful, the vanilla bean pods begin to develop. The vainillero and family can rest again. For the most part, caring for vanilla during this period is not labor intensive. Once the vanilla bean pods mature in September or October, they become targets for theft. Since at least the 1740s, authorities have established dates before which vanilla should not be harvested—usually in November or December.[44] The idea, as one vainillero explained it to me, was to ensure the quality of Mexican vanilla on the international market. Harvesting vanilla bean pods before full maturity results in a lower-quality product. Most published sources and interlocutors that I consulted were dubious about the efficacy of these prohibitions, but they do indicate a specific temporality at play in vanilla cultivation.

The risk of theft between maturation (September–October) and harvesting (December–January) creates the potential for violence. "Always, all vainilleros

FIG. 6. Harvested green vanilla, 2017. Photograph by the author.

have to care [for the vanilla]. . . . Back before, during the peak, I tell you, in the [19]50s, in the [19]60s, there were two or three people with shotguns in every vainillal," as Martín, a veteran vainillero, explained it to me. Labor, in these months, consisted of guarding one's vainillal: Martín recalled that he would spend two weeks at a time caring for his vanilla, day and night. Vanilla became a dangerous business, whether caring for the vainillal or leaving it unattended: "Harrowing tales are told of planters who have tried to protect their holdings and who have been murdered for their pains," but "a planter thinks twice before going to Papantla for weekly purchases because the harvest may be stolen during his absence."[45]

Assuming our hypothetical vainillero's crop has survived, they will soon be able to harvest. Harvesting vanilla bean pods must be done manually, but the process consists of simply cutting or twisting off the pod at the stem (see figure 6). Martín calculated that he would need eight or ten workers for an eight-hour day to harvest a hectare's worth of vanilla, for a yield of about 150 kilograms. Historically, at this point, the cultivators' labor would end. The vainillero will most likely sell their harvested green vanilla to the intermediaries (pejoratively called *acaparadores, acopiadores, picotilleros,* or *coyotes*), who resell the vanilla to curers, who dry the vanilla for export to international markets. If the vainillero is so inclined, they might keep some vanilla to cure for themselves, for individual sale or for processing into other products like extract, liquor, and handicrafts.

As suggested above, getting green vanilla to market also brought risk upon cultivators. Historically, vanilla had among the highest value-to-weight ratios of all Mexican export commodities.[46] In other words, it took relatively little vanilla by weight to make a substantial profit, in comparison with other products. In 1947–48, a *mancuerna*—a parcel weighing between about a kilogram and a kilogram and a half—of processed sugarcane, El Tajín's other historic cash crop, sold for "between $0.40 and $0.50; in Papantla, it is slightly higher."[47] A kilogram of green vanilla brought at least ten times as much: between $4 and $12, depending on whether it was sold earlier or later in the season.[48] For the prospective thief, a traveling vainillero made a tempting target, whether for vanilla or cash.

Given this profitability, whatever came to affect one's ability to cultivate vanilla constituted a threat to economic livelihood. Archaeology could be such a threat. Erasmo Rodríguez encountered vanilla cultivation around El Tajín on a number of occasions. In one 1934 account, he petitioned Ignacio Marquina on what to do: "As the owners of the Parcels in which the ruins are found are finishing the vanilla harvest, I beg you to instruct me whether or not I should remove the vines of the previously-mentioned vanilla such that they are not destroyed when the clearing that began this year is continued."[49] Vanilla became another axis of the conflicts between archaeologists and landowners. In a 1937 letter to the Secretaría de Educación Pública, landowners and brothers Agustín, Tirso, Albino, and Magdaleno Méndez protested the cutting of a new path along their parcel 50: "Erasmo Rodríguez ... opened a trail through our parcel, without even having asked us permission to open said trail and, as we have a vainillal, we fear that by taking the trail he will destroy it. ... We do not doubt that you will intervene ... so that the vainillal of reference will not be harmed, as it is our only patrimonio."[50] Authorities assured the brothers that they would be compensated for any losses and ordered Agustín García Vega to relocate the trail.[51] In his capacity as head of the excavation project, García Vega replied that the trail was necessary for delimiting the site, and that there was no vanilla.

Evoking the idiom of patrimony speaks to the value of vanilla; the landowners previously used the patrimony designation to argue for the protection of their private property (see chapter 1). One might suspect that the Méndez brothers sought to take advantage of the reconstruction work to solicit compensation. The SEP had suggested as much in 1935, when it noted that the landowning Juárez brothers had profited from the lumber cleared from the site.[52] However, the petitioners did not request indemnification: they asked that Rodríguez stop opening the trail. Perhaps there are differing conceptions of the landscape at play. García Vega and Rodríguez saw parcel 50 as a patch of monte to be cleared for access, a necessary precondition to any excavation or monumental reconstruction. However, the Méndez brothers would have known that vanilla flourishes in the acahual, whose shade and organic debris is necessary for nutrition.

The suggestion that the botanical necessities of vanilla facilitated a particular kind of misidentification on the part of outsider archaeologists provides another perspective on the case of María discussed in chapter 1. Charging that INAH officials had tried to pressure her and her husband into selling their land to facilitate archaeological research in the early 1990s, she recalled that workers began clearing the monte on her land. The available publications dealing with excavations in this part of the site only note that "work was interrupted because [the Building of the Columns] is on private land."[53] For her part, María noted that one of the family's key reasons for not wanting the workers to intrude was that "there was vanilla, which was only just about to be harvested." The vanilla, María continued, was important because it had a good price: 400–500 pesos in those days. The monte that made an obstacle for archaeological research was also necessary for the production of vanilla, which provided an important source of cash income in a context of land dispossession.

The violence wrought by the political economy of vanilla cultivation also became a concern for the managers of El Tajín. Writing in 1954, and recalling a similar request he had made in 1951, García Payón requested "a few Mauser [rifles] for the site's guardians, or, what would be more practical, that the military flying column based in Papantla extend its surveillance to the aforementioned archaeological site."[54] As an illustration, he noted that one Jacinto Simbrón had been murdered the previous month, and his house robbed. His son, Bartolo, was a regular mason at the site, and continued to live within its boundaries. While the response to this request was negative, the fact that the local police were also requested to accompany García Payón when he visited the site with workers' pay suggests the reality of the threat of violence and its effect on the operations of the archaeological site.[55] In 1960 García Payón again requested a military presence. The archaeologist noted that he had discussed the possibility with those who lived in El Tajín. Considering "their necessity for their own protection, because the entire region is infested with thieves and murders to rob the indigenous are frequently committed," the residents of El Tajín were willing to provide the construction materials for the military's potential lodging.[56] He noted, with apparent frustration, that his previous proposals to that effect and their corresponding requests for funding had gone unanswered. The INAH, it seems, was unwilling or unable to provide support in the matter. In the political economy of archaeology in El Tajín, the violence associated with vanilla created conditions for which archaeologists and Totonac communities were not directly responsible but that directly impinged on the possibilities of life at the site.

Curing Vanilla

Green vanilla is surprisingly nondescript. It looks like an underdeveloped bean pod and smells slightly botanical, but little more (see figure 6). Vendors have occasionally been known to douse the bean pods with vanilla extract to produce the aroma that tourists expect. To produce the eponymous flavor and aroma, another process is necessary: curing (*el beneficiado*). As I noted above, most vainilleros were not beneficiadores. But the deep historical roots of this relationship do not explain why this is so. The Totonac vainilleros that I discuss in this chapter cultivate and cure. Why, then, would most cultivators opt not to cure vanilla, as they tended not to do during the twentieth century? In short: it takes time.

The process of getting vanilla to bear fruit is a long one. The labor, however, is only relatively intensive during the fertilization, guarding, and harvesting processes. Even then, there is ample time for a cultivator to attend to other tasks. Curing does not require the same multiyear commitment. But it is a full-time task, and one that requires the practitioner to be attentive to minute changes in weather, vanilla feel, and a variety of other factors. When cultivators can earn the necessary funds through the sale of green vanilla, and have competing commitments with lands and households, selling green vanilla is the best balance between labor and earnings—when the price is right and the degree of exploitation is tolerable.

To understand why the temporality of cultivation is workable for vainilleros but the temporality of curing is less so, we might begin again with the green vanilla, now in the hands of a dedicated curer. Their objective is to reduce the pods to about 30 percent humidity content over several weeks, facilitating the development of vanillin.[57] First, the bean pods are sun-dried and "killed," which stops the maturation process. Second, the pods are gathered, wrapped, sweated, and enclosed to continue the drying process. Third, the bean pods are sun-dried once again. Fourth, the pods are "conditioned"—bundled, wrapped, and stored—to encourage full development of the vanilla aroma. These steps are repeated as many times as necessary until the vanilla can be classified and sold. Curing is resolutely empirical: current studies "have not revealed the exact nature of the reaction processes involved in the highly complex phenomena that take place during vanilla curing."[58]

This process requires a different kind of labor than does cultivation. Juan, a third-generation vainillero who, like Martín, learned the beneficio and cures his own vanilla, explained the process like this: "In the morning [the vanilla] is laid out in the sun, on the field or on the floor, so one waits for it to heat up, that the weather is good, logically.... When it's 11:00 a.m. or noon, once it's hot, approximately forty degrees [Celsius] one begins to store it in boxes, the boxes are covered with blankets.... One does this daily process of laying out the vanilla and later putting it in the box so it sweats." For Juan, if the vanilla was thick (between eighteen and twenty centimeters long) this process would be repeated over twenty-four mornings of sun (soles); shorter bean pods may take as few as eleven soles to be finished. Conditioning, for Martín, could take another two or three months. Afterward, the cured vanilla could be stored for as long as two or three years, as long as it is periodically aired out to prevent fungal growth.

The process of sun-drying the vanilla often takes much longer than twenty-four calendar days. As Martín explained, "Sometimes it's cloudy for a week, there's no sun and the vanilla doesn't dry, it's just laid out, it's just airing out, nothing more." He calculated that his vanilla should be exposed for a cumulative total of between ninety and ninety-five sun-hours at between forty and forty-five degrees Celsius. This might take two or three months of removing the vanilla from its containers, laying it out, and letting it soak up the sun. The bean pods also shrink during this process: Amelia, Martín's daughter and an experienced vainillera herself, expected to get eight kilograms of cured vanilla from thirty-five of green vanilla. Published sources agree, citing a ratio of about five kilograms of green vanilla to one kilogram of cured vanilla.[59]

During the curing process, the curer must attend to their vanilla constantly and consistently. Martín explained the dynamics of this process to me on a sunny April morning on the patio of his house. By the time I had arrived, he had already unwrapped the blanket-and-plastic bundles of vanilla, and laid the pods out in even rows on a covered table. Attending to the vanilla

FIG. 7. "Look at how the vanilla shines." Vanilla in the process of curing, 2017. Photograph by the author.

requires multisensory engagement. The vanilla should be robust and firm. If the bean pod was yellowing at the end, that meant that it was getting too mature and risked splitting during the curing process. If left out too long, the vanilla burns, peels, and turns brown ("It's like us," Martín wryly observed). Martín advised me on the camera angle that would let me appreciate the quality of his vanilla (see figure 7). The sun catches the surface of the vanilla beans for a crystalline glint: "Look at how the vanilla shines," Martín said. "This is vanilla's color." Martín periodically checks the density and texture of the vanilla with his fingertips: it had to be firm and not too juicy—but not too dry either. For checking the temperature, however, Martín uses the back of his hands: calloused finger pads were deceptive in matters of temperature. When he judges that the shine, texture, and firmness are appropriate, Martín collects the vanilla, wraps it in wax paper (which has no odor), and takes it inside to sweat or condition. At this point, the bean pods develop their indexical aroma. No birthday cake smelled better.

Knowing when the vanilla is finished curing also requires experience. Amelia explained that she would know when the curing was done "because it feels like it, when it doesn't have water . . . but it's not toasted, it's still a little bit soft but very dry." Only once vanilla has the right feel can it be sold. Those bean pods that are burned, split, or otherwise damaged are sold at a lower grade, used for flavoring, or fashioned into tourist crafts. The feel for vanilla also influences the grade and price at which it can be sold. One normative classification describes the highest quality of cured vanilla: "thick beans, flexible and lustrous, dark brown 'chocolate' color, sweet and delicate aroma, with a vanillin content greater than 2.5 percent of dry weight."[60]

During curing, one must be perpetually attentive to the vanilla and the weather. If there is no sun, the vanilla may still be tended, taken out, and left to ventilate. If the vanilla has not finished curing and is still too moist when stored, it may develop a fungus. But just three or four extra minutes of sun could cause the vanilla to burn; even master curers made such mistakes.[61] Amelia estimated that it took her and her mother two hours to lay the vanilla out, two hours to let it sun-dry, and another two to store again. Between the two of them, it was a full-time job, and one that could extend itself depending on the weather and changes in the vanilla's feel. Curing vanilla carries an opportunity cost that cultivating does not. However, those who could afford to dedicate themselves to curing reaped the benefits. In 1942 a Papantla cultivator was paid around $9.75 per green kilogram; on the New York market, the same quantity of whole cured vanilla sold for $154.38, nearly 1,500 percent more.[62]

During the late nineteenth and early twentieth centuries, the Spanish and Italian families made wealthy by the curing and export of vanilla directed their wealth toward other ends, including archaeology. In central Veracruz, Estefanía Salas de Broner, a Totonac vanilla producer married to a German merchant, collected archaeological material used in Hermann Strebel's pathbreaking research in the area; she regularly donated artifacts to Berlin's Museum of Ethnology.[63] Inspector of Monuments Leopoldo Batres described her as "of Totonac origins [and] well-known in Europe as a collector of archaeology, zoology, and botany, to the extent that in Germany they have given the name of this woman to some of the specimens discovered by her."[64] In El Tajín, and given a nascent governmental interest in the promotion of archaeology, Salas's Papantla counterparts played constitutive roles in the earliest efforts to manage and administer El Tajín. In so doing, they also used the site for their own political ends. This begins with the first conserje formally employed at the site: Agapito Fontecilla y Vidal, a member of Papantla's elite class, also known as the author of the "best source on Mexican vanilla in the nineteenth century."[65]

Family patriarch Agapito Fontecilla Agustina was born in Spain around 1804 and migrated to Mexico perhaps during the turbulent 1830s.[66] He became "one of Papantla's foremost notables—businessman, investor, [vanilla] curing expert, promotor of culture and education, man of letters, and crafty politician."[67] In 1848 the ambitious Fontecilla Agustina married Rosalía Vidal of Papantla, who was from a family active in local political and economic life for more than a century.[68] Juan Vidal, for example, "spent thirty-one years in Papantla as a Militia Captain, thirteen as Postal Administrator, and five as Tobacco Monopoly Administrator" during the late eighteenth century.[69] The Vidals' interest in vanilla was well established by Rosalía's marriage to Fontecilla Agustina, and those familial relationships very likely enabled their descendants' business ventures. By the time son Agapito Fontecilla y Vidal was appointed El Tajín's first conserje in 1886, he was already a noted curer; he won a gold medal for the quality of his vanilla at the Exposition Universelle of 1878 in Paris.[70] In turn, Fontecilla y Vidal's son with Florencia Fontecilla—Agapito Guillermo Fontecilla y Fontecilla—served as conserje between 1906 and 1913. The activities and controversies of the family in El Tajín illuminate the relationships between vanilla curing and local politics in the broader political economy of archaeology.

In 1889 Fontecilla y Vidal filed a report with Batres reporting that El Tajín had not suffered any damages, and recording the number of visitors.[71] In a different letter to Batres, published in *La Nacional* newspaper, Fontecilla y Vidal gave a general description of the Pyramid of the Niches, including the vegetation and measurements of the structure.[72] Later, Fontecilla y Fontecilla requested funds for tools and the labor of twenty men for thirty days: "Given the abundance of this land, the roots penetrating the junctures of the stones that form said monuments, they separate them, they disintegrate them, and push them as they get thicker, collapsing [the stones]."[73] Regular reports and maintenance were among the foundational responsibilities for site custodianship. Here, these activities are the pastimes of one particularly interested family of vanilla curers.

At the same time, the Fontecillas leveraged their work in El Tajín and their association with Batres in matters of local politics. In August 1909 one Luciano Decuir Lathiolait sent a letter to Fernando Marin in Mexico City.[74] Decuir was of the same merchant class as the Fontecillas, but of a different political persuasion. Decuir described to his friend Marin that Fontecilla y Fontecilla did not care for El Tajín, despite his salary. The site was practically abandoned and inaccessible. Could Marin approach the Secretaría de Instrucción Pública y Bellas Artes to have one Benjamín Cabrera appointed in Fontecilla y Fontecilla's place? The letter made it to the secretaría, which requested further information from Batres. The inspector of monuments defended Fontecilla, "a son of the place with abundant [economic] resources," noting that he was not only attentive to his duties but had been a conserje without a salary for many years beforehand.[75] Rivals of the Fontecillas did not let up. Two months later, in October 1909, another report arrived at the secretaría, this time from Governor Teodoro Dehesa.[76] Dehesa passed on a report from the state-appointed regional executive, who reported that El Tajín was abandoned. Fontecilla y Vidal replied to Batres with various arguments: the Inspectorate had authorized, but not disbursed, funds for clearing El Tajín; the vegetation's fecundity required more regular cleaning; and the Fontecillas would be soon submitting a proposal for a more thorough cleaning of the monuments.[77] Was it a coincidence that, one month later, vanilla merchant and landowner Isidoro O. Marié requested the conserje position?[78] Likely not. Despite letters of support from the mayor and regional executive, Marié was turned down because Fontecilla y Fontecilla still occupied the position.

The following year, Decuir again attacked the Fontecillas. In 1910 Decuir reported to Batres that Fontecilla y Fontecilla had moved to Tuxpan and, apparently, that he had let stones be taken from the site.[79] In response, Fontecilla y Vidal explained to Batres that he thought the attacks were political, painting Decuir as a corrupt and power-hungry murderer.[80] Fontecilla y Vidal concluded by warning Batres that "it would not be strange if the machinations continue, creating disturbances with the gossip of naysayers."[81] For his part, Marié's later interests appear commercial; a year later, he requested information on the site's boundaries to determine whether he could quarry certain stones near the site.[82] Nearly forty years later, one Alfonso Acosta told Ángel Palerm that around 1910 there "existed a pretty active trade in stone" between El Tajín and Papantla, with the stones sold by landowners in the archaeological site to the likes of Isidoro Marié, Pastor Gutiérrez, and Pedro Tremari, all otherwise known for their vanilla interests.[83] By the time inspector Pablo Henning brought the matter to federal attention again, in 1913, the political situation had changed: Díaz and Batres were gone, and the country was still reeling from Victoriano Huerta's coup d'état. That Fontecilla y Fontecilla was fired suggests the importance of the family's prior Porfirian political connections.[84]

Examining the activities of Papantla's vanilla merchants suggests that political economy of archaeology functioned as a channel to negotiate matters of local politics. The fecundity of the vegetation is a key theme in such debates. Trinidad Rico observes that the idea of "heritage at risk" naturalizes heritage as something that must be protected, while providing a conduit for other agendas to enter the picture.[85] From the perspectives of Papantla's merchant elite, El Tajín's state of conservation was a proxy for the efficacy of local political factions and, perhaps, the control of resources like stone. The presence of vegetation serves to naturalize El Tajín's state of conservation as a result of the implacable monte (as with the Fontecillas), to demonstrate the negligence of site authorities (as with Decuir, Marié, and the Fontecillas' other opponents), and to argue that others would be better suited to guard positions. It seems ironic that the destructive vegetation was, in fact, perfect for cultivating vanilla, as the Méndez brothers' complaints about Erasmo Rodríguez later in the century suggest.

Even after Mexico's vanilla booms ended, the merchant class proved a useful resource upon which others drew for negotiations with the federal administration vis-à-vis El Tajín. After the death of conserje Pedro Bautista in 1920, Honorato Méndez wrote to the national administration to request the position.[86] In support of his request, he sent along three letters of recommendation; two were signed by the heads of the well-known curing houses R. Curti and Brothers and Melquiades Patiño.[87] Méndez took advantage of the social capital offered by endorsements from members of Papantla's vanilla class to position himself for a federal conserje position, which he eventually received. When Méndez was accused of neglecting his duties, Patiño's firm would write Méndez a note for his file, praising his dedication, and describing the enthusiastic approval of tourists.[88]

Archaeologists, too, found themselves in mutually beneficial relationships with certain members of this vanilla-exporting class. During the 1940s García Payón corresponded with Raúl del Cueto Decuir, "one of the really important vanilla merchants . . . the only person in town who affects *traje de casimir* [cashmere suit] complete with necktie."[89] In one instance, del Cueto wrote to García Payón of his plan to develop a camping area near the entrance to the archaeological site. On February 28, 1945, del Cueto described how he had received a hectare from a local landowner that had a patch of monte good for exhibiting vanilla. "I can tell you," he continued, "that the parcel in front of Pedro's is completely the property of my father. So we dominate both sides of the road entering the site."[90] García Payón responded approvingly, and del Cueto's land evidently became part of the site's infrastructure: four decades later, head guard Pedro Pérez Bautista wrote of del Cueto's cession of twenty meters of property to the site, which were maintained accordingly.[91] When visiting El Tajín, Tatiana Proskouriakoff of the Carnegie Institution of Washington, whose groundbreaking work provided the initial definition of the Classic Veracruz style, stayed with del Cueto in Papantla.[92] The wealth gained by early twentieth-century vanilla curing and exporting could be transferred into other kinds of activities, like facilitating the improvement of tourist infrastructure and the potential for research in El Tajín.

With the decline of vanilla production after the 1960s, the orchid only sporadically emerges in archival materials related to the archaeological site. In El Tajín, vanilla is now most often encountered for sale to tourists or found on the outskirts of the site, thanks to Vicente. Much like the green vine, vanilla's relationships to violence and archaeology are inconspicuous, hidden in the shadow of the "City That Perfumed the World." Following the political economy of vanilla demonstrates how different forms of violence affected local livelihoods and extended to the administration of the site, and how the site could be leveraged in matters of local politics.

Conclusion

During the late nineteenth and early twentieth centuries, Papantla's vanilla booms drew on production that caused conflicts between cultivators and archaeologists in El Tajín. At the same time, the curers who profited most from the orchid also served as conserjes, carrying out the foundational responsibilities of heritage management while leveraging their positions in matters of local politics. Toward the middle of the twentieth century, vanilla's profitability made the broader Papantla landscape one of danger for cultivators, conditions that also became concerns for site managers. These diffuse ties suggest the broader processes at play in the political economy of archaeology, and the additional actors they implicate.

Since the 2000s vanilla has been subject to erratic boom-and-bust cycles. Tropical cyclones in Madagascar regularly damage farmers' livelihoods and vanilla production. Speculators take advantage of the scarcity and drive up prices.[93] In this context, more than a few Papantla cultivators have again chosen to plant vanilla. The backdrop of "normal" violence has changed. Narcoviolence, attacks on journalists, and impunity are now well known in the region. Still, the local antecedents of contemporary violence cast a long shadow. Older residents occasionally remark that the perpetrators of today were like the vanilla bandits of yesterday. The violence associated with profitable vanilla cultivation is not specific to midcentury Papantla.[94] But what does it mean to suggest that a commodity whose relations of production have historically resulted in violence for the Indigenous Totonac residents of El Tajín is integral to the political economy of archaeology? At a minimum, it means archaeology is implicated in the broader discussions of violence and the state in twentieth-century Mexico.

Still, tracing the changing place of vanilla cultivation and curing does not yield the same degree of interconnectedness that I suggest for the oil industry. These relationships had a specific end: the need to conserve Mexico's archaeological sites along broadly Western lines, an idea already naturalized by the late nineteenth century. This "conservation ethic"—understanding places like El Tajín as exemplars of a "non-renewable 'archaeological resource' while . . . championing its conservation in government and public spheres"—was a set of values upon which Batres, the Fontecillas, and their opponents agreed.[95] This continued to be the case during the twentieth century.

However, adhering to ideas of conservation did not ensure their efficacy, and neither did the state's appropriations of the past for nation-building and tourism development. To carry out these objectives, the state relied on more than the configurations of private property, the operations of oil companies, and the interests of vanilla merchants. Generations of largely, but not exclusively, Totonac labor made the ruins into an archaeological site. That labor was not monolithic: workmen, masons, and guards alike participated in different aspects of the research and management process: clearing vegetation, digging pits, reconstructing architecture, safeguarding the site, corresponding with the national administration, and more. Yet focusing on workers' contribution to archaeology alone overlooks how they used employment in the field to their own ends, and how that related to the broader conditions of their lives. I now turn to the wage laborers, custodios, and managers of El Tajín and their places in the political economy of archaeology.

Wage Labor

4

From Subsistence Farming to Archaeology

Everything that we see now wasn't like that before, they discovered El Tajín first, the Pyramid of Niches. . . . Everything was falling down, messy, the stones had fallen. . . . That's how it was, I still had the chance to help do that . . . accommodating the stones, with care, there were no machines, it was all on our shoulders.

—Gerardo

In 1955 archaeologist José García Payón published *Exploraciones en El Tajín: Temporadas 1953 y 1954*. In a discipline that destroys its data while it produces them, documenting research has long been considered a key professional responsibility. The 1953–54 report is straightforward, describing the excavation and reconstruction of El Tajín's precolonial architecture building by building. Yet for the reader not used to the conventions of the genre, the position of the narrator is curious. García Payón wrote mostly in the first-person plural, describing the labor as collective: "Our attention during all of the 1954 season was dedicated to 'Building C,' which we consider was the residence of some hierarch. . . . We began work on the south-east corner."[1] Who is the "we" in question? In other instances, the use of the passive voice provokes a similar question: "The Local Museum was fixed and a door was added to it, the roof and the storeroom's fence were changed out, and a flagpole was placed at the entrance to the site."[2] Occasionally, the reader gets a glimpse of the others erased in the first-person plural and obscured by the passive voice, the workers: "While the masons carried out this work . . ."[3] By contrast, the author named scholars like Agustín García Vega and Ignacio Marquina, as well as funders like Antonio J. Bermúdez of PEMEX.

"Archaeology is a practice we do with others," Gavin Lucas observes, "and there is a violence which accompanies this when people are silenced in the name of representation, the production of knowledge."[4] As with other scientific objects—from seventeenth-century air pumps to modern laboratories—the labor involved in the production of archaeological knowledge tends to go unacknowledged in text.[5] Project directors have the final say in interpretation and publication, and archaeological site reports tend to be written in an impersonal, abstract style.[6] García Payón's report is exemplary in this sense. But archaeology is work. Surveying an area, excavating a feature, stabilizing architecture, interpreting the finds, analyzing and cataloging the artifacts, and creating the infrastructure necessary for researchers requires laborers, often local and/or Indigenous. Much more research has been dedicated to understanding the precolonial past than the lives of those who bring history to light.

In archaeology, workers' contributions tend to be silenced. Allison Mickel convincingly argues that this silencing results from the constitutive divisions between the labors of manual excavation and scholarly interpretation, compensating workers for the performance of docility rather than embodied knowledge.[7] If workers' interpretations are not recorded or valorized, Mickel suggests, archaeologists lose out on valuable understanding of the past, and of archaeology itself. In addition to these interpretative losses, inattention to archaeological labor risks replicating longer histories of colonialism and racism: "When the hand that holds the trowel is black, it is as though holes dig themselves."[8] But is exclusion from archaeology's texts a problem for the workers themselves? Mary Leighton writes that "workers are only invisible if one already assumes the purpose of excavation is to generate texts," an assumption that many archaeologists and workers would find limiting.[9] This insight, that workers have uses for archaeology that go beyond the production of knowledge, provides an important complement to approaches that emphasize inclusion according to disciplinary frames of reference alone.

In El Tajín the people who do the work of clearing, excavating, and reconstructing are overlooked in ways that unfortunately resonate with studies of archaeology worldwide.[10] Scholars like Wendy Doyon, Ashish Avikunthak, and Paul Everill document the silencing, disciplining, and objectification of archaeological labor across time and space.[11] Scholarship on archaeology in the Middle East critiques the discipline's tendency to recreate the exploitative relationships with workers that are characteristic of capitalism.[12] Following workers through the political economy of archaeology requires situating labor in the context of regional history rather than in the evolving state of knowledge about the pre-Hispanic past.

In what follows, I analyze archaeological labor in El Tajín relative to regional patterns of production with an emphasis on seasonal wage labor. After discussing workers in early antiquarian expeditions, I move to the twentieth-century projects of Agustín García Vega and José García Payón. For these projects, I discuss the nature and variability of work in archaeology, how it compares to other employment opportunities, and how wage labor articulates with broader social and economic circumstances. An examination of *peón* labor illustrates the similarities of traditional campesino work and clearing site vegetation. Seasonal labor in archaeology provided opportunities for income when broader socioeconomic processes eroded the region's traditional agricultural base. The following discussion of masons (*albañiles*) demonstrates how employment in archaeology enabled the development of transferable skills. Exploring the work of site custodios shows that these possibilities depended on specific social and kin networks. I suggest that the long-term availability of archaeological labor facilitated regular income and social mobility in a context of agrarian compression, while excluding certain residents and contributing to broader socioeconomic stratification.

Totonac Labor in the Antiquarian Era

In the July 12, 1785, edition of the *Gazeta de México* newspaper, amid news of a hot-air balloon flight in Oaxaca and the death of Doña Paula Francisca Maldonado at the age of 104 in Michoacán, news from Papantla appeared. In March royal official Diego Ruiz was searching for illegal tobacco plantations when he encountered an unusual stepped pyramid.[13] Featuring a hypothetical reconstructive drawing signed by one García (see figure 8), the article's author described the structure and mentioned that "the Indians [*Indios naturales*] of the place did not ignore the structure, although they never revealed it to any Spaniard."[14]

This publication, and its omissions, circulated through the trans-Atlantic scholarly networks of the day.[15] Antiquarian José Antonio de Alzate y Ramírez noted the publication in his important *Descripción de las antigüedades de Xochicalco* of 1791.[16] In 1803 José Pichardo of the order of San Felipe Neri sent a copy of the *Gazeta* publication, along with Alzate's *Descripción*, to exiled Jesuit Andrés Cavo in Rome; Cavo, in turn, gave the documents to Pedro José Márquez.[17] In 1804 Márquez used these materials to write "the first work in Mexican archaeology to be published in Europe": *Due antichi*

FIG. 8. The first published depiction of the Pyramid of the Niches. *Gazeta de México*, July 12, 1785. Image from the collections of the National Library of Spain.

monumenti di architettura messicana.[18] For just over a half century, the anonymous *Gazeta* publication and the works derived from the same were the only published record of El Tajín. It seems unsurprising that the first report of an unusual precolonial structure, close to three hundred years after the end of the Aztec-Spanish War, should spend time describing the structure rather than the local culture or workers.

However, a comparative example demonstrates that this omission was contingent rather than necessary. The second actual visit to El Tajín was Luxembourger dragoon captain Guillermo Dupaix, who visited between 1791 and 1804 under the auspices of the Royal Antiquarian Expedition.[19] In contrast to the contemporaneous *Gazeta* account, Dupaix's notes describe his process: "I requested Indians from Subdelegado Estevan Tison [Tizón] and, as a consequence, I took for the effort some 80 Totonacs, armed with hatchets, machetes, etc. for the clearing [*desmonte*] of said Pyramid, bristling with thick trees, hiding itself under them and becoming confused with the surrounding jungle.... After many sessions, dangers, and much time, I could take charge of the architectural content of this Building."[20] However, for two centuries, Dupaix's visit was only known via Alexander von Humboldt's *Essai politique sur le royaume de la Nouvelle-Espagne* (1811).[21] Thanks to Leonardo

López Luján's research in the collections of the American Philosophical Society, Dupaix's notes were identified and published in 2008.[22] Moreso than the *Gazeta* account, Dupaix's references allow for some speculative reconstruction of labor in regional context.

The mention of the *subdelegado* redirects attention to the broader political-economic networks in which local colonial antiquarianism was enmeshed.[23] Esteban Tizón, a Cádiz-born merchant and militia commander based in the port of Veracruz, was subdelegado of Papantla from 1788 to 1803.[24] Tizón presided over a region whose economic circumstances were becoming increasingly difficult. Colonial Papantla featured "relatively low population densities, a rugged terrain, poor transport networks, and underdeveloped markets."[25] Rural life focused on the milpa, while the two most important cash crops were vanilla and tobacco; the latter also had important ritual significance for the Totonac.[26] By the time Tizón became subdelegado, the situation had changed. Among the wide-ranging reforms of the eighteenth-century Bourbon dynasty was the 1764 monopoly over the cultivation of tobacco.[27] This monopoly, which outlawed Totonac cultivation of the crop, upset the balance of political power in Papantla.[28] Georgina Moreno Coello proposes that Tizón willingly overlooked clandestine Totonac tobacco plantations—the same that Diego Ruiz sought to confiscate—for personal profit: Tizón was accused of complicity in the sale of tobacco products in his Papantla store in 1800, contravening the royal monopoly.[29] This set of relationships suggests that visits from the likes of Ruiz threatened the local balance of power in a way that Dupaix, who had no obligation to seek out tobacco plantations, did not. In this reading, El Tajín might not have revealed in the three decades preceding Ruiz's inspection because doing so may have exposed illegal tobacco plantations. The brief mention of a colonial official and Totonac labor shifts concerns away from Diego Ruiz's "discovery" to the local political-economic circumstances in which Totonac residents became "archaeological labor."

The next published account demonstrates how vague references and dry architectural descriptions silence the contemporary agency and labor of the area's Totonac residents while emphasizing a more distant past. Carl Nebel's account of the 1830s is sparse, and is notable for a lithograph still used to present El Tajín today (see figure 9). With regard to Totonac labor, the author only noted that he "had to take advantage of the arms of the Indians to fell the trees and branches that had the [Pyramid] covered, so much so that, being close to the base, nothing could be distinguished of it."[30]

FIG. 9. Carl Nebel's reconstructive lithograph of the Pyramid of the Niches. *Voyage pittoresque et archéologique dans la partie la plus intéressante du Mexique*, 1836.

The racism of this metonymy reflects broader understandings of Indigenous communities in nineteenth-century Mexico. Ostensibly, liberal reforms like equality of citizenship had done away with the discriminatory caste system that relegated Indigenous people to legal inferiority.[31] Ending legal distinctions between Indigenous and non-Indigenous Mexicans did not undo the "dominant ideologies of the colonial period, [in which] the indigenous race was inferior to the Spanish race . . . redeemable through Christian faith and procreation with Spaniards."[32] Following this logic of Indigenous deficiency, liberal theory considered Indigenous people as citizens in need of progressive modernization. Indigenous communities in Papantla and elsewhere took advantage of these new legal frameworks to advance their own aims, like negotiating local politics, preserving communal autonomy, and maintaining collective landownership.[33]

As interest in Mexico's pre-Hispanic past developed during the nineteenth century, Indigenous communities frequently acted as intermediaries between outsider expeditions and the remains of the past. The published notes from the Comisión Científica de Cempoala of 1891–92 offer insight into the place of labor in archaeology during the Porfiriato: "D. Marcelino Sánchez, Jefe

Político del Cantón, put at our disposal the congregation of Indians of El Tajín to clear the land near the Pyramid to an extent sufficient to bring it into view, removing the weeds and brush that covered it, which did much to lessen our workload: the Secretary of those congregations, Juan Pérez, also helped us plenty by smoothing out the difficulties that occurred with the Indians, which we would not have been able to overcome, because we did not know the Totonac language, the only one that is spoken there."[34] Marcelino Sánchez and Juan Pérez were necessary for del Paso y Troncoso and his expedition to get the workers necessary to clear El Tajín. For local communities, it appears that archaeological labor was like other kinds of work for which state officials like Sánchez solicited support. Yet the phrasing of this footnote says little about the nature of archaeological labor: was it like the communal labor used to maintain trails and town centers? Was it wage labor? Did workers have the choice to participate, and if so, why did they choose to do so? Even if researchers depended on intermediaries and local workers, these relationships were far from equal. Archaeological interventions began on a social, political, and economic plane structured by anti-Indigenous racism.

Already by the end of the nineteenth century, records show a few common trends emerging in the representation of labor in El Tajín that recall archaeological practice elsewhere.[35] Workers are rarely identified and, if mentioned, are only referred to in collective (as with "80 Totonacs") or metonym (as in "the arms of the Indians"). Authors rarely describe workers' labor as such. If they do, it is only preliminary to the researcher's labor of interpretation, as with the clearing. As García Payón's 1955 report suggests, modern reports reproduced colonial trends.

Archaeological Labor in El Tajín: A Panorama

At the turn of the twentieth century, El Tajín was a community of Totonac landowners who lived near their milpas, cultivating maize, beans, and chile for subsistence, and vanilla and sugarcane for cash. The state had forcibly ended communal land tenure in favor of private property, but land dispossession did not immediately follow in Ojital y Potrero (see chapter 1). Despite the turmoil of the Mexican Revolution and the challenges of rebuilding the state, continuity was the rule for rural Totonac lifeways.[36] The 1930s saw agrarian mobilizations elsewhere in the municipality and the state, but El Tajín remained a community of subsistence-oriented Totonac landowners who controlled land as private property.[37] By the 1950s the growth of the oil industry and paving of new roads made the region accessible as never before. Cattle ranchers, eager to take advantage of new pasture grasses, cattle breeds, barbed wire, and growing demand for beef, began to arrive in force.[38] Whether through legitimate purchase, outright swindle, or violent dispossession, cattle ranchers came to control much of the region. By the last decade of the twentieth century, anthropologist Carola Kasburg described El Tajín as "characterized by typical rural occupations, with a surplus of wage-dependent workers. . . . [Only archaeological labor], brickworks during the dry season, handicrafts, and the construction industry in the immediate vicinity offer new alternative occupations for the peasants who have become landless."[39] As I will illustrate, archaeology offered the possibility of employment in difficult circumstances for some, the potential for economic mobility and skill development for others, and increasing socioeconomic stratification for the community.

This process took shape during Agustín García Vega's 1934–38 excavations. By this decade, Mexican archaeology was a professionalizing, state-sponsored discipline based in field research and excavation. In monumental sites like Teotihuacan, Monte Albán, Mitla, and Tula, the state archaeologists of the Departamento de Monumentos Prehispánicos regularly employed wage laborers for seasonal projects. Archaeologists needed workers to clear terrain, dig excavation pits, and reconstruct pre-Hispanic monuments. The state considered that hiring local workers was not just "cheaper and more comfortable" but a "moral obligation" and intended to prevent hostility toward archaeological projects.[40]

Archived payroll records, which list names, positions, and wages, provide a window into what labor looked like for residents between 1934 and 1974.[41] For much of the century, employment was variable and seasonal. Projects occurred frequently, but not always, between August and January of the following year. The number of workers varied, but was often substantial, and required different skill sets. The quantity of positions contracted varied, from an average of 245 during the decade of the 1930s to an average of 382 by the decade of the 1970s. A sizable portion of the community's population participated (see table 4).[42]

The relative scale of employment is comparable to similar projects: Manuel Gamio's celebrated Teotihuacan project of 1917–21 hired around 500 workers at three times the normal daily wage.[43] The Carnegie Institution of Washington hired between 40 and 150 workers annually for its excavations in Chichén Itzá between 1927 and 1934, or nearly all the men from nearby

TABLE 4. Lista de raya positions compared with male population of El Tajín, 1930–70

YEAR	AVERAGE POSITIONS CONTRACTED	MALE POPULATION OF EL TAJÍN	EMPLOYMENT AS PROPORTION OF MALE POPULATION
1930	245	386	63%
1940	123	358	34%
1950	160	413	39%
1960	262	575	46%
1970	382	605	63%

Source: 1930–70 data from INEGI, Archivo Histórico de Localidades Geoestadísticas, AGEE Veracruz, AGEM 124-Papantla.

Pisté.[44] Later megaprojects were even more labor intensive. The Proyecto Teotihuacan of 1960–64 employed more than 800 workers, and the Proyecto Especial Cantona of 1992–94, around 500.[45] El Tajín's own Proyecto Tajín contracted more than 500 between 1988 and 1992.[46]

This labor force was organized into different positions requiring distinct skill sets. The most common position is peón, representing 58 percent of payroll entries. Peones were responsible for removing vegetation, digging, and transporting material. Grades of mason represent about 32 percent of positions.[47] These were responsible for consolidating, stabilizing, and rebuilding pre-Hispanic architecture. Other position titles represented about 9 percent of payroll entries. These varied by season and were likely otherwise collapsed into the peón/mason positions: supervisor (*sobrestante*), water-carrier (*aguador*, required for mixing cement), conservator (*conservador*, responsible for helping to stabilize architecture), and driver (*chofer*, usually non-Totonac). Not included in the payroll records are the subjects of the following chapter: the custodios. Custodios worked year-round and were paid directly by the INAH, rather than through archaeologists' seasonal projects. The custodios and their social networks were still important factors in seasonal worker employment, as I discuss below.

From Campesino to Peón

Through the 1940s El Tajín remained a community of dispersed Totonac subsistence farmers. Despite archaeological field seasons in 1946 and 1947–

48, seasonal employment and wage labor in archaeology is not mentioned in Kelly and Palerm's landmark ethnography, and emerges only tangentially in Kelly's unpublished materials: "Extremely few Tajín residents work for wages, and they are the landless and the least prosperous."[48] Whether wage labor in archaeology was not a salient feature of everyday life during Kelly's fieldwork, or whether Kelly did not recognize its incipient importance, the conditions that facilitated this exclusion would soon change.

The most commonly employed workers were referred to as peones. Though less derogatory than its English-language cognate, the title of "peón" carries important baggage. The term is especially associated with debt, serfdom, and hacienda labor.[49] Contemporary historical scholarship has done much to restore the agency of these workers, but the association of exploitative labor with archaeology is evocative.[50] Likewise suggestive is the term's derivation from terminology associated with the infantry of the Roman legions.[51] The connections between archaeology and militarism date to the discipline's foundations and continue to influence field practice.[52] However, these associations should not be pushed into etymological fallacy. Debt peonage, for instance, was not a feature of Papantla's so-called haciendas; their most valuable resource was the land, whether leased to tenants or put up for investment collateral.[53] It appears that the local use of the term *peón* is a transplant from elsewhere in the country, mediated via state archaeology.[54] The Porfirian Inspectorate of Monuments used the term as a title, along with *conserje* (see chapter 5).

Regardless of the title, residents of El Tajín knew this work well. Its key responsibilities—clearing low vegetation, felling trees, trimming branches, and removing brush—were integral to swidden milpa agriculture.[55] Planting a milpa further involved burning, planting, weeding, harvesting, and, as the soil was exhausted, rotation to an adjacent plot. Clearing El Tajín was like the preparation for rotation, especially clearing secondary growth (acahual). This was no minor commitment. Acahuales featured three to four meters of vegetation, and up to ten or twelve meters of tree cover.[56] Even with steel machetes, sickles, and axes, weeding the acahual is laborious. It can take between eight and ten days of work to clean a single hectare.[57]

This work was constant in an archaeological site open year-round. A 1947 account from García Payón speaks to the exuberance of the vegetation, and the nature of work otherwise glossed as "cleaning."[58] In August the archaeologist returned to El Tajín for the first time in two months. He was disappointed to find the access road overgrown, though the archaeological structures were clear. García Payón admonished the custodios, figuring that they had been less than dedicated to their work. They responded that, despite their efforts, the vegetation's fecundity had rendered regular clearing unmanageable. As proof, they offered their own house lots, which, overgrown at the edges, had likewise been impossible to keep clear. García Payón was convinced. In turn, he explained to his superiors that the fecundity of vegetation meant that cleaning worked in stages: cutting down the trees and plants (*desmontar*); removing the cut trunks, stems, and roots (*destroncar* and *desenraizar*); and cutting everything that grew back during the first two stages. Peones were responsible for this work, which covered about fifty hectares of the site by the 1940s.[59]

The Totonac campesinos of El Tajín had the skills to work as peones, but they were not hired randomly: local intermediaries like custodios played key roles in employment. Prior to the beginning of García Vega's project, state officials wrote to custodio Erasmo Rodríguez and honorary inspector Luis André to request information on the local costs of materials and salaries for peones and masons.[60] Rodríguez then received 3,000 pesos for worker payroll in February 1934, in advance of García Vega's arrival.[61] While there is relatively little documentation to the effect, it seems that Rodríguez and, later, García Payón worked through the local Sindicato Gremial de Albañiles y Similares "Gonzalo Juárez" to find workers during the 1930s and 1940s.

If the history, composition, and functions of this union are difficult to trace, its presence is not a surprise. In the aftermath of the Mexican Revolution, unions played a complex role in the development of Mexico's single-party system.[62] Politicians sought the support of organized labor with guarantees like the Constitution of 1917's Article 123, which enshrined labor rights like an eight-hour workday, a minimum wage, and the right to unionize. However, organized labor was not populous, extensive, or politically unified enough to act autonomously. During the 1920s and 1930s the political give-and-take between the state and labor became a relationship of unequal dependence.[63] The Congreso de Trabajadores Mexicanos (CTM)—of which the Sindicato Gremial de Albañiles y Similares "Gonzalo Juárez" was a small part—became the labor wing of Mexico's ruling PRI party: "The regime could reinforce its legitimacy by making a show of formal endorsements by labor and peasant organizations [and] could carry out political propaganda campaigns and organize mass demonstrations."[64]

Still, unions were capable of important activism. In 1939 the CTM referred the SEP to a request from the Sindicato Gremial de Albañiles y Similares

"Gonzalo Juárez."[65] The union gave the rates for work in Papantla (2.50 pesos for peones) and requested a 25 percent increase for work in El Tajín, in addition to free transportation. Eight days later, the workers stopped working, ostensibly because of a delay in pay.[66] The timing seems more than coincidental. After meeting with the workers, García Payón was able to resolve the conflict, though more funding was not forthcoming. Similar petitions during the 1940s met with similar responses, though references to unions in those petitions become scarce. Changes in broader state-labor relations may account for this change. In 1941 CTM leadership turned over to Fidel Velázquez, who "set the organization on a course of government adherence that branded [a] specific form of state-labor collaborationism" during the following half century.[67] Perhaps this move or its consequences proved debilitating to the likes of the Sindicato Gremial de Albañiles y Similares "Gonzalo Juárez." If nothing else, the use of union labor suggests that archaeology was one of several possibilities for employment in the region.

So why might a Totonac campesino in El Tajín seek peón employment? First, work as a peón was familiar. Peones who began working in the 1960s echo this analysis: it was basically campesino work (see figure 10). Labor involved clearing and removing vegetation with manual tools, though one had to be careful with pre-Hispanic stucco when weeding unexcavated mounds. While labor protections and benefits were either informal or nonexistent, the former workers with whom I spoke did not emphasize poor working conditions. Archaeology paid better than comparable campesino jobs (though consistently under minimum wage), and at one kilometer away, one could walk to work.[68] Workers did not spend earnings on transport or lunch.

Furthermore, it appears that seasonal labor in archaeology could be accommodated within the regular planting schedule. The overlaps between archaeological field seasons and the farming schedule appear to have been limited to a month or two. Field seasons from 1948 to 1960 tended to begin in April or May, while field seasons from 1960 to 1974 tended to begin in September or October. April and May would typically be busy months for the clearing and preparation of a milpa, while October and November would be occupied with harvesting. Outside of these overlaps, the most common milpa labor was the kind of weeding one would do in the archaeological site.

If work as a peón was like work in the fields, so too were its gendered associations. In El Tajín the gendered division of labor was fluid.[69] Normatively, men worked in the fields, and women in the household. Work in archaeology

FIG. 10. Communal labor dedicated to weeding the plaza of the community of El Tajín. "Faena: Desyerbando la plaza," ITKEA, series 5, box 55, binder 1, slide 066, DeGolyer Library, Southern Methodist University.

was more specifically gendered. Women do not appear in the payroll records, except occasionally as typists. In interviews with former peones, women's contributions consisted in making or bringing lunch to the site, a responsibility shared by children. This gendered division of labor may represent sexism on the part of archaeologists. An important line of research in archaeology has demonstrated the discipline's gender biases, arguing that certain types of labor are coded as masculine and valorized (fieldwork, excavation) and other forms of labor are coded as feminine and denigrated (lab-based and archival analyses).[70] These biases intersected with other forms of discrimination.[71] This division of labor may also represent archaeologists' efforts to accommodate what they saw as community norms in a rural, Indigenous region, as well as broader state-led development efforts that focused on male heads of households.

If the nature of the work and its gendered associations were familiar, the changing regional conditions I discuss in the first half of this book made employment even more attractive. Toward the 1950s El Tajín's status as a community of Totonac landowners and agriculturalists became increasingly precarious. Some ten kilometers northwest of El Tajín, a rustic oil camp became the epicenter of the Mexican oil industry: Poza Rica. Foreign firms drilled the first wells in 1930, and within eight years, journalist Ruth Sheldon considered that "for practical purposes, the Poza Rica field is really the Mexican oil industry."[72] As drilling in Poza Rica expanded, oil companies paved an old footpath that went east from the town of Coatzintla, facilitating access to El Tajín. Before long, new interstate highways linked Mexico City with the Gulf Coast, and new paved roads linked the burgeoning oil city of Poza Rica to the San Andrés oil fields to the south, making the region accessible as never before.[73]

Export-oriented cattle ranchers were among the beneficiaries. As one interviewee put it: "Indigenous people had land, but they passed it down. . . . And if the heirs sell? And if those lands weren't sold, the wealthy ranchers were those that took ownership [fueron los que se fueron adueñando]." This passive-voice phrasing (se fueron adueñando), with a verb that emphasizes outcome (adueñar), delicately alludes to the fact that cattle ranchers came to control much of the land previously owned by Totonac residents of El Tajín and the surrounding communities. At the same time, production of the region's principal cash crop, vanilla, declined between the 1940s and 1960s, outcompeted by Madagascar and synthetic vanillas on the international market (see chapter 3). In contrast to the independent farmers of the early twentieth century, the peones of the 1960s and 1970s tended to be landless workers relying on corporate employment, wage labor, and stores.[74] In a context of increasing land dispossession and agrarian compression, offering wage-labor positions to former subsistence farmers makes archaeology appear as one exploitative capitalist enterprise among many.[75] While archaeological labor alone did not cause the formation of a rural proletariat, it arguably took advantage of the circumstances to recruit workers for low pay.

In these circumstances, workers had to adapt. Peón employment enabled regular (if seasonal) cash income, and the potential for minor capital accumulation. This may have been the case for Tirso González Méndez. Born around 1912 to Modesto González and María Antonia Méndez, Tirso worked as a peón during seventeen field seasons between 1936 and 1970. One of Kelly's census records provides a snapshot of Tirso's life around 1948.[76] He owned a house on rented land, which he shared with wife María Ana Méndez and seven children. Though more residents of El Tajín owned land then rented, Tirso was hardly alone; around 30 percent of plantings were on rented land.[77] Absent the midcentury pressures on land, rent does not appear to have been a concern. Landowner Francisco Ferral charged 34 pesos annually, while in

1947 Tirso earned at least 188 pesos for seven nonconsecutive weeks of work as a peón.[78] Outside of the archaeological site, Tirso worked in the milpa and sold corn, vanilla, and chile. His harvests during the 1940s were abundant enough that he was able to gift corn to his parents, mother-in-law, and brother Rosalino González. With access to land providing the sustenance, cash was used to purchase clothes, dishware, kerosene, cane liquor, beer, salt, and other commodities produced outside of El Tajín.[79] For reference, Juan Castro's local store likely did not contain more than 200 pesos worth of products—rice, beans, lard, cookies, soft drinks, chewing gum, cigarettes, matches, soap, pens, notebooks, sugar, salt, raw tobacco, and aspirin—at any given time during the 1940s.[80]

For residents otherwise dedicated to subsistence agriculture and local commerce, archaeological labor could form part of a survival strategy in changing times. This interpretation resonates with the experiences of women who have worked in later projects.[81] One such worker explained to me that three years of work reintegrating murals for Proyecto Tajín (1988–92) had enabled her to pay off her house lot, have it titled in her name, and begin building a masonry dwelling. That kind of restoration, she explained, was considered women's work. The same is true today. What looks like a survival strategy at the household scale could nevertheless be exploitation at the communal scale, but examining the work of masons complicates an overemphasis on exploitation.

Mason Mobility

For masons, archaeological labor could facilitate skill development and social mobility. Unlike peón labor, masonry had few precedents in El Tajín. In 1947 the community had only two masonry buildings, both built by workers from Papantla.[82] During decades of work at the site and elsewhere, certain residents of El Tajín became expert masons. For individuals, learning masonry had a few possible outcomes. While some seem to have been content with seasonal employment, like their peón counterparts, others were able to develop skills over time, or parlay seasonal work into tenured custodio positions. The career of Faustino González Méndez illustrates the second trajectory. Another son of Modesto González and María Antonia Méndez, Faustino began as a peón during the 1940s. He spent a season as a mason's assistant in 1952 before becoming a mason during the 1960s and, finally, a first-grade mason during the 1970s. This trajectory of increasing specialization over time accords with broader descriptions of this archaeological labor force. A few years before Faustino began working, both García Vega and Luis André agreed that the Totonac were incompetent masons. The former noted in 1935 that he "could not count on competent personnel. . . . The masons and carpenters of the region are very unfamiliar with their trades, or their work is extremely deficient. . . . With patience and goodwill I managed to get the work back on track."[83] Patronizing and paternalistic, these comments contrast with later evaluations of El Tajín's Totonac workers as practical experts.

By 1959 García Payón noted that a specific group of Totonac residents living near the site had taken charge of the masonry work in El Tajín.[84] The archaeologist is recalled for respecting the skill of these workers. In an interview, archaeologist S. Jeffrey K. Wilkerson, a former student of García Payón, recalled the transportation of the carved columns from the Building of the Columns complex to the provisional site museum, a kilometer away. As Wilkerson recalled, García Payón directed a Totonac work crew to transport the column sections, and they asked when the stones needed to be at the new museum building. García Payón replied accordingly and left with Wilkerson. The latter wondered aloud why they had not explained how to transport the weighty pieces, carved with some of El Tajín's most famous iconography. "They know more about moving heavy stones than we'll ever know," as Wilkerson recalled García Payón's reply. With hardwood rails, vines, and overlying ropes, the Totonac workers transported the sections to the museum in the allocated time. García Payón had complete confidence in the Totonac workers, Wilkerson emphasized. A far cry from García Vega and André's concerns about the masons during the 1930s, the workers had become so expert that, by the 1970s, Wilkerson could describe them as having "it in their blood."

The masonry characteristic of El Tajín (see figure 11) is not specific to archaeology. Former masons stress the similarity of labor to construction work elsewhere: as one experienced worker put it, the work "was normal . . . moving stones, putting stones together with cement, like masonry . . . but it was another type of masonry because it was with stones," rather than bricks or concrete blocks. For these masons, employment taught skills—like measuring spaces, verifying alignments, mixing cement, and mortaring stone—that qualified one for work on other construction projects. For Faustino González Méndez and a select number of other workers, like Bartolo Simbrón de León, Celedonio Xochihua Pérez, and Santos García Pérez, employment as a peón provided an entry point for work as a mason, which enabled the development

FIG. 11. Masonry work on the South Ballcourt. Fototeca del Centro INAH Veracruz, núm. inv. 495. Reproduction authorized by the Instituto Nacional de Antropología e Historia.

of transferable skills (and paid better). Unlike the peón labor, whose similarity to work in the milpa was well known to residents, the development of expertise in masonry came about through generations of engagement with archaeological labor.

The career of Pedro Pérez Bautista best illustrates how employment in archaeological labor could facilitate social mobility (see chapter 5). Born in 1917, Pérez Bautista began working at El Tajín through his association with Modesto González, whom he regarded as an abuelo.[85] Like Faustino González, Pérez Bautista began as a peón with García Vega in the 1930s and graduated to mason by the 1950s. He worked as a first-grade mason into the 1960s. Thanks to his association with García Payón, Pérez Bautista was appointed head custodio (*encargado*) in 1964, replacing Teódulo González Méndez (son to Modesto and brother to Tirso and Faustino). As encargado, Pérez Bautista held a tenured position with a regular paycheck, vacations, and retirement, and was responsible for administrative tasks like organizing workers, tracking visitor statistics, and rendering reports until his retirement in 1994.

For wage laborers like Tirso González, employment in archaeological labor provided seasonal cash income in a context of land dispossession and changing economic opportunities. For the likes of Faustino González, wage labor enabled the development of skills that allowed for continued employment in the site, and could be useful elsewhere. Finally, for a fortunate few like Pedro Pérez Bautista, Epifanio de León Méndez, and Onésimo Juárez González, wage labor was a gateway to a lifetime of stable and well-paid custodio work, and the possibility of the same for one's descendants. However, not all residents of El Tajín had access to wage labor, and even fewer could become custodios.

Guardship and Kinship

Across Mexico, site custodios had a range of responsibilities: safeguarding monuments, responding to visitors, liaising between scholars and officials, and mediating between archaeologists and communities. As I discuss in the following chapter, custodios from across the country became part of a union delegation affiliated with the national teachers' union, the Sindicato Nacional de Trabajadores de la Educación, by the 1970s.[86] This process consolidated the custodios as the local elite class, with union benefits joining the stability and prestige of working for the federal government.[87] One younger custodio's recollection of this generation is illustrative: "Many of them lived better than you because you depend on work in the fields, for example, I used to sell water. . . . They earned like government workers and had a lot of benefits, vacations, bonuses, and everything, and you have nothing."

These custodios were a select group. El Tajín's custodio workforce expanded only gradually during the twentieth century, from two in 1936 to seven by 1974. The workers who filled these seven positions were all members of the most represented families on the payroll list. A 1974 petition for a custodio position makes the grounds for the request explicit, referencing the impacts of land dispossession while drawing on experience with wage labor. As Quintín Pérez wrote to García Payón, "I have always worked during the work seasons that you have ordered, recently in 1973 and 1974, I worked as a second-class mason." This work was necessary, Pérez continued, because "I have no land on which to plant, I survive on others' work."[88] The letter reflects shared understandings of the region's circumstances and the background useful for a custodio position, a perspective backed up by other materials from García Payón's archives.

Beyond the benefits to one's own family, employment as a site custodio had intergenerational impacts. Tenured custodio positions were passed down to sons according to agreements made between the INAH and the union.[89] A

1972 request from Faustino González Méndez recalls his labor in the site, while alluding to the position inheritance that gives custodio employment a long-lasting effect. "By virtue of the fact that my father, Modesto González González, left his position vacant upon his death, I request that, by your honorable conduct, I be given the opportunity to have the aforesaid vacancy, since I have worked in the archaeological site of El Tajín on various occasions beforehand, and as a result I know the jobs there, and regardless that position will have to be filled."[90] In petitions like Faustino's, workers drew on their experiences with wage labor and their genealogical relationships alike to make claims for custodio positions.

In addition to their employment benefits and intergenerational impacts, certain custodio positions like that of the encargado further influenced the employment of wage laborers. Echoing Erasmo Rodríguez's receipt of payroll funds in advance of García Vega's project, former workers recalled the importance of site encargados as labor intermediaries. As one former mason put it: "When García Payón [wasn't here] . . . they told us when there was going to be work, Don Teódulo [González Méndez] was the first to look for us, we were the first ones he sought." For one retired custodio and former mason, "Pedro Pérez . . . was the person in charge, so he would notify everyone. It was a chain, he would notify one or two and those people would be in charge of notifying the others." The similarity of these comments suggests that the hiring of workers was related to the structural position of the encargado rather than the personal characteristics of any individual official.

Nevertheless, the intermediary role alone does not account for who was hired and who was not. As the retired custodio further explained, "The people who were chosen were those that [the encargado] had known before, among others, his family and other families. . . . If he didn't know them, there was no work to be had." This effect is visible in the payroll data: about 10 percent of families account for fully 64 percent of individual payroll entries. Comparing the tenures of individual encargados further bears this perspective out. Modesto González González appears as encargado in 1940, and son Teódulo González Méndez was encargado between 1944 and 1964.[91] In total, González González's children and grandchildren account for at least 14 percent (887) of total entries in the payroll records. Compared with his predecessor, Pedro Pérez Bautista's period (1964–74/1994) saw fewer members of the González Méndez family, and more members of those related to Pérez Bautista. After González González's children, Pérez Bautista and his siblings are the second most represented family in the payroll lists. They account for about 4 percent of entries (252); if the second generation is included, the proportion rises to about 15 percent (955). Taking these figures as a minimum, close relatives of two encargados—Modesto González González and Pedro Pérez Bautista—account for nearly 30 percent (1,842) of all entries in payroll records for the 1936–74 period.

These associations are to be expected. In the Totonac region, kinship is a fundamental principle of social organization: "Consanguineal, affinal, and ritual kin are supposed to have a mutual bond and readiness to help. . . . Disinterested support among kin [is] the moral rule."[92] In forms of collective, reciprocal labor (known as *mano vuelta*), community members solicited their kin for assistance in large-scale projects like building houses, clearing milpas, and harvesting crops, with the expectation that the recipients, too, would provide labor when needed. As intermediaries, site encargados relied on similar networks to find labor. Those with limited access to these kin and social networks were excluded. However, even kinship and work history were no guarantees. Guard employment ultimately depended on the INAH's allocation of guard positions and admissions procedures. Quintín Pérez's and Faustino González's petitions were ultimately unsuccessful.

By regularly allocating funds to some, and not to others, employment in archaeology almost certainly contributed to local socioeconomic stratification; archaeology functioned to channel cash from the state to El Tajín and communities like it.[93] In a random sample of García Payón's budgets from this period—1947, 1958, 1963–64, and 1973–74—the archaeologist dispersed an average of around 42,700 pesos to the workers he employed. Indeed, worker payroll was consistently among the archaeologist's highest expenditures, accounting for between 37 percent and 64 percent of the total seasonal budget. In addition to the cash income, the possibility of becoming a custodio highlights the intergenerational effects of participating in wage labor. As of 2021, four custodios who began in the 2000s trace their positions back to custodio parents who began as wage laborers during the 1960s and 1970s. Not all Tajín residents would have the opportunity to work as peones, not all peones could become masons, not all masons could become custodios, and not all custodio positions could be passed down. Until recently, women were excluded from each of these positions.

Conclusion

The exclusion of workers from the production of knowledge in archaeology is an increasingly well-recognized phenomenon, likewise visible in the early history of research at El Tajín. In this case, beginning with the political economy of archaeology illustrated how twentieth-century research in El Tajín developed in a context of Totonac landowners and subsistence farmers, whose work in the site was like labor in the fields. Over time, some workers were able to continue working at the site, an opportunity that would have been attractive in the context of declining local land ownership. Others were able to specialize in masonry or parlay their seasonal jobs into permanent positions. This participation depended on specific kin and social networks related to the site encargados, meaning that not all had the same opportunities.

Regular employment of rural and Indigenous residents for archaeological research and heritage management projects remains common in Mexico and further afield. However, a further laboral tie between El Tajín and the archaeological site is relatively less common: the system of unionized, tenured custodios. Since 1885 these workers have been guards, landscapers, and civil servants at archaeological sites across the country. While their understandings of the pre-Hispanic past are specific to the cultures they claim, they have in common long—often intergenerational—histories of labor. As a result, following the political economy of archaeology relative to the custodios offers the chance to understand other ways of telling and writing the history of archaeology in Mexico, one structured by the generational succession of worker cohorts.

Custodios

Cohorts and Histories of Labor

5

> The first thing I'd tell [the INAH] is "*de nada*, thank you, for giving me
> my family, for giving me my home, giving me what I can appreciate
> in my work," twenty-three years working for the INAH.... I, at least,
> would say: "how magnificent it is to have a job like this." Who else
> would pay you not to get wet [outside]? Who else would pay you to
> be seated, to be in a place like this?
>
> —Armando

In 2011 I first came to know El Tajín as most visitors do: a tourist destination
and place to learn about Mexico's precolonial past. I returned with aspirations
of research—a project on "Totonac Perspectives on El Tajín"—in September
2012. The site's director, an architect, listened with interest as I explained what
I hoped to do. It being a Sunday, he recommended that I return the following
day to check out the library and site offices. I returned Monday afternoon.
As I entered the site's open-air installations, a custodio clad in a blue INAH
uniform eyed me expectantly from the ticket counter. I asked about the offices,
feeling that passing the counter without a ticket would be a transgression.
He gestured to a space behind the ticket counter and around a large, sculpted
pillar. The offices were there, he explained, "but they're closed." As I ambled
around the pillar, I double-checked the day: it was indeed Monday, and the
site was open. I checked my watch: it was 12:30 p.m., and the director had
said that the offices were open from 9 a.m. to 5 p.m. Was it a holiday? Had
I misunderstood the director?

As it turned out, I had misunderstood the meaning of "closed." It became
obvious when I approached the offices. The front patio was crowded with
landscaping equipment: wheelbarrows, riding mowers, weed trimmers, backpack sprayers, mops, rakes, and brooms. Behind this equipment was a table
with three chairs, and behind that table was a large standalone board that

FIG. 12. The custodios' protest, September 2012. Photograph by the author.

blocked entry to the site's offices (see figure 12). No fewer than fourteen signs decorated the display. On these signs, the site administration was accused of financial mismanagement, not following through on previously made agreements, and being a puppet; who controlled the strings was not specified. The signs demanded new tools for the archaeological sites of El Tajín, Cuyuxquihui, and Castillo de Teayo from both the site administration and the state of Veracruz.[1] Four signs demanded the firing of the director of El Tajín's Management Plan. Another five signs expressed support for Mexico's main heritage law, the Ley Federal de Monumentos y Zonas Arqueológicas of 1972, and organized labor, while rejecting the labor, fiscal, and energy reform proposed by President Felipe Calderón. Two others staked positions against the privatization of patrimony. I had no idea what any of this meant, but the staging suggested that it was important.

I loitered until the director, sitting with the rest of the staff in the adjacent cafeteria, beckoned me over. He introduced me to the rest of the staff.

Formally belonging to the site subdirectorate (*subdirección*), those I refer to as managers or *administrativos* included an administrator, an administrative assistant, two archaeologists, an anthropologist, a community psychologist, a conservator, and a maintenance worker. The director explained that the custodios had stopped work and closed the offices. When this happened, the custodios denied entrance to the offices, maintaining a permanent presence at the tables in front and operating only select positions inside the site. The staff was working in the cafeteria for the moment, and I was welcome to join them. I noticed that another ten signs hung in front of the site entrance, and at the entrance to the site museum. So that was what "closed" meant.

At two weeks, the September 2012 work stoppage was the longest for which I was present. But it was not unique in degree or kind. Similar stoppages in 2009, 2010, and 2011 had resulted in the firing of the site's directors, and I attended shorter stoppages in 2016 and 2017. The custodios' union, the Trabajadores Administrativos, Técnicos y Manuales del INAH (ATM), sometimes involved El Tajín's counterparts from the INAH's Veracruz offices and other archaeological sites across the state. When a stoppage occurred, there was little else to talk about. The staff kept busy by filling out affidavits attesting to what was going on, attempting to document every deviation from normal activity. The custodios met with INAH authorities in Veracruz and Mexico City to argue for their demands, using the smooth operation of the archaeological site as leverage. Newsreaders from Poza Rica to Xalapa caught headlines about the conflict: "Custodios del INAH Demand Work Material and Seize Installations, in Papantla"; "Archaeological Site Not Being Neglected"; "Legal Action Against INAH Workers."[2] Like the peones and masons discussed in the previous chapter, custodios like those employed in El Tajín are largely absent in published scholarship, rendering their work invisible. But with all those signs and headlines, "invisible" does not quite describe the custodios of El Tajín.

Because the state's ability to maintain and control El Tajín (and sites like it) depends on them, looking at the custodios offers another entry point into the political economy of archaeology. Since 1944 nearly all of El Tajín's custodios have come from the Totonac community of El Tajín.[3] While workers in archaeology are typically excluded from the production of knowledge, so too have archaeologists historically excluded Indigenous communities from the interpretation of the past.[4] Archaeologists using concepts like multivocality seek to redress this exclusion. As Alison Wylie notes, "The cornerstone of a commitment to multivocality [is] that the insights of diversely situated epistemic agents and communities should be taken seriously."[5] Archaeologists increasingly coauthor works with Indigenous collaborators, integrate Indigenous perspectives on the past into their research, and conduct outreach with stakeholder communities.[6] Scholars and advocates argue that the ancient, monumental past may not be the most relevant one to study, and descent may not be the most important way of determining stakeholdership.[7] Without attention to these perspectives in the historiography of El Tajín, the Totonac site custodios seem invisible both as workers and as Indigenous subjects.

But this double historiographic exclusion does not dictate how the Totonac custodios or their peers see themselves: "Obscurity is the product of standpoint."[8] Site administrators, local media, community residents, and the custodios themselves all considered the workers quite visible. The 2012 work stoppage illustrated this vividly: administrators complained about their inability to work without access to their offices. Construction projects went unsupervised, regular reports went unfiled, restoration projects slowed, and veiled threats abounded.[9] Daily headlines in newspapers and blogs related the custodios' demands and documented the administration's responses. The custodios themselves leveraged that visibility to advance their political objectives, and to criticize the administration.

Perhaps their historiographic exclusion was less a problem for the custodios than it was for me. I was tempted to make the custodios legible in the disciplinary terms discussed above, collecting interpretations of the pre-Hispanic past and putting them on the same analytical footing as archaeologists' studies; such had been my project's original intention. Yet using visibility as a proxy for inclusion risks perpetuating other kinds of inequality.[10] Is there another way to center Indigenous labor? Mark Rifkin suggests that understanding Indigenous temporality is "a matter of attending to peoples' own frames of reference for their experiences of time: not just as beliefs set within a supervening or underlying 'natural' timeline but as a basis for understanding the materiality of their ways of being and becoming."[11] Taking this cue, I sought to understand the categories according to which the Totonac custodians of El Tajín understood the site's past.

Collectively, custodios' narratives yielded a history structured by the succession of cohorts (generaciones), distinguished according to when a custodio began working. This history is closely linked not to the ancient past but to the political economy of archaeology, addressing topics like the contemporary possibilities for making a living, admission processes, the nature and division of labor, and other, less visible associations. Following these approaches and interests in the archives, I documented early custodial cohorts that had not persisted in local memory. The facts about the lives of the custodios were recorded, filed, and archived, even if they have only rarely made it from the archives to narratives, or from narratives to historiography.[12]

The Archaeological Site as Office

El Tajín is staffed twenty-four hours a day, seven days a week, and 365 days a year by about thirty-two custodios. Nearly all are Totonac men between twenty and sixty years old. A custodio, as they say, is a jack-of-all-trades (*un trabajador de mil usos*). The terms historically used to refer to these men attest to the scope of this labor: concierge (*conserje*), watchman (*vigilante*), guardian (*guardián*), guardian-conservator (*guardián conservador*), auxiliary (*auxiliar*), and *peón*.[13] These labels share a common theme: the safeguarding of an archaeological site. Nowadays, the work of a custodio is that of a civil servant and groundskeeper. Custodios sell tickets, manage the bag-check, clean museum pieces, record visitor statistics, give guided school tours, fumigate archaeological structures, mow grass, prune trees, observe visitors, file reports, and monitor the installations overnight.

At El Tajín, the workday for most custodios begins at 9:00 a.m. For someone like Eugenio, an administrative support custodio, this will involve a kilometer-long walk to the site or a ten-peso taxi. He will check in via a thumbprint scanner and get set up in his office in the site installations. During the day, he will collate daily visitor statistics, keep track of tickets, and work with the site's subdirectorate as necessary. Eugenio gets off work at 6:00 p.m., when the site closes to visitors. He leaves after making sure that the office is locked, unless the director is working late. For a site custodio (*custodio de zona*) like Ernesto, the day's work will depend on the day of the week. Often assigned to the plaza of the Pyramid of the Niches, Ernesto will spend the weekend days patrolling the plaza and responding to tourist concerns. Equipped with a whistle and radio, he will make sure that no tourists bypass the ropes that limit access to the buildings in the Pyramid of the Niches plaza. If today is a weekday, there will be fewer tourists that need supervising. Taking advantage of the quiet, Ernesto will coordinate with his colleagues to get the riding mower, weed trimmer, or backpack sprayer to cut the grass, keep the weeds at bay, or fumigate. He may come down to the site installations to eat lunch or use the bathroom, but otherwise his day will be spent in the site rather than in the installations. At around 5:00 p.m., he will collaborate with his counterparts in the other site areas—like Tajín Chico, the Gran Greca, and the Plaza del Arroyo—to close the site for the day, return to the installations, and corral tourists along the way.

Outside of the administrative offices and the site proper, other custodios work in the site museum and as educational assessors (in charge of school visits and outreach programs), night watchmen, and drivers. These positions are determined by a combination of job requirements, official appointments, and commissions, depending on custodios' qualifications and site needs. For example, if there is a shortage of night watchmen, a custodio who usually works in the archaeological site could be commissioned to work the night shift. As a workplace rationally governed by a series of abstract rules and roles, put into practice and fulfilled by salaried employees most equipped to do them, El Tajín is as much a bureaucracy staffed by civil servants as it is a pre-Hispanic urban center or visitor-friendly UNESCO World Heritage Site.[14]

Historicizing Archaeological Labor

Neither Eugenio nor Ernesto is a stranger to their work. Both hold tenured positions (*plazas*).[15] During my fieldwork, Eugenio was among the most senior custodios still working at El Tajín. Tall and robust, Eugenio preferred work amid the trees and wildlife of the archaeological site, where he might meet a visitor: "I've met a lot of people, politicians, ambassadors, I attended governors." However, he was one of the few trained in the administrative procedures necessary to run the site. He worked as the site encargado in the absence of a professional administrator. Reflecting on his predecessors and successors, Eugenio considered himself betwixt and between. He had been young when he started in 1980. For the veteran workers, Eugenio was "the kid [*el chamaco*], they called me, I was young in those days and they were all older men." These veterans were the *viejos trabajadores*: the men who had known Don Pepe (José García Payón) and his wife, Doña Magdalena (Magdalena García Ramos), and worked with machetes alone. They had all since retired, and Eugenio himself was well established by the time the new guys, *los nuevos*, like Ernesto, had taken their competitive exams and entered in 1993. "I'm the old guy and they're the kids, how the times have changed."

Eugenio and Ernesto understood their places in El Tajín relative to a broader succession of worker cohorts. Each of these cohorts is associated with a particular time in regional political economy and site history, and with their own ways of working. Veteran workers distinguished between these cohorts by date of entry or the years in which *plazas* opened: some charted nine or ten different cohorts. However, more than common dates define a cohort. There are less-visible considerations that enable a nuevo to distinguish himself from a viejo trabajador and vice versa.[16] These include the people with whom one worked, who they were, and how they organized themselves; the tools with which one worked; the environmental conditions of the site; and, for more recent workers, possibilities for education and the desire for social mobility for one's children. In this way, the viejos trabajadores likewise recall the first custodios (*los primeros*). Something of a mystery, these primeros worked at a site that was practically wilderness and saw few tourists.

Nearly all retired and working custodios graciously shared their perspectives with me during formal interviews. I began with interviews of retired custodios, locally recognized as authorities on the history of the site. I then moved on to interviews of all currently employed custodios, with the objective of understanding how work experiences changed over time. As I developed the periodization below, I followed custodios' suggestions to speak with relatives of an older cohort of site custodios—*los primeros*—about whom little was known. I took the historical references that El Tajín's custodios shared with me to the archives. Feedback from interested custodios like Eugenio aided me in finalizing this periodization of custodial cohorts (see figure 13).

The narrative below follows these cohorts according to the categories that most interested contemporary custodios, tied to the political economy of archaeology: What were things like back then? How did one become a custodio? What was work like? How was each cohort different from the others?

Los Conserjes (1886–1941)

Once a governmental space was dedicated to the safeguarding of Mexico's pre-Hispanic past, it was there for good. The Porfirian foundations of Mexican archaeology outlasted the fall of the regime and subsequent Revolution of 1910 (see introduction). Among these foundations was the establishment of a network of local guards known as conserjes. These "unsung heroes in Mexico's history of archaeology" were at once caretakers, sentinels, landscapers, and managers.[17] They were often the state's sole representatives at archaeological sites, serving as intermediaries between visitors, residents, and the federal government. Through the 1890s these conserjes were wealthy, local elites

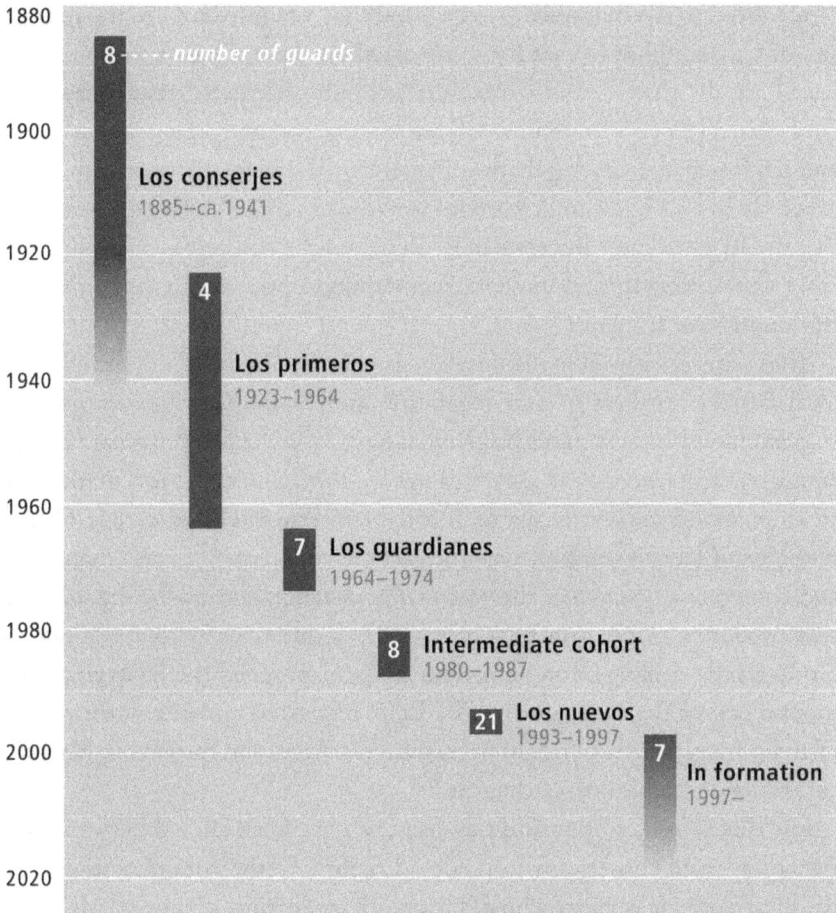

FIG. 13. Timeline of custodio cohorts in El Tajín since 1886. Erin Greb Cartography.

capable of monitoring a site, overseeing maintenance work, and communi-cating with the Inspectorate, without regular salaries.[18]

Spanish vanilla merchant Agapito Fontecilla y Vidal, appointed the first conserje of El Tajín in 1886, was one such elite (see chapter 3).[19] How Fon-tecilla y Vidal got the job is unclear, but his local prominence and relations with the Porfirian government were almost certainly responsible. Prefiguring a later trend, Fontecilla y Vidal's son, Agapito Guillermo Fontecilla y Fon-tecilla, was appointed conserje in 1906. The earliest archived report from Fontecilla y Vidal, dating from 1889, gives a sense of the conserje's work in El Tajín. Fontecilla y Vidal noted that there had been "no alteration worthy of mention" to the monuments, suggested that a family move to the nearby site of Cuyuxquihui to care for it, reported on the finding of a monument near Paso del Correo, and wrote that "it can be calculated that those who have visited [El Tajín's monuments] are some 480, among them 46 outsiders and ten foreigners: among them an American Woman journalist who came expressly to visit them and record information on them."[20] These notes indicate the Inspectorate's interests in El Tajín and the conserje's corresponding labor: conserving the monuments, maintaining a presence in the ruins, and tracking visitor statistics.

These conserjes lived in the municipal capital of Papantla and likely hired local Totonac workers to clear vegetation. As Larissa Kelly has shown, the Inspectorate's hiring patterns had shifted from local elites to proximate Indigenous residents as early as 1895.[21] However, this tendency is less marked in El Tajín, where the first verifiable Totonac conserje was hired in 1923. Other divisions of labor were similarly unclear: the conserjes were also managers and, sometimes, researchers themselves. For instance, Erasmo Rodríguez Jaac, employed from 1931 to 1939, took on a variety of duties for himself. Rodríguez hindered the drilling of an oil well in El Tajín, stopped the quarrying of a mound east of the community of El Tajín, requested updates on the status of archaeological sites in neighboring municipalities, and carried out his own excavations—to his bosses' chagrin.[22]

For this cohort, responsibilities seem to have been shared between the Papantla-based conserjes who rendered reports to the administration and the local Totonac workers who did the work of clearing. Honorato Méndez, conserje from 1921 to 1929, was reprimanded for attempting to obligate the residents of El Tajín to clear the site via unpaid collective labor during his first year of work.[23] He countered that peón Eugenio Salazar had refused to do the clearing, with the implication that it was Salazar's obligation.[24] Yet, in the complex and fast-moving institutional changes between the beginnings of site guardianship and the end of this cohort, these distinctions were not always clear to the actors themselves. Salazar, for instance, had written to the authorities after the death of conserje Pedro Bautista in 1919. Bautista had "accompanied [Salazar] in all of the clearing and inspection work," but successor Honorato Méndez had told Salazar that the work should be done alone. "Since he did not give me any other explanation," Salazar wrote, "I ask that you tell me what my obligations are and which are those of the conserje."[25] The porosity of these job responsibilities, combined with differences in residence (and likely language), may explain why early conserjes do not form a part of local historical memory in El Tajín. In other documentation, the likes of Salazar are referred to as peones, and we have already met one: Modesto González González. González, hired in 1923, is often recalled as the first custodio.[26] As such, his tenure also begins that of the following cohort, los primeros.

Los Primeros (1923–64)

Between the 1920s and the 1960s the Mexican state went from the challenges of rebuilding after a decade of revolution and civil war to a stable, single-party state lauded for its economic growth and apparent ability to buck hemispheric trends of dictatorship and civil war. State-sponsored archaeology, too, experienced "a transitional stage."[27] In the aftermath of the Mexican Revolution, state agencies dedicated to conserving the pre-Hispanic past were divided, consolidated, and reassigned across different federal entities. The presidency of Lázaro Cárdenas, best-known for the expansion of agrarian reform, the nationalization of the oil industry, and a party organization based on the campesino, urban-industrial, and middle classes, saw a renewed effort to institutionalize governmental anthropology writ large.[28]

Under the auspices of the Secretaría de Educación Pública, "nationalist intellectuals and researchers finally translated their previously disparate initiatives into a coordinated state cultural project," of which the Departamento de Monumentos Prehispánicos was a part.[29] In 1939 the state allocated the legal authority to protect and administer Mexico's pre-Hispanic past to the INAH. The labor of the custodios became increasingly standardized. A contemporary memorandum outlines custodios' normative responsibilities in five points: (1) live in the site and keep the monuments clear of vegetation; (2) assure that visitors do not cause damage to the monuments; (3) advise the national administration of any deterioration; (4) facilitate the work of technical personnel in the case of excavation or restoration; (5) file monthly reports on works.[30] These regulations suggest that the primeros were the first cohort to work as specialized custodios. No longer would the likes of Erasmo Rodríguez file reports in the technical archives.[31]

In El Tajín, García Payón regularly directed fieldwork and began developing the site's infrastructure. Isabel Kelly described the workplace installations as "one tumble-down 'bodega,' which houses a long-defunct pickup truck, plus stones, beams, and other building materials" as of 1947.[32] Today's viejos trabajadores recall the clearing of vegetation as the most common, and most persistent, task for their predecessors. An exemplary report documenting the labors of September 1–15, 1947, agrees: among the daily tasks are weeding, felling, and uprooting.[33] In contrast with later cohorts, the time of the primeros is recalled for having few tourists. While the number of annual visitors to the site rose sharply over their tenure—from perhaps 230 in 1925 to 12,789 in 1960 (see appendix)—the primeros still dedicated much of their labor to site maintenance.

By 1947 Modesto González was well established as the site's longest-serving custodio. Having died in 1971, and with a daughter and stepson still living in El Tajín during my fieldwork, González is still recalled as the "first custodio" of El Tajín, the archetypal primero (see figure 14). Few living residents knew him well, but older generations recall him as "a man with typical clothing from the region, not like us, he was *de blanco*, he spoke Totonac well," as one viejo trabajador told me, referring to his traditional all-white clothing.[34] Though he lived through the early years of the succeeding cohort, the now-retired workers recognized González's difference in clothing and language. How González became a custodio remains obscure. His having grown up near the archaeological site likely played a role.

As with the Fontecillas, labor at El Tajín was a family affair for los primeros. Two of González's sons, Teódulo and Rosalino González Méndez, also belong to this cohort. Teódulo began in 1940, and Rosalino in 1944.[35] Teódulo served as the site encargado, with reporting and administrative responsibilities, likely thanks to his primary-school education and fluency in Spanish.[36] Thus, the three consistent federal employees of the site—los primeros—were, until 1964, Modesto, Teódulo, and Rosalino González. Other residents of El Tajín labored in García Payón's seasonal projects, clearing vegetation or reconstructing monuments.[37] Around 1964 El Tajín had "an extraordinary mess."[38] There are different versions of what exactly happened, but the authorities agreed on the fact of financial mismanagement on the part of the site encargado. The result was that INAH fired "the [younger] Gonzálezes, who for so many years had been in control of the situation."[39] Modesto González, it seems, escaped the controversy and continued to work until a fall in the late 1960s left him unable to walk. He died in 1971, without having formally retired. The González Méndez brothers moved out of El Tajín and found work elsewhere.

FIG. 14. Modesto González González (c. 1880–1971) in 1947. "Modesto González," ITKEA, series 5, box 55, binder 1, slide 055, DeGolyer Library, Southern Methodist University.

Los Viejos Trabajadores (1961–74)

By midcentury, Mexican archaeology had entered a so-called Golden Age.[40] Institutions like the INAH, the affiliated Escuela Nacional de Antropología e Historia, and the Sociedad Mexicana de Antropología helped to professionalize the discipline. The concept of Mesoamerica—a geographical area roughly corresponding with modern Mexico and defined by a set of precolonial cultural traits—gave archaeologists a broad spatiotemporal framework with which to interpret the country's diverse cultures, sites, and time periods.[41] Institutional backing for this conceptual focus remained resilient, even during the disciplinary reaction to the social upheavals of 1968 and the negotiation of new archaeological theory from the United States.[42] The tourism industry, an important part of the state's economic development strategy since the 1940s, benefited from a postwar boom whose effects were visible in El Tajín: between 1961 and 1973 the number of annual visitors to El Tajín quadrupled, from 13,043 to 52,000 (see appendix). The INAH allocated more plazas to El Tajín, and the custodio workforce grew from three during the 1950s to six by the early 1970s. The most important institutional change for this cohort came toward the end of its entry dates: the establishment of the union.

In 1964 Pedro Pérez Bautista, a veteran mason of García Vega's and García Payón's projects, began his thirty-year tenure as site encargado.[43] His management of El Tajín and its workers is a reference point for the viejos trabajadores and the succeeding intermediate cohort. The custodios who entered between 1961 and 1974, most of whom worked until the 1990s or early 2000s, are known as the viejos trabajadores or, today, the retired ones (los jubilados). Like their encargado, all previously worked with García Payón in seasonal wage labor, they worked in the wilderness (puro monte) with machetes, and they labored before the coming of the union.

Unlike their primero predecessors, whose entries into the field remain obscure or followed kinship networks, and unlike their successors, who were hired via a bureaucratic examination process, the viejos trabajadores began work via association with García Payón and/or encargado Pérez Bautista. This association often came about through participation in seasonal excavation projects. To find workers for his excavations, García Payón worked through the encargado, who mobilized his kin and social networks in turn. It should come as no surprise, then, that all viejos trabajadores came from the families most often employed in wage labor (see chapter 4).

The viejos trabajadores describe their becoming custodios in a straightforward fashion. I asked hale septuagenarian Ángel about this process, during an interview on the patio of the house he had inherited from his father. Recalling how he had started working as a custodio in 1964, Ángel said, "I learned [that there would be a position] because Don Pedro is my tío. . . . Payón told him to look for a custodio and Don Pedro, since he's my tío, told me, 'there's a custodio job, you know, if you want it.' 'I'll think about it,' I told him. . . . I told him 'yes,' and he said, 'but for sure, you're not going to rest, from when you start until you die.'" The documentation agrees. For example, in 1972 García Payón wrote to Pérez Bautista for "a first-class person, honorable and hard-working, who has completed his military service requirement and has not had difficulties with the authorities" for an open custodio position.[44]

Pedro Pérez Bautista's quoted warnings about the difficulty of labor ring true for the viejos trabajadores. Contrasting themselves with los nuevos, the viejos trabajadores often discuss how they had to buy their own tools and work clothes, and labored without regular days off, vacations, or a schedule. As Ángel recalled, "At six in the morning, let's go. You'd go and your kids wouldn't see you . . . and you arrive [back home] at six at night, eight at night and they're already sleeping again. Every day, every day. We never rested." Moreover, the division of labor was such that the same custodios were also night watchmen. Mateo, who began in 1973, remembers staying in García Payón's encampment until after the visitors left, sometimes not until 11:00 p.m. or later. Only then could the site close.

The organization of labor became more complex to accommodate the additional custodios and tourists. No longer would everyone spend all day in weeding, felling, and uprooting alone. A 1977 report from Pérez Bautista describes different areas of work. One custodio ensured that visitors did not damage the structures. Two oversaw the clearing of the Pyramid of the Niches. Another two kept Tajín Chico clear of vegetation. A sixth sold tickets, while Pérez Bautista, as encargado, administered the museum, correspondence, and payroll.[45]

The physical labor for which the viejos trabajadores are known consists of "just the machete" (puro machete). Knowing how to wield a machete is a claim to a particular kind of masculinity. Santiago, whom I interviewed during his break from harvesting oranges in the field he bought after retiring, brought up the topic indirectly. I asked him about why all the custodios had come from the community of El Tajín. He replied that "the campesinos from here know how to wield the machete, to work. If someone from outside comes, well, they won't know how to work, they won't know how to wield the machete, they won't know how to do anything." Knowing how to wield a machete and knowing how to work (hard) are one and the same. The use of the machete is linked inextricably with the condition of the site during the 1960s and 1970s: forested, with relatively few excavated buildings, and site installations made from local materials (rather than cement). Nicolás, who began in 1973, recalled: "There was no electricity or anything, just the machete." The gendered associations of the machete are strong: "A man who doesn't know how to wield a machete isn't a man, they used to say in Tajín," as nuevo custodio Diego told me. Pride in the ability to wield a machete, therefore, is also a claim to campesino masculinity, linked with the ability to grow, harvest, and provide for the family.[46] Los primeros had lived during the time when lands were abundant, and one could live well as a farmer. The viejos trabajadores could not count on the same, but they were able to weather the region's broader socioeconomic transformations with secure federal jobs as their friends and families lost lands to cattle ranchers (see chapter 1).

One of the most important factors that differentiate the viejos trabajadores from their successors is presence of the union: the ATM del INAH, a division of the larger Sindicato Nacional de Trabajadores de la Educación (SNTE). The SNTE, one of the largest unions in Latin America, was historically noted for "a symbiotic [state-labor] relationship that strengthens their respective positions by seeing legislation and other union-friendly conditions handed on down from high in exchange for wild, 'spontaneous' shows of mass politics percolating up from below."[47] While custodios had technically been unionized since at least the 1930s, no custodios in El Tajín recalled a local union presence before the 1970s.

The "arrival" of the union may be related to the broader trajectory of organized labor during the economic downturns of the 1970s. In the aftermath of the legitimation crisis that followed the government's massacre of student protestors in 1968, the government of Luis Echeverría Álvarez (1970–76) undertook a series of liberalizing reforms known as the democratic opening. Among these were decentralizing efforts, considered "the best way to promote citizen participation in government policies and the solution to the social needs of the population."[48] Within the SNTE, a dissident movement that sought a more democratic approach to union politics emerged.[49] In these internecine conflicts, the Delegation D-III-24 of the Sección XI of the SNTE, which included the administrative, technical, and manual workers of the INAH, advocated for a new agreement on working conditions specific to the institution's work.[50] In 1978–79, union leadership sought to incorporate workers from across the country.[51]

Viejo trabajador Mateo recalled the coming of the union as a three-way dialogue between the workers, Pedro Pérez Bautista, and INAH archaeologist Ariel Valencia, who oversaw the site after García Payón died in 1977:

> [From Mexico City, they told us:] "You know what? We're sending you this pamphlet so that you read it, because the rights and obligations of the workers are in this pamphlet."
>
> We talked to Don Pedro: "you know what? We're going to adhere to these pamphlets, because here in this pamphlet it's showing us the times we start work and the time we leave."
>
> [Don Pedro replied]: "I don't have the authorization to adhere to these little pamphlets . . . you're going to continue working early until the night, when it gets dark."
>
> An archaeologist named Ariel [Valencia] . . . supported us a lot, he spoke to Don Pedro: "you know what? Your workers are going to stick to these rules, they're going to enter at 9 in the morning and they're going to leave at 6 p.m."
>
> Perfect, so that was how the work schedule got started.

Shortly thereafter, the union and INAH authorities negotiated the Condiciones Generales de Trabajo. Covering the hiring, firing, rights, and obligations of the workers, the document, and the negotiations behind it, were key in the transformation of the custodios' labor from that of a campesino to that of a civil servant.

The Condiciones Generales de Trabajo, in conjunction with other national union agreements, provided the permanence and benefits that allowed the viejos trabajadores to become a local elite class. Current custodios have access to extra funds for school supplies, eyeglasses, hearing aids, scholarships for their children, and loans for building their houses, among other benefits.[52] With the resulting job security, the viejos trabajadores invested their funds and energy elsewhere. For example, four of the seven viejos trabajadores owned brickworks, an important local industry during the 1980s. In addition to the arrival of the union, another key factor that differentiates the viejos trabajadores from their predecessors is the question of plaza inheritance.[53]

Based on agreements with the union, the viejos trabajadores had the opportunity to pass down their plazas to the next generation. Such heirs would eventually forge the cohort in consolidation during my fieldwork (1997–2017, "in formation").

Intermediate Cohort (1980–87)

The most recent three cohorts to start working in El Tajín have done so during Mexico's neoliberal era. Union activism and the political conditions of the mid-twentieth century created the conditions for the viejos trabajadores to become a local elite, but the results of continued neoliberal and democratizing reforms have been much more mixed. Given the extent to which labor benefited from the state's single-party government and import-substitution industrialization model, it comes as no surprise that unions have weakened since the beginning of Mexico's neoliberal period.[54] As Graciela Bensusán and Maria Lorena Cook argue, "The crisis of corporatism posed by political opening and neoliberalism, together with institutional features that increased conservative government and employer influence and established weak internal mechanisms of union affiliation and representation, resulted in a situation in which unions did not recover" into the 2000s.[55] Still, the Condiciones Generales de Trabajo have endured and the union has continued to benefit the custodios in El Tajín.

For friends and families, however, the situation was bleaker (see chapter 1). By the 1980s only about a dozen residents owned their own land.[56] Those who made a living in agriculture typically did so on rented land, while most worked in wage labor. Citrus cultivation and cattle ranching continued to expand at the regional scale. In El Tajín, campesino, day laborer, bricklayer, and excavator were among the most common occupations. Among the best off were those who still had land, teachers, artisans, and the custodios.[57] Locally, brickworks and Proyecto Tajín (1983–94) provided important sources of work. Although land was no longer plentiful, members of this intermediate cohort recall relatively little competition for custodio plazas.

The eight custodios who entered between 1980 and 1987, Eugenio among them, came in under the union rules and with the corresponding benefits. They worked a regular schedule, with two days off a week, and with vacations twice a year. The INAH provided them with the work clothes, tools, and materials necessary to do the job. They continued to work largely with machetes, and El Tajín had yet to see the large-scale transformation that came with the construction of the current site installations and museum between 1988 and 1992. Pedro Pérez Bautista was still the encargado when the intermediate cohort entered. They were the final cohort to work to learn from the tenured Totonac encargado rather than a contracted administrator. However, members of the intermediate cohort did not have the advantage of having known García Payón well. Viejo trabajador Fidencio Morales García did not recall him working in the site after 1968 or thereabouts, and the archaeologist's final reports on the site date from 1972 to 1973.[58]

The intermediate cohort was not subject to the same degree of competition as their successors for their plazas. Half of this cohort had relatives working at the site: two were brothers and two were children of viejos trabajadores. While this cohort typically learned of the opportunity to solicit a plaza from the viejos trabajadores, they recall the paperwork, rather than the relationships alone, necessary to become custodios. It appears that this was the first cohort to enter via a bureaucratic examination process.[59] Matías, who worked in the museum when I first met him, recounted how he learned about the contest for plazas: "The announcement came out, but in that time there wasn't a lot of demand.... Most people worked in the brickworks, in the fields.... Only ten of us took the exam." Matías noted that the stumbling block for failed aspirants was less the exam than the paperwork. The requirements were more stringent than for the preceding cohort: documentation of school attendance (primary school and, at most, secondary school), a birth certificate, proof of residence, a police clearance certification, and military service clearance. Those who did not have these documents could not participate. The next step was the exam. A written theoretical component asked questions on the definitions of cultural heritage, an archaeological site, and the INAH, and a practical component asked prospective custodios to demonstrate how to use manual tools like machetes to clear vegetation. In my interviews, most members of this cohort did not remember the exam as being particularly demanding. They found the questions simple and the practical portion even more so. It was the campesino work with which they had grown up.

The custodio workforce, however, was growing. The union fought for more positions, and in 1980, 1982, and 1987, one, two, and five plazas, respectively, were allocated to El Tajín. Pedro Pérez Bautista organized the workers, and the viejos trabajadores taught them. Matías recalled Pérez Bautista's instructions on the work: "Here, you will recommend yourselves alone.... Here are your machetes, everyone choose a machete, everyone with their whetstone and you will go with your colleagues who are already here, and they will tell you where to work." René, a member of this cohort, commented that the work was well organized, the workers ate together, and there were few hard feelings between colleagues. A more formal division of labor began with the expansion of the workforce. The site custodios and the night watchmen worked according to different schedules. By the end of 1992, the archaeological site had changed significantly: there were now forty-two structures excavated and open to the public, there was a new museum and set of site installations, and there was a shortage of workers.

Los Nuevos (1993)

The expansion of neoliberal reforms during the government of Carlos Salinas de Gortari (1988–94)—the end of land reform, the signing of the North American Free Trade Agreement (NAFTA), and attacks on traditional union leadership—changed the political-economic context in which seventeen new (nuevo) custodios began working at El Tajín. After NAFTA, for instance, farmers could not compete with cheap grains from the United States and the north of Mexico. In Totonacapan, a transition to corn husk (totomoxtle) production risked the "food security, risk insurance, employment for family members, and cultural values" provided by local maize.[60] Outmigration to urban centers like Mexico City, Reynosa, and Monterrey, and to the United States, became an increasingly common feature of rural life during the 1990s.[61]

In the communities around El Tajín, the panorama looked somewhat different. The influx of funds dedicated to Proyecto Tajín made the archaeological site a source of income for many families, whether through direct employment or the tourism sector. The construction of the new site installations and museum provoked no small amount of local and academic opposition (see chapter 6), but everyone appreciated the employment opportunities. As one former worker described it, the work was "very peaceful, no one watched you, except when you found a floor or some ceramic, that's when you'd tell the archaeologist." In contrast to the wage labor available in Papantla and Poza Rica, one could walk to work and rely on one's family for lunch and water during the day. More visitors arrived to see the new excavations: tourism grew from 76,761 visitors in 1977 to 181,371 by 1996 (see appendix).

Many nuevo custodios worked on this project. The nuevos were subject to the same examination process as the intermediate cohort. Beyond the exam, however, multiple nuevo custodios recounted how other factors had influenced their hiring: the preferences of project directors, the union delegation, and the viejos trabajadores.[62] One nuevo recalled having asked the current workers about the possibility of a plaza, and they had told him nothing. He only learned about the exam on the day it was held, and "they never taught us how to fumigate, how to prune, how to hedge, they didn't teach us. They chose their people [beforehand]." However, this worker's particular background led the encargado to recommend him, and he entered as a nuevo.

For others, the social and kin networks so much at play for previous cohorts remained a factor. One nuevo custodio, Diego, never wanted to work in El Tajín. One of his relatives, a viejo trabajador, invited him on two or three occasions during the 1980s, and he had declined. Around 1993, Diego's father finally convinced him that it would not cost the young man to go ask about a plaza. Diego was received by members of the viejo trabajador and intermediate cohorts. They verified that he had his paperwork in order and informed him of the exam. When the time came, Diego set himself apart from the rest using a makeshift hook to quickly clear the vegetation he had just felled with his machete: "This kid knows more than us, he knows, because he's a campesino," this nuevo recalled Pedro Pérez Bautista saying. As Diego concluded, "We seventeen were there, as they say, 'inside,' [and the exam] was just protocol."

Once the nuevos started, the union delegation clamored for a professionally trained administrator to run the site. At the arrival of the administrator, Pedro Pérez Bautista, who had run the site since being appointed by García Payón in 1964, was ordered to return to the custodio workforce. The transition was a bitter one, and Pérez retired shortly thereafter, in 1994. This marked another break between the nuevos and their predecessors. As one nuevo recalled, "In reality, with Don Pedro, we didn't see the command that he supposedly had with the others . . . never, we didn't see that power." The difference was not just one in personnel: the administrator of El Tajín was a contract position. Subsequent administrators only lasted for between three months and seven years at a time, while Eugenio handled the role of administrator in the absence of a professional appointment.

Tools and education further distinguish the nuevos from their predecessors. The nuevos began working with machetes, but for most of their tenure they have worked with machinery: lawn mowers, weed trimmers, and fumigation tanks. This created the corresponding obligation of the site administration to provide for this equipment, which became a focal point in conflicts like that of September 2012. The nuevos were also the first cohort to collectively take advantage of the INAH's educational benefits. This can be illustrated by contrast. One member of the intermediate cohort had wanted to continue his formal schooling during the early 1990s. That way, he could be promoted according to the INAH's system of civil service ranking. The viejos trabajadores, in this custodio's recollection, tried to prevent him from doing so: "Here, no one will be promoted, here we will all be the same." Eugenio recalled a similar admonition from Pérez Bautista: "You're here to work, not to study."

By contrast, when Diego decided to study in the early 2000s, the opposition he described came not from other workers but from oneself: "It's just you that says 'yes, I'm going to study an undergraduate degree, I'm going to finish high school' . . . but it's always when you want, [because] we all have these opportunities." Four nuevos have finished undergraduate degrees in fields like history, pedagogy, and law. Still others have finished secondary or high school in open programs. Education and promotion enabled custodios to access other positions like that of educational assessor, which led to a reallocation of work among custodios. Custodios that formerly worked in the archaeological site moved to other areas with their own responsibilities. As a result, they no longer participate in the archaeological site's division of labor between areas, creating occasional conflict and, paradoxically, a shortage of workers.

Cohort in Formation (1997–2017)

By 2003 El Tajín was a community of around 1,500, of which perhaps 80 percent depended on the archaeological site for income.[63] The service sector provided these opportunities: artisanry, cooperatives, food preparation, parking services, and the ritual Danza de los Voladores.[64] In 1999 the state government began planning for an annual music and cultural festival for the spring equinox, March 21: Cumbre Tajín. The event proved popular, if controversial (see chapter 6). Tourist numbers grew from 222,548 in 1997 to 426,176 by 2019, including a record 888,637 visitors in 2004 (see appendix). The union requested more plazas, but a new factor came to affect the composition of the newest cohort: retirement.

Of the seven viejos trabajadores, only three were able to will their plazas to their children. After the father's retirement, a period would be set for a son to submit the necessary paperwork and begin working. If he did not, the plaza would freeze (congela). By all accounts, a plaza congelada does not thaw. It is more straightforward to inherit a plaza in cases of illness or death. Since the last time plazas were opened in 1997, most members of the cohort in formation have entered via inheritance: for retirement (in three cases), illness (in one case), and death (in another case). All interviewees consider that plaza inheritance is now virtually impossible in cases of retirement, difficult for illness, and not easy even in cases of death: the Reforma Educativa of 2013 sought to replace plaza inheritance with merit-based hiring criteria.[65] As an illustration, after a car accident took the lives of two custodios in 1996, their relatives started as custodios about a week later. By contrast, after the illness and death of a custodio in 2017, his son had to wait six months before starting.

The question of plaza inheritance also affects how older cohorts understand the cohort in formation. All desire to pass down their plazas, but none want their children to have to receive them. Viejo trabajador Santiago explained it to me. When he was young, his parents' land had been occupied by a cattle rancher, who had sent hired gunmen to burn their house down. He and his family had fled, arriving landless to the neighboring community of El Tajín. Without land, "you have to work in the fields, with the machete, perhaps, or it could be the cattle, but it's not yours. . . . You have to work whether it's raining, thundering, or if it's hot, you have to be there, risking the danger of the cattle, risking the danger of the snakes, risking the danger of cutting yourself with the machete." After thirty years as a custodio in El Tajín, Santiago had built his house and purchased land, and his children had earned undergraduate degrees—with one exception. It was this son to whom he left his position. "For as much as I did to send him to school, [this son] didn't want to go. . . . I retired, and what am I going to do? Well, you can come [work] here . . . as a last resort. I never wanted to get my kids in there. Better that they come out as university graduates."

This cohort includes a number of such sons, who are well aware of the job's benefits—even if the work itself is not to their liking. Perhaps the most striking case was of a custodio trained in petroleum engineering and human resources management. Prior to becoming a custodio, he made a good living working offshore for a PEMEX contractor in Campeche. When his father began to consider retirement, the viejo trabajador preferred that another relation take his plaza. The union responded that only a son could enter. The plaza was valuable, and if frozen, it would leave the family forever, foreclosing any possibilities for future inheritance. Eventually, the engineer was convinced to accept the position. In the end, he is happy with the stability of the plaza and the proximity to family but remains keenly aware of the opportunities he left.

The cohort in formation has always worked with professional administrators and has long had access to the benefits for which the viejos trabajadores fought. However, this period also saw resurgent efforts to bring neoliberal market reforms to Mexico's cultural sector. One of the recent iterations of this process was the 2015 creation of the Secretaría de Cultura, and the movement of the INAH from the Secretaría de Educación Pública to the new secretaría.[66] The effects of this process are far from clear, but they began a series of cascading changes. One of the immediate ones was the formation of a new union, the Sindicato Nacional Democrático de los Trabajadores de la Secretaría de Cultura (SNDTSC). This union, though similar to the ATM, no longer formed a part of the SNTE. As a result, the negotiations that had resulted in the Condiciones Generales de Trabajo and other such benefits have to be renegotiated, a process that remains ongoing as of 2024. Custodios with whom I spoke thus considered the creation of the Secretaría de Cultura (and the movement of the INAH) an attack on the workers and their rights. The cohort in formation, as a result, is entering an uncertain work environment. While the nuevos, too, will be affected by these changes, they are nearing retirement. The cohort in formation will be defined by them.

Conclusion

"History," as Michel-Rolph Trouillot notes, "is always produced in a specific historical context. Historical actors are also narrators, and vice versa."[67] Following the content and form of custodios' ways of understanding the archaeological site and its past provided another entry point into the political economy of archaeology. In this view, these workers are neither invisible nor silent. When the custodios of El Tajín spoke about ways of working, they were more concerned with making sense of the past and anticipating the future than with restoring their rightful place in the interpretation of archaeological materials.

In 2017 I presented what became this chapter to a group of viejos trabajadores, members of the intermediate cohort, and a few nuevos. My presentation stressed how the development of the site had depended on the custodios and their predecessors. With no small amount of anxiety, I asked the audience members what they thought; I expected—perhaps—a demonstration of expertise.[68] The dialogue took a different path. Mateo recalled the hard work characteristic of his cohort, not to remind scholars like me to acknowledge them but to indirectly critique how the nuevos had changed the division of labor: "I see a lot of inequality [among the workers], whoever knows more comes out on top, [and] this shouldn't be done. We should advance together, and when we want something, we go together to fight the boss so that he'll give it to us. But if we're fighting [among ourselves] there's nothing." Santiago, too, indirectly commented on his successors' frequent conflicts with the administration: "We know how to do our jobs, we know the Condiciones Generales de Trabajo well, if that's my work, I can't go into management or research, so there has been a bit of a misunderstanding."

One vocal nuevo replied. A ritual dancer in his youth, this worker was fluent in Totonac, and his degree qualified him to work as an educational assessor. In this conversation, however, he was not concerned about epistemological equality between scholars and workers. Rather, he drew on this history of labor to both reply to his predecessors and comment on broader changes to Mexico's cultural sector:

> We can't work together, because some want to do what benefits them, others defend the law, others defend cultural heritage.... I think the goal of all INAH workers is to really do the hard labor [*ponerse la camiseta*] and work for the benefit of our cultural heritage.... We carry it in our blood, we have these roots that the workers who were here in the archaeological site [before] have passed down to us, and we'll keep doing it.... Unfortunately, it's the politics, even if it's true that we change a lot or a little, the politics are always changing.

Even in their disagreement, both the viejo trabajador and the nuevo drew on a shared understanding of what was important about the history of labor in El Tajín: the generational succession of workers and its relationship to broader structures of power.

The frame of reference with which this chapter began was that of the expert managers. We might assume that we know these experts well enough. We have already met Agustín García Vega and José García Payón, and we have seen the news stories and official reports from the more recent subdirectorate. Yet we might take the custodios' insights a step further and turn this political-economic perspective to these experts. The next chapter's engagement with the people ostensibly charged with managing, administering, and running the site will similarly show that the historiographic prominence of these experts fails to reflect El Tajín's lived realities.

Experts

6

Precarity and Opportunity

> It's been six months since we were paid, and, of course, that delays
> paying other expenses. . . . You could say it will become impossible for
> us to work, we have expenses for transportation, food, etcetera. . . . In
> terms of work, you could say that it's depressing, no? That you have
> to be doing your work without receiving payment for the same, it's
> unmotivating at times, ha.
>
> —Esmeralda

By September 2017 El Tajín's *administrativos*—who had welcomed me to the
cafeteria when the custodios' work stoppage closed their offices—knew me
well enough. Since my arrival in 2012, certain positions had changed: funding
for the anthropologist, community psychologist, and one of the archaeologists had run out, while the director, administrator, and administrative
assistant had changed. The director later recalled that the combination of
people and posts present in 2017 was particularly cohesive: not only did all
have experience with the site, but they worked well together. I often joined
them for lunches and after-work gatherings that sometimes lasted into the
morning. I expected nothing other than the normal conviviality when I
went to the site on September 5. The staff had been in a meeting with the
administrator of the Centro INAH Veracruz (CIV), regarding payroll delays.
For fourteen workers, including members of the staff and laborers employed
in the site's conservation projects, nine months had passed since their last
paycheck. Regular budgetary cycles meant that delays of a few months were
not uncommon, but this was unprecedented. The staff affected by the delays
thus took unprecedented steps. They had consulted state and federal labor
offices in nearby Poza Rica, and would cease working in the meantime. This
was a risk. Without the protection of a union, a work stoppage risked them
being fired.

Relations between the CIV and the site subdirectorate were strained. Personnel changes in the former had upset a cordial working relationship, and getting the CIV authorities to take the four-hour drive to Papantla had proven near impossible. Making the complaints had been one tactic, but there was still one more possibility: because the maintenance workers were among those who had gone unpaid, the staff could close the bathrooms. Tourists would complain, and these complaints would be redirected to the local press or the CIV, making this a useful, albeit last-ditch, pressure tactic. The bathrooms were indeed gated when I entered the site. Curious, I asked the custodio at the ticket counter; in more than two decades at the site, they had never seen that happen. The custodios had closed the offices, but never the staff. I continued through the installations, going to the outbuilding where the staff usually ate. On the way, I stopped to chat with the guides. What did they make of the bathroom closure? The tourists had complained, one guide commented, and he had felt foolish: why should the visitors suffer for problems that were internal to the site? The bathrooms were closed for less than a day, but the strategy had been successful: a meeting with the CIV was in progress.

The meeting had adjourned by the time I arrived. I joined the administrativos in the dining room and asked the conservator about how things had gone. Poorly, he said: the Centro INAH had tried to justify the delays, made excuses, and scolded them for making their complaints. The conservator, the administrator, her assistant, and the director's assistant ate in utter silence. Over the course of the day, I would hear the words desperate (*desesperado*), depressed (*agüitado*), and disheartened (*desanimado*) used to describe the atmosphere of the site's offices. After nine months, nearly all administrativos were indebted to various family and friends, having taken out short-term loans when they had been told, again and again, that their paychecks were on the way. As one of their cosigned letters to the INAH's director-general put it, "This situation violates our individual agreements and economies, as it even affects our ability to attend our workplace and to our basic expenses, in addition to the psychological distress produced by the uncertainty of whether we will be paid our salaries." Despite the assurances of the Centro INAH Veracruz, no one was confident that there would be any actual payment, at least anytime soon. "We really don't know what's going to happen," the administrator told me. "For those from Veracruz, it doesn't matter that the bathrooms are closed and that there's no [administration]."

By that Friday, September 8, nothing had been resolved but the staff returned to work, lest they be fired. But work had its own problems. The custodios were due to be paid today, because the regular payday fell on a Sunday. However, Hurricane Katia was preparing to make landfall somewhere between Martínez de la Torre and Tuxpan—a coastline that includes Papantla.[1] The banks closed early as a precaution. The custodios' regular paychecks would be thus delayed until the following Monday. I happened to be standing nearby when a group of custodios got the news; their consternation was visible and audible. Even though the site was closed early in anticipation of Katia's landfall, and most custodios had gone to secure their dwellings, a few stayed gathered around the site entrance. I walked by with the intention of saying goodbye, but heard them tersely discussing their delayed paychecks and decided not to interrupt. The site administrator was exasperated at the situation. The normal pay period did not actually end until the fifteenth of the month. It was because of a long-standing agreement that the custodios were paid five days before the end of the pay period. They would now be getting paid one day "late," according to their schedule, rather than two days early. Meanwhile, six members of the staff had gone nine months without a paycheck. Their efforts to pressure the Centro INAH Veracruz into a resolution had failed, as would their attempts to seek resolution from a variety of state and federal offices.

To the administrativos, the contrast was bitterly apparent. They had done their work well, carrying out the plans and projects necessary to keep the site functioning. Without the administration, there is little long-term planning, no regular attention to the concerns of tourists and residents, or new projects. Now, they had to spend long hours strategizing, meeting, and making their cases as to why they should be paid on time. By contrast, the site custodios occasionally closed the site and ceased working altogether—with no evident consequences, apparently, other than their demands being addressed. They could just as easily do so now, it seemed, and the result would more likely be the firing of an administrativo than a reprimand for the custodios. As a former administrativo put it, "We were always 'the forgotten ones.'"

The administrativos are the public faces of the INAH in El Tajín. Their reports, filed and archived, are available for consultation, and their research outcomes are sometimes presented at academic conferences. "Whose labor is visible thus depends on where one searches for signs of action and agency"; whether in the production of texts or the everyday life of the site, the administrativos seem especially visible.[2] Yet this visibility did not translate into quality working conditions. In this case, a close attention to the political economy of archaeology elucidates the precarity of expert labor and the opportunities it affords.[3]

In what follows, I will again examine political-economic changes in archaeological labor over time, but this time, the focus will be on the workers collectively referred to as administrativos. By examining the history and practice of managing the precolonial past, I will show that the epistemological authority used to interpret the past does not always translate into broader authority, despite legal regimes that grant it in theory. This chapter will follow the administrativos to understand how heritage management resulted in precarity for experts in El Tajín, and to what extent they may take advantage of the resulting flexibility. Between the 1930s and the 1990s, the day-to-day management of El Tajín was largely in the hands of the site encargado. This changed with neoliberal reforms that eventually led to Proyecto Tajín (1983–92) and the Cumbre Tajín (2001–present) event. These events show an expansion in state authority in the site, a drive for more planning and management, and a reconfiguration in funding structure that rendered expert labor precarious. Thanks to these processes, however, the administrativos were also well positioned to take advantage of novel opportunities.

Expertise and Labor

Managing archaeology is work. The custodios of the previous chapter may be closer to civil servants than their campesino predecessors, but the administrativos have always been civil servants and experts in the management, administration, and safeguarding of cultural heritage according to the standards set by the Mexican state via the INAH. During my 2016–17 fieldwork, the administrativos consisted of a director, the administrator, two assistants, the archaeologist in charge of the Technical and Legal Protection department, the site conservator and his project workers, the head of the maintenance department, and two maintenance workers responsible for the upkeep of the site installations. Together, they constituted the subdirectorate of the Zona de Monumentos Arqueológicos El Tajín, a dependency of the Centro INAH Veracruz, the state delegation of the federal INAH (see figure 15). By the 2010s there were twenty-four such subdirectorates across the country, including well-known sites like Palenque, Tula, and Monte Albán.[4]

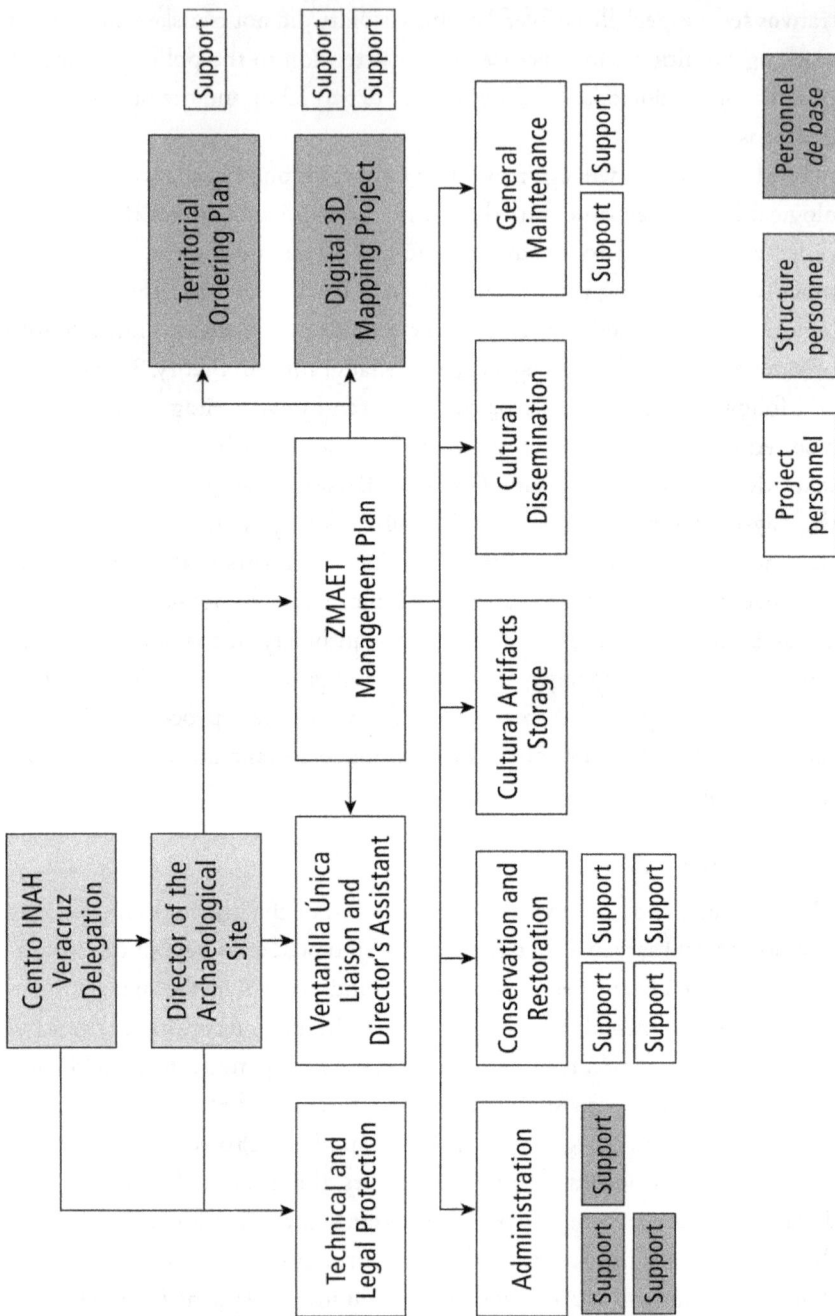

FIG. 15. Organizational diagram representing the site subdirectorate's administrative organization and means of contracting, 2017. Erin Greb Cartography.

As with the custodios, each of these roles has a corresponding set of bureaucratic responsibilities: in ideal terms, structured, hierarchical, managed, impersonal, disciplined, permanent, and rationally organized.[5] As one director explained to me, his responsibility was to communicate with the municipal, state, and federal governments, correspond with the INAH, and "coordinate the specialists that work here. . . . They get me the information about what their diverse research projects or the site needs." The director's assistant, in addition to supporting the director, attends the public. The administrator manages El Tajín's regular budget, project funds, payroll, ticket sales, and purchases. The conservator carries out restoration projects at the site. Most recently, these included constructing retaining walls to prevent erosion, reburying the Building 11 murals, and removing the impermeable cement of past conservation projects in favor of a moisture-filtering lime paste. The archaeologist in charge of the Technical and Legal Protection department supervises the area open to the public and evaluates construction projects in El Tajín's 1,221-hectare protected area. The maintenance workers clean the offices and bathrooms and assist with infrastructural improvement projects.

The primary distinction between administrativo and custodio is laboral, in terms of both contracting and professional responsibilities. In Mexico, workers in public institutions like the INAH have historically been divided into two groups: the rank-and-file (*de base*) and at-will employees (*de confianza*). The former, the custodios among them, are able to unionize. For the INAH, they cannot be fired after six months of service, except for cause. The latter are not unionized. For the INAH, they occupy specific, typically high-ranking posts like that of director-general.[6] While the Condiciones Generales de Trabajo set out these distinctions quite clearly, the reality is that the administrativos are, for the most part, contracted in such a way as to exclude them from either category.[7] Lawyer Arturo Alcalde Justiniani calls such contract workers the "undocumented workers of the INAH": by 2011 they included around two thousand employees "contracted outside the law and outside the INAH's norms."[8]

These laboral differences map onto other distinctions, without exactly mirroring them. In contrast with the Totonac custodios of the site, these experts are typically from outside of El Tajín and contracted for specific technical skills and knowledge: the director's assistant was finishing her undergraduate degree in administration when first hired, while the archaeologist, psychologist, and director were hired with the degrees that qualify them as professionals in their fields.[9] The conservator and other professionals contracted for projects administered through the subdirectorate had master's degrees or were working on doctorates.[10] The distinctions between administrativos and custodios were not absolute: for instance, the maintenance workers were from El Tajín and, in terms of background, closer to the custodios. Still, because of how they were contracted, their livelihoods more closely resembled those of the administrativos.

These administrativos are expert heritage managers. Along with the INAH and university-based archaeologists who periodically conduct research in El Tajín, they are the "binary other to various non-expert communities" like the custodios, site vendors, and Totonac communities of the region.[11] They are responsible for reproducing and implementing what Laurajane Smith describes as a "discourse of expertise that stresses the so-called common-sense aspects of heritage as monumental, material and innately of value to national narratives."[12] In El Tajín few question the importance of conserving the archaeological site with the best technical means available, because of the site's importance to the nation and the world. But what was all this authority and expertise good for when a paycheck comes nine months late, if at all? Time and time again, the contrast between the custodios' ability to mobilize and the administrativos' inability to defend their interests became clear.

Managing Archaeology, 1934–83

In Mexico, divisions between the production of knowledge about the pre-Hispanic past and the management of material remains in the present have historically been permeable. In the INAH, the concept of cultural heritage management as distinct from archaeology dates mostly from the 1990s.[13] Today, many of the INAH's archaeologists work in heritage management directed toward planning and conservation.[14] Those who work in the subdirectorate of El Tajín are responsible for keeping the site open, well conserved, and accessible to tourists. Meanwhile, the unionized researchers of the Centro INAH Veracruz, as well as the academic archaeologists of the Universidad Veracruzana and the Universidad Nacional Autónoma de México, participate in research projects. In El Tajín it is possible to trace the threads of site administration to the establishment of a state presence in the nation's archaeological sites during the Porfiriato. This led to the concentration of managerial, administrative, and safeguarding responsibilities in the conserje position (see chapter 5).[15]

In individual archaeological sites like Teotihuacan, the division of labor between research and management remained flexible during most of the twentieth century.[16] Agustín García Vega is often cited as among the first to conduct state-sponsored excavations in El Tajín, but less often noticed is that he was among the first to manage the site. As he wrote, in 1929 director José Reygadas Vértiz of the Dirección de Arqueología "commissioned this writer to formulate a budget for the conservation of the pyramid and as a result of the following report, agreed to conduct those works annually."[17] In the available documentation, research and administration are closely linked. The archived budgets refer to projects that could effectively do double duty: excavation and management alike required keeping the site clear of vegetation and sustaining the installations.

As the management of the pre-Hispanic past was formalized at the federal level, the administration of individual sites became increasingly standardized. A 1941 report listed fifty-nine administrative dependencies of the INAH's Dirección de Monumentos Prehispánicos, and fifty-two of these had encargados.[18] El Tajín was represented by short-lived conserje Fernando Ramírez Cortés and primero Modesto González. Encargados like these received correspondence and rendered regular reports to the national administration, reporting on site conservation, visitors, and needs for funds or tools. The likes of García Vega arrived with specific projects and legal authority over both the sites and workers. Projects like García Vega's and, later, José García Payón's, were most often funded by the INAH.

The organizational simplicity of this hierarchy—employing year-round personnel for safeguarding, funding seasonal projects for research, and circulating the paperwork associated with them—helped the state to maintain a presence in sites like El Tajín. The same processes helped to make El Tajín legible to the state, including it and other sites in the nation's portfolio of visitable archaeological sites. This was not a trivial problem. Getting a piece of mail from Mexico City to El Tajín in 1929, for example, required a trip through the rugged Sierra de Puebla: a train to Teziutlán, Puebla, a road trip to Zacapoaxtla and an automobile (or mule train, depending on the weather) through Cuetzalan, descending to San Pedro Miradores, Comalteco, Espinal, and Agua Dulce before arrival in Papantla.[19] From there, the recipient had to walk or ride to El Tajín—a trip of about an hour, and not without danger. Through the 1960s, transportation infrastructure improved, tourist traffic grew, and the custodio workforce expanded, but the basic INAH-archaeologist-encargado-custodio hierarchy remained resilient. After García Payón's last field season (1972–73) and before the beginning of Proyecto Tajín (1983), Pedro Pérez Bautista continued as encargado, rendering reports directly to the national administration.

The INAH was not exempt from the economic and political crises of the 1970s. Among the proposed solutions was decentralization. The populist administrations of Luis Echeverría (1970–76) and José López Portillo (1976–82) encouraged limited decentralization policies.[20] The neoliberal administration of Miguel de la Madrid (1982–88) declared the "decentralization of national life," enacting reforms to strengthen local governments as well as neoliberal economic policies like privatization and deregulation.[21] In the INAH, decentralization resulted in the founding of state- and regional-level offices (Centros Regionales) beginning in 1972 and renewed institutional support for community museums.[22] What became the Centro INAH Veracruz was founded in Xalapa in 1979; its relocation to the city of Veracruz in 1981 occasioned tensions with the Xalapa-based Universidad Veracruzana that would come to the fore during Proyecto Tajín.[23] This project brought a new set of political-economic conditions that transformed the management and administration of the archaeological site.

Proyecto Tajín (1983–92): Neoliberalism in Action

By 1999 it seemed that privatizing, liberalizing, and deregulating policies that had begun in the 1970s were finally reaching the nation's archaeological heritage. A senate proposal from the conservative National Action Party's Mauricio Fernández Garza sought to facilitate nongovernmental participation in heritage management, a mainstay of revolutionary nationalism that heretofore had avoided crass commercialization.[24] Popular reaction to private participation in cultural heritage management resulted in what Ana María Salazar calls patrimonialist movements, civil society-based organizations dedicated to critiquing "the arbitrariness of private capital which, for profitability, destroys the cultural vestiges of the past and de facto appropriates and exploits material cultural goods to improve capitalist profitability."[25] These fears—destruction of cultural property, the commodification of culture, and the withdrawal of the state—are common to many accounts of heritage and neoliberalism.

Yet while "neoliberalism" describes a set of economic ideas, especially policies supporting "strong private property rights, free markets, and free trade," the term also refers to broader projects to remake state and society alike.[26] "To focus on neo-liberal rationalities," Thomas Lemke suggests, "means to take seriously the programmatic dimension of government . . . tak[ing] programs at face value to uncover what they hide and exclude by identifying and framing certain problems, making them amenable to specific technical solutions, and producing distinctive forms of expertise."[27] The consequences of neoliberal reforms like decentralization can thus be unexpected, as I discuss below.[28] In El Tajín these effects are most visible in the form of an archaeological megaproject called Proyecto Tajín. At the closure of the project, President Carlos Salinas de Gortari explained the project's rationale to the press: in addition to the reclaiming of "historical memory," the president added that "the works developed by oil production in this area are passing . . . but those who are here will not. . . . For this reason we will promote the productive activity that tourism means to us."[29] Proyecto Tajín was framed as a means of generating knowledge and economic development through tourism, solving the problems of declining employment caused by downturns in PEMEX production. Notably left out from the discussion were the contested changes in land ownership (see chapter 1), the resulting changes in site management, and the possibility of further precarity.

A closer examination of Proyecto Tajín's funding scheme, management structure, and longer-term effects elucidates the trajectory of neoliberal reforms in Mexico's cultural sector. The reforms famously championed by Salinas de Gortari affected archaeology more in administration than ideology.[30] As Luis Vázquez León notes, Salinas's use of archaeology was very much in line with the traditional management of the pre-Hispanic past as state property.[31] Among the results was not wholesale privatization or commodification but a complex "devolution of authority to new agencies and coalitions of agencies, joint partnerships, public-private alliances, global-local or multi-scalar assemblages of NGOs, international authorities, and transnational agencies."[32] This devolution involved effects that, to residents and workers, looked more like an expansion of the state. Patrimonialists feared the dissolution of the INAH in favor of a McDonald's on top of the Pyramid of the Niches. What actually happened was arguably just as impactful, and is key to understanding the administrativos' current precarity.

Proyecto Tajín emerged from a 1983 agreement between the INAH and the Universidad Veracruzana, represented by Jürgen Brüggemann and Alfonso Medellín Zenil, respectively.[33] The state government funded Proyecto Tajín's year-long 1984 field season, with the objective of restoring the Pyramid of the

Niches. Brüggemann, in charge of the project, instead began by constructing drains to divert rainwater from the Plaza de los Nichos to stabilize the
structure—costing the approval and funding of the state government, though
the Universidad Veracruzana continued to contribute students and technical
personnel.[34] The three-month 1985 field season was funded by the INAH, while
no fieldwork was carried out during 1986 for lack of funds.[35] The University
of Münster and the German Research Foundation contributed funds for the
1987 field season. The 1988–92 period involved four years of continuous work,
including the support of the state-owned Petróleos Mexicanos. As the state
government's annual report put it: "We were joined by the invaluable support
of Petróleos Mexicanos, with whom we signed an agreement for the construction of . . . the Site Museum, rest area, public services, and the archaeological
site's administrative offices."[36] By 1992 laborers were working day and night to
finish the installations in order to accommodate a planned visit by President
Carlos Salinas de Gortari and the King and Queen of Spain, followed by
the declaration of El Tajín as a UNESCO World Heritage Site.[37] Under the
auspices of Proyecto Tajín, some five hundred workers, forty-two technical
personnel, and eighteen researchers carried out excavations, reconstructions,
and analyses, and built a new set of site installations, including the museum,
all at a cost of approximately 11.6 million pesos.[38] By 1994 Proyecto Tajín
had reconstructed about twenty-four hectares of the site, analyzed around
700,000 ceramic sherds, and produced ninety technical reports.[39]

What had once been a scaled devolution of authority from the INAH
in Mexico City through specific archaeologists and site encargados became
an uneven field of competing acronyms. This became clear when Proyecto
Tajín's institutional stakeholders—the INAH, the CIV, and the UV—came
into conflict. Though Proyecto Tajín was an agreement between the INAH
and the state government of Veracruz, the project did not always have the
support of the CIV. A contemporary periodical account describes the CIV's
opposition to the project: why uncover more structures when there were not
enough funds to conserve those already excavated? Proyecto Tajín, focused
on the excavation of structures and the improvement of site infrastructure for
the purposes of attracting tourism, included no long-term plan to continue
funding the site's maintenance after the end of the project.[40] CIV officials
made little effort to hide their critiques.

Other conflicts also stemmed from disagreement over methods.[41] In one
infamous case, a viejo trabajador custodio contacted the INAH regarding the

apparent destruction of fragments of the Pyramid of the Niches' original stucco finish. The alleged perpetrators were none other than an architect and workers commissioned by the UV. As another viejo trabajador explained it to me: "To straighten a niche, which was [crooked] but had its stucco, what they did was remove the stucco, remove the niche and they wanted to put it back but without stucco. . . . We said to not damage the stucco because it's original, we sent the petition to Mexico." The custodios effectively circumvented Proyecto Tajín's management, and the INAH dispatched officials from the CIV. When the CIV personnel arrived, they found the wholesale architectural reconstruction of the pyramid underway, supported by heavy machinery, rather than the supposed archaeological restoration. Centro INAH Veracruz officials formally suspended the work, provoking an angry response from Brüggemann and Proyecto Tajín's officials.[42] The restoration work on the Pyramid of the Niches was eventually completed, but animosity between Proyecto Tajín's constituent parties remained.

Management and Administration in the Wake of Proyecto Tajín, 1992–2000

By 2017 why had the staff gone unpaid for so long? One cause lies in the local development of a neoliberal management structure, an outcome of Proyecto Tajín. During the 1990s the importing of heritage management as a field distinct from archaeological knowledge production dovetailed with the political decentralization and neoliberal economic reforms discussed above. Nelly Robles García and Jack Corbett trace the growth of heritage management as such to the United Nations Educational, Scientific, and Cultural Organization (UNESCO) and its associated advisory bodies; the World Heritage Convention of 1972 was ratified by Mexico in 1984.[43] The resulting "technical managerialism" enshrined "particular modes of conservation and management" through instruments like Management Plans (see below).[44] Proyecto Tajín, which culminated in the declaration of El Tajín as a UNESCO World Heritage Site on December 14, 1992, followed this orientation and left a new management structure in its wake. After the arrival of los nuevos in 1993, and at behest of the custodios, the Centro INAH Veracruz sent a professional administrator, one Juan Antonio Ferrer, to take Pedro Pérez Bautista's place as encargado.

The functions of an encargado and administrator are related, but the technocratic orientation and contract nature of the latter highlights their differences. Local encargados, coming from the ranks of the custodios, were deeply tied into both their communities and the INAH. Though not without friction, this positioning gave the INAH a face in places like El Tajín, and provided residents a way to negotiate with the institution via a local interlocutor. Professional administrators like Ferrer, "equipped with both general knowledge and the ability to apply this knowledge to change the production and management environment" were not drawn from the ranks of the custodios, were not from El Tajín, and—crucially, for later administrativos—were contracted such that they were not subject to the Condiciones Generales de Trabajo.[45]

A comparison of Pérez Bautista's and Ferrer's trajectories elucidates the transition from encargados to administrators, and from local to technocratic management. Pérez Bautista, from El Tajín, was a campesino who cultivated vanilla and owned a mill for processing sugarcane during the 1940s. He began working in El Tajín with García Vega in 1936 and worked with García Payón during fourteen field seasons between 1946 and 1964. Starting his career as a peón, he eventually became a mason before succeeding Teódulo González as encargado in 1964.[46] He lived in El Tajín during retirement until his death at the age of 104. Juan Antonio Ferrer Aguilar, of Tabasco, earned his undergraduate degree in business administration from the Instituto Tecnológico de Tabasco in 1989 and his master's degree in executive business administration from the Universidad Olmeca in 2012.[47] His work in the INAH during the 1990s included directorial positions in the Centro INAH Chiapas and the Centro INAH Tabasco, as well as in the archaeological sites of Palenque, Bonampak, and Yaxchilán. Outside the INAH, he worked in administrative positions at the municipal and state levels in Tabasco, and was appointed director of the federal Instituto de Salud para el Bienestar in 2020.

Ferrer and his successors entered a complex management field involving diverse federal and state agencies. The financial participation of the state government continued in terms of land ownership (see chapter 1) and through the Instituto Veracruzano de la Cultura (IVEC).[48] The IVEC managed the site installations—bathrooms, an exposition area, and a first-aid clinic—and the INAH continued to maintain the site's pre-Hispanic structures.[49] Over time, this morphed into an informal agreement by which the IVEC effectively managed the site from the highway to the ticket counter, while the INAH managed the area from the ticket counter to the end of the archaeological site open to the public. However, the IVEC lacked the INAH's legal authority to regulate informal commerce, land use, and other day-to-day aspects of life in an archaeological site. The INAH, lacking legal ownership of the site's installations, was likewise unable to maintain them. By 2003 this wealth of acronyms and the corresponding allocations of authority was among the most pressing managerial issues facing the site.[50] The situation continued until 2010, when the IVEC's offices were moved to Papantla, though the institution remains the legal owner of the site installations.[51]

The INAH's local management structure developed from a single administrator during the 1990s to a full-fledged subdirectorate by 2005. That same year, El Tajín became part of a nationwide effort to implement management plans.[52] A delayed consequence of the site's declaration as World Heritage, the effort responded to a UNESCO recommendation that "States Parties are encouraged to prepare plans . . . for the safeguarding of each cultural property nominated."[53] The subdirectorate is charged with carrying out the "Plan de Manejo de la Zona de Monumentos Arqueológicos El Tajín," eventually published in 2009.[54] Outlining a series of management areas, including technical and legal protection, conservation, investigation, interpretation and divulgation, public use, social connection, and administration and management, the plan proposes a series of projects and personnel for three-, six-, and ten-year intervals.

As with Proyecto Tajín, the neoliberal management of cultural heritage resulted in the expansion of state control, now in the form of long-term planning. But technocratic management and devolutions of authority crossed paths to complicate funding schemes. The funding structure that supported the Management Plan and the archaeological site had evolved considerably since the days of INAH archaeologists' seasonal budgets and encargados' ad-hoc requests. By 2005 funding came from the INAH and the site's regular budget (*gasto básico*), specific projects approved and funded by the INAH (*recursos fiscales*), and projects approved by the INAH but funded by third parties (*terceros*).[55] The available data indicate that these third parties were a significant but wildly inconsistent source for site funds, from 93 percent in 2015 to less than 1 percent in 2018 (see table 5).[56] Recalling fears of neoliberal privatization, we might ask: Who were these terceros? What were they funding in El Tajín? Terceros included insurance payouts after natural disasters affected the site—a fire in 2016 and Cold Front No. 49 in 2018 for example—but the most common third party was the state government of Veracruz, this time via the Cumbre Tajín event.

TABLE 5. Selected funding sources and amounts for El Tajín, 2007–19

YEAR	SOURCE		
	Gasto básico	Projects	
		Recursos fiscales	Terceros
2007	697,507	1,245,910	
2008	699,900	1,912,971	
2009	900,000	3,884,405	
2010	810,000		6,449,641
2011	1,410,000		2,400,000
2012	1,410,000		3,000,000
2013	1,500,000		3,000,000
2014	1,500,000	337,750	3,800,412
2015	1,500,000	162,050	2,994,383
2016	1,000,000	144,980	1,232,102
2017	667,384.65	1,908,451.48	25,114
2018	536,030.47	1,733,668	370,554
2019	753,210.68	1,222,869	

Sources: Gasto básico 2007–17 data from Jesús Trejo González to María del Perpetuo Socorro Villarreal Escárrega, July 6, 2017, INAI, Folio 1115100046217, Oficio ZMAET 401.12C.6-2017/201. Gasto básico 2018–19 data from David H. García Ávila to María del Perpetuo Socorro Villarreal Escárrega, October 6, 2020, INAI, Folio 1115100080220, Oficio 401.12C.5-2020/1064. Projects 2007–9 data from "Anexo," INAI, Folio 1115100000110, Oficio CNRF/041/2010. Projects 2010–11 and 2014–19 data from Erik Romero Vázquez to José Manuel Bañuelos Ledesma, July 10, 2020, INAI, Folio 1115100061920, Oficio 401.10C.3-2020/633 BIS. Projects 2012–13 data from INAH, "Evaluación del Plan," 23.

Cumbre Tajín, 2000–Present

Despite the failure of legal efforts to facilitate private-sector intervention in Mexico's cultural heritage, it seems that the fears of patrimonialist movements have slowly come to pass since the 2000s. Efforts like the construction of a Bodega Aurrera (owned by Walmart) in Teotihuacan caused national scandals.[57] Other forms of neoliberal commercialization, like the Cumbre Tajín festival, were more episodic, and drew on longer histories of private-sector interest related to tourism.[58] The use of state-sponsored light-and-sound shows at Mexican archaeological sites, for instance, dates back to 1968 in

Teotihuacan.[59] Organizers now argue that "Cumbre Tajín is a benchmark for the work of safeguarding, regenerating, promoting, and cultural tourism."[60] More recent events like the Cumbre Olmeca suggest that the Cumbre Tajín is indeed a model worth emulating.[61]

Planning for what became Cumbre Tajín began in 1999, when the state government of Veracruz announced plans for an end-of-the-millennium festival. The contemporary press announced the effort to "call the country's and the world's attention to Veracruz, and particularly to Totonacapan, and that's just the beginning of an economic policy of regional development and the maximization of our Veracruzan cultural and natural wealth."[62] The event was to involve camping, a light-and-sound show, and concerts in El Tajín. These plans stalled when September 1999 saw one of the worst natural disasters to hit north Veracruz in a century: Tropical Depression Eleven caused between 1,000 and 1,300 millimeters of precipitation to fall in about a week.[63] The Tecolutla, Nautla, Tuxpan, and Cazones Rivers rose between 4.5 and 9 meters each, causing widespread flooding in the cities of Tuxpan, Poza Rica, and Gutiérrez Zamora.[64] The event was delayed until the following year.

In the lead-up to the event, patrimonialist movements formed and took action. Scholars, site custodios, university students, and professors joined in protest with organizations ranging from the local Alianza Ciudadana Papanteca (which had formed to support those affected by the 1999 floods) to the national Frente Zapatista de Liberación Nacional.[65] Their concerns were wide-ranging: damage to Mexico's archaeological heritage, the commercialization of traditional Totonac cultural expressions, and the exclusion of the communities whose culture was ostensibly being celebrated.[66] The state government highlighted the cultural promotion and economic effects of the 2000 event: twenty-three musical, dance, and theatrical events with around 14,500 visitors; the participation of three hundred members of Totonac communities; and an economic spillover of 14.8 million pesos.[67]

Critics were not mollified, and the protests became annual.[68] While they did not stop the event, activists were successful in pressing the state government to address certain criticisms. The state government constructed an event space, the Parque Temático Takhilsukut, about a kilometer outside the site's monumental core, in 2001.[69] Covering about seventeen hectares with a capacity of forty thousand people, this project caused further protest from local organizations because of its location inside the formal boundaries of the Zona de Monumentos Arqueológicos.[70] From then, the only official Cumbre

Tajín event held at the archaeological site was a nighttime light-and-sound show, which required extensive coordination with site administrators. This involved meetings with producers well in advance of the event, supervising the installation of temporary equipment, and, eventually, long hours of supervision during the show. To address protestors and highlight its commitment to Veracruz's cultural heritage, the state government of Veracruz began to pay the INAH an annual fee of 3 million pesos.

Tracing Cumbre Tajín's funding structure relative to the site illustrates another permutation of the neoliberal heritage management, in which "the grey area of the 'marketization' of national patrimony is often legitimated through [public-private] 'partnerships.'"[71] The state government and private corporations worked through a series of trusts to fund the event (see table 6) with the former contributing an average of about half the event's total cost over fourteen years.[72] Compared with the other costs of the event, the payment to the INAH—the only direct contribution to the archaeological site—is relatively minor. The payments to INAH, which funded the Management Plan, ranged from about 3–9 percent of the Cumbre Tajín's total cost during the years for which financial data are available.[73] However, the experts contracted under the Management Plan depended entirely on this revenue stream.

Unequal dependence was the result. The Management Plan, its projects, and its workers depended almost entirely on Cumbre Tajín, but after 2001 the event mostly needed the administration for the light-and-sound show. Otherwise, event planners used the proximity of the site to attract visitors, the image of the Pyramid of the Niches to promote musical acts, and the like, with no additional support for the site's management. This configuration made the system vulnerable to external shocks that affected third-party funding. For example, massive corruption in the government of Javier Duarte de Ochoa (2012–16) left the state unable to pay its bills, including to the INAH.[74] The links between the complexities of this funding scheme and the daily lives of Management Plan personnel became abundantly clear in 2015.

Precarious Livelihoods and Flexible Opportunities

Summer 2015: When I returned to El Tajín for the first time in a year, I was surprised to find the site quiet. The offices were practically empty, with the exception of the administrator and the director's assistant. The former commented that things had been difficult because of budget cuts. I did my

TABLE 6. Selected funds and costs for Cumbre Tajín in millones de pesos, 2006–20

YEAR	EVENT INCOME	STATE CONTRIBUTION	TOTAL COST	PRODUCTION IN EL TAJÍN	CONTRIBUTION TO INAH
2006	12.6	16.2	28.8	5.6	0
2007	6.9	26.4	33.3	8.8	3
2008	11.5	24.5	36	9.1	3
2009	8.8	31.1	39.9		3
2010	22.4	18.6	40.9	8.9	3
2011	27.1	19.9	47.1	9.4	2.2
2012	43.1	28.1	71.1	9	3
2013	96		96	15.4	3
2014	95.5		95.5	18.6	0
2015	52.4	23.6	76	0.1	0
2016	2.9	14.8	17.7	0.1	0
2017	7	12.2	19.2	0	0
2018	8	22.7	30.7	0	0
2019	3.3	36.4	39.6	0	0
2020	0.8	20.4	21.2	0	0

Source: Fideicomiso Público de Administración y Operación del Parque Temático Takhil-Sukut, INAI, Folio 301559400000321.

best to sympathize, though I then had only a vague notion of how the site was funded. Fortunately, the director's assistant—who was always willing to explain very basic things to me—was working that day. The state government, she explained, had ceased paying its fee for the Cumbre Tajín event, and the INAH did not have the funds to cover the projects that supported these positions.[75] Only the director's assistant, the administrator, the conservator, and maintenance personnel remained, because they were funded by recursos fiscales rather than terceros. Three of the administrativos that I'd known in 2012–14 were gone: a fellow anthropologist, the community psychologist, and the archaeologist in charge of materials storage. As the anthropologist later told me, one day in May a memo arrived saying that there was no money to fund the projects and they would no longer be paid. They lost their jobs overnight. The conservator, still working thanks to his INAH project funding, blamed the contract nature of the work: "You make contracts every three months. . . . If they want to switch you out, they switch you out, if they want to fire you, they fire you. . . . You don't have benefits, insurance, nothing." He had even periodically forgone his salary in order to pay his workers. Closer to the at-will government workers than the custodios, the administrativos' employment was precarious from the beginning.

However, following the political economy of heritage management at El Tajín demonstrates that the precarity was overdetermined. Corruption in the Duarte administration (2010–16) left the state government unable to pay the fees on which the Management Plan personnel depended. The funding structure of the Management Plan (2009) left its projects and workers vulnerable to changes in third-party funds. The creation of a subdirectorate (2005) staffed by contract workers made short-term employment a norm. The employment of technocratic administrators in place of local unionized encargados (1994) meant that outsiders would have to negotiate the everyday practices of heritage that had developed since the 1880s.[76]

Custodios have been working at El Tajín for the past 120 years, with a system of payroll that depends on the national INAH and that is backed by a well-established union. The eighteen-year-old subdirectorate has always been funded by a combination of gasto básico, recursos fiscales, and terceros. The substantive activities of the Management Plan relied fundamentally on contributions from the Cumbre Tajín event, which was itself subject to broader pressures from the state government, activists, and donors. Yet for the administrativos, the picture was not so bleak as the September meeting portended. The system in which they worked was characterized by a diversified funding scheme and flexible labor contracts that enforced precarious livelihoods but enabled novel opportunities.

The staff's ability to leverage precarity to make the best of a bad situation became unexpectedly clear to me during another custodios' protest in 2016. I spent a December day in a rural community south of Papantla learning about the process of vanilla curing. After returning, a habitual Facebook check produced the surprising news that the custodios had again occupied the offices, as they had in September 2012. The demands were similar to those that had ostensibly animated previous protests: the firing of certain personnel in El Tajín, the Centro INAH Veracruz, and INAH's Mexico offices; more funding with more plazas; and payment in cash rather than via direct

deposit. I arrived at the site the following day to see how the administrativos had reacted. As in 2012, all were working from the cafeteria. All seemed
resigned. "We're used to them treating us like this," said the administrator. The
director's assistant was noncommittal: this was nothing new. She thought it
would just be a matter of waiting until the proper negotiations with Mexico
City were carried out.

Before the administrativos learned of the closure, the director had invited
me to accompany him to a nearby ecotourism cooperative. He would be
meeting a group to discuss community-based tourism, one of his areas of
expertise. We headed out that morning. Over lunch, he described ecotourism
in Papantla, dialoguing about possibilities for similar collaborations with
the group. It was a convivial meeting, full of friendly chatter, the exchanging
of contact information, and plans for future collaborations. Throughout, I
was faintly surprised that the director was not staying in the site to attend
to the protest. I had imagined that there would be negotiations to attend to,
much like those I had witnessed in 2012. On the way back to El Tajín, the
director explained that he had already done what he could: this disparate
set of complaints could only be addressed at the state and federal levels.
Personally, he had no problems with the custodios: "I hope they give them
their [additional] plazas."

The director continued that he understood why the custodios felt so
involved with their jobs. If he were fired, he could go elsewhere. An anthropologist by training, he had worked on ecotourism projects in El Tajín and
cultural tourism projects in his Puebla hometown. Colleagues had invited him
to apply for master's programs in Mexico City and Xalapa. He had inherited
from his father a parcel of land where he would eventually build his house,
and he had cows, sheep, and chickens to maintain. He liked his work at El
Tajín, but he had contingency plans. By contrast, if some large-scale change
came to affect the structure of custodios' labor, where else would they go?
Some had taken advantage of the INAH's benefits to attend high school
or study for an undergraduate degree, but others had not. Most had been
custodios for decades and did not have the same kind of labor mobility. In
the director's view, because of the historical development and structure of
labor discussed in the preceding chapter, the custodios were relatively more
entangled with the site than were the administrativos. The site depends on
them for maintenance, and they depend on the site for regular pay, health
insurance, social security, vacations, and retirement. Once used to having these

benefits, it becomes much more difficult to leave. In the broader landscape of labor in Mexico, the custodios' stability was more the exception than the rule.[77]

The professional heritage managers, whose positions emerged in the neoliberal era, rarely had the same expectations of their work. They have always had to see themselves "in terms of corporate individualism—a flexible bundle of skills that reflexively manages oneself as though the self was a business."[78] In the same way that the director appreciated his mobility, the conservator appreciated being able to work on the kind of short-term contracts that took him to Egypt, Guatemala, and Yucatán, instead of staying in El Tajín on a full-time basis. While the administrativos undoubtedly suffer because of the uncertainty of their futures, the fact that their positions were institutionalized during the neoliberal era at least affords them certain flexible possibilities not afforded to the custodios.

Unfortunately, this flexibility proved useful. By 2018 not one administrativo from 2012–17 remained.[79] The administrator was replaced by an anthropologist said to be a friend of the INAH's director-general; she was eventually paid most of what she was owed in December 2018, more than a year late. Her assistant, preferring to not go through the trouble, found work in a PEMEX subcontractor after leaving—until those contracts, too, ran out. He eventually left for work in Monterrey and, later, the United States. The director's assistant, pessimistic about ever being paid, quit after her contract ended and returned to her home in the port of Veracruz; it was nine months before she found work again, in a lawyer's office. The director, though holding a kind of plaza that gave him job security, was unexpectedly fired in April 2018 and returned to his hometown. The conservator comes and goes depending on whether there is funding for his projects. On the outs with the current site authorities, he now returns to visit rather than to work. The archaeologist took a pay cut before quitting and returning to his home in Guanajuato to begin a master's degree.

I stayed in touch with the administrator after leaving the field, following up on her efforts to get what she was owed. She had little luck finding work, though she applied to positions all the way to Mexico City. Though initially stung by the difficulty of finding a steady job, she eventually made it work with a variety of projects, drawing on her particular bundle of skills and relationships: an assistantship in the planning of an academic conference, reselling Papantla artisanry at regional fairs, planting vanilla, importing coffee from neighboring Puebla, setting up a stall in Papantla's artisanry market, and eventually finding employment in a new government program aimed at improving agricultural outputs. She admitted that she was no longer looking for the kinds of administrative positions she had previously sought. It was nice not having to go into an office every day, and not needing to worry about disagreeable superiors in the Centro INAH Veracruz or in INAH's Mexico City offices. Of course, job security would have been better.

Conclusion

The experts I discuss here are the educated authors of reports filed in the INAH technical archives and published elsewhere. Largely a product of the neoliberal era, they are responsible for directing projects ranging from site conservation to attending to tourist complaints under the auspices of the federal heritage management agency. But they are subject to precarious livelihoods in ways not shared by the custodios. The staff, at least, consider themselves better positioned to take advantage of the opportunities offered by the flexible status forced upon them. For how much longer will this be the case?

Budget cuts will likely flatten this structural complexity. It is more probable that the custodios will lose their plazas than that the administrators will have their positions secured. More than a few custodios feared this future in 2017. No one knows quite what will happen with labor under the recently created Secretaría de Cultura. In addition to the numerous procedural complaints about the process—for instance, the fact that it operated for eleven months without any published regulations—the fact that January 2017 saw the announcement of a 21 percent budget cut to Mexico's cultural sector did not inspire optimism among INAH workers.[80] One custodio thought that the change, which would require a renegotiation of certain agreements related to worker benefits, like the Condiciones Generales de Trabajo, was nothing less than an effort to eliminate plazas. Perhaps the situation would be like in Teotihuacan, where police and other subcontractors increasingly do the work of custodios.[81] The 2023 deployment of the Guardia Nacional for vigilance purposes suggested as much.[82]

Others simply felt uncertain but pessimistic: the situation could stay the same, at best, but would probably get worse. A CIV archaeologist thought that the creation of the Secretaría de Cultura was just to get INAH to do "the same with a lower budget." At the national scale, custodios' and investigators' unions protested the creation of the secretaría when they saw the initial plans for its organization. As one anthropologist and union official explained it to me, the plan "was pretty terrible, it was to unmake the INAH and the Instituto Nacional de Bellas Artes. . . . The regulation was very violent." After protests and negotiations, the published regulations maintained the INAH more or less as it had existed since 1939: with administrative autonomy, judicial personhood, and patrimony.

Nevertheless, the INAH's institutional survival did not guarantee better working conditions. Ever-tighter budgets continued to affect workers like El Tajín's administrativos. The administrativos' counterparts elsewhere in the INAH forcefully call attention to this exclusion. Under the Twitter hashtags of #YaPágameINAH (pay me already, INAH), #contratodigno (both "with respectable treatment" and "respectable contract"), and #TodosSomosINAH (we are all INAH), many of those contracted in the same way as El Tajín's administrativos sought to publicize their precarious working conditions, characterized by short-term contracts, no benefits, and no possibility of retirement or a pension.[83]

As a nuevo custodio friend put it, "if the INAH goes, we all go." Over dinner, he thought out loud about what might happen with the new secretaría. He had been a union delegate in the past and was never shy about appearing in protests, but he was concerned about the possible disappearance of the custodios' benefits, if not positions. What would happen in that case? While all might lose their employment, as the administrativos with whom I worked had, the custodios are relatively less equipped to exercise their neoliberal agency than their administrative counterparts. This, then, is the custodios' disadvantage: moored to the site by intergenerational labor histories, stable plazas, and a variety of benefits, they have the most to lose in the broader political-economic shifts that inexorably transform Mexico's cultural sector.

Conclusion

<blockquote>
Even in relation to The Past our authenticity resides in the struggles of our present. Only in that present can we be true or false to the past we choose to acknowledge.

—Michel-Rolph Trouillot, *Silencing the Past: Power and the Production of History*
</blockquote>

The Pyramid of the Niches looms large. Its distinctive image and profile serve as a convenient visual shorthand for El Tajín, whether on national stamps, state license plates, or local advertisements. If you are like most visitors, you will find the pyramid particularly memorable: the contrast between the projection of the flying cornices and the depth of the niches, the delicate interplay of light and shadow across its facades, and its apparent authenticity. Yet if you observe closely, you might notice that certain niches are furnished with concrete rather than pre-Hispanic sandstone alone. You might notice a bit of the red-painted stucco finish that covered the structure in antiquity, and realize that today's mottled stone is a far cry from the crimson pyramid that would have awed pre-Hispanic visitors.

In its monumentality and mystery, the Pyramid of the Niches attests to a deep pre-Hispanic past that now stands in for the rest of El Tajín's recent history.[1] Recent research by Patricia Castillo Peña argues that this metonymy is archaeologically accurate.[2] If you had visited El Tajín around 1100 CE, you might have entered from the west. You would have seen the Pyramid of the Niches set against the backdrop of the three-hundred-meter-tall hill to the east. As you approach, the pyramid grows relative to the hill, also known as the Cerro de los Mantenimientos. By the time you enter the city center, the pyramid has eclipsed the Cerro. The message is clear. The pre-Hispanic rulers of El Tajín emphasized their sacred authority by mimicking the great Cerro in pyramid form, appropriating the hill's cosmological significance at human scale.

Behind the Pyramid of the Niches also lies a set of relationships between the local concerns of making a living and the broader trends of researching and managing the past that I have called the political economy of archaeology. Mexican heritage management emphasizes monumental urban centers representative of pre-Hispanic civilization, like El Tajín. Commonsense references like "archaeological site" reinforce this emphasis, alluding to specific periods of time brought to light through excavation and maintained as cultural heritage in the present. In this study, I addressed an imbalance in what Michel-Rolph Trouillot calls "the making of *history* in the final instance."[3] The range of commodities and labor that I discuss in this book have long been registered, archived, and retrieved. Some have extensive historiographies. The archaeology of El Tajín, too, is relatively well studied, even if scholarly consensus on basic facts is elusive. Less recognized were two facts: that Totonac communities consider these histories of landscape and labor important to understand their present conditions, and that these processes are constitutive of the history of archaeology in El Tajín.

In this view, events like the 2019 conflict that opened this book do not simply stem from negligence or malfeasance but are rooted in longer-term processes. The configuration of a private property regime in the late nineteenth century entailed a particular vision of space that facilitated communication between archaeologists and landowners, each of which drew on an idiom of patrimony to make claims. The resulting pragmatic accommodations, however, depended on a hegemonic view of land as property that eventually favored the state when an archaeological megaproject came in. Events like a landowner's efforts to clear a newly purchased parcel recalled this history, especially when the relevant legal restrictions seemed to fall more often on Totonac residents than wealthy outsiders. The rhetoric of conservation that justified such restrictions seemed less than convincing when evidence of past exploitation remained on the landscape, as with the sealed oil well inside the archaeological site. The presence of this foreign-drilled well further testified to a long-running history of cooperation (and occasional conflict) between state archaeologists and oil interests. This relationship strengthened and weakened at different moments after the mid-nineteenth century. Following the Totonac communities of the region, however, shows that these relationships are also of ongoing and cumulative environmental contamination. Still, not all industries were exploitative in the same ways. Papantla's Totonac farmers were once known for their vanilla wealth. Vanilla is far from obscure, but rural memories of the violence associated with the cultivation and curing of the spice are less known. Understanding this violence requires looking at the temporality of vanilla cultivation in the context of a durable political economy rooted in unequal relations of production. Those who profited most from vanilla used their wealth and influence in El Tajín and, in so doing, were well positioned to leverage the site in matters of local politics. For residents, however, the rumors of men carrying rifles and fears of organized crime that circulated in 2019 recalled the danger associated with cultivating and commercializing the crop.

As the events of August 2019 suggested, those employed by the same institution and ostensibly working toward the same goals did not always see things the same way. For as long as there has been research in El Tajín, scholars have needed Totonac labor. Wage laborers, frequently excluded from the interpretation of the materials they excavate, found work in archaeology a welcome possibility. In a context of land dispossession, archaeology provided the opportunity for a regular cash income, skill development, and the possibility of a permanent position. But those opportunities were not available to all. In unevenly distributing employment opportunities and income, archaeology could not help but contribute to local socioeconomic stratification. This is especially clear in the case of the custodios. Their presence is integral to the day-to-day functioning of the archaeological site. These workers are nowhere near as invisible as their lack of representation in the historiography suggests. Centering their pasts demonstrates that the custodios reckon their history according to the generational succession of worker cohorts, relative to the changing circumstances of twentieth-century Papantla. Long histories of labor and activism have consolidated the custodios as a local elite class, one capable of exercising authority to advance political aims. Their counterparts, the administrativos, suffer from precarious livelihoods despite their intellectual authority, relative historiographic prominence, and the legal authority of their positions, which would seem to give them the ability to prevent events like the 2019 conflict. I trace this precarity to neoliberal heritage management and its effects: an inconsistent system of funding that depends on the Cumbre Tajín event. Yet, as a result, the administrativos are relatively more equipped to exercise their neoliberal agency. The dynamics of the processes behind the 2019 conflict and others like it are not reducible to the state's appropriation of the past, the development of the tourism industry, or other historiographic tendencies typically used to explain the history and politics of archaeology in Mexico.

In this book, I sought to acknowledge disparate historical processes—from the employment of wage laborers to the cultivation of vanilla—as "valid histories in their own right" and as integral to the development of the archaeological site, with a political-economic focus as a common denominator.[4] Following these threads through the case of El Tajín illustrates the richness of recent Indigenous history, presents its importance for understanding the development of archaeology, and suggests that both tend to be overlooked in normative ways of investigating the pre-Hispanic past and the politics thereof in Mexico. At a conceptual level, I hope this work strengthens the historiography of archaeology and indigeneity in twentieth-century Mexico, and demonstrates the utility of interdisciplinary engagements with archaeology. Still, this book could have been written otherwise. Questions of state-led tourism and development, or cultural practice and Indigenous cosmovision, were tangential to my account.

Similarly tangential was the traditional subject matter of archaeology: the pre-Hispanic culture history of El Tajín and the changing approaches with which archaeologists have interpreted the past.[5] I instead started from the increasingly well-acknowledged insights that archaeological sites have recent pasts, that engaging with local communities offers a more informed understanding of the histories of archaeology, and that the archaeological literature can, and should, be populated by people living today.[6] However, considering the discipline's current situation in the United States, asking archaeologists to be ethnographers and historians seems foolhardy. Even before prospective archaeologists begin their graduate training and specialization in the analysis of material culture, they confront systemic discrimination, widespread precarity, and ever-higher bars for entry.[7]

Attention to these dimensions of the political economy of archaeology informed my discussion of the INAH. The institution is frequently subject to critique from those who oppose the state's monopoly on archaeology, as well as those who support it. Recent research drawing on settler-colonial studies forcefully argues that the structure and practice of archaeology in Mexico is the result of long-running efforts to expropriate diverse Indigenous pasts in favor of the state.[8] Mexican archaeologists have argued that the political orientation of the discipline means that archaeology frequently responds to the priorities of the state, limiting the potential for production of knowledge about the past.[9] For those who continue to justify the INAH's efforts along nationalist lines, the extent of pre-Hispanic materials in what is now Mexico means that fulfilling the institution's legal objectives is a monumental task, and impossible in practical terms.[10] Even during periods of strong state support for archaeology, sites as well known as El Tajín regularly faced funding shortfalls.[11] Financial challenges aside, the legal regulation of archaeology puts practitioners in challenging positions: "The law requires [the INAH] to operate in arenas where it has no legal authority and holds it accountable for outcomes over which it has no control."[12] These recognitions complicate any critique that treats the Mexican state, the INAH, and INAH archaeologists as though they were the same.

Archaeology and my fieldwork were not exempt from these trends or the changing circumstances of Mexico in the first decades of the twenty-first century. In this book's opening, rumors of men carrying rifles recalled not just the violence of midcentury agrarian compression or the risks of selling vanilla but the ongoing effects of Mexico's militarized antidrug operations. In 2018 *El Universal* described Veracruz as "an endless grave," following the excavations of 1,178 bodies in 601 clandestine mass burials.[13] The recurrent harassment, displacement, and murder of journalists gave the state its reputation as one of the most dangerous in the country, and Papantla was no exception.[14] Veteran journalist María Elena Ferral, whose coverage of the 2019 conflict I cite in the introduction, was murdered by masked gunmen in 2020.[15] Neither was Veracruz exempt from the long-running national crisis of femicide and impunity. The Universidad Veracruzana's Observatorio Universitario de Violencias contra las Mujeres documents ongoing intimate violence, femicide, and forced disappearances on a semesterly basis.[16]

In this context, the first case of COVID-19 in Mexico was registered in February 2020.[17] Mexico's archaeological sites were closed the following month. Some were periodically reopened in accordance with declining infection rates, but El Tajín was not. Officially, the site was closed for nearly two years, a closure without precedent.[18] Papantla's Association of Hotels, Motels, and Restaurants estimated losses of around $200,000 per month while the site was closed.[19] What are the implications for the rural communities around El Tajín? Ejido communities have been able to sustain themselves through agriculture, for the most part, and the communities closest to the archaeological site could depend on tourism for generally reliable patterns of visitation. In casual fieldwork conversations, interlocutors would sometimes cite the tourist economy as a reason for remaining in the community rather than migrating. That may soon change.

Ongoing violence—related to the drug trade, targeting journalists, and rooted in misogyny—and the duration of the COVID-19 pandemic thus became the backdrop for more "normal" disasters, like Hurricane Grace. Grace crossed the Yucatán Peninsula as a Category 1 hurricane on August 19, 2021, and spun up into a Category 3 with maximum sustained winds of 125 miles per hour before landing in Papantla on August 21. The loss of life was relatively small, and there was little coverage in the English-language press. But the material damages were enormous, estimated at between $300 and $500 million for Mexico.[20] The loss of housing and crops exacerbated food insecurity: prices of basic commodities spiked 400 percent in the immediate aftermath of the disaster.[21] Neither was aid immediately forthcoming from the municipal, state, or federal governments.[22] Even months later, civil society organizations continued to organize support for communities from the Sierra Norte de Puebla to the Gulf Coast of Veracruz. Questions of violence, pandemics, and natural disasters will continue to inform the political-economic landscape of life and labor around El Tajín.

In writing this book, I have leveraged the sources at my disposal to tell a story about how archaeology works in the world. I take for granted that the operations of archaeology generated real knowledge about the pre-Hispanic past, instead taking the opportunity to decenter the production of knowledge in favor of political economy. In this view, archaeology was a proximate cause for land dispossession, was deeply imbricated with an industry responsible for the degradation of Indigenous livelihoods, and was connected to a historic merchant elite that also profited from the exploitation of vanilla cultivators. The labor required for these outcomes also allowed some residents to access cash income in difficult circumstances, enabled a select few to achieve uncommon socioeconomic mobility, and facilitated precarious livelihoods for others. The details of landscape and labor may be specific to El Tajín, but the constitutive exclusions of what we take to be the past are not. By attending to them, we work toward histories that are both more empirically adequate and ethically engaged.

Appendix
Annual Visitors to El Tajín, 1925–2024

YEAR	RECORDED VISITORS	YEAR	RECORDED VISITORS
1925	230	1965	23,917
1926	250	1966	30,079
1927	281	1967	32,450
1928	256	1968	32,125
1931	660	1969	36,650
1934	2,092	1970	40,950
1935	2,723	1972	48,926
1936	7,814	1973	52,000
1937	1,644	1976	68,530
1946	1,000	1977	76,761
1947	1,400	1996	181,371
1948	900	1997	222,548
1949	900	1998	323,463
1950	927	1999	222,741
1951	3,425	2000	338,655
1952	5,579	2001	476,735
1953	4,080	2002	629,908
1954	4,293	2003	685,124
1955	4,273	2004	888,637
1956	5,115	2005	380,264
1957	4,935	2006	470,311
1958	9,970	2007	472,636
1959	16,333	2008	381,509
1960	12,789	2009	431,328
1961	13,043	2010	388,403
1962	15,172	2011	390,831
1963	14,966	2012	384,697
1964	20,801	2013	423,601

YEAR	RECORDED VISITORS
2014	330,331
2015	442,761
2016	414,601
2017	386,406
2018	395,698
2019	426,176
2020	84,344
2021	0
2022	290,280
2023	346,255
2024	334,408

For El Tajín, the first year for which I have been able to locate annual visitor statistics is 1925. Of the following ninety-nine years, I have located data for sixty-seven of them. The most complete data series are as follows. For 1925–28 see "Número de visitantes a las ruinas arqueológicas de la República," AM-DMP, exp. 1761. For 1934–37 see "Relación del número de visitantes," AM-DMP, exp. 1735. For 1946–49 see "Gráfica de visitantes a las zonas arqueológicas," AH-MNA, vol. 155, exp. 4, f. 29 (for "Veracruz"). For 1950–67 see "Estadística de Visitantes," AGEV-JGP, c. 28, exp. "Informes," f. 13. For 1968–70 see José García Payón to Ignacio Marquina, May 31, 1971, AGEV-JGP, c. 16, exp. 18. For 1996–2024 see *Sistema Institutional: Estadística de Visitantes*, Instituto Nacional de Antropología e Historia, accessed March 17, 2024, https://www.estadisticas.inah.gob.mx/.

Annual visitors are mentioned for individual years in the following sources. For 1931 see Erasmo Rodríguez to Ignacio Marquina, December 31, 1931, ADDMP, exp. "El Tajín," ref. B/311.32(z61-2)/I, leg. I. For 1972 see "Relación de los visitantes con pago durante el año de 1972 en la zona arqueológica de Tajín," AGEV-JGP, c. 25, exp. 5 "Varios." For 1973 see José García Payón to Ignacio Marquina, March 9, 1974, ADDMP, exp. "El Tajín," ref. B/3.04(z61-2) (02)/I. For 1976 see ADDMP, exp. "El Tajín," ref. B/3.04(z61-2)(02)/I, leg. 2 (note that this series is missing August, which I extrapolated by averaging monthly visitation between July and November). For 1977 see ADDMP, exp. "El Tajín," ref. B/3.04(z61-2)(02)/I, leg. 2. Otherwise, I have not adjusted the reported statistics.

Notes

Preface

1. Kelly, "In the Shadow of El Tajín," 22.
2. Younging, *Elements of Indigenous Style*, 18.
3. Younging, *Elements of Indigenous Style*, 65, 77.
4. Smail and Shryock, "History and the 'Pre,'" 713.
5. García Mora, "Mesoamérica."
6. For a more detailed consideration of this category, see Narotzky, "Where Have All the Peasants Gone?"
7. Younging, *Elements of Indigenous Style*, 113–15.
8. Weiss, "The Interlocutor Slot," 948.

Introduction

1. María Elena Ferral, "Avanza destrucción de vestigios arqueológicos en El Tajín," *El Heraldo de Poza Rica*, September 4, 2019, https://elheraldodepozarica.com .mx/estado/papantla/76097-avanza-destruccion-de-vestigios-arqueologicos -en-el-tajin.html; Rosalía Vergara, "Denuncian destrucción de patrimonio cultural en El Tajín," *Proceso*, August 23, 2019, https://www.proceso.com.mx /cultura/2019/8/23/denuncian-destruccion-de-patrimonio-cultural-en-el -tajin-229971.html; María Elena Ferral, "Se rompe el diálogo entre el INAH y los custodios de El Tajín," *Quinto Poder de Veracruz*, September 8, 2019 (site discontinued).
2. José Topete, "Pide AMLO castigo contra quienes dañaron zona arqueológica de El Tajín," *Al Calor Político*, August 29, 2019, https://www.alcalorpolitico.com /informacion/pide-amlo-castigo-contra-quienes-daniaron-zona-arqueologica -de-el-tajin-296914.html.
3. Pedro Matías, "Disputa de tierras comunales deja un muerto y dos heridos en Santa Cruz Xoxocotlán, Oaxaca," *Proceso*, November 19, 2019, https://www .proceso.com.mx/nacional/estados/2019/11/19/disputa-de-tierras-comunales -deja-un-muerto-dos-heridos-en-santa-cruz-xoxocotlan-oaxaca-video-234509 .html; Nahmad Molinari, "Problemática social."

4. Centro de Derechos Humanos Fray Bartolomé de Las Casas, A.C., "Informe preliminar."

5. See, among others, Benavides, *Making Ecuadorian Histories*; Mortensen, "Copán Past and Present"; Cojti Ren, "Maya Archaeology"; Escallón, "Afro-Descendant Heritage in Brazil"; Alexandrino Ocaña, "Seeking Rights."

6. Comparable to a county, borough, or parish, the Mexican municipality (municipio) is a second-level administrative division under a state government (in this case, Veracruz de Ignacio de la Llave). This administrative division, and the territorial extension to which it refers, varied over the course of the nineteenth and twentieth centuries. Belmonte Guzmán, *La organización territorial*.

7. Secretaría de Cultura, *Manual general*, 25.

8. Meskell, "Archaeological Ethnography," 84.

9. Clarke, "Archaeology," 6.

10. Cleere, "Introduction: The Rationale," discusses the development of heritage management in global context. For general characterizations of Mexican archaeology along these lines, see Gándara, *La arqueología oficial mexicana*; Martínez Muriel, "Archaeological Research"; Vázquez León, *El Leviatán arqueológico*; Robles García and Corbett, "Heritage Resource Management." Given their close associations, I do not sharply distinguish between archaeology and heritage management before the 1990s (see chapter 6).

11. Brading, "Manuel Gamio," 78.

12. For perspectives on Mesoamerica as an object of research, see Joyce, "Mesoamerica"; Vázquez León, *El Leviatán arqueológico*, 45–94.

13. Byrne, "Counter-Mapping," 611.

14. Trouillot, *Silencing the Past*, 29.

15. Castañeda, *In the Museum*, 98.

16. Leventhal et al., "Community Heritage Project"; Diserens Morgan and Leventhal, "Maya of the Past."

17. "Ley federal sobre monumentos," 7.

18. In archaeology, uses of "political economy" range from discussions of ancient state economies to contemporary questions of equality and knowledge production; compare uses of the term in Smith, "Ancient State Economies," 76–78, and Conkey and Williams, "Original Narratives," 111–14. My use is indebted to work in critical archaeology, heritage studies, and anthropological political economy. See Patterson, "Political Economy of Archaeology"; Niklasson, *Funding Matters*; Meskell, *Nature of Heritage*; Lafrenz Samuels, *Mobilizing Heritage*; Wolf, *Europe*; Roseberry, *Anthropologies and Histories*.

19. Engels, "Anti-Dühring," 135.

20. Hollowell and Mortensen, "Introduction," 10. See also MacEachern, "Seeing"; Plets, "Heritage Statecraft."

21. Cusicanqui, "Ch'ixinakax Utxiwa," 102.

22. Roseberry, "Political Economy," 179.

23. Meskell, "World Heritage and WikiLeaks," 73.
24. Trigger, "Alternative Archaeologies," 359. Trigger's work was key in calling archaeologists' attention to the politics of archaeology and helped to spawn an important literature on the topic. See Gathercole and Lowenthal, *Politics of the Past*; Fowler, "Uses of the Past"; Díaz-Andreu and Champion, *Nationalism and Archaeology*; Kohl and Fawcett, *Nationalism, Politics*; Kohl, "Nationalism and Archaeology"; Meskell, *Archaeology Under Fire*.
25. Bernal, "Effect of Settlement Pattern," 397; Lorenzo, "Archaeology South," 201; see also Gillingham, *Cuauhtémoc's Bones*.
26. Bernal, *History of Mexican Archaeology*, 14.
27. López Hernández, "Ruptura y tradición," 111.
28. On this period, see Garrigan, *Collecting Mexico*; Bueno, *Pursuit of Ruins*; Rutsch, *Entre el campo*; López Hernández, *En busca del alma*; Kelly, "Waking the Gods."
29. Considering the discipline's nineteenth-century (and colonial) inheritances productively complicates this view. See Achim, *From Idols to Antiquity*; Mucher, *Before American History*; Sellen, *In the Shadow of Charnay*; López Hernández, *En busca del alma*.
30. Salas Landa, "(In)Visible Ruins," 48.
31. Coggins, "Illicit Traffic"; Renfrew, *Loot*; Barker, "Looting."
32. Heath, "Economic Aspects"; Matsuda, "Ethics of Archaeology"; Bonilla, "Pothunter's Livelihood"; Luke, "Diplomats, Banana Cowboys."
33. For entry points into this vast literature, see Boone, *Collecting the Pre-Columbian Past*; Chase and Chase, *Market for Mesoamerica*. Outside of Mesoamerica, see González-Ruibal, "Ethics of Archaeology."
34. Joyce, "Making Markets," 5.
35. A study of Mesoamerican materials auctioned at Sotheby's U.S. branch recorded a total of 7 artifacts identified as "Tajín" auctioned between 1966 and 2010; by comparison, artifacts recorded as Maya numbered 3,263. Categories like "Totonac" (22) and "Veracruz" (1,174) could possibly include Tajín materials, but the latter likely includes Huastec, Nahua, and Olmec materials. Regardless, the proportion remains relatively minor. See Levine and Martínez de Luna, "Museum Salvage," 266.
36. Contrast Covert, "Reframing Guanajuato's Indigenous Past," on the Bajío.
37. "Anthropological practices of the nineteenth and twentieth centuries invented Maya *culture and civilization*, [and] the tourist industry of the region must be understood as the 'product' and extension of our science." Castañeda, *In the Museum*, 8. Italics in original.
38. Lorenzo, "Archaeology South," 201.
39. Covert, *San Miguel de Allende*; Jolly, *Creating Pátzcuaro, Creating Mexico*; see also López, *Crafting Mexico*.
40. See overviews in Wood, "Introduction"; Berger, *Development of Mexico's Tourism*; Saragoza, "Selling of Mexico."

41. Castellanos, *Indigenous Dispossession*; Córdoba Azcárate, *Stuck with Tourism*.

42. Córdoba Azcárate, *Stuck with Tourism*; see also Brulotte, *Between Art and Artifact*; Taylor, *On Being Maya*.

43. Nicholas and Hollowell, "Ethical Challenges"; Atalay, "Indigenous Archaeology"; McNiven, "Theoretical Challenges"; see reviews in Watkins, "Through Wary Eyes"; Colwell, "Collaborative Archaeologies."

44. This is the classic definition of Indigenous archaeology. See Nicholas and Andrews, "Indigenous Archaeology," 3.

45. Schneider and Hayes, "Epistemic Colonialism," 129.

46. The common ethnohistorical definition comes from Kelly and Palerm, *Tajín Totonac*. For an archaeological definition, see Medellín Zenil, *Cerámicas del Totonacapan*; and for a critical review and alternative definitions, see Mora, "Espacios." "Totonacapan" should not be confused with Totonicapán, Guatemala, named by the Tlaxcalans who participated in the conquest of Guatemala. See Christenson, *Title of Totonicapán*.

47. Lack of pre-twentieth-century linguistic material makes the study of Totonacan languages a challenge. See Morales Lara, "Estudios lingüísticos," 214; MacKay and Trechsel, "Bibliografía de las lenguas." Brown et al., "Totozoquean," 368, suggest that Totonacan and Mixe-Zoquean languages share a common ancestor whose antiquity is comparable to Proto-Indo-European. Others are more conservative; see MacKay and Trechsel, "Alternative Reconstruction."

48. INEGI, "Población."

49. For introductions to Totonac history and ethnography, see Masferrer Kan, "Las condiciones históricas"; Chenaut, *Aquellos que vuelan*; Deans-Smith, "Native Peoples"; Trejo Barrientos, "Los totonacos."

50. Torquemada, *Monarquía indiana*, 381–85. For the broader Sierra context of the period, see García Martínez, *Los pueblos*; for Teotihuacan, see Cowgill, *Ancient Teotihuacan*.

51. Interpreting the cultural history of north-central Veracruz shares some of the challenges of determining the ethnic identity of those who built El Tajín (see notes 106 and 107). For archaeological and historical evaluations of Huastec presence over time, see Wilkerson, "Eastern Mesoamerica"; Koontz, "Iconographic Relationships"; Maldonado Vite, "El antiguo Tochpan." The presence of early-colonial Totonac-Nahuatl bilingualism and the prevalence of Nahuatl place-names suggest the pre-Aztec antiquity of Nahuatl-speakers in the region. For the nature, timing, and implications of this presence, see Kelly and Palerm, *Tajín Totonac*, 16–24; Masferrer Kan, "Las condiciones históricas"; Wilkerson, "Nahua Presence"; Nahmad Molinari, "El debate"; Trejo Barrientos, "Paisaje de tormenta," 60–110.

52. For the Aztec conquests, see Maldonado Vite, "El antiguo Tochpan," 206–15; Kelly and Palerm, *Tajín Totonac*, 20–24.

53. Carballo, *Collision of Worlds*. The ethnolinguistic identities of Cempoala's inhabitants, and that identification's implications for Totonac history, are a matter of debate. See García Márquez, "El posclásico en Veracruz."

54. Wilkerson, "Eastern Mesoamerica," 46; Gerhard, *Guide*, 218–20.

55. The given figures are 15,000 or 16,000 men at Cortés's arrival and 300 at the time of writing; Acuña, "Relación de Hueytlalpa," 174. The same document, sometimes known as the *Relación de Papantla*, is reprinted in Brizuela Absalón, "Papantla en las Relaciones." Wilkerson discusses the estimate of 60,000; see "Eastern Mesoamerica," 46. Frederick considers it "assuredly exaggerated"; see *Riot!*, 16. The degree of decline, if not the exact figures, is supported by contemporary sources. For 1547–48, Papantla and "Tuspa and Tomilco," said to be coterminous, were reported to have a total of 1,515 men; see García Castro, *Suma de visitas*, 251. For 1610, de la Mota y Escobar reported "more than 300 married Indians, tributaries, which are all congregated at this site"; see *Memoriales*, 72.

56. Carballo, *Collision of Worlds*, 109, gives 10,500 residents; Márquez, "Cempoala," 10, gives a range of 15,000–20,000. For the 1609 figure, see de la Mota y Escobar, *Memoriales*, 56.

57. De la Mota y Escobar, *Memoriales*, 72.

58. De la Mota y Escobar, *Memoriales*, 74. De Tapia Sosa was the grandson of encomendero Andrés de Tapia, who received Papantla's tributes after the 1520s; see Gerhard, *Guide*, 218.

59. Brizuela Absalón, "Noticias," 50.

60. Gerhard, *Guide*, 219; Frederick, *Riot!*, 31.

61. Frederick, *Riot!*

62. Moreno Coello, "Alcaldes mayores y subdelegados."

63. Ducey, *A Nation of Villages*; Ducey, "La territorialidad indígena"; Ruiz Medrano, "Rebeliones indígenas"; Luna Santiago, "El motín de Papantla"; Frederick, "A Fractured Pochgui."

64. Frederick, *Riot!* For Afrodescendants and legacies in the region, see Hall, *Ethnographic Study of Afro-Mexicans*.

65. López Luján, "El Tajín," 76.

66. Cañizares-Esguerra, *How to Write*; Brading, *Origins of Mexican Nationalism*.

67. The most thorough chronology of visits to El Tajín is Ladrón de Guevara, *Imagen y pensamiento*, 123–36.

68. Ducey, "Village, Nation, and Constitution"; Ducey, "La comunidad liberal"; Ducey, "Indios liberales." The Totonacs were far from alone in theorizing liberal political practice for their own ends; see Caplan, *Indigenous Citizens*.

69. Ruiz Gordillo, *Serafín Olarte*; Santander Ontiveros, *Entre vainillales y fusiles*; compare the interpretations of Flores D., *La revolución de Olarte*; Masferrer Kan, "Los factores étnicos."

70. Chenaut, *Aquellos que vuelan*, 94–95.

71. Bausa, "Bosquejo geográfico," 379–80. De razón refers to a set of characteristics associated with Spanishness; these may include, but are not limited to, skin tone, manner of dress, and language.

72. Chenaut, *Aquellos que vuelan*, 118–223; Skerrit Gardner, *Colonos franceses y modernización*.

73. My overview draws from the useful syntheses of Rugeley, *Epic Mexico*; Sherman, Deeds, and Meyer, *Course of Mexican History*; Moreno-Brid and Ros, *Development and Growth*; Cárdenas, "La economía mexicana"; Bethell, *Mexico since Independence*; Dawson, *First World Dreams*; Alexander, "Mexican Politics."

74. Lurtz, *From the Grounds Up*, 6.

75. Bulmer-Thomas, *Economic History*, 46–81; Knight, "Export-Led Growth," 127.

76. Valiant, *Ornamental Nationalism*, 136–37.

77. Bueno, "Forjando Patrimonio"; Palacios, *Maquinaciones neoyorquinas*; Ruiz Martínez, *Género, ciencia y política*.

78. Tenorio-Trillo, *Mexico at the World's Fairs*; Rutsch, *Entre el campo*; Garrigan, *Collecting Mexico*; Valiant, *Ornamental Nationalism*.

79. Earle, *Return of the Native*, 183.

80. For introductions to the historiography, see Knight and Rodriguez, "Mexican Revolution, 1910–1940." Knight, *Mexican Revolution*, and Hart, *Revolutionary Mexico*, remain canonical accounts.

81. Gillingham, *Unrevolutionary Mexico*, 2.

82. Aviña, *Specters of Revolution*; McCormick, *Logic of Compromise*. The classic account of the Tlatelolco Massacre is Poniatowska, *La noche de Tlatelolco*.

83. Export-led development remained key during the first decades of the twentieth century. See Topik, "Revolution, the State." For ISI in comparative perspective, see Baer, "Import Substitution and Industrialization"; Cardoso and Helwege, *Latin America's Economy*, 84–99.

84. Moreno-Brid and Ros, *Development and Growth*, 107–12.

85. Moreno-Brid and Ros, *Development and Growth*, 6; Haber et al., *Mexico since 1980*, provide a contrasting interpretation.

86. Gamio, *Forjando patria (pro-nacionalismo)*; Alonso, "Territorializing the Nation."

87. See Dawson, *Indian and Nation*, and Saldívar, *Prácticas cotidianas del estado*, for entry points.

88. The Inspectorate of Monuments functioned as a part of the Secretaría de Justicia y Instrucción Pública (1886–1901) and, later, the Secretaría de Instrucción Pública y Bellas Artes (1901–16). The office briefly functioned as the Dirección de Estudios Arqueológicos y Etnográficos (1917–18) and the Dirección de Antropología (1919–25) as part of the Secretaria de Agricultura y Fomento. The Dirección de Antropología was moved to the Secretaría de Educación Pública in 1925. As part of the SEP, the office became the Departamento

de Antropología (1925) and the Dirección de Arqueología (1926–29). The Dirección de Arqueología was reorganized into the Departamento de Monumentos Prehispánicos (1930) of the Departamento de Monumentos Artísticos, Arqueológicos e Históricos; the former was absorbed into the INAH at its 1939 founding. On this period, see Gallegos Ruiz, *Antología de documentos*, 271; Martínez Acuña, *Catálogo selectivo*, 21–35; Vázquez León, "Mexico"; López Hernández, "La arqueología mexicana."

89. Lorenzo, "Mexico"; Robles García and Corbett, "Heritage Resource Management."

90. Gándara, *La arqueología oficial mexicana*.

91. Knight, "History, Heritage, and Revolution"; Lorenzo, "Archaeology South."

92. For the broader intellectual currents of the period, see Rosemblatt, *Science and Politics*. Canonical critiques are found in Warman et al., *Antropología mexicana*. More recent evaluations include Saldívar, *Prácticas cotidianas del estado*; Taylor, *Indigeneity*; Varner, *La Raza Cosmética*.

93. Recent research has approached these transitions in the context of global activism and regional history. See Lewis, *Rethinking Mexican Indigenismo*; Dillingham, *Oaxaca Resurgent*; Campos, "Rasgos del indigenismo participativo."

94. Moreno-Brid and Ros, *Development and Growth*, 128–29; Cárdenas, "La economía mexicana," 521.

95. Cárdenas, "La economía mexicana," 526.

96. Dawson, *First World Dreams*, 9–10; see also Williams, "Path of Economic Liberalism."

97. Williams, "Path of Economic Liberalism," 750. For the unexpected outcomes of ending land reform, see Perramond, "Rise, Fall, and Reconfiguration."

98. Dawson, *First World Dreams*, 44.

99. Centeno, *Democracy Within Reason*, 462.

100. Dawson, *First World Dreams*; compare Haber et al., *Mexico since 1980*.

101. Coffey, "From Nation to Community."

102. For Mexico, see Saldívar, "'It's Not Race'"; Saldívar, "Uses and Abuses." For broader hemispheric context, see Yashar, "Democracy, Indigenous Movements"; Hale, "Neoliberal Multiculturalism"; Gutiérrez Chong, "Ethnopolitics." Compare Escallón, "Afro-Descendant Heritage in Brazil"; Hale, "Resistencia Para Que?"; Hooker, *Black and Indigenous Resistance*.

103. McGuire, *Archaeology as Political Action*, 140–87; Vázquez León, *El Leviatán arqueológico*.

104. Tovar y de Teresa, "Hacia una nueva política"; for a critical evaluation, see Yáñez Reyes, "Antecedentes, trayectoria y cambios."

105. See, respectively, Benavides, *Making Ecuadorian Histories*; López Hernández, *En busca del alma*; Castañeda, *In the Museum*; Breglia, *Monumental Ambivalence*; Cox Hall, *Framing a Lost City*; Rice, *Making Machu Picchu*; Podgorny, "'Silent and Alone'"; Gallegos Ruiz, *Antología de documentos*.

106. For recent scholarly syntheses of Classic Veracruz and El Tajín, see Arnold and Pool, "Charting Classic Veracruz"; Koontz, *Lightning Gods*; Nahmad Molinari, "El debate." My account follows the line of research represented by Pascual Soto, *El Tajín*; Wilkerson, "Huastec Presence"; García Payón, "Archaeology of Central Veracruz." For an alternative perspective, especially on chronology, see Brueggemann, "El problema cronológica"; Reyes López, "Análisis cuantitativo"; Raesfeld, "New Discoveries."

107. For reviews, see Daneels, "El patrón de asentamiento," 37–63; Arnold, Pool, and Diehl, "Historical Currents"; Nahmad Molinari, "El debate." El Tajín was traditionally identified with the Totonacs. See Spinden, "Place of Tajin"; García Payón, "Quiénes construyeron el Tajín." Discussions of Huastec presence are found in Du Solier, "La cerámica arqueológica"; Wilkerson, "Huastec Presence." Other research prefers the "Tajín culture" designation; see Brüggemann, "Otra vez." See Pascual Soto, *El Tajín*, on the probable multiethnicity of the city's inhabitants.

108. Johnson, *Ideas of Landscape*, 3.

109. Scholars have critiqued the ideological baggage of the term "landscape," its emphasis on the visual, and its relationships with early-modern bourgeois ideas of power over nature. See Cosgrove, "Prospect"; Stewart, *What Nature Suffers*, 11–12.

110. Olivier, *Dark Abyss of Time*, 63.

111. When distinguishing between these places, I usually refer to the settlement as the "community of El Tajín," following local usage, and the state-managed facility as "the site."

112. Breglia, *Monumental Ambivalence*, 14.

113. These are the communities most often considered "local" to the archaeological site, and the 2001 declaration spurred important academic work. See Nahmad Molinari and Rodríguez Martínez, "Informe del programa"; Valdovinos Ortega, "El surgimiento"; Trejo González, "Los que siguen volando"; Cabrera Rodríguez, "Análisis socioecológico."

114. Meskell, "Archaeological Ethnography," 84.

115. Colwell-Chanthaphonh, "Archaeology on the Periphery," 254.

116. Meskell, "Archaeological Ethnography"; Holley-Kline, "Contextualizing Archaeology's 'Locals.'"

117. Holley-Kline and Papazian, "Heritage Trekking."

118. Kemper and Marcucci, "Ethnographic Archive"; on Kelly, see Fowler and Kemper, "Isabel T. Kelly."

119. Lewis, "Anthropology and Colonialism."

120. Deloria, "Deep Politics of Knowledge," 243.

121. Kelly and Palerm, *Tajín Totonac*, ix. On Kelly's legacy as a teacher, see Pérez Lizuar, "De Franz Boas."

122. Isabel T. Kelly to George Foster, January 27, 1947, NAA-RISA, Box 8.

123. Bruchac, *Savage Kin*, 19; see also Sullivan, *Unfinished Conversations*.

124. Murdock, Clellan, and Hudson, *Outline of Cultural Materials*.
125. During my research Kelly's field notes were housed in a filing cabinet designated Box 1. For locating these references, I refer to the Murdock classification (number and category) assigned by Kelly.
126. See Reyes Cruz, "Just Cite Graciela?"
127. After Meskell and Pels, "Introduction."

1. Lands

1. Signers redacted to CNDH, February 2, 2016, INAI, Folio 3510000069118, exp. CNDH/4/2016/2214/Q, f. 7.
2. Signers redacted to CNDH, February 2, 2016, INAI, Folio 3510000069118, exp. CNDH/4/2016/2214/Q, f. 7.
3. Breglia, *Monumental Ambivalence*.
4. Meskell, *Nature of Heritage*, 20; West, Igoe, and Brockington, "Parks and Peoples"; see also Colchester, "Conservation Policy"; Brockington, *Fortress Conservation*.
5. Herzfeld, *Evicted from Eternity*; Abu El Haj, *Facts on the Ground*.
6. Wakild, *Revolutionary Parks*, 14.
7. The relationship between natural and cultural conservation in Mexico warrants further study. One reason for the divergence may have to do with the Porfirian debates around partage policies, which have no parallel in Porfirian forestry; see Cámara de Diputados, *Diario de los debates*, 1:542, and commentary by Kelly, "Waking the Gods," 83–92; Díaz y de Ovando, *Memoria de un debate*. On Porfirian forestry, see Wakild, *Revolutionary Parks*, 22–27.
8. Walsh Sanderson, *Land Reform in Mexico*.
9. Perramond, "Rise, Fall, and Reconfiguration," 357.
10. Following the calculations of Cohen and Solinis-Casparius, "Micropolitics of Public Archaeology," 331, 343; see also Ardren, "Conversations."
11. After González-Robles, "Limbos arqueológicos."
12. Roseberry, "Hegemony," 361.
13. See Li, "What Is Land?"; Blomley, "Making Space for Property"; Blomley, "Making Private Property." For Mexico and Veracruz, see Craib, *Cartographic Mexico*.
14. Olivier, *Dark Abyss of Time*, 62–63.
15. Kourí, *A Pueblo Divided*, 71.
16. Kourí, *A Pueblo Divided*, 75–78.
17. Kourí, *A Pueblo Divided*, 60–62. On defining Papantla haciendas, see Xochihua García, "Dinámicas económicas," 17–20.
18. Ducey, *A Nation of Villages*, 134.
19. *Memoria leída*, 30; Hojital likely refers to the community now known as Ojital Viejo, from which San Antonio Ojital split in the 1930s. See Brizuela Absalón, "Un asentamiento campesino," 115–19.

20. Velasco Toro and García Ruiz, *Perfiles de la desamortización*; Kourí, *A Pueblo Divided*; Gatti and Chenaut, *La costa totonaca*. Compare Johnson, *Ideas of Landscape*, on enclosure and Chang, "Enclosures of Land," on allotment.

21. Hale, *Transformation of Liberalism*, 4.

22. De la Luz Enríquez, "Memoria," 2304.

23. Kourí, *A Pueblo Divided*.

24. See Pérez Castañeda, "Condueñazgos in Mexico."

25. Elsewhere, condueñazgos continued to exist until well into the twentieth century. See Ohmstede and Schryer, "Las sociedades agrarias."

26. Santiago Simbrón to Ángel Palerm, May 28, 1948, ITKEA, s. 2. b. 1, 103 Lands. Polutla is a community located to the northeast of Papantla.

27. Kourí, *A Pueblo Divided*, 187–289.

28. Kourí, *A Pueblo Divided*, 280.

29. Kourí, *A Pueblo Divided*, 283.

30. Brizuela Absalón, "Desamortización de bienes."

31. Kourí, *A Pueblo Divided*, 74, 148.

32. Callon, "Some Elements of a Sociology," 211–14.

33. Chenaut, "Comunidad y ley," 86.

34. Kelly and Palerm, *Tajín Totonac*, 55.

35. For this calculation, I began with the list of landowners in 1896, from "Acta general de reparto de los terrenos del Lote No. 19 denominado 'Ojital y Potrero,' entre 205 condueños," AHPM, Fondo Expropriación, c. 1566, exp. 44050. To infer locality, I cross-referenced listed recipients of Ojital y Potrero parcels with the merchant elite discussed by Kourí, *A Pueblo Divided*, and "Tajín (property, inheritance)," ITKEA, s. 2, b. 42, fol. 330332, which describes individuals as "de Papantla" (i.e., identified as nonlocal by Isabel Kelly's interlocutors in 1947). This approach identifies the owners of 43 parcels (21 percent) as nonlocal, or 162 (79 percent) as probably local. The identification of nonlocals should thus be regarded as a minimum.

36. Modesto González to Ángel Palerm, May 21, 1948, ITKEA, s. 2, b. 1, 411 Oral Historical.

37. The original source is no longer accessible. The most complete transcription I have located is "Informe de actividades generals y balance del estado de la investigación del programa No. 9: Demografía y etnografía de Tajín, correspondiente al año de 1991," AT-CNA, Estado de Veracruz, vol. 29-85, f. 23. See also Brizuela Absalón, "Desamortización de bienes," 5.

38. Dunnell and Dancey, "Siteless Survey," 271.

39. Muñoz was a nephew of Porfirio Díaz and was a Veracruz state congressman. See Kourí, *A Pueblo Divided*, 260.

40. This control was formalized with the Law of Archaeological Monuments of 1897. See Litvak King, González R., and del Refugio González, *Arqueología y derecho*, 187, for the relevant portion of the Ley sobre ocupación y enajenación

de terrenos baldios of 1894. For the law and state archaeology, see Bueno, *Pursuit of Ruins*, 80–88. Bausa, "Bosquejo geográfico," 411, notes that El Tajín was under the dominion of the national government, but there is no evidence that this apparent legal ownership had any effect on life in and around the site.

41. Compare Gallegos Tellez Rojo, "Teotihuacan," 262–64, and see Bueno, *Pursuit of Ruins*, 81, on the conflict between the Law of Monuments and private property rights.

42. See Agapito G. Fontecilla to Leopoldo Batres, April 29, 1910, AGN-IPBA, c. 112, exp. 71, f. 7–9.

43. Lorenzo Xochihua to José Luis Lorenzo, February 3, 1947, ITKEA, s. 2, b. 1, 3424 Objects and Sacred Places.

44. Modesto González and Lorenzo Xochihua to Isabel Kelly, May 14, 1947, ITKEA, s. 2, b. 1, 103 Lands.

45. Gallegos Tellez Rojo, "Teotihuacan"; López Palacios, "Algunos aspectos."

46. Leopoldo Armengual to Leopoldo Batres, March 16, 1904, ADDMP, exp. "El Tajín," ref. B/311.32(z61-2)/1, leg. 1.

47. Brading, "Manuel Gamio"; Saldívar, "'It's Not Race.'"

48. Bueno, *Pursuit of Ruins*; Kelly, "Waking the Gods."

49. García Vega, "Exploraciones en El Tajín."

50. Salas Landa, "(In)Visible Ruins," 47.

51. See Gustavo Segura to Ignacio García Téllez, June 12, 1935, ADDMP, exp. "El Tajín," ref. B/311.1(z61-2)/1, f. 26.

52. Agapito, Espiridion, and Francisco Juárez to C. Secretario de Instrucción Pública, May 20, 1935, ADDMP, ref. B/311.1(z61-2)/1, f. 20–20r; José María and Rosalía García to C. Secretario de Instrucción Pública, May 20, 1935, ADDMP, ref. B/311.1(z61-2)/1, f. 21–21r; Marciano Juárez to C. Secretario de Instrucción Pública, May 20, 1935, ADDMP, ref. B/311.1(z61-2)/1, f. 22. Kelly's genealogy for José María García lists him as the son of Francisco García. See "José María García," ITKEA, s. 2, b. 16, fol. 33012187.

53. Agapito, Espiridion, and Francisco Juárez to Lázaro Cárdenas, May 20, 1935, ADDMP, exp. "El Tajín," ref. B/311.1(z61-2)/1, f. 15. *Chijol* (*Piscidia piscipula*), *frijolillo* (*Cojoba arborea*), and *alzaprima* (*Carpodiptera ameliae* Lundell) are local tree species.

54. Ferry, *Not Ours Alone*, 13; see also 211–14.

55. Rozental, "Nature of Patrimonio."

56. Agapito, Espiridion, and Francisco Juárez to C. Secretario de Instrucción Pública, May 20, 1935, ADDMP, ref. B/311.1(z61-2)/1, f. 20r.

57. Agapito, Espiridion, and Francisco Juárez to C. Secretario de Instrucción Pública, May 20, 1935, ADDMP, ref. B/311.1(z61-2)/1, f. 20r.

58. Alfonso Toro to Agapito Juarez and demás firmantes, July 9, 1935, ADDMP, exp. "El Tajín," ref. B/311.1(z61-2)/1, f. 25.

59. Vázquez León, *El Leviatán arqueológico*; Rozental, "Nature of Patrimonio."

60. Interestingly, there is a file regarding a 1950 ejido solicitation for El Tajín. See "El Tajín," AGEV–Archivo Administrativo, Fondo Comisión Agraria Mixta, Mpio. Papantla, exp. 4205. The solicitation was apparently discontinued after 1958, when few of the original solicitants still lived in El Tajín.

61. Armstrong-Fumero, "Artifactual Surface," 1304–5.

62. Wakild, *Revolutionary Parks*, 122–48.

63. Daneels, "José García Payón," 31.

64. "Map from copy loaned by Rosalino González," ITKEA, s. 2, b. 1, 103 Lands.

65. Modesto González to Isabel Kelly, May 18, 1948, ITKEA, s. 2, b. 1, 1072 Population Distribution.

66. Parcel 76 was reportedly sold after the owner died intestate, by "a lawyer who ended the disputes, [by] himself buying [from] the majority of the claimants, and the lawyer later sold to the Stanford [Company]. . . . This lawyer was also the proxy or legal representative of the [Stanford] Company." Jacinto García to Ángel Palerm, May 29, 1948, ITKEA, s. 2, b. 1, 1533 Extractive Industries.

67. "Tajín (property, wealth, inheritance)," ITKEA, s. 2, b. 42, fol. 330232.

68. Ojital y Potrero was not representative in this sense. By the conclusion of land reform in 1992, about 42 percent (145,404.54 ha) of the ex-cantón (approx. 350,000 ha) and about 40 percent (58,250 ha) of the municipality of Papantla (145,650 ha) were ejidos. See Ramírez Melgarejo, *La política del Estado*, Cuadro A2.

69. Isabel Kelly to George Foster, January 27, 1947, NAA-RISA, b. 7.

70. Tutino, "Rural Economy and Society," 705; see Tutino, *From Insurrection to Revolution*.

71. Ortiz Espejel, *La cultura asediada*, 52.

72. Velázquez Hernández, *Cuando los arrieros*, 103–4.

73. González-Montagut, "Factors That Contributed," 109.

74. Velázquez Hernández, *Cuando los arrieros*, 102; Villanueva, "Region and Power," 252. See Ortiz Espejel, *La cultura asediada*, 41–45, on deforestation.

75. Villanueva, "Region and Power," 252.

76. Between 1940 and 2000 the communities of Lagunilla, Zapotal Santa Cruz, and San Lorenzo Tajín fissioned off from El Tajín (formerly Potrero), and San Antonio Ojital and Ojital Nuevo fissioned off from Ojital, now known as Ojital Viejo.

77. "Appendix (1965) property and wealth," ITKEA, s. 2, b. 42, fol. 331718. See also Harvey and Kelly, "The Totonac," 664.

78. "Memoria descriptive de los trabajos topográficos relativos al deslinde de la zona arqueológica de El Tajín," ADDMP, exp. "El Tajín," ref. B/311.1(z61-2)/1.

79. See, for example, García Payón, "El Tajín, descripción y comentarios."

80. José García Payón to Ignacio Marquina, June 22, 1973, ADDMP, exp. "El Tajín," ref. B/311.32(z61-2)/1, leg. 5.

81. Kasburg, *Die Totonaken*, 112.

82. Source and access limitations prevent me from determining the rate of land loss, but diverse sources independently agree on the general extent. See Kasburg, *Die Totonaken*, 86–87; Brizuela Absalón, "Marco geográfico y cultural," 39–40; Villanueva, "Region and Power," 55–56, 249–51.

83. For 1947 I have preferred Kelly's unpublished data, found in "Tajín (property, wealth, inheritance)," ITKEA, s. 2, b. 42, fol. 330232. Kelly's calculation is based on an analysis of 175 parcels, or 85 percent of Ojital y Potrero. I follow her in considering this figure representative. Even if the 30 parcels for which Kelly did not have data was owned by a nonlocal, that would result in a total of 152 parcels (74 percent) owned by Totonac residents of the area. For 1989 I have relied on Kasburg, *Die Totonaken*. Brizuela Absalón, "Marco geográfico y cultural," 40, reports a slightly lower number: 354 hectares owned by 26 residents.

84. Brüggemann, "Tajín en números," 57.

85. Alfonso Medellín Zenil and Jurgen Kurt Bruggemann to Joaquin García Barcena, January 6, 1984, AT-CIV, Tajín (Proyecto) Originales. Notably, this was the response to the INAH's request for clarification on the issue. See Joaquin García-Barcena to Alfonso Medellín Zenil and Jurgen Kurt Bruggemann, December 16, 1983, AHI-INAH, Colección Coordinación Nacional de Centros Regionales, c. 1, exp. 13, f. 7.

86. Rogelio Franco Castán to Isaías Trejo Sánchez, August 21, 2017, INAI, Folio 3510000069118, exp. CNDH/4/2016/2214/Q, f. 687–88. See also Brizuela Absalón, "Un asentamiento campesino."

87. See "Convenio," INAI, Folio 3510000069118, exp. CNDH/4/2016/2214/Q, f. 548.

88. Isaías Trejo Sánchez to recipient redacted, October 30, 2017, INAI, Folio 3510000069118, exp. CNDH/4/2016/2214/Q, f. 891–92.

89. Isaías Trejo Sánchez to recipient redacted, October 30, 2017, INAI, Folio 3510000069118, exp. CNDH/4/2016/2214/Q, f. 898.

90. Isaías Trejo Sánchez to recipient redacted, October 30, 2017, INAI, Folio 3510000069118, exp. CNDH/4/2016/2214/Q, f. 905.

91. Isaías Trejo Sánchez to recipient redacted, October 30, 2017, INAI, Folio 3510000069118, exp. CNDH/4/2016/2214/Q, f. 898.

92. Zúñiga Bravo, "Las transformaciones del territorio"; Maciel Martínez, "Preservación del patrimonio cultural"; Reyes García, "Ante Cumbre Tajín."

93. See "Decreto."

94. On Zonas de Monumentos Arqueológicos, see Paredes Gudiño, "Proceso de declaratorias."

95. "El Tajín, Expediente Técnico," November 2000, AT-CIV, 080 H47T, 2000, f. 50. For the 1976 delimitation, conducted by the INAH but with little apparent impact on life or land tenure at the site, see Ortiz Ceballos and Arellanos Melgarejo, "Delimitación de zonas arqueológicas."

96. Espinosa Rodríguez, "Estrategias y gestión," 124–25.

97. Nahmad Molinari and Rodríguez Martínez, "Informe del programa."
98. Herzfeld, "Spatial Cleansing."
99. For other examples of related outcomes, see Escallón, "Afro-Descendant Heritage in Brazil"; Hale, "Resistencia Para Que?"; Hooker, *Black and Indigenous Resistance*.
100. Signers redacted to CNDH, February 2, 2016, INAI, Folio 3510000069118, exp. CNDH/4/2016/2214/Q, f. 3–4.
101. AGN, Fondo Departamento de Petróleo, c. 231, exp. 2, f. 40.
102. Pascual Soto, *Guerreros de El Tajín*, 15–30. Perhaps the damage is more extensive but understudied, thanks to a lack of problem-oriented research in El Tajín; see review in Arnold, Pool, and Diehl, "Historical Currents."
103. Grove, *Discovering the Olmecs*, 135–65.

2. Oil

1. Salas Landa, "(In)Visible Ruins," 63–70.
2. Nahmad Molinari, "Informe de la temporada," 81; Trejo González, "Proyecto comunitario alternativo," 15.
3. Trejo González, "Ruta ecológica y cultural," 18.
4. Pascual Soto, *Guerreros de El Tajín*, 21.
5. The brick's only visible identification is "Evens H, ACM, S M." The mark likely refers to an Acme-brand brick manufactured by Evens & Howard Fire Brick Company of St. Louis between the mid-nineteenth and early twentieth centuries. "S M" may refer to the stiff-mud manufacturing process.
6. "Estado actual de la exploración y de los trabajos de conservación de los monumentos de la zona arqueológica del Tajín," AT-CIV, Estado de Veracruz, Tajín, vol. III, 1940–1953.
7. Lombardo de Ruiz and Solís Vicarte, *Antecedentes de las leyes*, 29; Vázquez León, *El Leviatán arqueológico*, 105.
8. Alexandrino Ocaña, "Seeking Rights"; on the Crown and mining, see Brading and Cross, "Colonial Silver Mining," 560–66; Brown, *History of Mining*.
9. Vázquez León, *El Leviatán arqueológico*, 104–22.
10. Riguzzi and Gerali, "Los veneros del emperador," 751–52.
11. Brown, *Oil and Revolution*, 93. Haber, Razo, and Maurer, *Politics of Property Rights*, 240–43, emphasize that subsoil wealth remained invested in the nation; only certain products (oil among them) gave ownership of the surface.
12. *Political Constitution*, 27.
13. For classic and contemporary entry points into the vast literature on this topic, see Meyer, *Mexico and the United States*; Brown and Knight, *Mexican Petroleum Industry*; Brown, *Oil and Revolution*; Santiago, *Ecology of Oil*, 205–356; Vergara, *Fueling Mexico*, 133–75. Government of Mexico, *Mexico's Oil*, offers a comprehensive portrait of the industry at expropriation.
14. Rodríguez García, *La arqueología en México*, 79–80.

15. Breglia, *Living with Oil*, 1–8; Ferry, *Not Ours Alone*, 207–14.

16. López Hernández and Pruneda Gallegos, "Dimes y diretes."

17. Frehner, *Finding Oil*.

18. Coombe and Baird, "Limits of Heritage," 338.

19. Knight, "Rise and Fall," 280.

20. For archaeological bitumen in El Tajín, see Krotser and Krotser, "Topografía y cerámica," 186–88. For Olmec uses of the same, see Wendt and Cyphers, "Olmec Used Bitumen."

21. On this period, see Gerali and Riguzzi, "Los inicios"; Álvarez de la Borda, *Los orígenes*; Brown, "Structure."

22. For legal background, see Haber, Maurer, and Razo, "When the Law." For international context, see Black, *Crude Reality*, 91–143.

23. Gerali and Riguzzi, "Los inicios," 77. On the Pennsylvania oil boom and its aftermath, see Black, *Petrolia*.

24. DeGolyer and Norman, "Furbero Oil Field," 270.

25. Autrey's name is also spelled Adolfo or Adolpho. Born in Alabama and raised in Texas, Adolphus Preston John Autrey (1835–1904) received his medical degree from the University of Nashville (now the Vanderbilt University School of Medicine) in 1856. Sympathetic to the Confederate faction of the American Civil War (1861–65), Autrey moved to Mexico in 1857 and was living in Papantla by around 1859. See "Dr. A. Autrey Dead," *Galveston Daily News*, February 25, 1904; Autrey de Ziebe, "Centenario de Casa Autrey," 88.

26. DeGolyer and Norman, "Furbero Oil Field," 270.

27. "La Firma Autrey y Autrey y Sucs," *Pan-American Review*, 1920, Edición especial extraordinaria dedicada al Estado de Tamaulipas; Adriana Ojeda and Kermith Zapata, "Los Autrey pierden hasta la casa," *El Universal*, February 10, 2000, https://archivo.eluniversal.com.mx/finanzas/4346.html.

28. Adolpho Autrey to John F. Dowling, March 2, 1892, AHPM, Fondo Expropriación, c. 3091, exp. 79548. The letter is translated and analyzed in Álvarez de la Borda, "Adolfo Autrey."

29. Adolpho Autrey to John F. Dowling, March 2, 1892, AHPM, Fondo Expropriación, c. 3091, exp. 79548, f. 29.

30. Adolpho Autrey to John F. Dowling, March 2, 1892, AHPM, Fondo Expropriación, c. 3091, exp. 79548, f. 33.

31. Fannie B. Ward, "The Papantla Pyramid: In the Depths of a Mexican Wilderness," *Boston Daily Globe*, May 31, 1886.

32. Adolpho Autrey to John F. Dowling, March 2, 1892, AHPM, Fondo Expropriación, c. 3091, exp. 79548, f. 30.

33. Adolpho Autrey to John F. Dowling, March 2, 1892, AHPM, Fondo Expropriación, c. 3091, exp. 79548, f. 31.

34. Adolpho Autrey to John F. Dowling, March 2, 1892, AHPM, Fondo Expropriación, c. 3091, exp. 79548, f. 32.

35. Adolpho Autrey to John F. Dowling, March 2, 1892, AHPM, Fondo Expropriación, c. 3091, exp. 79548, f. 32.
36. Autrey de Ziebe, "Centenario de Casa Autrey," 88. I have been unable to locate the original award.
37. Furber, *I Took Chances*, 91–101.
38. López Vallejo, "Entre la vainilla," 13–41.
39. "Furber's Properties," AHPM, Fondo Expropriación, c. 3182, exp. 81392, f. 71.
40. Capitanachi Luna, *Furbero*, 55; see López Vallejo, "Entre la vainilla." For measurements, see A. E. Buchanan to T. J. Ryder, May 27, 1906, AHPM, Fondo Expropriación, c. 3182, exp. 81392, f. 37.
41. Rodríguez Badillo, *La maquinita*; Holley-Kline, "El patrimonio industrial."
42. On Pearson, see Garner, *British Lions*.
43. Brown, *Oil and Revolution*, 59.
44. "Entrevista," f. 18. See also Santiago, *Ecology of Oil*, 83–84, 133–44; Kuecker, "Desert in a Tropical Wilderness," 310–18.
45. "Entrevista," f. 21.
46. Santiago, *Ecology of Oil*, 135.
47. Hamilton, *Oil Tales of Mexico*, 76.
48. Kuecker, "'Greatest and the Worst.'"
49. After Carrillo Dewar, *Industria petrolera*, 32.
50. Vergara, *Fueling Mexico*, 142.
51. See Vergara, *Fueling Mexico*, 159. Reasons for the decline are debated. Haber, Maurer, and Razo, "When the Law," argue that accessible oil simply ran out.
52. Carrillo Dewar, *Industria petrolera*, 42.
53. Capitanachi Luna, *Furbero*, 25–30.
54. Capitanachi Luna, *Furbero*, 155–59.
55. Quintal Avilés, "Industria petrolera," 78.
56. Straub, "Pre-Hispanic Mortuary Pottery," 218.
57. Brizuela Absalón, "Las compañías petroleras extranjeras," 6.
58. The concession was solicited by engineer Eduardo Prieto y Souza in 1929, as the representative of a number of landholders in Ojital y Potrero and the adjacent lots. "Concesión para explorer y explorer diversas parcelas de Ojital y Potrero," AGN, Fondo Departamento de Petróleo, c. 206, exp. 4, leg. 1. For details on the administrative history of the well's drilling, see Holley-Kline, "Nationalist Archaeology."
59. Also known as the Compañía Stanford, Stanford y Compañía was a Tampico-based and Mexico-registered company founded in 1925 that formed part of the American Sinclair conglomerate. See Government of Mexico, *Mexico's Oil*, 544.
60. Erasmo Rodríguez to Ignacio Marquina, December 16, 1935, ADDMP, exp. "El Tajín," ref. B/311.41(z61-2)/1, leg. 1, f. 97–98.
61. Alfonso Toro to Erasmo Rodríguez, December 23, 1935, AHPM, Fondo Expropriación, c. 1570, exp. 44170, f. 132.

62. Alfonso Toro to Miguel R. Cárdenas, December 31, 1935, AHPM, Fondo Expropriación, c. 1570, exp. 44170, f. 126.

63. Ignacio Marquina to Luis R. Ruíz, January 8, 1936, AHI-INAH, Subfondo Coordinación Nacional de Recursos Humanos (CNRH), Luis R. Ruíz Gaviño, Serie Expedientes Personales (60), 401.A(18)60-2819, c. 61, f. 18.

64. Luis R. Ruíz to C. Jefe de la Oficina de Monumentos Prehispánicos, January 16, 1935, ADDMP, exp. "El Tajín," ref. B/311.41(z61-2)/1, leg. 1, f. 142.

65. A. A. Sepúlveda to James J. Quoyeser, January 16, 1936, AHPM, Fondo Expropriación, c. 1570, exp. 44170, f. 96.

66. A. A. Sepúlveda to James J. Quoyeser, January 16, 1936, AHPM, Fondo Expropriación, c. 1570, exp. 44170, f. 96.

67. Procter Armstrong to James J. Quoyeser, January 9, 1936, AHPM, Fondo Expropriación, c. 1570, exp. 44170, f. 104.

68. M. M. Cárdenas to W. G. Tschudin, January 27, 1936, AHPM, Fondo Expropriación, c. 1570, exp. 44170, f. 92.

69. "Memoria relativa a la localización del pozo proyectado 'Ojital Número Uno,'" ADDMP, exp. "El Tajín," ref. B/311.41(z61-2)/1, leg. 1, f. 123–25.

70. Rodríguez Badillo, *La maquinita*.

71. "Memoria relativa a la localización del pozo proyectado 'Ojital No. 2,'" AHPM, Fondo Expropriación, c. 1570, exp. 44170, f. 9–10. See also Capitanachi Luna, *Furbero*, 319.

72. Alafita Méndez, "Perforación y perforadores," 156–59.

73. Erasmo Rodríguez to Ignacio Marquina, January 23, 1936, ADDMP, exp. "El Tajín," ref. B/311.32(z61-2)/1, leg. 1.

74. Luis R. Ruíz to C. Jefe de la Oficina de Monumentos Prehispánicos, January 16, 1935, ADDMP, exp. "El Tajín," ref. B/311.41(z61-2)/1, leg. 1, f. 143.

75. "Informe de los trabajos de exploración de las Ruinas del Tajín," AT-DMP, tomo 36, Estado de Veracruz, Tajín, vol. 2, 1936–40, f. 4.

76. "Informe de los trabajos de exploración de las Ruinas del Tajín," AT-DMP, tomo 36, Estado de Veracruz, Tajín, vol. 2, 1936–40, f. 10–11.

77. "Informe de los trabajos de exploración de las Ruinas del Tajín," AT-DMP, tomo 36, Estado de Veracruz, Tajín, vol. 2, 1936–40, f. 12.

78. "Memoria relativa a la localización del pozo proyectado 'Ojital Número Uno,'" ADDMP, exp. "El Tajín," ref. B/311.41(z61-2)/1, leg. 1, f. 123–25.

79. James J. Quoyeser to W. G. Tschudin, July 13, 1937, AHPM, Fondo Expropriación, c. 1570, exp. 44170, f. 45.

80. García Vega, "Exploraciones en El Tajín," 82.

81. Juan B. La Riviere to James J. Quoyeser, June 25, 1937, AHPM, Fondo Expropriación, c. 1570, exp. 44170, f. 59.

82. Luis André to Secretaría de Educación Pública, ADDMP, exp. "El Tajín," ref. B/311.41(z61-2)/1, leg. 1, f. 147.

83. "Pozo de Exploración:'Ojital No. 1,'" Petróleos Mexicanos, Gerencia de Exploración, Región Norte, Archivo Técnico, f. 14–15.

84. Capitanachi Luna, *Furbero*, 2:7–13.

85. "Informe de los trabajos de exploración y restauración llevados a cabo en la zona arqueológica del Tajín, Ver., durante la temporada de 1945–1946," AT-CIV, Estado de Veracruz, Tajín, vol. 3, 1940–53.

86. Kelly and Palerm, *Tajín Totonac*, 74; Holley-Kline,"Nationalist Archaeology," 88–89.

87. Santiago, *Ecology of Oil*, 122–47.

88. Uhthoff López,"La industria del petróleo."

89. By 1955 oil and natural gas represented 75 percent of the country's gross energy consumption. See Vergara, *Fueling Mexico*, 178.

90. Morales,"Consolidation and Expansion"; Álvarez de la Borda, *Crónica del petróleo*, 88–92. In the context of Mexico's economic performance over time, see Moreno-Brid and Ros, *Development and Growth*, 94–103.

91. Sordo and López, *Exploración*, 28.

92. Petróleos Mexicanos, *Los veinte años*, 407.

93. The description is likely based on the Escolin fields, to the immediate north of El Tajín. See Ramírez Melgarejo, *La política del Estado*, 277–78.

94. Schöneich, *Time Bomb*; Aguilar León,"Transformaciones socioterritoriales"; Cruz,"Gobierno mediante normas privadas"; Cruz,"Property in Pieces."

95. Ramírez Melgarejo, *La política del Estado*, 177–79; Velázquez Hernández, *Cuando los arrieros*, 104.

96. José García Payón to Benito Coquet, April 15, 1955, AGEV-JGP, c. 23, exp."Correspondencia García Payón-Benito Coquet."

97. José García Payón to Benito Coquet, January 5, 1955, AGEV-JGP, c. 23, exp. "Correspondencia García Payón-Benito Coquet."

98. José García Payón to Benito Coquet, January 12, 1955, AGEV-JGP, c. 23, exp. "Correspondencia García Payón-Benito Coquet."

99. García Payón, *Exploraciones en El Tajín*. See also "Cantidades aportadas por el INAH," AGEV-JGP, c. 28, exp."Informes," f. 6.

100. See, for example, aspirations for PEMEX funding from 1961 in Román Piña Chan to José García Payón, January 24, 1961, AGEV-JGP, c. 25 exp. 7 (1961), and from 1969 in Ignacio Bernal to Jesús Reyes Heroles, March 17, 1969, ADDMP, exp."El Tajín," ref. B/311.32(z61-2)/1, leg. 3.

101. Respectively: José García Payón to Eduardo Noguera, March 7, 1951, AH-CIV, Serie Jefatura de Servicio del INAH y Dirección del Depto. Arqueológico del Estado de Veracruz, c. 7, exp. 7;"Inventario de las herramientas y demás objetos al cuidado de los guardianes," AH-CIV, Serie Jefatura de la Zona Oriental, c. 5, exp. 16; José García Payón to José Luis Lorenzo, April 24, 1967, ADDMP, exp."El Tajín," ref. B/311.32(z61-2)/1, leg. 2.

102. García Payón,"El Tajín, trabajos," 76.

103. José García Payón to Raúl López Saucedo, June 20, 1967, ADDMP, exp. "El Tajín," ref. B/311.32(z61-2)/1, leg. 2 (1958).

104. José García Payón to Rodolfo Domínguez Calzada, February 8, 1966, ADDMP, exp. "El Tajín," ref. B/311.32(z61-2)/1, leg. 2 (1958).

105. José García Payón to José Luis Lorenzo, December 5, 1966, ADDMP, exp. "El Tajín," ref. B/311.32(z61-2)/1, leg. 2 (1958).

106. García Payón, *Exploraciones en El Tajín*, 7; "Exploraciones arqueológicas en El Tajín, durante la temporada de 1961–1962," AT-DMP, tomo 130, Estado de Veracruz, Tajín, vol. 6, 1959–62.

107. García Payón, "Ensayo de interpretación." On the panels' iconography, see Koontz, *Lightning Gods*, 55–62.

108. José García Payón to José Luis Lorenzo, March 28, 1966, ADDMP, exp. "El Tajín," ref. B/311.32(z61-2)/1, leg. 2; José García Payón to Rodolfo Domínguez Calzada, December 5, 1966, ADDMP, exp. "El Tajín," ref. B/311.32(z61-2)/1, leg. 2.

109. These included a theodolite, alidade, and measuring tape. A theodolite is a surveying tool used to measure horizontal and vertical angles, while an alidade (also known as a turning board) is used for measuring lines of sight on distant objects. Krotser and Krotser, "Topografía y cerámica," 178. José García Payón to Lita Osmundsen and Janet Grandinetti, February 15, 1971, AGEV-JGP, c. 7, exp. 13: El Tajín y correlativo (1971).

110. José García Payón to Manuel Gutiérrez Katthain, September 21, 1962, AGEV-JGP, c. 25, exp. 8 (1962).

111. "Plano general de la region de Poza Rica de Hgo. Ver.," AGEV-JGP, c. 20, exp. "Plano."

112. Mario Lazzeri V. to INAH, September 27, 1972, ADDMP, exp. "El Tajín," ref. B/311.32(z61-2)/1, leg. 4 (1970).

113. "Memoria descriptive de los trabajos topográficos relativos al deslinde de la zona arqueológica de El Tajín," ADDMP, exp. "El Tajín," ref. B/311.1(z61-2)/1.

114. Krotser and Krotser, "Topografía y cerámica," 179, 183. The Krotser map was only supplanted by PEMEX-sponsored LIDAR research in the 2010s.

115. "La 'Raza de Bronce' Lanza su Queja Contra los Políticos," September 21, 1979, BLT-AE, exp. "Totonacas," 10-4374.

116. See Braunschweig, "Repercusiones económicas." For San Antonio Ojital, see José García Payón to Manuel Contreras, June 13, 1962, AH-CIV, Serie Jefatura de la Zona Oriental del INAH, c. 4, exp. 21. For El Tajín, see Jacinto García to Ángel Palerm, May 29, 1948, ITKEA, s. 2, b. 1, 1533 Extractive Industries.

117. Holley-Kline, "El patrimonio industrial," 308–9.

118. Schöneich, *Time Bomb*, 84–86; Cruz, "Property in Pieces," 188.

119. McCabe and Clayton, "Air Pollution"; Goldsmith, "20-Minute Disaster"; Capitanachi Luna, *Furbero*, 2:187–95.

120. Del Palacio Langer, "Agrarian Reform, Oil Expropriation," 146.

121. *Macrobrachium acanthurus*, a species of river prawn commonly eaten in the area.

122. Checa-Artasu, "Los efectos," 28. See also Vergara, *Fueling Mexico*, 183–88; Salas Landa, "Crude Residues"; Santiago, "Oil and Environment"; Fry and Hilburn, "Distributional Justice"; Schöneich, *Time Bomb*.

123. Morales, "PEMEX during the 1960s," 233.

124. Álvarez de la Borda, *Crónica del petróleo*, 112; see also Morales, "PEMEX during the 1960s."

125. Breglia, *Living with Oil*, 31; see Black, *Crude Reality*, 374–425, for global context.

126. Cárdenas, "La economía mexicana," 525.

127. See Breglia, *Living with Oil*, 197–232.

128. Breglia, *Living with Oil*, 35–36.

129. Fry, "Shifting Volumetric Imaginaries," 83.

130. Cruz, "Property in Pieces," 100.

131. Comisión Nacional de Hidrocarburos, "Aceite Terciario del Golfo."

132. Zona de Monumentos Arqueológicos El Tajín, "Informe de actividades," 403.

133. For the agreement, see INAI, Folio 1115100030621, Oficio 401.12C.5-2021/0386. PGS Mexicana is a subsidiary of Petroleum Geo-Services ASA, a Norwegian-headquartered company that was awarded a US$165 million PEMEX contract for a seismic survey in Veracruz and Puebla between 2008 and 2012. Immediate antecedents to this relationship include Proyecto Tajín. See Delgado, *Sexto informe del gobierno*, 74. Unfortunately, the available sources do not allow me to quantify PEMEX support during that project. The sharing of equipment seems to have continued; see Joaquin García-Barcena to Enrique Florescano Mayet, January 9, 1985, ADDMP, exp. "El Tajín," ref. B/311.41(z61-2)/1, leg. 2 (1948–52).

134. "Convenio de colaboración para llevar a cabo las labores de prospección arqueológica," INAI, Folio 1115100030621, Oficio 401.12C.5-2021/0386/.

135. Castillo Peña, *Culturas del Golfo*.

136. Castillo Peña, *Culturas del Golfo*, 31–32. Light detection and ranging (LIDAR) is a remote-sensing method that uses lasers to measure precise distances between points on a landscape and a sensor.

137. Vázquez Prada and Flores Lot, "La contribución de PEMEX."

138. Chenaut, "Impactos sociales y ambientales"; Román Segura, "Proyecto ATG"; Aguilar Sánchez, "Explotación petrolera y resistencia." The extent of ongoing fracking is difficult to assess; environmentalist NGO CartoCrítica calculates that, between the first fracking applications in 1996 and 2018, nearly a quarter of all wells (7,879 of 32,464) were hydraulically fractured at some point. See CartoCrítica, "Actualidad de la fracturación," but compare Cruz, "Property in Pieces," 202–3, on the reliability of fracking figures.

139. Miguel Ángel Guerrero, "Pozos artesianos, contaminados en Emiliano Zapata," *Papantla al Momento*, April 4, 2024, https://www.facebook.com/PPantlaal momento/posts/pfbid0JTH6vdfAJfYW9mamZkNc5B5iJyHG1UyHZw PAtP3Y6B7BZH8xiYewaCzyLzgSE7Lpl; Luis Ángel Valera, "Fuga de hidro-

carburo en Cerro Grande Escolin," *Papantla al Momento*, March 24, 2019, https://www.facebook.com/PPantlaalmomento/posts/pfbid0u 7j8yYaGf9dvfgFXGP93cQbyEgggp45rcGHEBrTkF7zLe9tWyVup3rH 4HFuP7ADCl; Miguel Ángel Guerrero, "Papantla, municipio contaminado por PEMEX," *Papantla al Momento*, September 13, 2022, https://www.facebook .com/PPantlaalmomento/posts/pfbid02jouAsJP2TVgwitug2AqaUHgx BPSi3K9A5HL4LUYhSgNx4dbo7RLyKS6y1iBAtXXDl.

140. Santiago, *Ecology of Oil*.

141. Hernández, *Cumbres y barrancas*, 232.

3. Vanilla

1. Todos Santos is All Saints' Day (November 1), though it generally refers to the period between October 31 and November 4. Involving altars, tamales, and the cleaning of family graves, it is the most important celebration of the year.

2. For diverse disciplinary entry points, see Bruman, "Culture History"; Kourí, *A Pueblo Divided*; Lubinsky, "Historical and Evolutionary Origins"; Odoux and Grisoni, *Vanilla*; Araya Fernández et al., *I Seminario Internacional*.

3. As a result, Plan de Hidalgo is a popular place for research. See Lara Mojica, "Estudio Socioeconómico"; Rodríguez Morrill, "Cambio y continuidad"; and Ortiz Espejel, *La cultura asediada*, among others.

4. Žižek, *Violence*; Galtung, "Violence, Peace."

5. See reviews in Gillingham and Smith, "Introduction"; Vaughan, "Mexico, 1940–1968."

6. Aviña, *Specters of Revolution*; McCormick, *Logic of Compromise*.

7. On Manuel Parra, see Santoyo, *La Mano Negra*; Gillingham, "Who Killed Crispín Aguilar?"; for Jaime J. Merino, see del Palacio Langer, "Jaime Merino"; Román del Valle, *Sangre y lucha*.

8. Cano González, "Monografía," 14. Compare references in Ramírez Melgarejo, *La política del Estado*, 266–68; Rodríguez Morrill, "Cambio y continuidad," 71–72; Cruz, "Property in Pieces," 64–65.

9. Since 2001 the federal Pueblo Mágico program has promoted smaller cities and towns as tourist destinations. Recognition as a Pueblo Mágico requires the presence of certain tourist attractions (archaeological, historical, cultural, environmental, etc.) and infrastructure (transportation, hotels, restaurants, etc.). See Velázquez García, "La formulación"; Pérez Gil, "Papantla, Veracruz."

10. Žižek, *Violence*, 2.

11. Žižek, *Violence*, 2.

12. Kourí, *A Pueblo Divided*, 33.

13. Bruman, "Culture History," 370.

14. Villa-Señor y Sánchez, *Teatro Americano*, 1:318; Bruman, "Culture History," 369.

15. In 1718 the rights to annual trade fairs held after the arrival of merchant convoys were allocated exclusively to Xalapa. As a result, local links to Xalapa's

merchant elite were likely key in the maintenance of these relations of production. See Moore, *Forty Miles*, 3.

16. Kelly and Palerm, *Tajín Totonac*, 150; García-Salazar et al., "Quién obtiene," 40.

17. Von Humboldt, *Political Essay*, 2:26.

18. "Tajín (commerce)," ITKEA, s. 2, b. 42, fol. 331932, f. 30.

19. Kelly and Palerm, *Tajín Totonac*, 126.

20. Villanueva, "Region and Power," 242.

21. Compared with the twentieth-century transformations of other agricultural products, vanilla production is fundamentally conservative (certain innovations notwithstanding). See Ramírez Melgarejo, *La política del Estado*, 331–55; Pendley, "'Betting' on Vanilla."

22. Kourí, *A Pueblo Divided*, 29.

23. Turnbow, Raffetto, and Tracy, *Ice Cream Industry*, 6.

24. Kourí, *A Pueblo Divided*, 112.

25. "Tendencias del mercado," May 1938, BLT-AE, Vainilla-Mercados, Estados Unidos, P03598-P03598. Kourí, *A Pueblo Divided*, 296, gives the lower figure of 113,117 kilograms for the 1900–1901 fiscal year; in this case, the relative growth is more important than the absolute figures.

26. Secretaria de Agricultura y Fomento, "Monografias Comerciales," 375–76. This source considered that the "productive region of Papantla," whose boundaries extend beyond the former Cantón of Papantla to include the central Veracruz municipalities of Misantla and Martínez de la Torre, as well as municipalities in neighboring Puebla, actually accounted for 98.7 percent of production. I recompiled the production by municipality figures to maintain consistency with materials cited elsewhere.

27. Kourí, *A Pueblo Divided*, 18, 109–10.

28. Correll, "Vanilla," 346.

29. For concision's sake, I have combined territories colonized by France in the West Indies and Pacific, with the exception of Madagascar.

30. For 1925–41, see Secretaria de Agricultura y Fomento, "Monografias Comerciales," 372–74. Note that 1944, 1948, 1954, and 1959 are the combined averages for the preceding five years; see Cipagaula Valenzuela and Sánchez Río, *La vainilla en México*, 14. For 1961–90, see Food and Agriculture Organization of the United Nations, "FAOSTAT Statistical Database."

31. "Vainilla," AGN, Fondo Secretaría de Gobernación, sección Dirección de Investigaciones Políticas y Sociales, c. 84, exp. 1, f. 39–43.

32. The frost is said to have destroyed 60 percent of Papantla's vanilla plantations. See Curti Díaz, *Cultivo y beneficiado*, 3; Ramírez Melgarejo, *La política del Estado*, 352.

33. Rendered in Spanish as Taracatloco, "Trakgátlokg" is often said to be a Totonac-language onomatopoeia for the sound of a horse pulling its hoof from deep mud. The horse plunges a hoof into the mud, making a sound like *kgá* (a

voiceless postvelar stop) and pulls it out, making a suction sound: *tlokg*. Kgá-tlokg, kgá-tlokg, kgá-tlokg—Trakgátlokg.

34. Isabel Kelly to George Foster, September 13, 1950, NAA-RISA, b. 8.
35. "Pietro Tremari," *XX Settembre*, September 20, 1903, 39; see also López Vallejo, "Entre la vainilla," 42–71.
36. Salas García, *Cachiquín*, 64; Chenaut, *Aquellos que vuelan*, 158.
37. "La Casa Bartolomeo Zardoni y Cia, Papantla (Veracruz)," *XX Settembre*, September 20, 1903, 35–36.
38. Ismael de la Fuente, "Don Raúl del Cueto Decuir," *El Dictamen*, October 29, 1951.
39. While I assume the reader has an idea of the common taste and aroma evoked by the term "vanilla," the social and chemical meaning of vanilla is surprisingly enigmatic. See Berenstein, "Making a Global Sensation"; Sinha, Sharma, and Sharma, "Comprehensive Review."
40. Vanilla is particularly sensitive to temperature fluctuations. See Curti Díaz, *Cultivo y beneficiado*, 3. This vulnerability to natural disasters and inclement weather is not unique to Mexican vanilla. See Brown, "Madagascar's Cyclone Vulnerability."
41. Direct observation of the pollination process in the wild has never been recorded or published. See Lubinsky, "Historical and Evolutionary Origins," 55.
42. Vanilla's current means of cultivation are inextricably linked with French colonialism and the exploitation of enslaved Africans' labor. See Lucas, "Vanilla's Debt." Albius's technique spread throughout the French colonies via Paris, and the process seems to have arrived in Mexico between 1874 and 1877 via the French colonies of San Rafael and Jicaltepec, south of Papantla. See Kourí, *A Pueblo Divided*, 110–11; Pointeau, "La transmisión de saberes." Artificial pollination was used in Papantla by around 1910. See Kourí, *A Pueblo Divided*, 191.
43. Hernández-Hernández, "Mexican Vanilla Production," 16.
44. Bruman, "Culture History," 370. During my fieldwork, the date was November 15.
45. Kelly and Palerm, *Tajín Totonac*, 126.
46. Kourí, *A Pueblo Divided*, 83.
47. Kelly and Palerm, *Tajín Totonac*, 131.
48. Kelly and Palerm, *Tajín Totonac*, 126; compare de la Peña, *Veracruz económico*, 2:137.
49. Erasmo Rodríguez to Ignacio Marquina, December 24, 1934, ADDMP, exp. "El Tajín," ref. B/311.32(z61-2)/1, leg. 1.
50. Agustín Méndez y Hnos. to C. Secretario de Instrucción Pública, June 5, 1937, ADDMP, exp. "El Tajín," ref. B/311.41(z61-2)/1, leg. 1, f. 195.
51. Enrique Juan Palacios to Agustín García Vega, June 20, 1937, ADDMP, exp. "El Tajín," ref. B/311.41(z61-2)/1, leg. 1, f. 201.
52. Alfonso Toro to Agapito Juarez and demás firmantes, July 9, 1935, ADDMP, exp. "El Tajín," ref. B/311.1(z61-2)/1, f. 25.
53. Cuevas Fernández et al., *El Tajín*, 93.

54. José García Payón to Ignacio Marquina, August 3, 1954, AH-CIV, Serie Jefatura de Servicio del INAH y Dirección del Depto. Arqueológico del Estado de Veracruz, c. 12, exp. 9.

55. Otilio Robles Nava to Felipe Ganeros S., August 3, 1954, AH-CIV, Serie Jefatura de Servicio del INAH y Dirección del Depto. Arqueológico del Estado de Veracruz, c. 12, exp. 9.

56. José García Payón to Román Piña Chan, June 3, 1960, ADDMP, exp. "El Tajín," ref. B/03.01(72-61)(02)/1, f. 27–27r.

57. Hernández-Hernández, "Mexican Vanilla Production," 20.

58. Odoux, "Vanilla Curing," 185.

59. Hernández-Hernández, "Mexican Vanilla Production," 21; see also Fontecilla, *Breve tratado*.

60. Hernández-Hernández, "Mexican Vanilla Production," 21.

61. Fontecilla, *Breve tratado*, 28.

62. De la Peña, *Veracruz económico*, 2:138; Secretaria de Agricultura y Fomento, "Monografías Comerciales," 388.

63. For Salas de Broner, see Fewkes, *Certain Antiquities*, 233–36; García Payón, "Exploraciones arqueológicas"; König, "Invisible." On Strebel and his legacy, see Daneels, "El patrón de asentamiento," 37–63.

64. Leopoldo Batres to Ezequiel A. Chávez, August 19, 1904, AGN-IPBA, c. 167b, exp. 66, f. 2.

65. Kourí, *A Pueblo Divided*, 91, on Fontecilla, *Breve tratado*.

66. For Fontecilla Agustina's vital statistics, see "Agapito Fontecilla," Mexico, Select Church Records, 1537–1966, FamilySearch, Salt Lake City, film no. 004689525.

67. Kourí, *A Pueblo Divided*, 91.

68. Ducey, *A Nation of Villages*, 45–46; Kourí, *A Pueblo Divided*, 69–72.

69. Hamnett, *Roots of Insurgency*, 230.

70. *Memoria que en cumplimiento*, 378; see also chapter 5. For the medal, see Rosario Hernández, "Editorial," *El Caudillo: Periódico independiente; de política, agricultura, industria, comercio y variedades*, April 29, 1888.

71. Agapito Fontecilla y Vidal to Leopoldo Batres, May 25, 1889, ADDMP, exp. "El Tajín," ref. B/311.32(z61-2)/1, leg. 1.

72. Lombardo de Ruiz, *El pasado prehispánico*, 1:185–86.

73. Agapito G. Fontecilla to Secretaría de Instrucción Pública y Bellas Artes, November 10, 1906, AGN-IPBA, c. 152, exp. 23, f. 1.

74. L. Decuir L. to Fernando Marin, August 17, 1909, AGN-IPBA, c. III, exp. 7, f. 10–12. Note that the specific identification is my inference based on initials and context. Like Fontecilla y Vidal, Decuir was the scion of a family with interests in land and vanilla. See Kourí, *A Pueblo Divided*, 207–8.

75. Leopoldo Batres to Secretaría de Instrucción Pública y Bellas Artes, September 23, 1909, AGN-IPBA, c. III, exp. 7, f. 4.

76. Teodoro Dehesa to Secretaría de Instrucción Pública y Bellas Artes, October 26, 1909, AGN-IPBA, c. III, exp. 7, f. 6.

77. Leopoldo Batres to Secretaría de Instrucción Pública y Bellas Artes, November 18, 1909, AGN-IPBA, c. III, exp. 7, f. 8.

78. Isidoro O. Marié to Leopoldo Batres, November 19, 1909, AGN-IPBA, c. III, exp. 8. f. 1. Marié was described elsewhere as the owner of a 230-hectare tract, "an old Frenchman . . . ex-rebel, ex-smuggler, etc. but a very nice old fellow, who is in rather hard circumstances as he has an immense family depending on him. . . . He has lived in [Papantla] for some fifty years and knows every inch of land in the Cantón of Papantla." See A. E. Buchanan to T. J. Ryder, May 27, 1906, AHPM, Fondo Expropriación, c. 3182, exp. 81392, f. 49.

79. L. Decuir to Secretaría de Instrucción Pública y Bellas Artes, April 16, 1910, AGN-IPBA, c. 112, exp. 71, f. 3–5, 7–9.

80. Leopoldo Batres to Secretaría de Instrucción Pública y Bellas Artes, April 29, 1910, AGN-IPBA, c. 112, exp. 71, f. 7–9.

81. Leopoldo Batres to Secretaría de Instrucción Pública y Bellas Artes, April 29, 1910, AGN-IPBA, c. 112, exp. 71, f. 7–9.

82. Y. O. Marín to Secretaría de Instrucción Pública y Bellas Artes, August 3, 1910, AGN-IPBA, c. 112, exp. 94, f. 1–2. See also Holley-Kline, "Contextualizing Archaeology's 'Locals.'"

83. Alfonso Acosta to Ángel Palerm, March 23, 1948, ITKEA, s. 2, b. 1, 25 Trade and Exchange.

84. Roberto Esteva Ruiz to Agapito G. Fontecilla, December 20, 1913, AH-MNA, vol. 310, exp. 30, f. 207.

85. Rico, "Heritage at Risk."

86. Honorato Méndez to C. Director de Estudios Arqueológicos y Etnográficos, June 30, 1919, AHI-INAH, Subfondo CNRH, Honorato Méndez, Serie Expedientes Personales (60), 401.A(18)60-2442, c. 43, f. 1.

87. R. Curti y Hermanos to Sr. Director General de Estudios Arqueológicos y Etnográficos, November 9, 1920, AHI-INAH, Subfondo CNRH, Honorato Méndez, Serie Expedientes Personales (60), 401.A(18)60-2442, c. 43, f. 8–9; Melquiades Patiño to Sr. Director General de Estudios Arqueológicos y Etnográficos, November 9, 1920, AHI-INAH, Subfondo CNRH, Honorato Méndez, Serie Expedientes Personales (60), 401.A(18)60-2442, c. 43, f. 9.

88. Ernesto Patiño to Honorato Méndez, October 29, 1926, AHI-INAH, Subfondo CNRH, Honorato Méndez, Serie Expedientes Personales (60), 401.A(18)60-2442, c. 43, f. 102.

89. Isabel Kelly to George Foster, January 27, 1947, NAA-RISA, b. 7.

90. Raúl del Cueto to José García Payón, February 28, 1945, AGEV-JGP, c. 23, exp. 1943.

91. Pedro Pérez Bautista to Edmundo Martínez Zaleta, April 19, 1986, ADDMP, exp. "El Tajín," ref. B/311.1(z61-2)/1, f. 12.

92. On a 1945 trip with Bodil Christensen, Proskouriakoff stayed with friends of Christensen "who ran a lucrative vanilla bean business and who put them up in luxurious rooms in their home." See Solomon, *Tatiana Proskouriakoff*, 87. Proskouriakoff mentions calling on del Cueto, specifically, on a 1950 trip. See Proskouriakoff field diary, March 20, 1950, CIW Department of Archaeology Records, 1914–1955, Group III-I#18, f. 27–28. On the Classic Veracruz style, see Proskouriakoff, *Varieties*; Koontz, *Lightning Gods*, 10.

93. Zhu, "Hot Money, Cold Beer."

94. See Osterhoudt, "'Nobody Wants to Kill.'"

95. Byrne, "Western Hegemony," 230.

4. Wage Labor

1. García Payón, *Exploraciones en El Tajín*, 10.

2. García Payón, *Exploraciones en El Tajín*, 14.

3. García Payón, *Exploraciones en El Tajín*, 10. Among these masons were Pedro Pérez Bautista, Faustino González Méndez, and Bartolo Simbrón de León.

4. Lucas, *Critical Approaches to Fieldwork*, 13.

5. See the pioneering work of Shapin, "Invisible Technician"; Latour and Woolgar, *Laboratory Life*. For archaeology, see Shepherd, "'When the Hand'"; Berggren and Hodder, "Social Practice"; Mickel, *Why Those Who Shovel*.

6. Hodder, "Writing Archaeology."

7. Mickel, *Why Those Who Shovel*.

8. Shepherd, "'When the Hand,'" 340. See also Bernbeck and Pollock, "Political Economy"; Quirke, *Hidden Hands*; Doyon, "On Archaeological Labor."

9. Leighton, "Indigenous Archaeological Field Technicians," 751.

10. See Holley-Kline and Mickel, "Introduction"; Mickel, *Why Those Who Shovel*, 114–29.

11. Mickel and Byrd, "Cultivating Trust, Producing Knowledge"; Everill, *Invisible Diggers*; Shepherd, "'When the Hand'"; Chadha, "Visions of Discipline"; Paynter, "Field or Factory?"

12. Pollock, "Decolonizing Archaeology"; Mickel, "Essential Excavation Experts."

13. "Gazeta de México."

14. "Gazeta de México," 351.

15. Medina González and García Uranga, "Los antiguos monumentos"; López Luján, "El Tajín."

16. Alzate y Ramírez, *Descripción*.

17. López Luján, "First Steps," 84.

18. Keen, *Aztec Image*, 300; see Márquez, *Due antichi monumenti*.

19. López Luján and Le Brun-Ricalens, "Guillermo Dupaix." See also Achim, "Writing Lessons in Antiquarianism."

20. López Luján, "El Tajín," 78.

21. See Von Humboldt, *Political Essay*, 2:412.

22. López Luján, "El Tajín."

23. A Bourbon-era replacement for the *alcalde mayor* position, the subdelegate was responsible for receiving the Crown's tribute, enforcing its laws, and centralizing authority more generally in rural Spanish America. See Ducey, *A Nation of Villages*, 13.

24. Moreno Coello, "Alcaldes mayores y subdelegados," 224–27.

25. Ducey, *A Nation of Villages*, 22.

26. Stresser-Pean, *Sun God*, 225–26.

27. Collectively, the political, economic, and military reforms associated with the Bourbon dynasty are known as the Bourbon Reforms. See Andrien, "Bourbon Reforms."

28. Frederick, *Riot!*, 56–75.

29. Moreno Coello, "Alcaldes mayores y subdelegados," 225–26.

30. Nebel, *Viaje pintoresco*, 30.

31. See Caplan, *Indigenous Citizens*, 4–9.

32. Lomnitz, *Deep Mexico, Silent Mexico*, 50.

33. For Indigenous communities in Totonacapan, see Chenaut, *Aquellos que vuelan*, 225–27; Ducey, *A Nation of Villages*. The literature on liberalism and Indigenous communities is vast. For useful entry points, see Caplan, *Indigenous Citizens*; Chassen-López, *From Liberal to Revolutionary Oaxaca*. For classic cases from neighboring regions, see Schryer, "Peasants and the Law"; Thomson, "Agrarian Conflict."

34. Galindo y Villa, *Las ruinas de Cempoala*, cli. See also Casanova, "La fotografía."

35. Compare Mickel, "Essential Excavation Experts."

36. Kourí, *A Pueblo Divided*, 283; Villanueva, "Region and Power," 221.

37. On Papantla, see López Vallejo, "Entre la vainilla," 83–118; Xochihua García, "Dinámicas económicas," 162–222. For the state, see Fowler Salamini, *Agrarian Radicalism in Veracruz*.

38. González-Montagut, "Factors That Contributed," 106–9.

39. Kasburg, *Die Totonaken*, 43, 45.

40. AHI-INAH, Colección Archivo Histórico de la Dirección del INAH, vol. 59, exp. 11.

41. Throughout the chapter, references to payroll refer to the records known as *listas de raya*. The records themselves do not contain full (paternal and maternal) last names before the 1960s and 1970s, making positive identification of the relationships I discuss here a challenge. To identify specific families, I cross-referenced payroll records with material from the Isabel T. Kelly Ethnographic Archive, as well as similar information I collected during my fieldwork. Most of these nominal record linkages involved adding maternal last names and differentiating families that shared identical last names. I only did so in cases where the worker in question could be positively identified in Kelly's archives, later payroll records, or my own fieldwork. The numbers registered here should thus be regarded

as conservative. After selection, transcription, and cleaning with OpenRefine, the data consisted of 6,390 entries, of which 4,851 (76 percent) were complete (paternal and maternal last names, position, and wage). I consider the resulting data set broadly representative, though I also identified shortcomings. Payroll records document seasonal employment in 1936–37, 1945–50, 1952–54, 1956–65, and 1968–74. While field research at El Tajín was not conducted annually, certain field seasons are missing in the payroll records: 1934–35, 1951, 1955, 1966, and 1967. Furthermore, the available technical reports do not always record the season's starting and ending dates, making it difficult to assess the extent to which payroll records represent entire field seasons. Given that certain years (1937, 1945, 1957, and 1961) are represented only by single months, I suspect that they do not. For technical reports, see García Moll, *Indice del Archivo Técnico*.

42. Figures from 1970 do not include gender; I inferred them based on a 1:1 human sex ratio.

43. Knight, "History, Heritage, and Revolution," 304–5.

44. Castañeda, *In the Museum*, 59.

45. Medina González and Ortega Cabrera, "Reconstrucciones en Teotihuacan 1960–1962," 59; Vázquez León, *El Leviatán arqueológico*, 215.

46. Brüggemann, "Tajín en números." Unfortunately, despite extensive searching, I have been unable to locate administrative material (including payroll records) for this project.

47. In an interview, archaeologist S. Jeffrey K. Wilkerson described the criteria that distinguished degrees of mason in northern Veracruz during the 1960s and 1970s: an *albañil de 3a* or an *ayudante de albañil* could follow direction on mixing and pouring cement, as well as excavating and carrying water. An *albañil de 2a* could handle cement and was adept with basic volumetric measurements. An *albañil de 1a*, now often called a *maestro albañil*, could do everything required of a *2a* and *3a* and could use a level with knowledge of geometry and measurements.

48. "Wealth," ITKEA, s. 2, b. 42, fol. 330232.

49. See, for example, Turner, *Barbarous Mexico*.

50. For entry points, see Bauer, "Rural Workers"; Knight, "Mexican Peonage"; Monteiro, "Labor Systems."

51. Malkiel, "La historia lingüística."

52. Podgorny, "Towards a Bureaucratic History"; Meskell and LaPorte, "'Your Mysterious Instruments.'" For Mexico, see Vázquez León, "Hobbes en la metáfora."

53. Xochihua García, "Dinámicas económicas," 231.

54. For agricultural labor in Papantla, *jornalero* or *labrador* seem more common than *peón*. In the archaeology of the period, *mozo* is used as a synonym elsewhere in the country.

55. For the milpa, see Kourí, *A Pueblo Divided*, 41–46; Kelly and Palerm, *Tajín Totonac*, 99–150.

56. Secretaría de Desarrollo Regional, *Programa de manejo*, 17.

57. Kourí, *A Pueblo Divided*, 45.

58. "Informe de las labores efectuadas en la zona arqueológica del Tajín entre el 26 de julio y 14 de agosto de 1947," AT-CNA, Estado de Veracruz, informe 29-177, f. 397–98.

59. José García Payón to Ignacio Marquina, August 18, 1952, AHI-INAH, Colección Archivo Histórico de la Dirección del INAH, vol. 48, sección 4, f. 147.

60. Ignacio Marquina to Erasmo Rodríguez, January 10, 1934, ADDMP, exp. "El Tajín," ref. B/311.41(z61-2)/1, leg. 1, f. 62; Ignacio Marquina to Luis André, January 10, 1934, ADDMP, exp. "El Tajín," ref. B/311.41(z61-2)/1, leg. 1, f. 64.

61. José Reygadas Vértiz to Jefe del Departamento Administrativo, February 27, 1934, ADDMP, exp. "El Tajín," ref. B/311.41(z61-2)/1, leg. 1, f. 66.

62. See Middlebrook, *Paradox of Revolution*; Bensusán and Middlebrook, *Organized Labour and Politics*; Collier, *Contradictory Alliance*; Lenti, *Redeeming the Revolution*.

63. Middlebrook, *Paradox of Revolution*, 72–106.

64. Collier, *Contradictory Alliance*, 44.

65. Elías Terán Gómez to C. Secretario de Educación Pública, May 2, 1939, ADDMP, exp. "El Tajín," ref. B/311.41(z61-2)/1, leg. 1, f. 253.

66. José García Payón to Ignacio Marquina, May 11, 1939, ADDMP, exp. "El Tajín," ref. B/311.41(z61-2)/1, leg. 1, f. 256.

67. Lenti, *Redeeming the Revolution*, 20.

68. For the 1964–74 period, minimum wage in the Poza Rica–Tuxpan area rose from 21 to 62.60 pesos per day. See INEGI, *Estadísticas Históricas de México*, 1:178. Over the same period, the wages recorded in the corresponding listas de raya for peones rose from 16 to 30 pesos per day.

69. Kelly and Palerm, *Tajín Totonac*, 99, 173–74.

70. For entry points into this literature, see Gero, "Socio-Politics"; Moser, "On Disciplinary Culture"; Heath-Stout, "Who Writes about Archaeology?" For Mexico, see Ruiz Martínez, *Género, ciencia y política*, 171–208.

71. Claassen, "Women at Irene Mound."

72. Sheldon, "Poza Rica Field," 26.

73. See chapter 2 of this book; Velázquez Hernández, *Cuando los arrieros*, 98–104; Ramírez Melgarejo, *La política del Estado*, 177–91.

74. Mintz, "Rural Proletariat," 319.

75. See Mickel, "Essential Excavation Experts."

76. "Tirzo González," ITKEA, s. 2, b. 16, fol. 33022187.

77. Kelly and Palerm, *Tajín Totonac*, 61.

78. See AH-CIV, Serie Jefatura de Servicio del INAH y Dirección del Depto. Arqueológico del Estado de Veracruz, c. 4, exp. 1.

79. See ITKEA, s. 2, b. 42, fol. 331932 (Commerce).

80. "Tajín (commerce)," ITKEA, s. 2, b. 42, fol. 331932, f. 24.

81. Hernández García, "Las mujeres del Proyecto."

82. Kelly and Palerm, *Tajín Totonac*, 176.

83. "Descubrimiento de la Zona Arqueológica del Tajín," AT-DMP, tomo 125, Estado de Veracruz, Tajín, vol. 1, 1924–35.

84. José García Payón to Jorge Acosta, April 22, 1959, AH-CIV, Serie Jefatura de la Zona Oriental, c. 2, exp. 11.

85. Heladio Castro, "Custodia El Tajín desde hace 9 décadas," *Imagen del Veracruz*, 2011 (site discontinued). Pérez Bautista's maternal great-grandparents, the family of Ignacio de la Cruz, were Modesto González's godparents; they raised González after the deaths of his parents. For Pérez's parentage, see "Datos que deberá llenar el interesado," AHI-INAH, Colección CNRH, c. 3, exp. 15, f. 94. For González's family, see Modesto González to Ángel Palerm, May 21, 1948, ITKEA, S. 2, b. 1, 411 Oral Historical.

86. Ávila Hernández, "Proceso de trabajo."

87. Breglia, "Keeping World Heritage."

88. Quintín Pérez González to José García Payón, July 12, 1974, AGEV-JGP, c. 16, exp. 7.

89. Article 21 of the Condiciones Generales de Trabajo allocates admission authority to a Comisión Mixta de Admisión, composed of representatives from the INAH and the union, while Article 21 of the Reglamento de Admisión establishes a preference for a spouse or son to inherit the plaza in the event of a worker's death. See *Condiciones Generales de Trabajo*, 19; *Reglamento de Admisión*, 9. However, the process of plaza inheritance likely draws from similar procedures elsewhere in the public sector and antecedents in archaeology. See Carrasco and Kent, "Power, Identity and Discourse," and Kelly, "Waking the Gods," 129–32, respectively.

90. Faustino González Méndez to José García Payón, February 14, 1972, AGEV-JGP, c. 34, exp. 9.

91. "Relación de las Ruinas Arqueológicas de la República y personal," AHI-INAH, Colección Archivo Histórico de la Dirección del INAH, vol. 22, exp. 352, f. 120. See also chapter 5 of this book.

92. Govers, *Performing the Community*, 60.

93. Documentation permitting, a fuller analysis might draw on household-level income data or analogies; however, Kelly noted residents' reticence to discuss details of commerce for fear that higher taxes might result. See Kelly and Palerm, *Tajín Totonac*, xii, 117.

5. Custodios

1. Cuyuxquihui and Castillo de Teayo are small, proximate archaeological sites whose administration is often routed through that of El Tajín.

2. Concepción Moreno, "Custodios del INAH exigen material de trabajo y tomaron instalaciones, en Papantla," *Al Calor Político*, September 21, 2012, https://www.alcalorpolitico.com/informacion/custodios-del-inah-exigen-material-de

-trabajo-y-tomaron-instalaciones-en-papantla-100754.html; Sabino Bautista Juárez, "Que no está descuidada la zona arqueológica," *Diario de Poza Rica,* September 21, 2012; Juan Olmedo, "Acciones legales contra trabajadores del INAH," *Tribuna Papanteca,* September 29, 2012.

3. The first Totonac custodio of the site seems to have been Modesto González, hired in 1923; see Holley-Kline, "El guardián Modesto González," 20. Local normativity holds that Tajín's custodios are Totonac. My usage reflects this ideal. While the majority of custodios do identify as Totonac, there are occasional exceptions. INAH custodios can transfer to different archaeological sites, and at different times El Tajín has had up to two custodios who identify with other Indigenous communities. At least one considers that his nonlocal origin has negatively affected his relationships with his coworkers.

4. Nicholas and Hollowell, "Ethical Challenges"; see also Schneider and Hayes, "Epistemic Colonialism."

5. Wylie, "Integrity of Narratives," 209.

6. See review in Colwell, "Collaborative Archaeologies." For Mesoamerican examples, see Leventhal et al., "Community Heritage Project"; McAnany, *Maya Cultural Heritage*; Dedrick, "Photovoice."

7. See McNiven, "Theoretical Challenges," 33–34; Parks, "Collision of Heritage and Economy"; Breglia, "Keeping World Heritage."

8. Schneider and Hayes, "Epistemic Colonialism," 130.

9. See DOS-INAH, exp. IA 9.

10. On the perils of recognition, see especially Hale, "Neoliberal Multiculturalism"; Coulthard, *Red Skin, White Masks*; Escallón, *Becoming Heritage.*

11. Rifkin, *Beyond Settler Time,* 31.

12. Holley-Kline, "El guardián Modesto González," after Trouillot, *Silencing the Past.*

13. The gendered designation is purposeful: the work is generally considered masculine, the employment of two female custodians notwithstanding.

14. Weber, "Bureaucracy."

15. In technical terms, a *plaza* is "the budgetary position supporting a post in the occupational structure or establishment plan, which can only be occupied by a civil servant and which has a particular assignment." See Secretaría de Cultura, *Manual general,* 17.

16. In Chichén Itzá the key factor that distinguishes *antiguo* from *nuevo* custodios is a history of residence in Chichén Pueblo, demolished in the 1980s. See Breglia, "Keeping World Heritage."

17. Bueno, *Pursuit of Ruins,* 100.

18. Kelly, "Waking the Gods," 114.

19. *Memoria que en cumplimiento,* 378.

20. Agapito Fontecilla y Vidal to Leopoldo Batres, May 25, 1889, ADDMP, exp. "El Tajín," ref. B/311.32(z61-2), leg. 1.

21. Kelly, "Waking the Gods," 114.

22. See chapter 2 of this book; "Constancias en el expediente del C. Erasmo Rodríguez," AHI-INAH, Subfondo CNRH, Erasmo Rodríguez Jaack, Serie Expedientes Personales (60), 401.A(18)60-2695, c. 14, f. 121; Erasmo Rodríguez to various, January 24, 1934, ADDMP, exp. "El Tajín," ref. B/311.32(z61-2), leg. 1; Erasmo Rodríguez to Ignacio Marquina, June 24, 1936, ADDMP, exp. "El Tajín," ref. B/311.32(z61-2), leg. 1.

23. José Reygadas Vértiz to Honorato Méndez, October 22, 1921, AHI-INAH, Subfondo CNRH, Honorato Méndez, Serie Expedientes Personales (60), 401.A(18)60-2442, c. 43, f. 38.

24. José Reygadas Vértiz to Honorato Méndez, November 18, 1921, AHI-INAH, Subfondo CNRH, Honorato Méndez, Serie Expedientes Personales (60), 401.A(18)60-2442, c. 43, f. 45.

25. Eugenio Salazar to C. Director de Antropología, August 23, 1921, AHI-INAH, Subfondo CNRH, Honorato Méndez, Serie Expedientes Personales (60), 401.A(18)60-2442, c. 43, f. 29.

26. José Reygadas Vértiz to C. Oficial Mayor Segundo, May 22, 1923, AHI-INAH, Subfondo CNRH, Modesto González González, Serie Expedientes Personales (60), 401.A(18)60-1239, c. 30, f. 1. See also see Holley-Kline, "El guardián Modesto González."

27. López Hernández, "La arqueología mexicana."

28. On Cardenismo, see Rugeley, *Epic Mexico*, 202–10. For Cardenista indigenismo, see Dawson, *Indian and Nation*; López Hernández, "De la gloria prehispánica."

29. López, *Crafting Mexico*, 137.

30. "Atribuciones de la Dirección de Monumentos Prehispánicos," AHI-INAH, sección Dirección de Monumentos Prehispánicos, Serie Correspondencia, c. 2, exp. 30, f. 6.

31. See García Moll, *Indice del Archivo Técnico*, 78, 82.

32. Isabel Kelly to George Foster, January 1, 1947, NAA-RISA, b. 7.

33. "Informe de las labores efectuadas en la zona arqueológica del Tajín en el período del 1 al 15 de septiembre," AT-CNA, Estado de Veracruz, vol. 29-177, f. 405–6.

34. *De blanco* refers to a Totonac person who wears the traditional *calzón de manta* of the region. Currently more prevalent among older generations, it is an important local index of indigeneity. On dress, see Vázquez Valdés, "Entre naguas y calzones."

35. Teódulo González's formal appointment dates from 1959, but he was evidently paid via the lista de raya beginning in 1940; García Payón repeatedly sought to have him appointed during this interim, and he seems to have been recognized as encargado. See AHI-INAH, Subfondo CNRH, Teódulo González Méndez, Serie Expedientes Personales (60), 401.A(18)60-44, c. 8, f. 27–63. For Rosalino González, see "Hoja de servicios de Rosalino González Méndez," AHI-INAH, Colección CNRH, s. Personal, c. 5, exp. 60, f. 8–9.

36. Teódulo's administrative responsibilities are detailed in José García Payón to Eusebio Dávalos Hurtado, July 27, 1962, AH-CIV, Serie Jefatura de la Zona Oriental del INAH, c. 4, exp. 22. See also Alazraki, *Raíces*, for Teódulo's on-screen role as the father of a Totonac woman pursued by a lascivious foreign archaeologist.
37. Bartolo Simbrón de León seems to have been employed between 1946 and 1951. See José García Payón to Bartolo Zimbrón, February 25, 1946, AH-CIV, Serie Jefatura de Arqueólogos del INAH y Encargado del Departamento Arqueológico del Estado de Veracruz, c. 2, exp. 10; José García Payón to Eduardo Noguera, August 15, 1951, AHI-INAH, Subfondo CNRH, Teódulo González Méndez, Serie Expedientes Personales (60), 401.A(18)60-44, c. 8, f. 48. Though both seem to have been employed during the same period, Simbrón de León's plaza passed to Teódulo González after the former resigned.
38. María Loreto to Isabel Kelly, May 29, 1964, ITKEA, s. 2, b. 1, 4164 Administración de la zona arqueológica.
39. María Loreto to Isabel Kelly, May 29, 1964, ITKEA, s. 2, b. 1, 4164 Administración de la zona arqueológica.
40. Vázquez León, "Mexico," 78; Robles García and Corbett, "Heritage Resource Management," 112.
41. Kirchhoff, "Mesoamérica"; see commentaries by Jácome González, "Mesoamérica"; Vázquez León, *El Leviatán arqueológico*.
42. On theory and politics in Mesoamerican archaeology, see Gándara, "Short History of Theory." Litvak King, "Posiciones teóricas"; Yadeun, "Arqueología de la arqueología"; Panameño and Nalda, "Arqueología"; and Matos Moctezuma, "Las corrientes arqueológicas," present important contemporary perspectives on these debates.
43. Nahmad Molinari, "Una visión propia," 4–9.
44. José García Payón to Pedro Pérez Bautista, March 10, 1972, AGEV-JGP, c. 34, exp. 9, "Tajín y correlativo 1972."
45. Pedro Pérez Bautista to Eduardo Matos Moctezuma, January 26, 1977, ADDMP, exp. "El Tajín," ref. B/311.32(z61-2)/1, leg. 6.
46. See also Breglia, *Monumental Ambivalence*, 120.
47. Lenti, *Redeeming the Revolution*, 21.
48. Street, "Burocracia y educación," 239; see also Dillingham, *Oaxaca Resurgent*, 120–23.
49. Dillingham, *Oaxaca Resurgent*, 120–23. This was also a reaction to the brand of union leadership known as *charrismo*, in which "a leader . . . puts himself at the bosses' bidding in return for political favors or advancement." See Foweraker, *Popular Mobilization in Mexico*, 28.
50. Albarrán Chávez, "Historia de los trabajadores," 82.
51. Ávila Hernández, "Proceso de trabajo," 131–88. On the union's early history, see Albarrán Chávez, "Historia de los trabajadores," 40–43.
52. See *Convenio de prestaciones socioeconómicas*.

53. The inheritance of plazas was common in, but not exclusive to, the SNTE. See Carrasco and Kent, "Power, Identity and Discourse."

54. Zepeda Martínez, *Decline of Labor Unions*.

55. Bensusán and Cook, "State-Corporatist Legacies," 162–63.

56. Kasburg, *Die Totonaken*, 22.

57. Kasburg, *Die Totonaken*, 43.

58. Morales García, "Don José García Payón." The 1972–73 reports are located in AGEV-JGP, c. 25, exp. 1973.

59. Admissions procedures for INAH workers were formalized at the national level in 1980. See *Reglamento de Admisión*; Albarrán Chávez, "Historia de los trabajadores," 103.

60. King, "Trade and Totomoxtle," 38; Beltrán Rosas, "Estudio etnográfico."

61. The timing, extents, and motivations for migration are highly variable in Totonacapan. See Popke and Torres, "Neoliberalization, Transnational Migration"; Moctezuma-Pérez, "La migración de indígenas"; García Martínez, "Juventud indígena"; Schiller, "Buscando hogar"; Pérez Monterosas, "Las migraciones." Compare Govers, *Performing the Community*, 79–114, on the Sierra de Puebla.

62. This was by design, at least to some extent. Article 21 of the Condiciones Generales de Trabajo allocates admission authority to a Comisión Mixta de Admisión, composed of representatives from the INAH and the union. See *Condiciones Generales de Trabajo*, 19; *Reglamento de Admisión*, 9.

63. Nahmad Molinari and Rodríguez Martínez, "Informe del programa," 40.

64. Jaimes Reyes, "Turismo cultural"; Zúñiga Bravo, "Nuevos usos del patrimonio"; Rivera Sandoval, "Consumo cultural."

65. For an overview of this project, see Islas, Calef, and Aparicio, "2013 Mexico's Education Reform."

66. Rojas Ruiz, "La Secretaría de Cultura."

67. Trouillot, *Silencing the Past*, 22.

68. Compare Mickel, *Why Those Who Shovel*, 4.

6. Experts

1. Fortunately, Katia's damage was minor. See Avila, "Hurricane Katia."

2. Leighton, "Indigenous Archaeological Field Technicians," 751.

3. In contrast with the inherent precariousness of life, precarity here designates a "politically induced condition in which certain populations suffer from failing social and economic networks of support and become differently exposed to injury, violence, and death." See Butler, *Frames of War*, 24–26. The fact that precarity is political and differential is key here.

4. Secretaría de Cultura, *Manual general*, 8–12.

5. Weber, "Bureaucracy."

6. For the INAH, see *Condiciones Generales de Trabajo*, 13–14; see also Grindle, *Bureaucrats, Politicians, and Peasants*, 43.

7. The positions of site director and head of the Legal and Technical Protection Department were considered *de estructura*, closer to the classification of *de confianza*. The other positions were considered *de proyecto*, with their positions entirely dependent on specific projects approved by the INAH.

8. Arturo Alcalde Justiniani, "Los indocumentados del INAH," *La Jornada*, August 27, 2011, https://www.jornada.com.mx/2011/08/27/opinion/025a1pol.

9. Locality, in this case, has a limited reach: the community of El Tajín or communities that originally formed part of the same, like San Lorenzo Tajín and Zapotal Santa Cruz. Thus, for instance, one site administrator from Papantla complained of his treatment by the custodios during the 2012 strike by saying that he was from here, just like they were. The custodios saw things differently.

10. See "Anexo," INAI, Folio 1115100067618, Oficio CIV/2596/2018, 401.3S.18/2018.

11. Hølleland and Skrede, "Heritage Experts?," 826; Rico, "Stakeholders in Practice."

12. Smith, "Editorial," 537.

13. Robles García and Corbett, "Heritage Resource Management," 111–12.

14. López Wario and Púlido Méndez, "Forjando arqueólogos"; on management, see Byrne, "Western Hegemony."

15. Bueno, *Pursuit of Ruins*, 94.

16. Avelar Gabi, "La administración," 87.

17. García Vega, "Exploraciones en El Tajín," 78.

18. "Relación de las Ruinas Arqueológicas de la República y personal," AHI-INAH, Colección Archivo Histórico de la Dirección del INAH, vol. 22, exp. 352, f. 116–21.

19. Arturo M. Elías to C. Director de Arqueología, June 5, 1929, ADDMP, exp. "El Tajín," ref. B/311.32(z61-2)/1, leg. 1. On road-building as state formation, see Bess, *Routes of Compromise*.

20. Rodríguez, *Decentralization in Mexico*, 61–87; McGinn and Street, "Educational Decentralization," 484–89.

21. Rodríguez, *Decentralization in Mexico*, 65.

22. Olivé Negrete, INAH, *una historia*, 1:461–63; Lorenzo, "Mexico," 97. On museums in the neoliberal era, see Coffey, "From Nation to Community"; Hoobler, "To Take Their Heritage."

23. "Centro Regional Veracruz: Un balance," AHI-INAH, Colección Secretaría Técnica, c. 13, exp. 7, "Informe 1983–1988." While this institution was known as the Centro Regional Veracruz for much of its history, I call it the Centro INAH Veracruz for consistency's sake.

24. Breglia, *Monumental Ambivalence*, 5–28.

25. Salazar Peralta, "Los movimientos patrimonialistas," 76. Compare Alexandrino Ocaña, "Seeking Rights," on heritage grassroots organizations in the Peruvian context.

26. Harvey, *Brief History of Neoliberalism*, 2; Lemke, "'Birth of Bio-Politics'"; see also Foucault, *Society Must Be Defended*.

27. Lemke, *Foucault, Governmentality, and Critique*, 83.

28. Hilgers, "Historicity of the Neoliberal." See, for example, Albro, "Neoliberal Cultural Heritage."

29. "Salinas entregó El Tajín restaurado, que permitirá crear empleos en la region," November 13, 1992, BLT-AE, Arqueología-Veracruz, Tajín, NO1777.

30. For an introduction to the Salinas administration, see Dawson, *First World Dreams*, 23–45.

31. Vázquez León, *El Leviatán arqueológico*, 211–14.

32. Coombe, "Managing Cultural Heritage," 378.

33. Unlike most Mexican universities, the Universidad Veracruzana was not autonomous until 1996 (see "Ley de autonomía"). As a result, the UV's research historically responded to the priorities of the state government of Veracruz. See Daneels, "José García Payón"; Holley-Kline, "José García Payón."

34. "Proyecto Tajín," AT-CIV, "Memoria sexenal, 1989–1994, VII Proyectos Especiales (Anexos), 8—Tajín."

35. Brueggemann, "Proyecto Tajín," 29.

36. Delgado, *Sexto informe del gobierno*, 74.

37. Colburn, "Anger at El Tajin."

38. "Proyecto Tajín," AT-CIV, "Memoria sexenal, 1989–1994, VII Proyectos Especiales (Anexos), 8—Tajín." This is equivalent to approximately 100 million pesos in 2021.

39. Brüggemann, "Tajín en números."

40. Miguel Ángel Flores, "El Proyecto Tajín estará listo en octubre del 92, pese al desacuerdo del INAH-Veracruz," *Proceso*, August 17, 1991.

41. See, for example, the disagreement between Brueggemann, "Apuntes para la restauración," and Ramírez Castilla, "La restauración de monumentos."

42. The disagreement is documented in ADDMP, exp. "El Tajín," ref. B/311.41(z61-2)/1, leg. 2 (1948–52).

43. Robles García and Corbett, "Heritage Resource Management," 114. For UNESCO in Mexico, see Espinosa Rodríguez, "Estrategias y gestión."

44. Meskell, *Future in Ruins*, 87; Robles García and Corbett, "Heritage Resource Management," 115.

45. Lorey, *Rise of the Professions*, 54–55, uses this definition for professionals.

46. On Pérez, see Nahmad Molinari, "Una visión propia"; Holley-Kline, "Archaeology, Wage Labor," 212–13.

47. See "Juan Antonio Ferrer Aguilar," INAI, Currícula de funcionarios, Instituto de Salud para el Bienestar, Ejercicio 2021.

48. Founded in 1987, the IVEC was charged with "researching, rescuing, and developing authentic elements of popular culture, preserving and making the most of our traditions, and religious and state artisanry." See "Ley que crea el Instituto Veracruzano," 1.

49. See Nahmad Molinari and Rodríguez Martínez, "Informe del programa," 54–56.

50. Nahmad Molinari and Rodríguez Martínez, "Informe del programa," 56.

51. The site installations, built with PEMEX support during Proyecto Tajín, were transferred to the IVEC in 2006. "Folio 923," INAI, Folio 3510000069118, exp. CNDH/4/2016/2214/Q, f. 670.

52. Valadez Moreno and Huitrón Santoyo, "Balance y perspectiva," 116–18.

53. UNESCO, "Operational Guidelines," 5.

54. Castillo Peña et al., "Plan de Manejo."

55. El Tajín was assigned the administrative category necessary to receive an annual budget in 2005. See Nahúm Noguera Rico to Luciano Cedillo A., December 26, 2005, DOS-INAH, exp. "Veracruz, Tajín."

56. Unfortunately, these numbers are frequently in disagreement, particularly for the *gasto básico*. The INAH authorities consider this a result of administrative turnover and failure to complete the necessary verifications of spending. See INAH, "Evaluación del Plan," 76. I have generally preferred sources that include original documentation or were produced closer to the spending in question. I have also omitted payroll for *personal de estructura* (the director, administrator, and site custodios), which does not directly depend on the funding structure I discuss here.

57. David Barstow and Alejandra Xanic von Bertrab, "How Wal-Mart Used Payoffs to Get Its Way in Mexico," *New York Times*, December 18, 2012, https://www.nytimes.com/2012/12/18/business/walmart-bribes-teotihuacan.html.

58. Castañeda, *In the Museum*; Breglia, *Monumental Ambivalence*. For concerts in Chichén Itzá, see, for example, Arturo Cruz Bárcenas and Luis Boffil, "Emocionan Plácido Domingo y Manzanero en Chichén Itzá," *La Jornada*, October 5, 2008, https://www.jornada.com.mx/2008/10/05/index.php?section=espectaculos&article=a37n1esp.

59. Villalobos Acosta, "Light Shows."

60. Bazbaz Lapidus, "Cumbre Tajín," 8.

61. Gobierno del Estado de Veracruz, "Cumbre Olmeca es de todas y todos para preservar la cultura y reactivar la economía del sur de Veracruz," September 21, 2022, http://www.veracruz.gob.mx/2022/09/21/cumbre-olmeca-es-de-todas-y-todos-para-preservar-la-cultura-y-reactivar-la-economia-del-sur-de-veracruz/; Martínez Cabral, "Festivales y Mercantilización Cultural," 92.

62. Brizuela Absalón, "De la Cumbre Tajín."

63. Wilkerson, "Waters Took Them."

64. Vera Cortés, "Totonacapan, 1999," 72.

65. Chenaut, "Las paradojas del Estado"; Reyes García, "Ante Cumbre Tajín."

66. Gameros, "Cumbre Tajín como espacio."

67. Alemán Velazco, *Segundo informe de gobierno*.

68. Reyes García, "Ante Cumbre Tajín," 108–58.

69. Gameros, "Cumbre Tajín como espacio," 255–57.

70. Alavez Segura and Vaca Espino, "Cumbre Tajin."

71. Breglia, "Business of Wonder," 212.

72. The funding of the event is also tied to the Duarte case. See Arturo Ángel, "Joyas, propiedades, parientes en nómina: La red de Karime Macías, esposa de Javier Duarte," *Animal Político*, April 19, 2017, https://animalpolitico.com/2017 /04/joyas-propiedades-parientes-en-nomina-la-red-de-karime-macias-esposa -de-javier-duarte.

73. The most complete data source to which I have access was returned via email in response to a Plataforma Nacional de Transparencia request to the Fideicomiso Público de Administración y Operación del Parque Temático Takhil-Sukut, INAI, Folio 301559400000321. Given the difficulty of accessing original documentation, and because general trends and relative proportions are most relevant for this discussion, I have preferred these figures for consistency's sake—with the exception of the contributions to INAH (2011–13) and their cessation, noted in INAH, "Evaluación del Plan," 23. However, it is worth noting that published sources are inconsistent; compare Marín Carreón, "El turismo como base," 116–29; Leopoldo Lara González to Concepción Moreno, April 9, 2010, INAI, Folio 00073410, Oficio UAIP/255/2010.

74. The Duarte case broke in 2016. For details, see Arturo Ángel and Víctor Hugo Artega, "El caso de las empresas fantasma de Veracruz," *Animal Político*, May 24, 2016, https://www.animalpolitico.com/2016/05/desaparece-el-gobierno -de-veracruz-645-millones-de-pesos-entrega-el-dinero-a-empresas-fantasma/. The governor resigned, fled to Guatemala, and was captured in 2017. See Zorayda Gallegos, "El exgobernador mexicano Javier Duarte es condenado a nueve años de prisión tras declararse culpable," *El País*, September 27, 2018, https://elpais.com/internacional/2018/09/27/mexico/1537999590_041505 .html.

75. See also INAH, "Evaluación del Plan," 23.

76. Breglia, *Monumental Ambivalence*, 11–14.

77. See Munck, "The Precariat"; compare Armstrong-Fumero, "Ouija Boards," 335–36.

78. Gershon, "Neoliberal Agency," 546.

79. This tendency is specific to neither El Tajín nor the INAH. For at-will workers, changes in presidential administration meant a cascade of firings and hirings, with ample opportunity for mobility in all directions. See Grindle, *Bureaucrats, Politicians, and Peasants*, 41–69. At least the INAH's director-general survived the transition: appointed in 2017, he remained in the post through early 2025.

80. Rojas Ruiz, "La Secretaría de Cultura," 18.

81. While there are 137 custodios in Teotihuacan, there are another forty subcontracted maintenance workers and thirty-eight police officers. In the words of one analyst, those in their department "operate basically according to internal agreements, leaving them in an undefined legal situation with respect to their functions." See Delgado Rubio, "Zona arqueológica de Teotihuacan," 142–43.

82. Guardia Nacional, "En Veracruz, Guardia Nacional realiza recorridos de seguridad y proximidad en la Zona Arqueológica El Tajín," June 17, 2023, http://www.gob.mx/guardianacional/prensa/en-veracruz-guardia-nacional-realiza-recorridos-de-seguridad-y-proximidad-en-la-zona-arqueologica-el-tajin?idiom=es.
83. Omar Espinosa Severino, "¿Quién protege a los protectores del patrimonio?" *Paso Libre*, February 9, 2020, https://pasolibre.grecu.mx/quien-protege-a-los-protectores-del-patrimonio/.

Conclusion

1. Castañeda, "Approaching Ruins."
2. Castillo Peña, "Planteamientos y perspectivas," 194–95, 217–27; Castillo Peña, "El Edificio"; contrast Brüggemann, "De la expansión."
3. Trouillot, *Silencing the Past*, 26.
4. Nicholas and Hollowell, "Ethical Challenges," 63.
5. See introduction of this book, notes 51, 106, and 107, and Bernal, *History of Mexican Archaeology*; Gándara, *La arqueología oficial mexicana*.
6. Meskell, "Archaeological Ethnography," 84. See, among others, Ardren, "Conversations"; Atalay, "Indigenous Archaeology"; Diserens Morgan and Leventhal, "Maya of the Past"; Cojti Ren, "Maya Archaeology"; Dedrick, "Photovoice"; Leventhal et al., "Community Heritage Project"; Nicholas and Hollowell, "Ethical Challenges"; Schneider and Hayes, "Epistemic Colonialism"; Watkins, "Through Wary Eyes."
7. Heath-Stout, *Identity, Oppression, and Diversity*.
8. Leathem, "History (Dis)Possessed"; Mucher, *Before American History*; Ocampo, *Where We Belong*.
9. Gándara, *La arqueología oficial mexicana*; Yadeun, "Arqueología de la arqueología"; Litvak King, "Posiciones teóricas"; Matos Moctezuma, "Las corrientes arqueológicas"; Panameño and Nalda, "Arqueología."
10. Martínez Muriel, "Archaeological Research."
11. Holley-Kline, "José García Payón."
12. Robles García and Corbett, "Heritage Resource Management," 113.
13. Edgar Ávila, "Veracruz, fosa sin fin; van mil 178 víctimas en entierros clandestinos," *El Universal*, September 11, 2018, http://www.eluniversal.com.mx/estados/veracruz-fosa-sin-fin-van-mil-178-victimas-en-entierros-clandestinos.
14. Del Palacio and Olvera, "Acallar las voces"; Del Palacio Montiel, "Resistencia, resiliencia y luchas."
15. Miguel Ángel León Carmona, Marcos Muedano, and Ignacio Alzaga, "La red política y criminal que asesinó a María Elena Ferral en Veracruz," *Alianza de Medios MX*, January 23, 2022, https://alianzademediosmx.org/noticias/la-red-politica-y-criminal-que-asesino-a-maria-elena-ferral-en-veracruz/995.
16. González, "Impunidad e invisibilización."

17. Suárez et al., "Epidemiología de COVID-19."

18. Luis Alberto Xochihua, "Así podrás disfrutar las atracciones de El Tajín, tras reapertura," *Diario de Xalapa*, February 8, 2022, https://www.diariodexalapa .com.mx/local/la-zona-arqueologica-de-el-tajin-reabre-sus-puertas-aunque-lo -hace-con-una-serie-de-restricciones-7834322.html.

19. The quoted figure was 4 million pesos per month; I used a rough conversion rate of 20 pesos to the dollar. Vanguardia de Veracruz, "El Tajín cerrado ocasiona pérdidas de 4 mdp mensuales," *Vanguardia de Veracruz*, May 26, 2021, https://www.vanguardiaveracruz.mx/el-tajin-cerrado-ocasiona-perdidas-de-4 -mdp-mensuales/.

20. Matthew Lerner, "Grace's Damage in Mexico, Caribbean Pegged at about $330M," *Business Insurance*, August 26, 2021, https://www.businessinsurance .com/grace%C2%92s-damage-in-mexico-caribbean-pegged-at-about-330m/; Aon plc, "Global Catastrophe Recap: August 2021," accessed September 16, 2021, http://thoughtleadership.aon.com/Documents/20210009_analytics-if -august-global-recap.pdf.

21. Eirinet Gómez, "Suben hasta 400% precios de básicos en Veracruz," *La Jornada*, August 27, 2021, https://www.jornada.com.mx/notas/2021/08/27 /estados/suben-hasta-400-precios-de-basicos-en-veracruz/.

22. Noé Zavaleta, "Los daños de 'Grace' en Veracruz: Tiempos de indolencia," *Proceso*, September 5, 2021, http://www.proceso.com.mx/reportajes/2021/9/5/los -danos-de-grace-en-veracruz-tiempos-de-indolencia-271333.html; Vanguardia de Veracruz, "Incalculables pérdidas generó 'Grace' a su paso por Tecolutla," *Vanguardia de Veracruz*, August 23, 2021, https://vanguardiaveracruz.com /incalculables-perdidas-genero-grace-a-su-paso-por-tecolutla/.

Bibliography

Archives and Manuscript Materials

ADDMP. Archivo de la Dirección del Departamento de Monumentos Prehispánicos. Instituto Nacional de Antropología e Historia, Mexico City.

AGEV-JGP. Archivo General del Estado de Veracruz, Archivo Histórico, Fondo Archivos Particulares, Sección José García Payón. Gobierno del Estado de Veracruz, Xalapa.

AGN-IPBA. Archivo General de la Nación, Fondo Instrucción Pública y Bellas Artes. Mexico City.

AH-CIV. Archivo Histórico del Centro INAH Veracruz, Fondo Incorporado 1934–1973 (José García Payón). Centro INAH Veracruz, Veracruz.

AHI-INAH. Archivo Histórico Institucional del INAH. Instituto Nacional de Antropología e Historia, Mexico City.

AH-MNA. Archivo Histórico del Museo Nacional de Antropología. Instituto Nacional de Antropología e Historia, Mexico City.

AHPM. Archivo Histórico de Petróleos Mexicanos, Fondo Expropriación. Petróleos Mexicanos, Mexico City.

AM-DMP. Archivo Muerto del Departamento de Monumentos Prehispánicos. Instituto Nacional de Antropología e Historia, Mexico City.

AT-CIV. Archivo Técnico del Centro INAH Veracruz. Centro INAH Veracruz, Veracruz.

AT-CNA. Archivo Técnico de la Coordinación Nacional de Arqueología. Instituto Nacional de Antropología e Historia, Mexico City.

AT-DMP. Archivo Técnico del Departamento de Monumentos Prehispánicos. Instituto Nacional de Antropología e Historia, Mexico City.

BLT-AE. Biblioteca Lerdo de Tejada, Archivos Económicos. Secretaría de Hacienda y Credito Público, Mexico City.

CIW Department of Archaeology Records, 1914–1955, Group III-I#18, Proskouriakoff, T. original field diaries, 1950: Mexico, Tajin. Peabody Museum of Archaeology and Ethnology, Cambridge, Massachusetts.

DOS-INAH. Dirección de Operación de Sitios del INAH. Instituto Nacional de Antropología e Historia, Mexico City.

INAI. Instituto Nacional de Acceso a la Información, Mexico City. https://home
.inai.org.mx/.

ITKEA. Isabel T. Kelly Ethnographic Archive, MSS 0122. Southern Methodist University, DeGolyer Library, Dallas.

NAA-RISA. Records of the Institute of Social Anthropology, Kelly, Isabel, Series
4: Correspondence, National Anthropology Archives. Smithsonian Institution,
Washington DC.

Published Works

Abu El Haj, Nadia. *Facts on the Ground: Archaeological Practice and Territorial Self-Fashioning in Israeli Society*. Chicago: University of Chicago Press, 2001.

Achim, Miruna. *From Idols to Antiquity: Forging the National Museum of Mexico*.
Lincoln: University of Nebraska Press, 2017.

———. "Writing Lessons in Antiquarianism: Guillermo Dupaix's Manuscripts."
Colonial Latin American Review 29, no. 2 (2020): 316–39. https://doi.org/10.1080
/10609164.2020.1755942.

Acuña, René, ed. "Relación de Hueytlalpa y su partido." In *Relaciones geográficas del
siglo XVI: Tlaxcala*, vol. 2, 147–94. Mexico City: UNAM, 1985.

Aguilar León, Irvin E. "Transformaciones socioterritoriales asociadas a la política
de extracción de petróleo en México: El caso de la comunidad Emiliano Zapata,
Papantla, Veracruz (1954–2012)." Maestría thesis, El Colegio de Veracruz, 2017.

Aguilar Sánchez, Martín. "Explotación petrolera y resistencia en la región Papantla-
Poza Rica." In *Protestas y movilizaciones sociales en el Golfo de México*, edited by
Martín Aguilar Sánchez, 80–93. Xalapa: Universidad Veracruzana, 2020.

Alafita Méndez, Leopoldo. "Perforación y perforadores: 1906–1938." *Anuario: Centro
de Estudios Históricos, Universidad Veracruzana* 7 (1990): 147–59.

Alavez Segura, Francisco, and Rosa María Vaca Espino. "'Cumbre Tajín': A Controversial Indigenous Cultural Event." In *Tourism, Festivals and Cultural Events in
Times of Crisis*, edited by Lise Lyck, Phil Long, and Allan Xenius Grige, 107–17.
Copenhagen: Copenhagen School of Business, 2012.

Alazraki, Benito, dir. *Raíces*. Mexico City: Teleproducciones, 1953.

Albarrán Chávez, Rafael. "Historia de los trabajadores ATM del INAH: Institución,
patrimonio cultural y conflicto sindical." Licenciatura thesis, Escuela Nacional de
Antropología e Historia, 2008.

Albro, Robert. "Neoliberal Cultural Heritage and Bolivia's New Indigenous Public."
In *Ethnographies of Neoliberalism*, edited by Carol J. Greenhouse, 146–61. Philadelphia: University of Pennsylvania Press, 2010.

Alemán Velazco, Miguel. *Segundo informe de gobierno, 1999–2000*. Xalapa: Gobierno
del Estado de Veracruz, 2000.

Alexander, Ryan. "Mexican Politics, Economy, and Society, 1946–1982." In *Oxford
Research Encyclopedia of Latin American History*. Oxford University Press, 2016.
https://doi.org/10.1093/acrefore/9780199366439.013.261.

Alexandrino Ocaña, Grace. "Seeking Rights to a City of Huacas: Cultural Heritage Management and Urban Citizenship in Lima, Peru." Doctoral thesis, Stanford University, 2020.

Alonso, Ana María. "Territorializing the Nation and 'Integrating the Indian': 'Mestizaje' in Mexican Official Discourses and Public Culture." In *Sovereign Bodies: Citizens, Migrants, and States in the Postcolonial World*, edited by Thomas Blom Hansen and Finn Stepputat, 39–60. Princeton: Princeton University Press, 2005.

Álvarez de la Borda, Joel. "Adolfo Autrey y el petróleo de El Cuguas." *Historias* 90 (2015): 99–108.

———. *Crónica del petróleo en México: De 1863 a nuestros días*. Mexico City: Petróleos Mexicanos, 2006.

———. *Los orígenes de la industria petrolera en México 1900–1925*. Mexico City: Archivo Histórico de PEMEX, 2005.

Alzate y Ramírez, José Antonio de. *Descripción de las antigüedades de Xochicalco*. Mexico City: Don Felipe de Zúñiga y Ontiveros, 1791.

Andrien, Kenneth J. "The Bourbon Reforms." *Oxford Bibliographies*, 2018. https://doi.org/10.1093/obo/9780199766581-0043.

Araya Fernández, Carlos, Roberto Cordero Solórzano, Amelia Paniagua Vásquez, and José Bernal Azofeifa Bolaños, eds. *I Seminario Internacional de Vainilla: Promoviendo la investigación, la extensión y la producción de vainilla en Mesoamérica*. Heredia: Instituto de Investigación y Servicios Forestales/Universidad Nacional de Costa Rica, 2014.

Ardren, Traci. "Conversations about the Production of Archaeological Knowledge and Community Museums at Chunchucmil and Kochol, Yucatán, México." *World Archaeology* 34, no. 2 (2002): 379–400. https://doi.org/10.1080/0043824022000007161.

Armstrong-Fumero, Fernando. "Artifactual Surface and the Limits of Inclusion: Blurring the Boundary Between Materiality and Intangible Heritage." *Anthropological Quarterly* 91, no. 4 (2018): 1303–28. https://doi.org/10.1353/anq.2018.0066.

———. "Ouija Boards, Shape Shifters, and Dropouts: Moral Panics and Neoliberal Precarity in Rural Yucatan." *Dialectical Anthropology* 43, no. 3 (2019): 333–46. https://doi.org/10.1007/s10624-019-09548-3.

Arnold, Philip J., III, and Christopher A. Pool. "Charting Classic Veracruz." In *Classic Period Cultural Currents in Southern and Central Veracruz*, edited by Philip J. Arnold III and Christopher A. Pool, 1–21. Cambridge: Dumbarton Oaks Research Library and Collection, 2008.

Arnold, Philip J., III, Christopher A. Pool, and Richard A. Diehl. "Historical Currents in Classic Veracruz Research." In *Classic Period Cultural Currents in Southern and Central Veracruz*, edited by Philip J. Arnold III and Christopher A. Pool, 23–53. Cambridge: Dumbarton Oaks Research Library & Collection, 2008.

Atalay, Sonya. "Indigenous Archaeology as Decolonizing Practice." *American Indian Quarterly* 30, no. 3/4 (2006): 280–310. https://doi.org/10.1353/aiq.2006.0015.

Autrey de Ziebe, Lorenza. "Centenario de Casa Autrey." In *Farmacias y Farmacéuticos en México*, edited by Efraín Castro Morales, María Concepción Amerlinck de Corsi, and Lorenza Autrey de Ziebe, 85–123. Mexico City: Casa Autrey, 1992.

Avelar Gabi, Margarita. "La administración de los bienes arqueológicos de Teotihuacán en los años 1916 y 1920." Licenciatura thesis, ENAH, 2022.

Avila, Lixion A. "Hurricane Katia, 5–9 September 2017." Tropical Cyclone Report. Miami: National Hurricane Center, February 14, 2019.

Ávila Hernández, Julieta. "Proceso de trabajo y democratización sindical en el Instituto Nacional de Antropología e Historia (INAH) (1975–1985): Caso de la Delegación Sindical D-III-24." Licenciatura thesis, UNAM, 1988.

Aviña, Alexander. *Specters of Revolution: Peasant Guerrillas in the Cold War Mexican Countryside*. New York: Oxford University Press, 2014.

Baer, Werner. "Import Substitution and Industrialization in Latin America: Experiences and Interpretations." *Latin American Research Review* 7, no. 1 (1972): 95–122. https://doi.org/10.1017/S0023879100041224.

Barker, Alex W. "Looting, the Antiquities Trade, and Competing Valuations of the Past." *Annual Review of Anthropology* 47, no. 1 (2018): 455–74. https://doi.org/10.1146/annurev-anthro-102116-041320.

Bauer, Arnold J. "Rural Workers in Spanish America: Problems of Peonage and Oppression." *Hispanic American Historical Review* 59, no. 1 (1979): 34–63. https://doi.org/10.1215/00182168-59.1.34.

Bausa, José M. "Bosquejo geográfico y estadístico del partido de Papantla." *Boletín de la Sociedad Mexicana de Geografía y Estadística* 5 (1857): 374–426.

Bazbaz Lapidus, Salomón. "Cumbre Tajín: Modelo de gestion de patrimonio cultural de Veracruz." In *I Primer Congreso Latinoamericano de Gestión Cultural*. Santiago, Chile, 2014. http://observatoriocultural.udgvirtual.udg.mx/repositorio/handle/123456789/160.

Belmonte Guzmán, María de la Luz. *La organización territorial de Veracruz en el siglo XIX*. Xalapa: Universidad Veracruzana, 1987.

Beltrán Rosas, Karla. "Estudio etnografíco de la producción y distribución de la hoja de maíz en la comunidad Gildardo Muñoz de Papantla, Veracruz." Licenciatura thesis, Universidad Autonoma Metropolitana Iztapalapa, 2020.

Benavides, O. Hugo. *Making Ecuadorian Histories: Four Centuries of Defining Power*. Austin: University of Texas Press, 2004.

Bensusán, Graciela, and Kevin J. Middlebrook. *Organized Labour and Politics in Mexico: Changes, Continuities and Contradictions*. London: Institute for the Study of the Americas, 2012.

Bensusán, Graciela, and Maria Lorena Cook. "State-Corporatist Legacies and Divergent Paths: Argentina and Mexico." In *Working through the Past: Labor and Authoritarian Legacies in Comparative Perspective*, edited by Teri L. Caraway, Maria Lorena Cook, and Stephen Crowley, 142–63. Ithaca: Cornell University Press, 2015.

Berenstein, Nadia. "Making a Global Sensation: Vanilla Flavor, Synthetic Chemistry, and the Meanings of Purity." *History of Science* 54, no. 4 (2016): 399–424. https://doi.org/10.1177/0073275316681802.

Berger, Dina. *The Development of Mexico's Tourism Industry: Pyramids by Day, Martinis by Night.* New York: Palgrave Macmillan, 2006.

Berggren, Asa, and Ian Hodder. "Social Practice, Method, and Some Problems of Field Archaeology." *American Antiquity* 68, no. 2 (2003): 421–34. https://doi.org/10.2307/3557102.

Bernal, Ignacio. "The Effect of Settlement Pattern Studies on the Archaeology of Central Mexico." In *Prehistoric Settlement Patterns: Essays in Honor of Gordon R. Willey,* edited by Evon Z. Vogt and Richard M. Leventhal, 389–98. Alburquerque: University of New Mexico Press, 1983.

———. *A History of Mexican Archaeology: The Vanished Civilizations of Middle America.* New York: Thames and Hudson, 1980.

Bernbeck, Reinhard, and Susan Pollock. "The Political Economy of Archaeological Practice and the Production of Heritage in the Middle East." In *A Companion to Social Archaeology,* edited by Lynn Meskell and Robert W. Preucel, 335–52. Malden MA: Blackwell, 2007.

Bess, Michael K. *Routes of Compromise: Building Roads and Shaping the Nation in Mexico, 1917–1952.* Lincoln: University of Nebraska Press, 2017.

Bethell, Leslie, ed. *Mexico since Independence.* Cambridge: Cambridge University Press, 1991.

Black, Brian. *Crude Reality: Petroleum in World History.* New York: Rowman & Littlefield, 2012.

———. *Petrolia: The Landscape of America's First Oil Boom.* Baltimore: The Johns Hopkins University Press, 2000.

Blomley, Nicholas. "Making Private Property: Enclosure, Common Right and the Work of Hedges." *Rural History* 18, no. 1 (2007): 1–21. https://doi.org/10.1017/S0956793306001993.

———. "Making Space for Property." *Annals of the Association of American Geographers* 104, no. 6 (2014): 1291–306. https://doi.org/10.1080/00045608.2014.941738.

Bonilla, Mónica Aguilar. "The Pothunter's Livelihood: Huaquerismo and Costa Rican Law in Defense of the National Archaeological Heritage." *Anthropology of Work Review* 28, no. 2 (2007): 8–12. https://doi.org/10.1525/awr.2007.28.2.8.

Boone, Elizabeth Hill, ed. *Collecting the Pre-Columbian Past.* Washington DC: Dumbarton Oaks Research Library and Collection, 1993.

Brading, David A. "Manuel Gamio and Official Indigenismo in Mexico." *Bulletin of Latin American Research* 7, no. 1 (1988): 75–89. https://doi.org/10.2307/3338441.

———. *The Origins of Mexican Nationalism.* Cambridge: Cambridge Centre of Latin American Studies, 1985.

Brading, David A., and Harry E. Cross. "Colonial Silver Mining: Mexico and Peru." *Hispanic American Historical Review* 52, no. 4 (1972): 545–79. https://doi.org/10.2307/2512781.

Braunschweig, Elisabeth. "Repercusiones económicas, sociales y culturales en comunidades Totonacos, afectadas por PEMEX." Instituto Nacional de Pueblos Indígenas, Biblioteca Juan Rulfo, Mexico City, Fondo Documental INI, DC 30/0133, 1981.

Breglia, Lisa. "The Business of Wonder: Public Meets Private at a World Heritage Site." In *World Heritage on the Ground: Ethnographic Perspectives*, edited by Christopher Brumann and David Berliner, 193–216. New York: Berghahn Books, 2016.

———. *Living with Oil: Promises, Peaks, and Declines on Mexico's Gulf Coast.* Austin: University of Texas Press, 2013.

———. *Monumental Ambivalence: The Politics of Heritage.* Austin: University of Texas Press, 2006.

Breglia, Lisa C. "Keeping World Heritage in the Family: A Genealogy of Maya Labour at Chichén Itzá." *International Journal of Heritage Studies* 11, no. 5 (2005): 385–98. https://doi.org/10.1080/13527250500337421.

Brizuela Absalón, Álvaro. "De la Cumbre Tajín." *El Jejen: Nota que hincha*, n.d. http://eljejen.com/_ttn/_fls/120925_DelaCumbreTajin_ABrizuelaA.htm.

———. "Desamortización de bienes en Ojital y Potrero." *Altepetl: Geografía histórica, social y estudios regionales*, no. 4 (2011).

———. "Las compañías petroleras extranjeras en Ojital y Potrero." Museo de Antropología de Xalapa, n.d.

———. "Marco geográfico y cultural." In *Tajín*, edited by Juergen K. Brueggemann, 21–46. Xalapa: Gobierno del Estado de Veracruz, 1992.

———. "Noticias de la población afromexicana en la región de Papantla, Veracruz, a principios del siglo XIX." In *¿Dónde están? Investigaciones sobre afromexicanos*, edited by Emiliano Gallaga Murrieta, 47–53. Tuxtla Gutiérrez: UNICACH, 2010.

———. "Papantla en las Relaciones Geográficas del Obispado de Tlaxcala, Siglo XVI." *Altepetl: Geografía histórica, social y estudios regionales* 3 (2011): 54–70.

———. "Un asentamiento campesino en un sitio arqueológico." *Revista Mexicana de Estudios Antropólogicos* 45–46 (2000): 115–19.

Brockington, Dan. *Fortress Conservation: The Preservation of the Mkomazi Game Reserve, Tanzania.* Bloomington: Indiana University Press, 2002.

Brown, Cecil H., David Beck, Grzegorz Kondrak, James K. Watters, and Søren Wichmann. "Totozoquean." *International Journal of American Linguistics* 77, no. 3 (2011): 323–72. https://doi.org/10.1086/660972.

Brown, Jonathan C. *Oil and Revolution in Mexico.* Berkeley: University of California Press, 1993.

———. "The Structure of the Foreign-Owned Petroleum Industry in Mexico, 1880–1938." In *The Mexican Petroleum Industry in the Twentieth Century*, edited by Jonathan C. Brown and Alan Knight, 1–35. Austin: University of Texas Press, 1992.

Brown, Jonathan C., and Alan Knight, eds. *The Mexican Petroleum Industry in the Twentieth Century*. Austin: University of Texas Press, 1992.

Brown, Kendall W. *A History of Mining in Latin America: From the Colonial Era to the Present*. Albuquerque: University of New Mexico Press, 2012.

Brown, Margaret L. "Madagascar's Cyclone Vulnerability and the Global Vanilla Economy." In *The Political Economy of Hazards and Disasters*, edited by Eric C. Jones and Arthur D. Murphy, 241–64. Lanham MD: Rowman & Littlefield, 2009.

Bruchac, Margaret M. *Savage Kin: Indigenous Informants and American Anthropologists*. Tucson: University of Arizona Press, 2018.

Brueggemann, Juergen K. "Apuntes para la restauración de edificios prehispánicos en México." *Antropología: Boletín oficial del Instituto Nacional de Antropología e Historia*, no. 29 (1990): 32–39.

———. "El problema cronológica del Tajín." *Arqueología*, no. 9–10 (1993): 61–72.

———. "Proyecto Tajín." *Consejo de Arqueología: Boletín*, 1990, 29–33.

Brüggemann, Jürgen K. "De la expansión a la anarquía: La ciudad de Tajín." *Arqueología mexicana* 1, no. 5 (1994): 26–56.

———. "¡Otra vez la cuestión totonaca!" *Antropología: Boletín oficial del Instituto Nacional de Antropología e Historia*, no. 34 (1991): 84–85.

———. "Tajín en números." *Arqueología mexicana* 1, no. 5 (1994): 57.

Brulotte, Ronda L. *Between Art and Artifact: Archaeological Replicas and Cultural Production in Oaxaca, Mexico*. Austin: University of Texas Press, 2012.

Bruman, Henry. "The Culture History of Mexican Vanilla." *Hispanic American Historical Review* 28, no. 3 (1948): 360–76. https://doi.org/10.1215/00182168-28.3.360.

Bueno, Christina. "Forjando Patrimonio: The Making of Archaeological Patrimony in Porfirian Mexico." *Hispanic American Historical Review* 90, no. 2 (2010): 215–45. https://doi.org/10.1215/00182168-2009-133.

———. *The Pursuit of Ruins: Archaeology, History, and the Making of Modern Mexico*. Albuquerque: University of New Mexico Press, 2016.

Bulmer-Thomas, Victor. *The Economic History of Latin America since Independence*. New York: Cambridge University Press, 2003.

Butler, Judith. *Frames of War: When Is Life Grievable?* London: Verso Books, 2009.

Byrne, Denis. "Counter-Mapping in the Archaeological Landscape." In *Handbook of Landscape Archaeology*, edited by Bruno David and Julian Thomas, 609–16. Walnut Creek CA: Left Coast Press, 2008.

———. "Western Hegemony in Archaeological Heritage Management." *History and Anthropology* 5, no. 2 (1991): 269–76. https://doi.org/10.1080/02757206.1991.9960815.

Cabrera Rodríguez, Luis. "Análisis socioecológico de la apropiación del territorio en la comunidades de San Antonio Ojital y Nuevo Ojital, Papantla, Ver." Maestría thesis, Universidad Veracruzana, 2018.

Callon, Michel. "Some Elements of a Sociology of Translation: Domestication of the Scallops and the Fisherman of St. Brieuc Bay." In *Power, Action and Belief: A*

New Sociology of Knowledge?, edited by John Law, 196–233. London: Routledge & Kegan Paul, 1986.

Cámara de Diputados. *Diario de los debates de la Cámara de Diputados, Décima Legislatura Constitucional de la Union.* Vol. 1. Mexico City: Tipografía Literaria de F. Mata, 1880.

Campos, Alexia. "Rasgos del indigenismo participativo en Papantla, Veracruz: Identidad, intermediarios y formación de nuevos sujetos indígenas (1972–1982)." Maestría thesis, CIESAS-Golfo, 2021.

Cañizares-Esguerra, Jorge. *How to Write the History of the New World: Histories, Epistemologies, and Identities in the Eighteenth-Century Atlantic World.* Stanford: Stanford University Press, 2001.

Cano González, Onésimo. "Monografía de la Ranchería Jorge Serdán." Dirección General de Culturas Populares, Indígenas y Urbanas, Centro de Información y Documentación Alberto Beltrán, Mexico City, Fondo Documental D/MO-ES/19, 1983.

Capitanachi Luna, Sinesio. *Furbero, Palma Sola y Poza Rica: Historia del petróleo y memorias de un trabajador jubilado en la industria petrolera.* 2 vols. Xalapa: Gobierno del Estado de Veracruz, 1983.

Caplan, Karen D. *Indigenous Citizens: Local Liberalism in Early National Oaxaca and Yucatán.* Stanford: Stanford University Press, 2009.

Carballo, David M. *Collision of Worlds: A Deep History of the Fall of Aztec Mexico and the Forging of New Spain.* Oxford: Oxford University Press, 2020.

Cárdenas, Enrique. "La economía mexicana en el dilatado siglo XX, 1929–2009." In *Historia económica general de México, de la colonia a nuestros días,* edited by Sandra Kuntz Ficker, 503–48. Mexico City: El Colegio de México, 2010.

Cardoso, Eliana, and Ann Helwege. *Latin America's Economy: Diversity, Trends, and Conflicts.* Cambridge: MIT Press, 1993.

Carrasco, Alma, and Rollin Kent. "Power, Identity and Discourse in the Institutionalization of Basic Education in Mexico." *Counterpoints* 387 (2011): 195–208.

Carrillo Dewar, Ivonne. *Industria petrolera y desarrollo capitalista en el Norte de Veracruz 1900–1990.* Xalapa: Universidad Veracruzana, 1993.

CartoCrítica. "Actualidad de la fracturación hidráulica en México." *CartoCrítica: Investigación, mapas y datos para la sociedad civil,* January 24, 2019. https://cartocritica.org.mx/2019/actualidad-de-la-fracturacion-hidraulica-en-mexico/.

Casanova, Rosa. "La fotografía en el Museo Nacional y la expedición científica de Cempoala." *Dimensión Antropológica* 42 (2008): 55–92.

Castañeda, Quetzil. "Approaching Ruins: A Photo-Ethnographic Essay on the Busy Intersections of Chichén Itzá." *Visual Anthropology Review* 16, no. 2 (2000): 43–70. https://doi.org/10.1525/var.2000.16.2.43.

——— . *In the Museum of Maya Culture: Touring Chichén Itzá.* Minneapolis: University of Minnesota Press, 1996.

Castellanos, M. Bianet. *Indigenous Dispossession: Housing and Maya Indebtedness in Mexico.* Stanford: Stanford University Press, 2020.

Castillo Peña, Patricia, ed. *Culturas del Golfo: Salvamento arqueológico y nuevas tecnologías*. Mexico City: INAH/PEMEX, 2011.

———. "El Edificio de los Nichos de El Tajín: Arquitectura para comunicarse con los dioses." In *Un patrimonio universal: Las pirámides de México; Cosmovisión, cultura y ciencia*, edited by Pedro Francisco Sánchez Nava. Mexico City: INAH, 2018.

———. "Planteamientos y perspectivas para la arqueología del paisaje en el antiguo Tajín: Tiempo, espacio y agencia." Doctoral thesis, ENAH, 2016.

Castillo Peña, Patricia, Daniel Nahmad Molinari, Omar Ruíz Gordillo, and Laura Anitua Valdovinos. "Plan de Manejo: Zona de Monumentos Arqueológicos El Tajín." Mexico City: Instituto Nacional de Antropología e Historia, 2009.

Centeno, Miguel Ángel. *Democracy Within Reason: Technocratic Revolution in Mexico*. University Park: Penn State University Press, 1997.

Centro de Derechos Humanos Fray Bartolomé de Las Casas, A.C. "Informe preliminar sobre la masacre de Chinkultic." October 6, 2008. https://frayba.org.mx/sites/default/files/081006_informe_ejecuciones_en_chinkultic.pdf.

Chadha, Ashish. "Visions of Discipline: Sir Mortimer Wheeler and the Archaeological Method in India (1944–1948)." *Journal of Social Archaeology* 2, no. 3 (2001): 378–401. https://doi.org/10.1177/146960530200200305.

Chang, David A. "Enclosures of Land and Sovereignty: The Allotment of American Indian Lands." *Radical History Review*, no. 109 (2011): 108–19. https://doi.org/10.1215/01636545-2010-018.

Chase, Arlen F., and Diane Z. Chase, eds. *The Market for Mesoamerica: Reflections on the Sale of Pre-Columbian Antiquities*. Gainesville: University Press of Florida, 2019.

Chassen-López, Francie R. *From Liberal to Revolutionary Oaxaca: The View from the South: Mexico, 1867–1911*. University Park: Pennsylvania State University Press, 2004.

Checa-Artasu, Martín M. "Los efectos en el territorio de la explotación de hidrocarburos en México: Recuento bibliográfico." In *El petróleo en México y sus impactos sobre el territorio*, edited by Martín M. Checa-Artasu and Regina Hernández Franyuti, 17–48. Mexico City: Instituto de Investigaciones Dr. José María Luis Mora, 2016.

Chenaut, Victoria. *Aquellos que vuelan: Los totonacos en el siglo XIX*. Mexico City: CIESAS/Instituto de Ecología, A.C., 1995.

———. "Comunidad y ley en Papantla a fines del siglo XIX." In *La costa totonaca: Cuestiones regionales II*, edited by Luis María Gatti and Victoria Chenaut, 65–89. Mexico City: CIESAS, 1987.

———. "Impactos sociales y ambientales de la explotación de hidrocarburos en el municipio de Papantla, Veracruz (México)." *E-Cuadernos* CES, no. 28 (2017): 94–117.

———. "Las paradojas del Estado mexicano en un municipio de Veracruz." In *Pueblos indígenas y Estado en México: La disputa por la justicia y los derechos*, edited by Santiago Bastos and María Teresa Sierra, 126–60. Mexico City: CIESAS, 2017.

Chirikure, Shadreck. "'Where Angels Fear to Tread': Ethics, Commercial Archaeology, and Extractive Industries in Southern Africa." *Azania: Archaeological Research in Africa* 49, no. 2 (2014): 218–31. https://doi.org/10.1080/0067270X.2014.909166.

Christenson, Allen J., ed. *The Title of Totonicapán.* Boulder: University Press of Colorado, 2022.

Cipagaula Valenzuela, Adel, and Armando Sánchez Río. *La vainilla en México: Producción, industrialización y comercialización.* Mexico City: Secretaria de Agricultura y Recursos Hidraulicos, 1979.

Claassen, Cheryl. "Black and White Women at Irene Mound." *Southeastern Archaeology* 12, no. 2 (1993): 137–47.

Clarke, David. "Archaeology: The Loss of Innocence." *Antiquity* 47, no. 185 (1973): 6–18. https://doi.org/10.1017/S0003598X0003461X.

Cleere, Henry. "Introduction: The Rationale of Archaeological Heritage Management." In *Archaeological Heritage Management in the Modern World*, edited by Henry Cleere, 1–19. London: Routledge, 1989.

Coffey, Mary K. "From Nation to Community: Museums and the Reconfiguration of Mexican Society under Neoliberalism." In *Foucault, Cultural Studies, and Governmentality*, edited by Jack Z. Bratich, Jeremy Packer, and Cameron McCarthy, 207–41. Albany: State University of New York Press, 2003.

Coggins, Clemency. "Illicit Traffic of Pre-Columbian Antiquities." *Art Journal* 29, no. 1 (1969): 94–96, 98–114. https://doi.org/10.1080/00043249.1969.10794675.

Cohen, Anna S., and Rodrigo Solinis-Casparius. "The Micropolitics of Public Archaeology: Working with the Ejido in Michoacán, Mexico." *Journal of Social Archaeology* 17, no. 3 (2017): 326–48. https://doi.org/10.1177/1469605317724526.

Cojti Ren, Avexnim. "Maya Archaeology and the Political and Cultural Identity of Contemporary Maya in Guatemala." *Archaeologies* 2, no. 1 (2006): 8–19. https://doi.org/10.1007/s11759-006-0003-4.

Colburn, Forrest D. "Anger at El Tajin." *New Leader* 75, no. 12 (1992): 11.

Colchester, Marcus. "Conservation Policy and Indigenous Peoples." *Environmental Science & Policy* 7, no. 3 (2004): 145–53. https://doi.org/10.1016/j.envsci.2004.02.004.

Collier, Ruth Berins. *The Contradictory Alliance: State-Labor Relations and Regime Change in Mexico.* Berkeley: University of California, Berkeley, International and Area Studies, 1992.

Colwell, Chip. "Collaborative Archaeologies and Descendant Communities." *Annual Review of Anthropology* 45, no. 1 (2016): 113–27. https://doi.org/10.1146/annurev-anthro-102215-095937.

Colwell-Chanthaphonh, Chip. "Archaeology on the Periphery: Locating a 'Last Great Place.'" In *Ethnographies and Archaeologies: Iterations of the Past*, edited by Julie Hollowell and Lena Mortensen, 240–60. Gainesville: University Press of Florida, 2009.

Comisión Nacional de Hidrocarburos. "Proyecto Aceite Terciario del Golfo: Primera revisión y recomendaciones." Mexico City: Secretaría de Energía, 2010. https://www.gob.mx/cms/uploads/attachment/file/109350/Proy_aceite _terciario_del_golfo._Primera_rev_y_recomendaciones.pdf.

Condiciones Generales de Trabajo. 2nd ed. Mexico City: INAH/CONACULTA, 1980.

Conkey, Margaret W., and Sarah H. Williams. "Original Narratives: The Political Economy of Gender in Archaeology." In *Gender at the Crossroads of Knowledge Feminist Anthropology in the Postmodern Era,* edited by Michaela di Leonardo, 102–39. Berkeley: University of California Press, 1991.

Convenio de prestaciones socioeconómicas bienio 2009–2011. INAH/Consejo Nacional para la Cultura y las Artes, 2009.

Coombe, Rosemary. "Managing Cultural Heritage as Neoliberal Governmentality." In *Heritage Regimes and the State,* edited by Regina Bendix, Aditya Eggert, and Arnika Peselmann, 375–87. Göttingen: Universitätsverlag Göttingen, 2012.

Coombe, Rosemary, and Melissa Florence Baird. "The Limits of Heritage: Corporate Interests and Cultural Rights on Resource Frontiers." In *A Companion to Heritage Studies,* edited by William Logan, Máiréad Nic Craith, and Ullrich Kockel, 337–54. London: John Wiley & Sons, 2016.

Córdoba Azcárate, Matilde. *Stuck with Tourism: Space, Power, and Labor in Contemporary Yucatán.* Berkeley: University of California Press, 2021.

Correll, Donovan S. "Vanilla: Its Botany, History, Cultivation and Economic Import." *Economic Botany* 7, no. 4 (1953): 291–358. https://doi.org/10.1007 /BF02930810.

Cosgrove, Denis. "Prospect, Perspective and the Evolution of the Landscape Idea." *Transactions of the Institute of British Geographers,* new series 10, no. 1 (1985): 45–62. https://doi.org/10.2307/622249.

Coulthard, Glen Sean. *Red Skin, White Masks: Rejecting the Colonial Politics of Recognition.* Minneapolis: University of Minnesota Press, 2014.

Covert, Lisa Pinley. "Reframing Guanajuato's Indigenous Past: Archaeological Field Notes and Development Priorities." *The Latin Americanist* 65, no. 1 (2021): 35–54. https://doi.org/10.1353/tla.2021.0003.

———. *San Miguel de Allende: Mexicans, Foreigners, and the Making of a World Heritage Site.* Lincoln: University of Nebraska Press, 2017.

Cowgill, George L. *Ancient Teotihuacan: Early Urbanism in Central Mexico.* Cambridge: Cambridge University Press, 2015.

Cox Hall, Amy. *Framing a Lost City: Science, Photography, and the Making of Machu Picchu.* Austin: University of Texas Press, 2017.

Craib, Raymond B. *Cartographic Mexico: A History of State Fixations and Fugitive Landscapes.* Durham: Duke University Press, 2004.

Cruz, Margaret. "Gobierno mediante normas privadas: Pemex y la creación de un ejido ilegible." *Iztapalapa: Revista de ciencias sociales y humanidades* 40, no. 87 (2019): 45–70. https://doi.org/10.28928/ri/872019/atc2/cruzm.

———. "Property in Pieces: Land, Oil and Uncertainty in a Mexican Ejido." Doctoral thesis, City University of New York, 2022.

Cuevas Fernández, Hectór, Juan Sánchez Bonilla, Alfonso García y García, Yamile Lira López, and Jaime Ortega Guevara. *El Tajín: Estudios monográficos*. Xalapa: Universidad Veracruzana, 1995.

Curti Díaz, Erasmo. *Cultivo y beneficiado de la vainilla en México*. Papantla: Fondo Regional de Solidaridad del Totonacapan, 1995.

Cusicanqui, Silvia Rivera. "Ch'ixinakax Utxiwa: A Reflection on the Practices and Discourses of Decolonization." *South Atlantic Quarterly* 111, no. 1 (2012): 95–109. https://doi.org/10.1215/00382876-1472612.

Daneels, Annick. "El patrón de asentamiento del período clásico en la cuenca baja del río Cotaxtla, centro de Veracruz: Un estudio de caso de desarrollo de sociedades complejas en tierras bajas tropicales." Doctoral thesis, UNAM, 2002.

———. "José García Payón y Alfonso Medellín Zenil, pioneros de la arqueología del centro de Veracruz." *Anales de antropología* 40, no. 1–2 (2006): 9–40.

Dawson, Alexander. *First World Dreams: Mexico since 1989*. London: Zed Books, 2006.

———. *Indian and Nation in Revolutionary Mexico*. Tucson: University of Arizona Press, 2004.

Deans-Smith, Susan. "Native Peoples of the Gulf Coast from the Colonial Period to the Present." In *The Cambridge History of the Native Peoples of the Americas*, vol. 2, *Mesoamerica, Part 2*, edited by Richard E. W. Adams and Murdo J. MacLeod, 274–302. Cambridge: Cambridge University Press, 2000.

"Decreto por el que se declara zona de monumentos arqueológicos el área conocida como El Tajín, ubicada en el Municipio de Papantla de Olarte, en el Estado de Veracruz." *Diario Oficial de la Federación*, March 30, 2001.

Dedrick, Maia. "Photovoice as a Method for the Development of Collaborative Archaeological Practice." *Journal of Community Archaeology & Heritage* 5, no. 2 (2018): 85–100. https://doi.org/10.1080/20518196.2018.1442659.

DeGolyer, E., and A. B. Norman. "The Furbero Oil Field, Mexico." *Transactions of the American Institute of Mining Engineers* 52 (1916): 268–80. https://doi.org/10.2118/916268-G.

de la Luz Enríquez, Juan. "Memoria presentada ante la H. Legislatura del Estado de Veracruz-Llave por el C. gobernador constitucional general [...], en la sesión del 17 de septiembre de 1886, y que corresponde al período de su administración comprendido entre el 1 de enero de 1885 y el 30 de junio de 1886." In *Estado de Veracruz: Informes de sus gobernadores, 1826–1986*, vol. 5, edited by Carmen Blázquez Domínguez, 2263–714. Xalapa: Gobierno del Estado de Veracruz, 1986.

de la Mota y Escobar, Alonso. *Memoriales del Obispo de Tlaxcala: Un recorrido por el Centro del México a prinicipios del siglo XVII*. Edited by Alba González Jácome. Mexico City: Secretaría de Educación de Pública, 1985.

de la Peña, Moisés T. *Veracruz económico*. 2 vols. Mexico City: Gobierno del Estado de Veracruz, 1946.

Delgado, Dante. *Sexto informe del gobierno*. Xalapa: Gobierno del Estado de Veracruz, 1992.

Delgado Rubio, Jaime. "Zona arqueológica de Teotihuacan: Problemas y conflictos en torno a su conversación." Maestría thesis, UNAM, 2008.

Deloria, Philip J. "Red Earth, White Lies, Sapiens, and the Deep Politics of Knowledge." In *Decolonizing "Prehistory": Deep Time and Indigenous Knowledges in North America*, edited by Gesa Mackenthun and Christen Mucher, 231–48. Tucson: University of Arizona Press, 2021.

del Palacio, Celia, and Alberto J. Olvera. "Acallar las voces, ocultar la verdad: Violencia contra los periodistas en Veracruz." *Argumentos* 30, no. 85 (2017): 17–35.

del Palacio Langer, Julia. "Agrarian Reform, Oil Expropriation, and the Making of National Property in Postrevolutionary Mexico." Doctoral thesis, Columbia University, 2015.

——. "Jaime Merino: The Oil Cacique of Poza Rica, Veracruz, 1941–1959." *The Extractive Industries and Society* 3, no. 2 (2016): 426–34. https://doi.org/10.1016/j.exis.2016.01.009.

del Palacio Montiel, Celia. "Resistencia, resiliencia y luchas por la memoria de la violencia: Los periodistas en Veracruz, México." *Chasqui: Revista Latinoamericana de comunicación*, no. 143 (2020): 199–214.

Díaz-Andreu, Margarita, and Timothy Champion, eds. *Nationalism and Archaeology in Europe*. London: University College London Press, 1996.

Díaz y de Ovando, Clementina. *Memoria de un debate (1880): La postura de México frente al patrimonio arqueológico nacional*. Mexico City: UNAM, 1990.

Dillingham, A. S. *Oaxaca Resurgent: Indigeneity, Development, and Inequality in Twentieth-Century Mexico*. Stanford: Stanford University Press, 2021.

Diserens Morgan, Kasey, and Richard M. Leventhal. "Maya of the Past, Present, and Future: Heritage, Anthropological Archaeology, and the Study of the Caste War of Yucatan." *Heritage* 3, no. 2 (2020): 511–27. https://doi.org/10.3390/heritage3020030.

Doyon, Wendy. "On Archaeological Labor in Modern Egypt." In *Histories of Egyptology: Interdisciplinary Measures*, edited by William Carruthers, 141–56. New York: Routledge, 2015.

Ducey, Michael T. "Indios liberales y liberales indigenistas: Ideología y poder en los municipios rurales de Veracruz, 1821–1890." In *El siglo XIX en las Huastecas*, edited by Antonio Escobar Ohmstede and Luz Carregha Lamadrid, 111–36. Mexico City: CIESAS/El Colegio de San Luis, 2002.

——. "La comunidad liberal: Estrategias campesinas y la política liberal durante la República Restaurada y el Porfiriato en Veracruz." In *Prácticas populares, cultura política y poder en Mexico: Continuidades y contrastes entre los siglos XVIII y XIX*, edited by Brian Connaughton, 302–32. Mexico City: Universidad Autónoma Metropolitana Iztapalapa, 2008.

————. "La territorialidad indígena y las reformas borbónicas en la tierra caliente mexicana: Los tumultos totonacos de Papantla de 1764–1787." *Historia Social*, no. 78 (2014): 17–41.

————. *A Nation of Villages: Riot and Rebellion in the Mexican Huasteca, 1750–1850*. Tucson: University of Arizona Press, 2004.

————. "Village, Nation, and Constitution: Insurgent Politics in Papantla, Veracruz, 1810–1821." *Hispanic American Historical Review* 79, no. 3 (1999): 463–93. https://doi.org/10.1215/00182168-79.3.463.

Dunnell, Robert C., and William S. Dancey. "The Siteless Survey: A Regional Scale Data Collection Strategy." *Advances in Archaeological Method and Theory* 6 (1983): 267–87. https://doi.org/10.1016/B978-0-12-003106-1.50012-2.

Du Solier, Wilfrido. "La cerámica arqueológica de El Tajín." *Anales del Museo Nacional de Arqueología, Historia y Etnografía* 5, no. 3 (1945): 1–76.

Earle, Rebecca. *The Return of the Native: Indians and Myth-Making in Spanish America, 1810–1930*. Durham: Duke University Press, 2007.

Engels, Frederick. "Anti-Dühring: Herr Eugen Dühring's Revolution in Science." In *Marx/Engels Collected Works*, edited by Valentina Smirnova, translated by Emile Burns, 25:5–312. 1894. Reprint, London: Lawrence & Wishart, 1987.

"Entrevista al Sr. Gonzalo Bada Ramírez realizada por Lief Adelson, en Tampico, Tamaulipas." Dirección de Estudios Históricos del INAH, Mexico City, Proyecto de Historia Oral 4/91.

Escallón, María Fernanda. *Becoming Heritage: Recognition, Exclusion, and the Politics of Black Cultural Heritage in Colombia*. Cambridge: Cambridge University Press, 2023.

————. "Rights, Inequality, and Afro-Descendant Heritage in Brazil." *Cultural Anthropology* 34, no. 3 (2019): 359–87. https://doi.org/10.14506/ca34.3.03.

Espinosa Rodríguez, María Guadalupe. "Estrategias y gestión para la conservación del patrimonio arqueológico en México." Doctoral thesis, Universitat de Barcelona, 2017.

Everill, Paul. *The Invisible Diggers: A Study of British Commercial Archaeology*. Oxford: Oxbow, 2009.

Ferry, Elizabeth Emma. *Not Ours Alone: Patrimony, Value, and Collectivity in Contemporary Mexico*. New York: Columbia University Press, 2005.

Fewkes, Jesse Walter. *Certain Antiquities of Eastern Mexico*. Washington DC: Government Printing Office, 1907.

Flores D., Jorge. *La revolución de Olarte en Papantla (1836–1838)*. Mexico City: Imprenta Mundial, 1938.

Fontecilla, Agapito. *Breve tratado sobre el cultivo y beneficio de la vainilla*. Mexico City: Imprenta de Andrade y Escalante, 1861.

Food and Agriculture Organization of the United Nations. "FAOSTAT Statistical Database." 2019. https://www.fao.org/faostat.

Foucault, Michel. *"Society Must Be Defended": Lectures at the Collège de France, 1975–1976*. New York: Picador, 2003.

Foweraker, Joe. *Popular Mobilization in Mexico: The Teachers' Movement 1977–87.* Cambridge: Cambridge University Press, 1993.

Fowler, Catherine S., and Robert V. Kemper. "Isabel T. Kelly: A Life in the Field." In *Their Own Frontier: Women Intellectuals Re-Visioning the American West,* edited by Shirley A. Leckie and Nancy J. Parezo, 139–79. Lincoln: University of Nebraska Press, 2008.

Fowler, Don D. "Uses of the Past: Archaeology in the Service of the State." *American Antiquity* 52, no. 2 (1987): 229–48. https://doi.org/10.2307/281778.

Fowler Salamini, Heather. *Agrarian Radicalism in Veracruz, 1920–38.* Lincoln: University of Nebraska Press, 1971.

Frederick, Jake. "A Fractured Pochgui: Local Factionalism in Eighteenth-Century Papantla." *Ethnohistory* 58, no. 4 (2011): 560–83. https://doi.org/10.1215/00141801-1333670.

———. *Riot! Tobacco, Reform, and Violence in Eighteenth-Century Papantla, Mexico.* Sussex: Sussex Academic Press, 2016.

Frehner, Brian. *Finding Oil: The Nature of Petroleum Geology, 1859–1920.* Lincoln: University of Nebraska Press, 2011.

Fry, Matthew. "Shifting Volumetric Imaginaries of Oil Potential in Mexico's Chicontepec Basin: Investible Asset, Reserve Replacement, and Oilfield Services Zone." *Journal of Latin American Geography* 17, no. 3 (2018): 73–101. https://doi.org/10.1353/lag.2018.0042.

Fry, Matthew, and Andrew Hilburn. "The Distributional Justice of Oil Industry Social Development Projects and Oil Field Production Activities." *Extractive Industries and Society* 7, no. 2 (2020): 647–59. https://doi.org/10.1016/j.exis.2020.03.017.

Furber, Percy Norman. *I Took Chances: From Windjammers to Jets.* Leicester: Edgar Backus, 1954.

Galindo y Villa, Jesús. *Las ruinas de Cempoala y del Templo del Tajín (Estado de Veracruz) exploradas por el director del Museo Nacional de Arqueología, Historia y Etnología, in misión en Europa, Don Francisco del Paso y Troncoso.* Mexico City: Museo Nacional de Arqueología, Historia y Etnología, 1912.

Gallegos Ruiz, Roberto, ed. *Antología de documentos para la historia de la arqueología de Teotihuacan.* Mexico City: INAH, 1997.

Gallegos Tellez Rojo, José Roberto. "Teotihuacan: La formación de la primera zona arqueología en México." In *Patrimonio histórico y cultural de México: IV Semana Cultural de la Dirección de Etnología y Antropología Social,* edited by María Elena Morales Anduaga and Francisco Javier Zamora Quintana, 255–79. Mexico City: INAH, 2001.

Galtung, Johan. "Violence, Peace, and Peace Research." *Journal of Peace Research* 6, no. 3 (1969): 167–91. https://doi.org/10.1177/002234336900600301.

Gameros, Manuel. "Cumbre Tajín como espacio global: Puente entre lo local y lo global." In *Espacios globales,* edited by Carmen Bueno and Margarita Pérez Negrete, 249–74. Mexico City: Plaza y Valdes, 2006.

Gamio, Manuel. *Forjando patria (pro-nacionalismo)*. Mexico City: Librería de Porrúa Hermanos, 1916.

Gándara, Manuel. *La arqueología oficial mexicana: Causas y efectos*. Mexico City: INAH, 1992.

———. "A Short History of Theory in Mesoamerican Archaeology." In *The Oxford Handbook of Mesoamerican Archaeology*, edited by Deborah L. Nichols and Christopher A. Pool, 31–46. Oxford: Oxford University Press, 2012.

García Castro, René, ed. *Suma de visitas de pueblos de la Nueva España, 1548–1550*. Toluca: Universidad Autónoma del Estado de México, 2013.

García Márquez, Agustín. "El posclásico en Veracruz: Los nahuas de Cempoala." Doctoral thesis, UNAM, 2014.

García Martínez, Ariel. "Juventud indígena en el Totonacapan veracruzano." *LiminaR: Estudios sociales y humanísticos* 10, no. 1 (2012): 75–88. https://doi.org/10.29043/liminar.v10i1.38.

García Martínez, Bernardo. *Los pueblos de la sierra: El poder y el espacio entre los indios del norte de Puebla hasta 1700*. Mexico City: El Colegio de México, 1987.

García Moll, Roberto. *Indice del Archivo Técnico de la Dirección de Monumentos Prehispánicos del INAH*. Mexico City: INAH, 1982.

García Mora, Carlos. "Mesoamérica: Un proyecto científico y un programa político." *Dimensión Antropológica* 19 (2000): 65–95.

García Payón, José. "Archaeology of Central Veracruz." In *Handbook of Middle American Indians*, vol. 11, edited by Robert Wauchope, 502–42. Austin: University of Texas Press, 1971.

———. "El Tajín, descripción y comentarios." *Universidad Veracruzana, revista trimestral* 3, no. 4 (1954): 18–59.

———. "El Tajín, trabajos de conservación realizados en 1951." *Anales del Instituto Nacional de Antropología e Historia* 5 (1951): 75–91.

———. "Ensayo de interpretación de los bajorrelieves de los cuatro tableros del Juego de Pelota Sur del Tajín, Ver." *El México antiguo: Revista internacional de arqueología, etnología, folklore, prehistoria, historia antigua y lingüística mexicana* 9 (1959): 445–60.

———. "Exploraciones arqueológicas en el Totonacapan meridional (región de Misantla, Ver.)." *Anales del Instituto Nacional de Antropología e Historia* 2 (1947): 73–111.

———. *Exploraciones en El Tajín: Temporadas 1953 y 1954*. Mexico City: INAH, 1955.

———. "Quiénes construyeron el Tajín y resultados de las últimas exploraciones en la temporada 1961–1962." *La Palabra y el Hombre*, no. 26 (1963): 243–52.

García-Salazar, José Alberto, Vianeth Méndez-Cortés, Rocío Ramírez-Jaspeada, and José Saturnino Mora-Flores. "¿Quién obtiene las mayores ganancias en la comercialización de vainilla (Vanilla planifolia J.) en Papantla, Veracruz? Productores o intermediarios." *Agro Productividad* 12, no. 9 (2021): 35–40. https://doi.org/10.32854/agrop.v12i9.1383.

García Vega, Agustín. "Exploraciones en El Tajín: Temporadas 1934 a 1938." In *Vigesimoseptimo Congreso Internacional de Americanistas: Actas de la primera sesión, celebrada en la Ciudad de México en 1939*, edited by INAH, 78–87. Mexico City: SEP/INAH, 1939.

Garner, Paul. *British Lions and Mexican Eagles: Business, Politics, and Empire in the Career of Weetman Pearson in Mexico, 1889–1919*. Stanford: Stanford University Press, 2011.

Garrigan, Shelley E. *Collecting Mexico: Museums, Monuments, and the Creation of National Identity*. Minneapolis: University of Minnesota Press, 2012.

Gathercole, Peter, and David Lowenthal, eds. *The Politics of the Past*. London: Routledge, 1990.

Gatti, Luis María, and Victoria Chenaut. *La costa totonaca: Cuestiones regionales II*. Mexico City: CIESAS, 1987.

"Gazeta de México del Martes 12 de Julio de 1785." In *Gazeta de México (enero a julio de 1785)*, edited by David Marley, 347–51. Windsor: Rolston-Bain, 1986.

Gerali, Francesco, and Paolo Riguzzi. "Los inicios de la actividad petrolera en México, 1863–1874: Una nueva cronología y elementos de balance." *Boletín del Archivo Histórico de Petróleos Mexicanos* 13 (2013): 63–88.

Gerhard, Peter. *A Guide to the Historical Geography of New Spain*. Norman: University of Oklahoma Press, 1993.

Gero, Joan M. "Socio-Politics and the Woman-at-Home Ideology." *American Antiquity* 50, no. 2 (1985): 342–50. https://doi.org/10.2307/280492.

Gershon, Ilana. "Neoliberal Agency." *Current Anthropology* 52, no. 4 (2011): 537–55. https://doi.org/10.1086/660866.

Gillingham, Paul. *Cuauhtémoc's Bones: Forging National Identity in Modern Mexico*. Albuquerque: University of New Mexico Press, 2011.

———. *Unrevolutionary Mexico: The Birth of a Strange Dictatorship*. New Haven: Yale University Press, 2021.

———. "Who Killed Crispín Aguilar? Violence and Order in the Postrevolutionary Countryside." In *Violence, Coercion, and State-Making in Twentieth-Century Mexico*, edited by Wil G. Pansters, 91–112. Stanford: Stanford University Press, 2012.

Gillingham, Paul, and Benjamin T. Smith. "Introduction: The Paradoxes of Revolution." In *Dictablanda: Politics, Work, and Culture in Mexico, 1938–1968*, edited by Paul Gillingham and Benjamin T. Smith, 1–44. Durham: Duke University Press, 2014.

Goldsmith, John R. "The 20-Minute Disaster: Hydrogen Sulfide Spill at Poza Rica." In *Environmental Epidemiology*, edited by John R. Goldsmith, 65–71. Boca Raton FL: CRC Press, 1986.

González, Estela Casados. "Impunidad e invisibilización de los feminicidios en Veracruz." *Clivajes: Revista de ciencias sociales* 3, no. 6 (2016): 58–78.

González-Montagut, Renée. "Factors That Contributed to the Expansion of Cattle Ranching in Veracruz, Mexico." *Mexican Studies/Estudios Mexicanos* 15, no. 1 (1999): 101–30. https://doi.org/10.2307/1051944.

González-Robles, Víctor. "Limbos arqueológicos: Sitios extraoficiales en México." Maestría thesis, UNAM, 2020.

González-Ruibal, Alfredo. "Ethics of Archaeology." *Annual Review of Anthropology* 47, no. 1 (2018): 345–60. https://doi.org/10.1146/annurev-anthro-102317 -045825.

Gould, Peter G. "Collision or Collaboration? Archaeology Encounters Economic Development: An Introduction." In *Collision or Collaboration: Archaeology Encounters Economic Development*, edited by Peter G. Gould and K. Anne Pyburn, 1–14. Cham, Switzerland: Springer, 2017.

Government of Mexico. *Mexico's Oil: A Compilation of Official Documents in the Conflict of Economic Order in the Petroleum Industry, with an Introduction Summarizing Its Causes and Consequences*. Mexico City: Government of Mexico, 1940.

Govers, Cora. *Performing the Community: Representation, Ritual, and Reciprocity in the Totonac Highlands of Mexico*. Berlin: Lit Verlag, 2006.

Grindle, Merilee. *Bureaucrats, Politicians, and Peasants in Mexico: A Case Study in Public Policy*. Berkeley: University of California Press, 1977.

Grove, David C. *Discovering the Olmecs: An Unconventional History*. Austin: University of Texas Press, 2014.

Gutiérrez Chong, Natividad. "Ethnopolitics and the Democratization of the Latin American State." In *Comparative Indigeneities of the Américas: Towards a Hemispheric Approach*, edited by M. Bianet Castellanos, Lourdes Gutiérrez Nájera, and Arturo J. Aldama, 173–83. Tucson: University of Arizona Press, 2012.

Haber, Stephen, Armando Razo, and Noel Maurer. *The Politics of Property Rights: Political Instability, Credible Commitments, and Economic Growth in Mexico, 1876–1929*. Cambridge: Cambridge University Press, 2003.

Haber, Stephen, Herbert S. Klein, Noel Maurer, and Kevin J. Middlebrook. *Mexico since 1980*. Cambridge: Cambridge University Press, 2008.

Haber, Stephen, Noel Maurer, and Armando Razo. "When the Law Does Not Matter: The Rise and Decline of the Mexican Oil Industry." *Journal of Economic History* 63, no. 1 (2003): 1–32. https://doi.org/10.1017/S0022050703001712.

Hale, Charles A. *The Transformation of Liberalism in Late Nineteenth-Century Mexico*. Princeton: Princeton University Press, 1989.

Hale, Charles R. "Neoliberal Multiculturalism: The Remaking of Cultural Rights and Racial Dominance in Central America." POLAR: *Political and Legal Anthropology Review* 28, no. 1 (2005): 10–28. https://doi.org/10.1525/pol.2005.28.1.10.

———. "Resistencia Para Que? Territory, Autonomy and Neoliberal Entanglements in the 'Empty Spaces' of Central America." *Economy and Society* 40, no. 2 (2011): 184–210. https://doi.org/10.1080/03085147.2011.548947.

Hall, Raymond A. *An Ethnographic Study of Afro-Mexicans in Mexico's Gulf Coast: Fishing, Festivals, and Foodways*. Lewiston ME: Edwin Mellen Press, 2008.

Hamilton, Charles W. *Early Day Oil Tales of Mexico*. Houston: Gulf Publishing, 1966.

Hamnett, Brian R. *Roots of Insurgency: Mexican Regions, 1750–1824.* Cambridge: Cambridge University Press, 1986.

Hart, John Mason. *Revolutionary Mexico: The Coming and Process of the Mexican Revolution.* Berkeley: University of California Press, 1987.

Harvey, David. *A Brief History of Neoliberalism.* Oxford: Oxford University Press, 2005.

Harvey, H. R., and Isabel Kelly. "The Totonac." In *Handbook of Middle American Indians,* vol. 8, edited by Robert Wauchope, 638–81. Austin: University of Texas Press, 1969.

Heath, Dwight B. "Economic Aspects of Commercial Archaeology in Costa Rica." *American Antiquity* 38, no. 3 (1973): 259–65. https://doi.org/10.2307/279713.

Heath-Stout, Laura E. *Identity, Oppression, and Diversity in Archaeology: Career Arcs.* New York: Routledge, 2025.

———. "Who Writes about Archaeology? An Intersectional Study of Authorship in Archaeological Journals." *American Antiquity* 85, no. 3 (2020): 407–26. https://doi.org/10.1017/aaq.2020.28.

Hernández, Porfirio. *Cumbres y barrancas: Viajes a pie y a caballo a través de la República Mexicana.* Mexico City: Talleres Gráficos Núm. 1 de la SEP, 1947.

Hernández García, Metztli Sarai. "Las mujeres del Proyecto Tajín: Memoria histórica en la Zona de Monumentos Arqueológicos El Tajín." Licenciatura thesis, Universidad Autonoma Metropolitana Iztapalapa, 2018.

Hernández-Hernández, Juan. "Mexican Vanilla Production." In *Handbook of Vanilla Science and Technology,* edited by Daphna Havkin-Frenkel and Faith C. Belanger, 3–25. Oxford: Wiley-Blackwell, 2011.

Herzfeld, Michael. *Evicted from Eternity: The Restructuring of Modern Rome.* Chicago: University of Chicago Press, 2009.

———. "Spatial Cleansing: Monumental Vacuity and the Idea of the West." *Journal of Material Culture* 11, no. 1–2 (2006): 127–49. https://doi.org/10.1177/1359183506063016.

Hilgers, Mathieu. "The Historicity of the Neoliberal State." *Social Anthropology* 20, no. 1 (2012): 80–94. https://doi.org/10.1111/j.1469-8676.2011.00192.x.

Hodder, Ian. "Writing Archaeology: Site Reports in Context." *Antiquity* 63, no. 239 (1989): 268–74. https://doi.org/10.1017/S0003598X00075980.

Hølleland, Herdis, and Joar Skrede. "What's Wrong with Heritage Experts? An Interdisciplinary Discussion of Experts and Expertise in Heritage Studies." *International Journal of Heritage Studies* 25, no. 8 (2018): 8–25. https://doi.org/10.1080/13527258.2018.1552613.

Holley-Kline, Sam. "Archaeology, Wage Labor, and Kinship in Rural Mexico, 1934–1974." *Ethnohistory* 69, no. 2 (2022): 197–221. https://doi.org/10.1215/00141801-9522189.

———. "Contextualizing Archaeology's 'Locals': A Scalar Approach from El Tajín, Mexico." *Archaeologies* 11, no. 1 (2015): 70–92. https://doi.org/10.1007/s11759-015-9268-9.

———. "El guardián Modesto González y la historiografía de la arqueología mexicana." *Complutum* 30, no. 1 (2019): 13–28. https://doi.org/10.5209/cmpl.64505.

———. "José García Payón y el manejo de la arqueología durante la Época Dorada (1930–1970)." *Dimensión Antropológica*, forthcoming.

———. "Nationalist Archaeology and Foreign Oil Exploration in El Tajín, Mexico, 1935–1940." *Archaeological Dialogues* 26, no. 2 (2020): 79–93. https://doi.org/10.1017/S1380203820000100.

Holley-Kline, Sam, and Allison Mickel. "Introduction: Archaeological Labor in Historical Contexts." *Bulletin of the History of Archaeology* 34, no. 1 (2024): 1–8. https://doi.org/10.5334/bha-726.

Holley-Kline, Sam, and Sabrina Papazian. "Heritage Trekking: Toward an Integrated Heritage Studies Methodology." *Journal of Field Archaeology* 45, no. 7 (2020): 527–41. https://doi.org/10.1080/00934690.2020.1807241.

Holley-Kline, Samuel. "El patrimonio industrial como patrimonio negativo: El caso de la industria petrolera en Papantla, Veracruz." In *Y se detuvieron las máquinas: Lenguajes, reconversión y espacios simbólicos del Patrimonio Industrial*, edited by Moisés Gámez and Francisco Alberto Núñez Tapia, 299–321. San Luis Potosí: El Colegio de San Luis, 2020.

Hollowell, Julie, and Lena Mortensen. "Introduction: Archaeologies and Ethnographies." In *Ethnographies and Archaeologies: Iterations of the Past*, edited by Julie Hollowell and Lena Mortensen, 1–20. Gainesville: University Press of Florida, 2009.

Hoobler, Ellen. "'To Take Their Heritage in Their Hands': Indigenous Self-Representation and Decolonization in the Community Museums of Oaxaca, Mexico." *American Indian Quarterly* 30, no. 3 (2006): 441–60. https://doi.org/10.1353/aiq.2006.0024.

Hooker, Juliet, ed. *Black and Indigenous Resistance in the Americas: From Multiculturalism to Racist Backlash*. Translated by Giorleny Altamirano Rayo, Aileen Ford, and Steven Lownes. Lanham MD: Lexington Books, 2020.

INAH. *Sistema Institutional: Estadística de Visitantes*. Instituto Nacional de Antropología e Historia, accessed July 27, 2022. https://www.estadisticas.inah.gob.mx/.

———. "Zona de Monumentos Arqueológicos El Tajín, Veracruz: Evaluación del Plan de Manejo 2009–2018." Coordinación Nacional de Arqueología, Dirección de Operación de Sitios, 2018.

INEGI. *Estadísticas Históricas de México*. Vol. 1. Aguascalientes: INEGI, 1994.

———. "Población de 5 años y más hablante de Totonaca (Totonaco) (Personas)." Banco de Indicadores, Demografía y Sociedad, Población, Lengua indígena, 2010.

Islas, Paul Moch, Anne K. Calef, and Cristina Aparicio. "2013 Mexico's Education Reform: A Multi-Dimensional Analysis." In *Implementing Deeper Learning and 21st Century Education Reforms: Building an Education Renaissance after a Global Pandemic*, edited by Fernando M. Reimers, 79–107. Cham, Switzerland: Springer International, 2021.

Jácome González, Alba. "Mesoamérica: Un desarrollo teórico." *Dimensión Antro-pológica* 19 (2000): 121–52.

Jaimes Reyes, Jazmin. "Turismo cultural, una actividad económica y sus distintas formas de organización laboral en la Zona Arqueológica 'El Tajín' (Estudio de caso entre artesanos, comerciantes y prestadores de servicios)." Licenciatura thesis, Universidad Autonoma Metropolitana Iztapalapa, 2017.

Johnson, Matthew. *Ideas of Landscape*. Malden MA: Blackwell, 2008.

Jolly, Jennifer. *Creating Pátzcuaro, Creating Mexico: Art, Tourism, and Nation-Building under Lázaro Cárdenas*. Austin: University of Texas Press, 2018.

Joyce, Rosemary A. "Making Markets for Mesoamerican Antiquities." In *The Market for Mesoamerica: Reflections on the Sale of Pre-Columbian Antiquities*, edited by Cara G. Tremain and Donna Yates, 1–15. Gainesville: University Press of Florida, 2019.

———. "Mesoamerica: A Working Model for Archaeology." In *Mesoamerican Archaeology: Theory and Practice*, edited by Julia A. Hendon and Rosemary A. Joyce, 1–42. Malden MA: Blackwell, 2003.

Kasburg, Carola. *Die Totonaken von El Tajín: Beharrung und Wandel über vier Jahzehnte*. Münster, Germany: Lit Verlag, 1992.

Keen, Benjamin. *The Aztec Image in Western Thought*. New Brunswick NJ: Rutgers University Press, 1971.

Kelly, Isabel. "In the Shadow of El Tajín." *Mexican Life* 26, no. 1 (1952): 22–24.

Kelly, Isabel, and Angel Palerm. *The Tajín Totonac*. Washington DC: Government Printing Office, 1952.

Kelly, Larissa Kennedy. "Waking the Gods: Archaeology and State Power in Porfirian Mexico." Doctoral thesis, University of California, Berkeley, 2011.

Kemper, Robert V., and John Marcucci. "The Isabel T. Kelly Ethnographic Archive: A Descriptive Guide." In *Homenaje a Isabel Kelly*, edited by Yólotl González, 59–70. Mexico City: INAH, 1989.

King, Amanda. "Trade and Totomoxtle: Livelihood Strategies in the Totonacan Region of Veracruz, Mexico." *Agriculture and Human Values* 24, no. 1 (2007): 29–40. https://doi.org/10.1007/s10460-006-9031-3.

Kirchhoff, Paul. "Mesoamérica: Sus límites geográficos, composición étnica y caracteres culturales." *Acta americana* 1, no. 1 (1943): 92–107.

Knight, Alan. "Export-Led Growth in Mexico, c. 1900–30." In *An Economic History of Twentieth-Century Latin America*, vol. 1, edited by Enrique Cárdenas, José Antonio Ocampo, and Rosemary Thorp, 119–51. London: Palgrave Macmillan, 2000.

———. "History, Heritage, and Revolution: Mexico, c .1910–c .1940." *Past & Present* 226, no. 10 (2015): 299–325. https://doi.org/10.1093/pastj/gtu021.

———. "Mexican Peonage: What Was It and Why Was It?" *Journal of Latin American Studies* 18, no. 1 (1986): 41–74. https://doi.org/10.1017/S0022216X00011160.

———. *The Mexican Revolution*. 2 vols. Cambridge: Cambridge University Press, 1986.

———. "The Rise and Fall of Cardenismo, c. 1930–c. 1946." In *Mexico since Independence*, edited by Leslie Bethell, 241–320. Cambridge: Cambridge University Press, 1991.

Knight, Alan, and Jaime Rodriguez. "The Mexican Revolution, 1910–1940." *Oxford Bibliographies*, 2011. https://doi.org/10.1093/obo/9780199766581-0033.

Kohl, Philip L. "Nationalism and Archaeology: On the Constructions of Nations and the Reconstructions of the Remote Past." *Annual Review of Anthropology* 27 (1998): 223–46. https://doi.org/10.1146/annurev.anthro.27.1.223.

Kohl, Philip L., and Clare Fawcett, eds. *Nationalism, Politics, and the Practice of Archaeology*. Cambridge: Cambridge University Press, 1995.

König, Viola. "Invisible: Female Collectors in Colonial and Postcolonial North and Central America." In *The Gender of Ethnographic Collecting*, edited by Carl Deußen and Mary Mbewe, 13–20. Bonn: Boasblogs, 2021.

Koontz, Rex. "Iconographic Relationships between the Huastec and El Tajín Traditions." In *The Huasteca: Culture, History, and Interregional Exchange*, edited by Katherine A. Faust and Kim N. Richter, 152–67. Norman: University of Oklahoma Press, 2015.

———. *Lightning Gods and Feathered Serpents: The Public Sculpture of El Tajín*. Austin: University of Texas Press, 2009.

Kourí, Emilio. *A Pueblo Divided: Business, Property, and Community in Papantla, Mexico*. Stanford: Stanford University Press, 2004.

Krotser, Ramón, and Paula H. Krotser. "Topografía y cerámica de El Tajín, Ver." *Anales del Instituto Nacional de Antropología e Historia*, época 7a (1973): 177–221.

Kuecker, Glen David. "A Desert in a Tropical Wilderness: Limits to the Porfirian Project in Northeastern Veracruz, 1870–1910." Doctoral thesis, Rutgers, The State University of New Jersey, 1988.

———. "'The Greatest and the Worst': Dominant and Subaltern Memories of the Dos Bocas Well Fire of 1908." In *The Memory of Catastrophe*, edited by Peter Gray and Kendrick Oliver, 65–78. Manchester: Manchester University Press, 2004.

Ladrón de Guevara, Sara. *Imagen y pensamiento en El Tajín*. Xalapa: Universidad Veracruzana/INAH, 1999.

Lafrenz Samuels, Kathryn. *Mobilizing Heritage: Anthropological Practice and Transnational Prospects*. Gainesville: University Press of Florida, 2018.

Lara Mojica, José Narciso. "Estudio socioeconómico y médico de la congregación de Plan de Hidalgo, Municipio de Papantla." Licenciatura thesis, Universidad Veracruzana, 1980.

Latour, Bruno, and Steve Woolgar. *Laboratory Life: The Construction of Scientific Facts*. Princeton: Princeton University Press, 1986.

Leathem, Hilary Morgan V. "History (Dis)Possessed: Haunting, Theft, and the Making of Monumental Heritage in Oaxaca, Mexico." Doctoral thesis, University of Chicago, 2022.

Leighton, Mary. "Indigenous Archaeological Field Technicians at Tiwanaku, Bolivia: A Hybrid Form of Scientific Labor." *American Anthropologist* 118, no. 4 (2016): 742–54. https://doi.org/10.1111/aman.12682.

Lemke, Thomas. "'The Birth of Bio-Politics': Michel Foucault's Lecture at the Collège de France on Neo-Liberal Governmentality." *Economy and Society* 30, no. 2 (2001): 190–207. https://doi.org/10.1080/03085140122085.

———. *Foucault, Governmentality, and Critique*. London: Routledge, 2012.

Lenti, Joseph U. *Redeeming the Revolution: The State and Organized Labor in Post-Tlatelolco Mexico*. Lincoln: University of Nebraska Press, 2017.

Leventhal, Richard M., Carlos Chan Espinosa, Eladio Moo Pat, and Demetrio Poot Cahun. "The Community Heritage Project in Tihosuco, Quintana Roo, Mexico." *Public Archaeology* 13, no. 1–3 (2014): 213–25. https://doi.org/10.1179/1465518714Z.00000000069.

Levine, Marc N., and Lucha Martínez de Luna. "Museum Salvage: A Case Study of Mesoamerican Artifacts in Museum Collections and on the Antiquities Market." *Journal of Field Archaeology* 38, no. 3 (2013): 264–76. https://doi.org/10.1179/0093469013Z.00000000053.

Lewis, Diane. "Anthropology and Colonialism." *Current Anthropology* 14, no. 5 (1973): 581–602. https://doi.org/10.1086/201393.

Lewis, Stephen E. *Rethinking Mexican Indigenismo: The INI's Coordinating Center in Highland Chiapas and the Fate of a Utopian Project*. Albuquerque: University of New Mexico Press, 2018.

"Ley de autonomía de la Universidad Veracruzana." *Gaceta Oficial: Órgano del Gobierno del Estado de Veracruz-Llave*, November 30, 1996. Last reformed June 28, 2000.

"Ley federal sobre monumentos y zonas arqueológicos, artísticos e históricos." *Diario Oficial de la Federación*, May 6, 1972. Last reformed February 16, 2018.

"Ley que crea el Instituto Veracruzano de la Cultura," *Gaceta Oficial: Órgano del Gobierno del Estado de Veracruz-Llave*, February 10, 1987. Last reformed February 22, 2010.

Li, Tania Murray. "What Is Land? Assembling a Resource for Global Investment." *Transactions of the Institute of British Geographers* 39, no. 4 (2014): 589–602. https://doi.org/10.1111/tran.12065.

Litvak King, Jaime. "Posiciones teóricas en la arqueología mesoamericana." In *Sociedad Mexicana de Antropología, XIII Mesa Redonda: Balance y perspectiva de la antropología de Mesoamérica y del centro de México*, edited by Sociedad Mexicana de Antropología, 11–29. Mexico City: Sociedad Mexicana de Antropología, 1975.

Litvak King, Jaime, Luis González R., and María del Refugio González, eds. *Arqueología y derecho en México*. Mexico City: UNAM, 1980.

Lombardo de Ruiz, Sonia. *El pasado prehispánico en la cultura nacional (memoria hemerográfica 1877–1911)*. 2 vols. Mexico City: INAH, 1994.

Lombardo de Ruiz, Sonia, and Ruth Solís Vicarte. *Antecedentes de las leyes sobre monumentos históricos (1536–1910)*. Mexico City: INAH, 1988.

Lomnitz, Claudio. *Deep Mexico, Silent Mexico: An Anthropology of Nationalism.* Minneapolis: University of Minnesota Press, 2001.

López, Rick A. *Crafting Mexico: Intellectuals, Artisans, and the State after the Revolution.* Durham: Duke University Press, 2010.

López Hernández, Haydeé. "De la gloria prehispánica al socialismo: Las políticas indigenistas del Cardenismo." *Cuicuilco* 20, no. 57 (2013): 47–74.

———. *En busca del alma nacional: La arqueología y la construcción del origen de la historia nacional en México (1867–1942).* Mexico City: INAH, 2018.

———. "La arqueología mexicana en un periodo de transición 1917–1938." Licenciatura thesis, ENAH, 2003.

———. "Ruptura y tradición en las historias de la arqueología, parte I: Ciencia universal y revolucionaria." *Saberes: Revista de historia de las ciencias y las humanidades* 1, no. 4 (2018): 96–114.

López Hernández, Haydeé, and Elvira Pruneda Gallegos. "Dimes y diretes: Polémicas sobre la práctica arqueológica en México." *Trace: Travaux et Recherches dans les Amériques du Centre*, no. 67 (2015): 39–61. https://doi.org/10.22134/trace.67.2015.16.

López Luján, Leonardo. "El Tajín en el siglo XVIII: Dos exploraciones pioneras en Veracruz." *Arqueología mexicana* 15, no. 89 (2008): 74–81.

———. "The First Steps on a Long Journey: Archaeological Illustration in Eighteenth-Century New Spain." In *Past Presented: Archaeological Illustration and the Ancient Americas*, edited by Joanne Pillsbury, 69–106. Washington DC: Dumbarton Oaks Research Library and Collection, 2012.

López Luján, Leonardo, and Foni Le Brun-Ricalens. "Guillermo Dupaix y sus correrías previas a la Real Expedición Anticuaria en Nueva España (1791–1804)." In *La arqueología ilustrada americana: La universalidad de una disciplina*, edited by Jorge Maier Allende and Leonardo López Luján, 297–322. Seville: Enredars Publicaciones, 2021.

López Palacios, José Antonio. "Algunos aspectos sobre la delimitación de zonas arqueológicas realizadas por la Inspección y Conservación de Monumentos Arqueológicos de la República Mexicana (1885–1911)." In *Memoria del registro arqueológico en México: Treinta años*, edited by Silvia Mesa Dávila, María Teresa Castillo Mangas, Pedro Francisco Sánchez Nava, and Miguel Medina Jaén, 367–72. Mexico City: INAH, 2009.

López Vallejo, Francisco Javier. "Entre la vainilla y el petróleo: Tenencia, industria petrolera y reparto agrario en las tierras de Papantla; El caso de la hacienda petrolera Palma Sola, 1880–1936." Licenciatura thesis, UNAM, 2020.

López Wario, Luis Alberto, and Salvador Púlido Méndez. "Forjando arqueólogos: Los planes de estudio de arqueología en la ENAH, 1941–1991." *Cuicuilco* 26 (1991): 83–96.

Lorenzo, José Luis. "Archaeology South of the Rio Grande." *World Archaeology* 13, no. 2 (1981): 190–208. https://doi.org/10.1080/00438243.1981.9979825.

————. "Mexico." In *Approaches to the Archaeological Heritage: A Comparative Study of World Cultural Resource Management Systems*, edited by Henry Cleere, 89–100. Cambridge: Cambridge University Press, 1984.

Lorey, David E. *The Rise of the Professions in Twentieth-Century Mexico: University Graduates and Occupational Change since 1929.* Los Angeles: UCLA Latin American Center Publications, 1992.

Lubinsky, Pesach. "Historical and Evolutionary Origins of Cultivated Vanilla." Doctoral thesis, University of California, Riverside, 2007.

Lucas, Gavin. *Critical Approaches to Fieldwork: Contemporary and Historical Archaeological Practice.* London: Routledge, 2001.

Lucas, Raoul. "Vanilla's Debt to Reunion Island." In *Vanilla*, edited by Eric Odoux and Michel Grisoni, 261–72. Boca Raton FL: CRC Press, 2011.

Luke, Christina. "Diplomats, Banana Cowboys, and Archaeologists in Western Honduras: A History of the Trade in Pre-Columbian Materials." *International Journal of Cultural Property* 13, no. 1 (2006): 25–57. https://doi.org/10.1017/S0940739106060036.

Luna Santiago, Germán. "El motín de Papantla de 1767: Un análisis histórico jurídico." *Historia Mexicana* 67, no. 1 (2017): 125–67. https://doi.org/10.24201/hm.v67i1.3442.

Lurtz, Casey Marina. *From the Grounds Up: Building an Export Economy in Southern Mexico.* Stanford: Stanford University Press, 2019.

MacEachern, Scott. "Seeing like an Oil Company's CHM Programme: Exxon and Archaeology on the Chad Export Project." *Journal of Social Archaeology* 10, no. 3 (2010): 347–66. https://doi.org/10.1177/1469605310378801.

Maciel Martínez, Xóchitl del Carmen. "Preservación del patrimonio cultural de El Tajín frente al contexto global y cambio cultural." Licenciatura thesis, ENAH, 2008.

MacKay, Carolyn J., and Frank R. Trechsel. "An Alternative Reconstruction of Proto-Totonac-Tepehua." *International Journal of American Linguistics* 84, no. 1 (2018): 51–92. https://doi.org/10.1086/694609.

————. "Bibliografía de las lenguas totonacas y tepehuas." In *Las lenguas totonacas y tepehuas: Textos y otros materiales para su estudio*, edited by Paulette Levy and David Beck, 545–90. Mexico City: UNAM, 2012.

Maldonado Vite, María Eugenia. "El antiguo Tochpan: Aspectos de economía política en la frontera sur de la Huasteca Veracruzana." Doctoral thesis, ENAH, 2016.

Malkiel, Yakov. "La historia lingüística de peón." *Thesaurus: Boletín del Instituto Caro y Cuervo* 7, no. 1–3 (1951): 201–44.

Marín Carreón, Luz de Abril. "El turismo como base de desarrollo económico del municipio de Papantla, Veracruz, caso Cumbre Tajín 1999–2009." Licenciatura thesis, Universidad Veracruzana, 2010.

Márquez, Agustín García. "Cempoala: Territorio y población en una provincia prehispánica de Veracruz." *Estudios Mesoamericanos*, no. 1 (2000): 3–13.

Márquez, Pietro. *Due antichi monumenti di architettura messicana*. Roma: Presso il Salomoni, 1804.

Martínez Acuña, Octavio. *Catálogo selectivo de la documentación de personal del Archivo Histórico Institucional del INAH*. Mexico City: INAH, 2010.

Martínez Cabral, Lizeth Adriana. "Festivales y Mercantilización Cultural: Cumbre Tajín, un estudio de caso." Maestría thesis, Universidad de la Américas Puebla, 2005.

Martínez Muriel, Alejandro. "Archaeological Research in Mexico's Monumental Sites." In *Archaeological Research and Heritage Preservation in the Americas*, edited by Robert D. Drennan and Santiago Mora Camargo, 56–62. Washington DC: Society for American Archaeology, 2001.

Masferrer Kan, Elio. "Las condiciones históricas de la etnicidad entre los totonacos." *America Indígena* 46, no. 4 (1986): 733–49.

———. "Los factores étnicos en la rebelión totonaca de Olarte de Papantla (1836–1838)." *Cuicuilco* 14/15, no. 4 (1984): 24–31.

Matos Moctezuma, Eduardo. "Las corrientes arqueológicas en México." *Nueva antropología: Revista de ciencias sociales* 3, no. 12 (1979): 7–25.

Matsuda, David. "The Ethics of Archaeology, Subsistence Digging, and Artifact Looting in Latin America: Point, Muted Counterpoint." *International Journal for Cultural Property* 7, no. 1 (1998): 87–97. https://doi.org/10.1017/S0940739198770080.

McAnany, Patricia A. *Maya Cultural Heritage: How Archaeologists and Indigenous Communities Engage the Past*. Lanham MD: Rowman & Littlefield, 2016.

McCabe, L. C., and G. D. Clayton. "Air Pollution by Hydrogen Sulfide in Poza Rica, Mexico: An Evaluation of the Incident of Nov. 24, 1950." *AMA Archives of Industrial Hygiene and Occupational Medicine* 6, no. 3 (1952): 199–213.

McCormick, Gladys. *The Logic of Compromise in Mexico: How the Countryside Was Key to the Emergence of Authoritarianism*. Chapel Hill: University of North Carolina Press, 2016.

McGinn, Noel, and Susan Street. "Educational Decentralization: Weak State or Strong State?" *Comparative Education Review* 30, no. 4 (1986): 471–90. https://doi.org/10.1086/446631.

McGuire, Randall H. *Archaeology as Political Action*. Berkeley: University of California Press, 2008.

McNiven, Ian J. "Theoretical Challenges of Indigenous Archaeology: Setting an Agenda." *American Antiquity* 81, no. 1 (2016): 27–41. https://doi.org/10.7183/0002-7316.81.1.27.

Medellín Zenil, Alfonso. *Cerámicas del Totonacapan: Exploraciones arqueológicas en el centro de Veracruz*. Xalapa: Universidad Veracruzana-Instituto de Antropología, 1960.

Medina González, José Humberto, and Baudelina Lydia García Uranga. "Los antiguos monumentos de El Tajín, Xochicalco, San Juan de los Llanos (Cantón o Cantona) y la isla del Nutka en la *Gazeta de México* y la *Gazeta de Literatura de México*." *Arqueología*, no. 57 (2019): 78–97.

Medina González, José Humberto, and Verónica Ortega Cabrera. "Exploraciones y reconstrucciones en Teotihuacan 1960–1962: Intervenciones previas al 'Proyecto Teotihuacán.'" *Figūras: Revista académica de investigación* 2, no. 1 (2020): 24–64. https://doi.org/10.22201/fesa.figuras.2020.2.1.128.

Memoria leída por el C. Gobernador del Estado ante la H. Legislatura del Mismo, el día 13 de octubre de 1871. Veracruz: Tip. del "Progreso" de R. Lainé y Ca., 1872.

Memoria que en cumplimiento del precepto constitucional presenta al Congreso de la Unión el C. Lic. Joaquin Baranda, Secretario de Estado y del despacho de Justicia e Instrucción Pública. Mexico City: Imprenta del Gobierno, en el ex-arzobispado, 1887.

Meskell, Lynn. "Archaeological Ethnography: Conversations around Kruger National Park." *Archaeologies* 1, no. 1 (2005): 81–100. https://doi.org/10.1007/s11759-005-0010-x.

———, ed. *Archaeology Under Fire: Nationalism, Politics and Heritage in the Eastern Mediterranean and Middle East*. New York: Routledge, 1998.

———. *A Future in Ruins: UNESCO, World Heritage, and the Dream of Peace*. Oxford: Oxford University Press, 2018.

———. "Mapungubwe Cultural Landscape: Extractive Economies and Endangerment on South Africa's Borders." In *World Heritage on the Ground: Ethnographic Perspectives*, edited by Christopher Brumann and David Berliner, 273–93. New York: Berghahn Books, 2016.

———. *The Nature of Heritage: The New South Africa*. Oxford: Wiley-Blackwell, 2011.

———. "World Heritage and WikiLeaks: Territory, Trade, and Temples on the Thai-Cambodian Border." *Current Anthropology* 57, no. 1 (2016): 72–95. https://doi.org/10.1086/684643.

Meskell, Lynn, and Peter Pels. "Introduction: Embedding Ethics." In *Embedding Ethics: Shifting Boundaries of the Anthropological Profession*, edited by Lynn Meskell and Peter Pels, 1–26. New York: Berg, 2005.

Meskell, Lynn, and Sarah LaPorte. "'Your Mysterious Instruments': American Devices and Imperial Designs in Cold War Archaeology." *Journal of Field Archaeology* 47, no. 4 (2022): 212–27. https://doi.org/10.1080/00934690.2022.2041279.

Meyer, Lorenzo. *Mexico and the United States in the Oil Controversy, 1917–1942*. Austin: University of Texas Press, 1977.

Mickel, Allison. "Essential Excavation Experts: Alienation and Agency in the History of Archaeological Labor." *Archaeologies* 15, no. 2 (2019): 181–205. https://doi.org/10.1007/s11759-019-09356-9.

———. *Why Those Who Shovel Are Silent: A History of Local Archaeological Knowledge and Labor*. Boulder: University Press of Colorado, 2021.

Mickel, Allison, and Nylah Byrd. "Cultivating Trust, Producing Knowledge: The Management of Archaeological Labour and the Making of a Discipline." *History of the Human Sciences* 35, no. 2 (2022): 3–28. https://doi.org/10.1177/09526951211015855.

Middlebrook, Kevin J. *The Paradox of Revolution: Labor, the State, and Authoritarianism in Mexico.* Baltimore: Johns Hopkins University Press, 1995.

Mintz, Sidney W. "The Rural Proletariat and the Problem of Rural Proletarian Consciousness." *Journal of Peasant Studies* 1, no. 3 (1974): 291–325. https://doi.org/10.1080/03066157408437893.

Moctezuma-Pérez, Sergio. "Factores que intervienen en la migración de indígenas totonacos de Veracruz." *Ra Ximhai: Revista de Sociedad, Cultura y Desarrollo Sustentable* 7, no. 3 (2011): 415–25. https://doi.org/10.35197/rx.07.03.2011.10.sm.

Monteiro, John. "Labor Systems." In *The Cambridge Economic History of Latin America*, vol. 1, *The Colonial Era and the Short Nineteenth Century*, edited by John Coatsworth, Roberto Cortes-Conde, and Victor Bulmer-Thomas, 185–234. Cambridge: Cambridge University Press, 2005.

Moore, Rachel A. *Forty Miles from the Sea: Xalapa, the Public Sphere, and the Atlantic World in Nineteenth-Century Mexico.* Tucson: University of Arizona Press, 2011.

Mora, Víctor Vacas. "Espacios, lugares, territorios y regiones: Hacia una (re)definición del Totonacapan como región." *Revista Española de Antropología Americana* 50 (2020): 167–89. https://doi.org/10.5209/reaa.71749.

Morales, Isidro. "The Consolidation and Expansion of PEMEX, 1947–1958." In *The Mexican Petroleum Industry in the Twentieth Century*, edited by Jonathan C. Brown and Alan Knight, 208–32. Austin: University of Texas Press, 1992.

———. "PEMEX during the 1960s and the Crisis in Self-Sufficiency." In *The Mexican Petroleum Industry in the Twentieth Century*, edited by Jonathan C. Brown and Alan Knight, 233–55. Austin: University of Texas Press, 1992.

Morales García, Fidencio. "Don José García Payón (1896–1977)." *Anales Antropológicos* 2 (1986): 123.

Morales Lara, Saúl. "Estudios lingüísticos del Totonacapan." *Anales de antropología* 42 (2008): 201–25.

Moreno-Brid, Juan Carlos, and Jaime Ros. *Development and Growth in the Mexican Economy: A Historical Perspective.* Oxford: Oxford University Press, 2009.

Moreno Coello, Georgina. "Alcaldes mayores y subdelegados frente a la siembra clandestina de tabaco: Papantla, 1765–1806." *América Latina en la Historia Económica* 19, no. 3 (2012): 206–34. https://doi.org/10.18232/alhe.v19i3.533.

Mortensen, Lena. "Copán Past and Present: Maya Archaeological Tourism and the Ch'orti' in Honduras." In *The Ch'orti' Maya Area: Past and Present*, edited by Brent E. Metz, Cameron L. McNeil, and Kerry M. Hull, 246–57. Gainesville: University Press of Florida, 2009.

Moser, Stephanie. "On Disciplinary Culture: Archaeology as Fieldwork and Its Gendered Associations." *Journal of Archaeological Method and Theory* 14, no. 3 (2007): 235–63. https://doi.org/10.1007/s10816-007-9033-5.

Mucher, Christen. *Before American History: Nationalist Mythmaking and Indigenous Dispossession.* Charlottesville: University of Virginia Press, 2022.

Munck, Ronaldo. "The Precariat: A View from the South." *Third World Quarterly* 34, no. 5 (2013): 747–62. https://doi.org/10.1080/01436597.2013.800751.

Murdock, George P., Ford S. Clellan, and Alfred E. Hudson. *Outline of Cultural Materials.* New Haven: Yale University Press, 1945.

Nahmad Molinari, Daniel. "El debate sobre la orígen cultural de El Tajín." *Xihmai* 17, no. 33 (2022): 219–50. https://doi.org/10.37646/xihmai.v17i33.548.

———. "El Tajín: Una visión propia." *Ciencias*, no. 49 (1998): 4–9.

———. "Informe de la temporada 2011 del Proyecto de Ordenamiento Territorial para la conservación de la Zona de Monumentos Arqueológicos de El Tajín." Instituto Nacional de Antropología e Historia, 2012.

———. "Problemática social en el patrimonio arqueológico de Monte Albán: Peritaje antropológico en el caso de Xoxocotlán, Oaxaca." In *INAH 80 años construidos por sus trabajadores: Ciencias antropológicas*, edited by Allan Ortega Muñoz, H. Antonio García Zúñiga, and Milton Gabriel Hernández García, 649–70. Mexico City: Sindicato Nacional de Profesores de Investigación Científica y Docencia del INAH, 2021.

Nahmad Molinari, Daniel, and María del Carmen Rodríguez Martínez. "Informe del programa de difusión de la declaratoria federal de la zona de monumentos arqueológicos del Tajín y diagnóstico social de la zona de monumentos." Veracruz: Centro INAH Veracruz, 2003.

Narotzky, Susana. "Where Have All the Peasants Gone?" *Annual Review of Anthropology* 45, no. 1 (2016): 301–18. https://doi.org/10.1146/annurev-anthro-102215 -100240.

Nebel, Carlos. *Viaje pintoresco y arqueolójico sobre la parte más interesante de la República Mejicana, en los años transcurridos desde 1829 hasta 1834.* Paris: Imprenta de P. Renouard, 1840.

Nicholas, George, and Julie Hollowell. "Ethical Challenges to a Postcolonial Archaeology: The Legacy of Scientific Colonialism." In *Archaeology and Capitalism: From Ethics to Politics*, edited by Yannis Hamilakis and Philip Duke, 59–82. Walnut Creek CA: Left Coast Press, 2007.

Nicholas, George P., and Thomas D. Andrews. "Indigenous Archaeology in the Post-Modern World." In *At a Crossroads: Archaeology and First Peoples in Canada*, edited by George P. Nicholas and Thomas D. Andrews, 1–18. Burnaby BC: Archaeology Press, Simon Fraser University, 1997.

Niklasson, Elisabeth. *Funding Matters: Archaeology and the Political Economy of the Past of the EU.* Stockholm: Stockholm University, 2016.

Ocampo, Daisy. *Where We Belong: Chemehuevi and Caxcan Preservation of Sacred Mountains.* Tucson: University of Arizona Press, 2023.

Odoux, Eric. "Vanilla Curing." In *Vanilla*, edited by Eric Odoux and Michel Grisoni, 173–89. Boca Raton FL: CRC Press, 2011.

Odoux, Eric, and Michel Grisoni, eds. *Vanilla.* Boca Raton FL: CRC Press, 2011.

Ohmstede, Antonio Escobar, and Frans J. Schryer. "Las sociedades agrarias en el norte de Hidalgo, 1856–1900." *Mexican Studies/Estudios Mexicanos* 8, no. 1 (1992): 1–21. https://doi.org/10.2307/1051798.

Olivé Negrete, Julio César, ed. INAH, *una historia*. 2 vols. Mexico City: INAH, 1995.

Olivier, Laurent. *The Dark Abyss of Time: Archaeology and Memory*. Lanham MD: Rowman & Littlefield Publishers, 2011.

Ortiz Ceballos, Ponciano, and Ramón Arellanos Melgarejo. "Delimitación de zonas arqueológicas en el estado de Veracruz." *Revista Mexicana de Estudios Antropólogicos* 23 (1986): 235–45.

Ortiz Espejel, Benjamín. *La cultura asediada: Espacio e historia en el trópico veracruzano (el caso del Totonacapan)*. Mexico City: CIESAS/Instituto de Ecología, A.C., 1995.

Osterhoudt, Sarah R. "'Nobody Wants to Kill': Economies of Affect and Violence in Madagascar's Vanilla Boom." *American Ethnologist* 47, no. 3 (2020): 249–63. https://doi.org/10.1111/amet.12911.

Palacios, Guillermo. *Maquinaciones neoyorquinas y querellas porfirianas: Marshall H. Saville, El American Museum of Natural History de Nueva York y los debates en torno a las leyes de Protección del Patrimonio Arqueológico Nacional, 1896–1897*. Mexico City: El Colegio de México, 2014.

Panameño, Rebeca, and Enrique Nalda. "Arqueología: ¿Para quién?" *Nueva antropología* 3, no. 12 (1979): 111–24.

Paredes Gudiño, Blanca. "Proceso de declaratorias de zonas de monumentos arqueológicos." In *Memoria del registro arqueológico en México: Treinta años*, edited by Silvia Mesa Dávila, María Teresa Castillo Mangas, Pedro Francisco Sánchez Nava, and Miguel Medina Jaén, 611–58. Mexico City: INAH, 2009.

Parks, Shoshaunna. "The Collision of Heritage and Economy at Uxbenká, Belize." *International Journal of Heritage Studies* 16, no. 6 (2010): 434–48. https://doi.org/10.1080/13527258.2010.505031.

Pascual Soto, Arturo. *El Tajín: Arte y poder*. Mexico City: UNAM/INAH, 2009.

———. *Guerreros de El Tajín: Excavaciones en un edificio pintado*. Mexico City: UNAM-IIE, 2016.

Patterson, Thomas C. "The Political Economy of Archaeology in the United States." *Annual Review of Anthropology* 28 (1999): 155–74. https://doi.org/10.1146/annurev.anthro.28.1.155.

Paynter, Robert. "Field or Factory? Concerning the Degradation of Archaeological Labor." In *The Socio-Politics of Archaeology*, edited by Joan M. Gero, David M. Lacy, and Michael L. Blakey, 17–29. Amherst: Department of Anthropology, University of Massachusetts, 1983.

Pendley, Joy Leigh. "'Betting' on Vanilla: Rural Producers and Development in Papantla, Veracruz, Mexico." Doctoral thesis, University of Oklahoma, 2007.

Pérez Castañeda, Juan Carlos. "Condueñazgos in Mexico during the Nineteenth Century." *Signos Históricos* 20, no. 40 (2018): 178–231.

Pérez Gil, Valeria Ysunza. "Papantla, Veracruz: El regreso y la disputa de lo mágico." In *Pueblos mágicos: Una visión interdisciplinaria*, vol. 3, edited by Liliana López Levi, Carmen Valverde Valverde, and María Elena Figueroa Díaz, 375–98. Mexico City: UAM/UNAM–Facultad de Arquitectura, 2017.

Pérez Lizuar, Marisol. "De Franz Boas a Ángel Palerm." *Destacos*, no. 45 (2014): 13–26.

Pérez Monterosas, Mario. "Las migraciones en el norte de Veracruz, México: Redes, rutas y ruralidades." *Si Somos Americanos* 18, no. 2 (2018): 34–52.

Perramond, Eric P. "The Rise, Fall, and Reconfiguration of the Mexican Ejido." *Geographical Review* 98, no. 3 (2008): 356–71.

Petróleos Mexicanos. *Los veinte años de la industria petrolera nacional: Informes 18 de marzo 1938–1958*. Mexico City: PEMEX, 1958.

Plets, Gertjan. "Heritage Statecraft: When Archaeological Heritage Meets Neoliberalism in Gazprom's Resource Colonies, Russia." *Journal of Field Archaeology* 41, no. 3 (2016): 368–83. https://doi.org/10.1080/00934690.2016.1184534.

Podgorny, Irina. "'Silent and Alone': How the Ruins of Palenque Were Taught to Speak the Language of Archaeology." In *Comparative Archaeologies: A Sociological View of the Science of the Past*, edited by Ludomir R. Lozny, 527–53. New York: Springer, 2011.

————. "Towards a Bureaucratic History of Archaeology: A Preliminary Essay." In *Historiographical Approaches to Past Archaeological Research*, edited by Gisela Eberhardt and Fabian Link, 47–67. Berlin: Edition Topoi, 2015.

Pointeau, Noémie. "La transmisión de saberes: La producción de vainilla en la colonia francesa de San Rafael, Veracruz (1874–1891)." Paper presented at the Jornada de los Jovenes Americanistas, 2011. https://halshs.archives-ouvertes.fr/halshs-00672268/document.

The Political Constitution of the Mexican United States. Translated by Carlos Pérez Vázquez. Mexico City: UNAM, 2005.

Pollock, Susan. "Decolonizing Archaeology: Political Economy and Archaeological Practice in the Middle East." In *Controlling the Past, Owning the Future: The Political Uses of Archaeology in the Middle East*, edited by Ran Boytner, Lynn Swartz Dodd, and Bradley J. Parker, 196–216. Tucson: University of Arizona Press, 2010.

Poniatowska, Elena. *La noche de Tlatelolco: Testimonios de historia oral*. 1971. Reprint, Mexico City: Ediciones Era, 1998.

Popke, Jeff, and Rebecca Maria Torres. "Neoliberalization, Transnational Migration, and the Varied Landscape of Economic Subjectivity in the Totonacapan Region of Veracruz." *Annals of the Association of American Geographers* 103, no. 1 (2013): 211–29. https://doi.org/10.1080/00045608.2011.652871.

Proskouriakoff, Tatiana. *Varieties of Classic Central Veracruz Sculpture*. Washington DC: Carnegie Institution of Washington, 1954.

Quintal Avilés, Ella F. "Industria petrolera, migración y movilidad social en la zona Poza Rica-Coatzintla, Veracruz." Licenciatura thesis, Universidad de Yucatán, 1981.

Quirke, Stephen. *Hidden Hands: Egyptian Workforces in Petrie Excavation Archives, 1880–1924*. London: Duckworth, 2010.

Raesfeld, Lydia. "New Discoveries at El Tajin, Veracruz." *Mexicon: News and Studies on Mesoamerica* 12, no. 5 (1990): 93–95.

Ramírez Castilla, Gustavo A. "En torno a la restauración de monumentos arqueológicos en México." *La Palabra y el Hombre*, no. 84 (1992): 165–78.

Ramírez Melgarejo, Ramón. *La política del Estado mexicano en los procesos agrícolas y agrarios de los totonacos*. Xalapa: Universidad Veracruzana, 2002.

Reglamento de Admisión. Mexico City: INAH, 1980.

Renfrew, Colin. *Loot, Legitimacy and Ownership: The Ethical Crisis in Archaeology*. London: Bloomsbury Academic, 2000.

Reyes Cruz, Mariolga. "What If I Just Cite Graciela? Working Toward Decolonizing Knowledge Through a Critical Ethnography." *Qualitative Inquiry* 14, no. 4 (2008): 651–58. https://doi.org/10.1177/1077800408314346.

Reyes García, Patricia Eréndira. "Ante Cumbre Tajín, el otro Tajín: El moviemento social en contra de la Cumbre Tajín." Licenciatura thesis, ENAH, 2011.

Reyes López, Marco Antonio. "Análisis cuantitativo de la cerámica de El Tajín, Ver." Licenciatura thesis, Universidad Veracruzana, 1996.

Rice, Mark. *Making Machu Picchu: The Politics of Tourism in Twentieth-Century Peru*. Chapel Hill: University of North Carolina Press, 2018.

Rico, Trinidad. "Heritage at Risk: The Authority and Autonomy of a Dominant Preservation Framework." In *Heritage Keywords: Rhetoric and Redescription in Cultural Heritage*, edited by Kathryn Lafrenz Samuels and Trinidad Rico, 147–62. Boulder: University Press of Colorado, 2015.

———. "Stakeholders in Practice: 'Us,' 'Them,' and the Problem of Expertise." In *Archaeologies of "Us" and "Them": Debating History, Heritage and Indigeneity*, edited by Charlotta Hillerdal, Anna Karlström, and Carl-Gösta Ojala, 38–52. New York: Routledge, 2017.

Rifkin, Mark. *Beyond Settler Time*. Durham: Duke University Press, 2017.

Riguzzi, Paolo, and Francesco Gerali. "Los veneros del Emperador: Impulso petrolero global, intereses y política del petróleo en México durante el Segundo Imperio, 1863–1867." *Historia Mexicana* 65, no. 2 (2015): 747–808. https://doi.org/10.24201/hm.v65i2.3162.

Rivera Sandoval, Eleuterio Enrique. "Consumo cultural en la zona arqueológica del Tajín." Licenciatura thesis, Universidad Veracruzana, 2008.

Robles García, Nelly M., and Jack Corbett. "Heritage Resource Management in Mexico." In *Cultural Heritage Management: A Global Perspective*, edited by Phyllis Mauch Messenger and George S. Smith, 111–23. University Press of Florida, 2010.

Rodríguez, Victoria. *Decentralization in Mexico: From Reforma Municipal to Solidaridad to Nuevo Federalismo*. New York: Routledge, 1997.

Rodríguez Badillo, José Luis. *La maquinita Cobos-Furbero*. Mexico City: Imprenta Serrano Hermanos, 2008.

Rodríguez García, Ignacio. *La arqueología en México: Cultura y privatización*. Mexico City: H. Cámara de Diputados, LXIII Legislatura, 2016.

Rodríguez Morrill, Evelyn I. "Cambio y continuidad en el uso de los recursos naturales entre los totonacas de la costa del Golfo." Licenciatura thesis, Universidad Veracruzana, 1987.

Rojas Ruiz, Minerva. "La Secretaría de Cultura federal mexicana: Tensiones entre dos modelos de administración cultural." *Córima: Revista de investigación en gestión cultural* 2, no. 3 (2017). https://doi.org/10.32870/cor.a2n3.6576.

Román del Valle, Mario A. *Sangre y lucha democrática en Poza Rica*. Xalapa: Códice-Taller Editorial, 2019.

Román Segura, María del Socorro. "Proyecto ATG: Medio ambiente y afectaciones sociales a comunidades totonacas de Papantla, Veracruz." *Clivajes: Revista de ciencias sociales* 5, no. 9 (2018): 153–69. https://doi.org/10.25009/clivajes-rcs.v0i9.2545.

Roseberry, William. *Anthropologies and Histories: Essays in Culture, History, and Political Economy*. New Brunswick NJ: Rutgers University Press, 1989.

———. "Hegemony and the Language of Contention." In *Everyday Forms of State Formation: Revolution and the Negotiation of Rule in Modern Mexico*, edited by Gilbert M. Joseph and Daniel Nugent, 355–66. Durham: Duke University Press, 1994.

———. "Political Economy." *Annual Review of Anthropology* 17 (1988): 161–85. https://doi.org/10.1146/annurev.anthro.17.1.161.

Rosemblatt, Karin Alejandra. *The Science and Politics of Race in Mexico and the United States, 1910–1950*. Chapel Hill: University of North Carolina Press, 2018.

Rozental, Sandra. "On the Nature of Patrimonio: 'Cultural Property' in Mexican Contexts." In *The Routledge Companion to Cultural Property*, edited by Jane Anderson and Haidy Geismar, 237–57. New York: Routledge, 2017.

Rugeley, Terry. *Epic Mexico: A History from Earliest Times*. Norman: University of Oklahoma Press, 2020.

Ruiz Gordillo, J. Omar. *Serafín Olarte: Un insurgente totonaco*. Papantla: Comisión para Investigar la Vida de Serafín Olarte, 1998.

Ruiz Martínez, Apen. *Género, ciencia y política: Voces, vidas y miradas de la arqueología mexicana*. Mexico City: INAH, 2016.

Ruiz Medrano, Carlos Rubén. "Rebeliones indígenas en la época colonial: El tumulto indígena de Papantla de 1767." *Mesoamérica* 32 (1996): 339–53.

Rutsch, Mechthild. *Entre el campo y el gabinete: Nacionales y extranjeros en la profesionalización de la antropología mexicana (1877–1920)*. Mexico City: INAH/UNAM-IIA, 2007.

Salas García, Luis. *Cachiquín*. Xalapa: Editora Graphos, 1979.

Salas Landa, Mónica. "Crude Residues: The Workings of Failing Oil Infrastructure in Poza Rica, Veracruz, Mexico." *Environment and Planning A* 48, no. 4 (2016): 718–35. https://doi.org/10.1177/0308518X15594618.

———. "(In)Visible Ruins: The Politics of Monumental Reconstruction in Postrevolutionary Mexico." *Hispanic American Historical Review* 97, no. 1 (2018): 43–76. https://doi.org/10.1215/00182168-4294456.

Salazar Peralta, Ana María. "La democracia cultural y los movimientos patrimonialistas en México." *Cuicuilco* 13, no. 38 (2006): 73–88.

Saldívar, Emiko. "'It's Not Race, It's Culture': Untangling Racial Politics in Mexico." *Latin American and Caribbean Ethnic Studies* 9, no. 1 (2014): 89–108. https://doi .org/10.1080/17442222.2013.874644.

———. *Prácticas cotidianas del estado: Una etnografía del indigenismo.* Puebla: Universidad Iberoamericana, 2008.

———. "Uses and Abuses of Culture: Mestizaje in the Era of Multiculturalism." *Cultural Studies* 32, no. 3 (2018): 438–59. https://doi.org/10.1080/09502386 .2017.1420092.

Santander Ontiveros, Juan Carlos. *Entre vainillales y fusiles: Rebelión indígena en el Totonacapan, 1836–1838.* Mexico City: Ediciones Navarra, 2016.

Santiago, Myrna. *The Ecology of Oil: Environment, Labor, and the Mexican Revolution, 1900–1938.* Cambridge: Cambridge University Press, 2006.

———. "Oil and Environment in Mexico." *Oxford Bibliographies*, 2016. https://doi .org/10.1093/acrefore/9780199366439.013.319.

Santoyo, Antonio. *La Mano Negra: Poder regional y Estado en México (Veracruz, 1928–1943).* Mexico City: CONACULTA, 1995.

Saragoza, Alex. "The Selling of Mexico: Tourism and the State, 1929–1952." In *Fragments of a Golden Age: The Politics of Culture in Mexico since 1940*, edited by Gilbert M. Joseph, Anne Rubenstein, and Eric Zolov, 90–115. Durham: Duke University Press, 2001.

Schiller, Katalin. "Buscando hogar: Jóvenes totonacos buscando lugar para establecerse." *Acta Hispanica* 23 (2018): 325–39. https://doi.org/10.14232/actahisp .2018.23.325-339.

Schneider, Tsim, and Katherine Hayes. "Epistemic Colonialism: Is It Possible to Decolonize Archaeology?" *American Indian Quarterly* 44, no. 2 (2020): 127–48. https://doi.org/10.1353/aiq.2020.a756930.

Schöneich, Svenja. *Living on a Time Bomb: Local Perspectives and Responses on Oil and Gas Extraction in a Rural Community in Veracruz, Mexico.* New York: Berghahn Books, 2022.

Schryer, Frans J. "Peasants and the Law: A History of Land Tenure and Conflict in the Huasteca." *Journal of Latin American Studies* 18, no. 2 (1986): 283–311. https:// doi.org/10.1017/S0022216X00012037.

Secretaria de Agricultura y Fomento. "Monografias Comerciales: Vainilla." *Boletín mensual de la Dirección de Economía Rural*, no. 204 (1943): 372–90.

Secretaría de Cultura. *Manual general de organización del Instituto Nacional de Antropología e Historia.* Mexico City: INAH, 2017.

Secretaría de Desarrollo Regional. *Programa de manejo: Entorno de El Tajín.* Xalapa: Gobierno del Estado de Veracruz, 2001.

Sellen, Adam T. *In the Shadow of Charnay: The Federal Inspector for Archaeology in Mexico, Lorenzo Pérez Castro.* Mérida: UNAM, 2021.

Shapin, Steven. "The Invisible Technician." *American Scientist* 77, no. 6 (1989): 554–63.

Sheldon, Ruth. "Poza Rica Field Backbone of Oil Industry in Mexico." *Oil and Gas Journal* 38, no. 2 (1939): 26–29.

Shepherd, Nick. "'When the Hand That Holds the Trowel Is Black . . .': Disciplinary Practices of Self-Representation and the Issue of 'Native' Labour in Archaeology." *Journal of Social Archaeology* 3, no. 3 (2003): 334–52. https://doi.org/10.1177 /14696053030033003.

Sherman, William L., Susan M. Deeds, and Michael C. Meyer. *The Course of Mexican History.* New York: Oxford University Press, 2017.

Sinha, Arun K., Upendra K. Sharma, and Nandini Sharma. "A Comprehensive Review on Vanilla Flavor: Extraction, Isolation and Quantification of Vanillin and Others Constituents." *International Journal of Food Sciences and Nutrition* 59, no. 4 (2009): 299–326. https://doi.org/10.1080/09687630701539350.

Skerrit Gardner, David. *Colonos franceses y modernización en el Golfo de México.* Xalapa: Universidad Veracruzana, 1995.

Smail, Daniel Lord, and Andrew Shryock. "History and the 'Pre.'" *American Historical Review* 118, no. 3 (2013): 709–37. https://doi.org/10.1093/ahr/118.3.709.

Smith, Laurajane. "Editorial: A Critical Heritage Studies?" *International Journal of Heritage Studies* 18, no. 6 (2012): 533–40. https://doi.org/10.1080/13527258 .2012.720794.

Smith, Michael E. "The Archaeology of Ancient State Economies." *Annual Review of Anthropology* 33, no. 1 (2004): 73–102. https://doi.org/10.1146/annurev.anthro .33.070203.144016.

Solomon, Char. *Tatiana Proskouriakoff: Interpreting the Ancient Maya.* Norman: University of Oklahoma Press, 2002.

Sordo, Ana María, and Carlos Roberto López. *Exploración, Reservas y producción de petróleo en México, 1970–1985.* Mexico City: El Colegio de México, 1988.

Spinden, Ellen S. "The Place of Tajin in Totonac Archaeology." *American Anthropologist* 35, no. 2 (1933): 225–70. https://doi.org/10.1525/aa.1933.35.2.02a00010.

Stewart, Mart A. *"What Nature Suffers to Groe": Life, Labor, and Landscape on the Georgia Coast, 1680–1920.* Athens: University of Georgia Press, 2002.

Straub, Walther. "Pre-Hispanic Mortuary Pottery, Sherd Deposits and Other Antiquities of the Huasteca." *El México antiguo: Revista internacional de arqueología, etnología, folklore, prehistoria, historia antigua y lingüística mexicana* 1 (1921): 218–37.

Street, Susan. "Burocracia y educación: Hacia un análisis político de la desconcentración administrativa en la Secretaría de Educación Pública (SEP)." *Estudios Sociológicos* 1, no. 2 (1983): 239–61.

Stresser-Pean, Guy. *The Sun God and the Savior: The Christianization of the Nahua and Totonac in the Sierra Norte de Puebla, Mexico*. Boulder: University Press of Colorado, 2009.

Suárez, V., M. Suarez Quezada, S. Oros Ruiz, and E. Ronquillo de Jesús. "Epidemiología de COVID-19 en México: Del 27 de febrero al 30 de abril de 2020." *Revista Clinica Espanola* 220, no. 8 (2020): 463–71. https://doi.org/10.1016/j.rce.2020.05.007.

Sullivan, Paul R. *Unfinished Conversations: Mayas and Foreigners Between Two Wars*. Berkeley: University of California Press, 1991.

Taylor, Analisa. *Indigeneity in the Mexican Cultural Imagination: Thresholds of Belonging*. Tucson: University of Arizona Press, 2009.

Taylor, Sarah R. *On Being Maya and Getting By: Heritage Politics and Community Development in Yucatán*. Boulder: University Press of Colorado, 2018.

Tenorio-Trillo, Mauricio. *Mexico at the World's Fairs: Crafting a Modern Nation*. Berkeley: University of California Press, 1996.

Thomson, Guy P. C. "Agrarian Conflict in the Municipality of Cuetzalan (Sierra de Puebla): The Rise and Fall of 'Pala' Agustin Dieguillo, 1861–1894." *Hispanic American Historical Review* 71, no. 2 (1991): 205–58. https://doi.org/10.1215/00182168-71.2.205.

Topik, Steven. "The Revolution, the State, and Economic Development in Mexico." *History Compass* 3, no. 1 (2005): 1–36. https://doi.org/10.1111/j.1478-0542.2005.00117.x.

Torquemada, Juan de. *Monarquía indiana*. Edited by Miguel León-Portilla. Mexico City: UNAM-IIH, 1983.

Tovar y de Teresa, Rafael. "Hacia una nueva política cultural." In *El patrimonio nacional de Mexico*, edited by Enrique Florescano, 87–107. Mexico City: Fondo de Cultura Económica, 1997.

Trejo Barrientos, Leopoldo. "Los totonacos a través de su etnografía." In *Las lenguas totonacas y tepehuas: Textos y otros materiales para su estudio*, edited by Paulette Levy and David Beck, 467–518. Mexico City: UNAM, 2012.

———. "Paisaje de tormenta: Etnografía del huracán en el Totonacapan." Doctoral thesis, UNAM, 2023.

Trejo González, Jesús. "Los que siguen volando: La danza de los voladores entre los totonacos de Papantla." Licenciatura thesis, Universidad Autonoma Metropolitana Iztapalapa, 2012.

———. "Proyecto comunitario alternativo en la comunidad de San Antonio Ojital, aledaña a la Zona Arqueológico El Tajín." INAH, 2012.

———. "Ruta ecológica y cultural en San Antonio Ojital." Presented in San Antonio Ojital, Papantla, Veracruz, 2012.

Trigger, Bruce G. "Alternative Archaeologies: Nationalist, Colonialist, Imperialist." *Man* 19, no. 3 (1984): 355–70. https://doi.org/10.2307/2802176.

Trouillot, Michel-Rolph. *Silencing the Past: Power and the Production of History*. Boston: Beacon Press, 1995.

Turnbow, Grover Dean, Lloyd Andrew Raffetto, and P. H. Tracy. *The Ice Cream Industry*. New York: J. Wiley & Sons, 1947.

Turner, John Kenneth. *Barbarous Mexico*. Chicago: Charles H. Kerr, 1910.

Tutino, John. *From Insurrection to Revolution in Mexico: Social Bases of Agrarian Violence, 1750–1940*. Princeton: Princeton University Press, 1989.

———. "Rural Economy and Society: 1821–1910." In *Concise Encyclopedia of Mexico*, edited by Michael Werner, 697–705. Chicago: Fitzroy Dearborn Publishers, 2001.

Uhthoff López, Luz María. "La industria del petróleo en México, 1911–1938: Del auge exportador al abastecimiento del mercado interno; Una aproximación a su estudio." *América Latina en la Historia Económica* 17, no. 1 (2010): 5–30. https://doi.org/10.18232/alhe.v17i1.427.

UNESCO. "Operational Guidelines for the Implementation of the World Heritage Convention." Paris: UNESCO World Heritage Center, 1999.

U.S. Bureau of the Census. *Foreign Commerce and Navigation of the United States*. Washington DC: Government Printing Office, 1920–40.

———. *United States Imports of Merchandise for Consumption: Commodity by Country of Origin*. Washington DC: Government Printing Office, 1950–70.

Valadez Moreno, Moisés, and Luis Antonio Huitrón Santoyo. "Balance y perspectiva de los planes de manejo en el INAH." *Hereditas* 15/16 (2011): 50–59.

Valdovinos Ortega, Irving Ezequiel. "El surgimiento de un nuevo centro de población totonaca en el norte de Veracruz: El caso del Zapotal Santa Cruz." Licenciatura thesis, Universidad Autonoma Metropolitana Iztapalapa, 2007.

Valiant, Seonaid. *Ornamental Nationalism: Archaeology and Antiquities in Mexico, 1876–1911*. Leiden: Brill, 2017.

Varner, Natasha. *La Raza Cosmética: Beauty, Identity, and Settler Colonialism in Postrevolutionary Mexico*. Tucson: University of Arizona Press, 2020.

Vaughan, Mary Kay. "Mexico, 1940–1968 and Beyond: Perfect Dictatorship? Dictablanda? Or PRI State Hegemony?" *Latin American Research Review* 53, no. 1 (2018): 167–76. https://doi.org/10.25222/larr.294.

Vázquez León, Luis. *El Leviatán arqueológico: Antropología de una tradición científica en México*. Mexico City: CIESAS, 2003.

———. "Hobbes en la metáfora del arqueólogo enemigo." In *Arqueología, realidades, imaginaciones: Un recuento de la arqueologia por quienes la practican*, edited by Ana María Crespo, Carlos Viramontes, and Ignacio Rodríguez, 31–46. Mexico City: SNTE Delegación D-II-IA-1, 1996.

———. "Mexico: The Institutionalization of Archaeology, 1885–1942." In *History of Latin American Archaeology*, edited by Augusto Oyuela-Caycedo, 69–89. Hampshire: Ashgate Publishing, 1994.

Vázquez Prada, Manuel Llano, and Carla Flores Lot. "La contribución de PEMEX a la emergencia climática: Análisis de emisiones por campo petrolero desde 1960." Mexico City: CartoCrítica, 2019.

Vázquez Valdés, Veronica. "Entre naguas y calzones: La vestimenta de los totonacos de El Tajín de 1947–1951 a partir de la mirada de Isabel Kelly." Doctoral thesis, ENAH, 2014.

Velasco Toro, José, and Luis J. García Ruiz. *Perfiles de la desamortización civil en Veracruz*. Xalapa: Gobierno del Estado de Veracruz, 2009.

Velázquez García, Mario Alberto. "La formulación de las políticas públicas de turismo en México: El caso del programa federal 'Pueblos Mágicos' 2001–2012." *Diálogos Latinoamericanos* 14, no. 21 (2013): 89–110. https://doi.org/10.7146/dl .v14i21.113255.

Velázquez Hernández, Emilia. *Cuando los arrieros perdieron sus caminos: La conformación regional del Totonacapan*. Zamora, Michoacán: El Colegio de Michoacán, 1995.

Vera Cortés, Gabriela. "Totonacapan, 1999: El Año de la Bestia." In *Devastación y éxodo: Memoria de seminarios sobre reubicaciones por desastres en México*, edited by Gabriela Vera Cortés, 59–80. Mexico City: CIESAS, 2009.

Vergara, Germán. *Fueling Mexico: Energy and Environment, 1850–1950*. Cambridge: Cambridge University Press, 2021.

Villalobos Acosta, Cesar. "Light Shows and Narratives of the Past." *International Journal of Historical Archaeology* 17, no. 2 (2013): 332–50. https://doi.org/10.1007 /s10761-013-0224-3.

Villanueva, Margaret Ann. "Region and Power: The Contested Terrains of Nature, Race, Gender, and Class in Totonacapan, Gulf Coast, Mexico, 1492–1992." Doctoral thesis, University of California, Santa Cruz, 1991.

Villa-Señor y Sánchez, Joseph Antonio. *Teatro Americano: Descripción general de los Reinos, y Provincias de la Nueva-España y sus jurisdicciones*. 2 vols. Mexico City: Imprenta de la Viuda de Joseph Bernardo de Hogal, 1746.

von Humboldt, Alexander. *Political Essay on the Kingdom of New Spain*. Edited by Vera M. Kutzinski and Ottmar Ette. Translated by J. Ryan Poynter, Kenneth Berri, and Vera M. Kutzinski. 2 vols. Chicago: University of Chicago Press, 2019.

Wakild, Emily. *Revolutionary Parks: Conservation, Social Justice, and Mexico's National Parks, 1910–1940*. Tucson: University of Arizona Press, 2011.

Walsh Sanderson, Susan R. *Land Reform in Mexico: 1910–1980*. Orlando: Academic Press, 1984.

Warman, Arturo, Margarita Nolasco, Guillermo Bonfil Batalla, Enrique Valencia, and Mercedes Olivera. *De eso que llaman antropología mexicana*. Mexico City: Editorial Nuestro Tiempo, 1970.

Watkins, Joe. "Through Wary Eyes: Indigenous Perspectives on Archaeology." *Annual Review of Anthropology* 34 (2005): 429–49. https://doi.org/10.1146 /annurev.anthro.34.081804.120540.

Weber, Max. "Bureaucracy." In *Max Weber on Charisma and Institution Building*, edited by S. N. Eisenstadt, 66–77. Chicago: University of Chicago Press, 1968.

Weiss, Margot. "The Interlocutor Slot: Citing, Crediting, Cotheorizing, and the Problem of Ethnographic Expertise." *American Anthropologist* 123, no. 4 (2021): 948–53. https://doi.org/10.1111/aman.13639.

Wendt, Carl J., and Ann Cyphers. "How the Olmec Used Bitumen in Ancient Mesoamerica." *Journal of Anthropological Archaeology* 27, no. 2 (2008): 175–91. https://doi.org/10.1016/j.jaa.2008.03.001.

West, Paige, James Igoe, and Dan Brockington. "Parks and Peoples: The Social Impact of Protected Areas." *Annual Review of Anthropology* 35, no. 1 (2006): 251–77. https://doi.org/10.1146/annurev.anthro.35.081705.123308.

Wilkerson, S. Jeffrey K. "And the Waters Took Them: Catastrophic Flooding and Civilization on the Mexican Gulf Coast." In *El Niño, Catastrophism, and Culture Change in Ancient America*, edited by Daniel H. Sandweiss and Jeffrey Quilter, 243–71. Cambridge: Dumbarton Oaks Research Library and Collection, 2008.

————. "Eastern Mesoamerica from Pre-Hispanic to Colonial Times: A Model of Cultural Continuance." In *Actas du XLII Congrès International des Amèricanistes*, vol. 8, 41–55. Paris: Fondation Singer-Polignac, 1979.

————. "Huastec Presence and Cultural Chronology in North-Central Veracruz, Mexico." In *Actas du XLII Congrès International des Amèricanistes*, vol. 9B, 31–47. Paris: Fondation Singer-Polignac, 1979.

————. "Nahua Presence on the Mesoamerican Gulf Coast." In *Chipping Away on Earth: Studies in Prehispanic and Colonial Mexico in Honor of Arthur J.O. Anderson and Charles E. Dibble*, edited by Eloise Quiñones Keber, 177–86. Lancaster CA: Labyrinthos, 1994.

Williams, Mark Eric. "The Path of Economic Liberalism." In *The Oxford Handbook of Mexican Politics*, edited by Roderic Ai Camp, 744–76. Oxford: Oxford University Press, 2012.

Wolf, Eric R. *Europe and the People without History*. Berkeley: University of California Press, 2010.

Wood, Andrew Grant. "Introduction: Travel History's Checkered Past as Prelude to Future Catastrophe?" In *The Business of Leisure: Tourism History in Latin America and the Caribbean*, edited by Andrew Grant Wood, 1–20. Lincoln: University of Nebraska Press, 2021.

Wylie, Alison. "The Integrity of Narratives: Deliberative Practice, Pluralism, and Multivocality." In *Evaluating Multiple Narratives: Beyond Nationalist, Colonialist, Imperialist Archaeologies*, edited by Junko Habu, Clare Fawcett, and John M. Matsunaga, 201–12. New York: Springer, 2008.

Xochihua García, Brehnis Daniel. "Dinámicas económicas, demográficas y sociales en la hacienda San Miguel del Rincón, Papantla, 1890–1940: La propiedad, el capital, la mano de obra y el ejido." Maestría thesis, Universidad Veracruzana, 2024.

Yadeun, Juan. "Arqueología de la arqueología." *Revista Mexicana de Estudios Antropológicos* 24, no. 2 (1978): 147–212.

Yáñez Reyes, Sergio. "El Instituto Nacional de Antropología e Historia: Antecedentes, trayectoria y cambios a partir de la creación del CONACULTA." *Cuicuilco* 13, no. 38 (2006): 47–72.

Yashar, Deborah J. "Democracy, Indigenous Movements, and the Postliberal Challenge in Latin America." *World Politics* 52, no. 1 (1999): 76–104. https://doi.org/10.1017/S0043887100020037.

Younging, Gregory. *Elements of Indigenous Style: A Guide for Writing by and about Indigenous Peoples.* Edmonton AB: Brush Education, 2018.

Zepeda Martínez, Roberto. *The Decline of Labor Unions in Mexico during the Neoliberal Period.* Cham, Switzerland: Palgrave Macmillan, 2021.

Zhu, Annah. "Hot Money, Cold Beer: Navigating the Vanilla and Rosewood Export Economies in Northeastern Madagascar." *American Ethnologist* 45, no. 2 (2018): 253–67. https://doi.org/10.1111/amet.12636.

Žižek, Slavoj. *Violence: Six Sideways Reflections.* New York: Picador, 2009.

Zona de Monumentos Arqueológicos El Tajín. "Informe de actividades del programa integral de actividades, febrero-diciembre 2010." Veracruz: Centro INAH Veracruz, 2010.

Zúñiga Bravo, Federico Gerardo. "Las transformaciones del territorio y el patrimonio cultural en el Totonacapan Veracruzano, basadas en la actividad turística como estrategia de desarrollo regional." *Cuadernos de Turismo* 34 (2014): 351–72.

———. "Nuevos usos del patrimonio arqueológico de El Tajín, a través de los procesos de turistificación, mercantilización y espectularización." *Anales de antropología* 48, no. 2 (2014): 151–82. https://doi.org/10.1016/S0185-1225(14)70247-4.

Index

Page numbers in italics refer to illustrations.

practice, 16; of Veracruz, 158. *See also* heritage management

Cumbre Tajín, 46, 138, 145, 155–60, 167

curing, vanilla, 76–77, 80, 83, 88–92, 94, 95–96, 160, 167

Curti, Rodolfo, 83

custodios, 1–4, 16, 20–21, 50, 73, 75, 96, 99, 105, 107, 114–24, 127–28, 130–45, 147–50, 153–54, 160–64, 167, 207n9, 209n56; cohort in formation, 139–40; cohort timeline, 125; intermediate cohort, 130, 134–38, 140; *nuevo*, 132, 136–37, 164, 203n16; tenure and, 111, 117; in Teotihuacan, 210n81; Totonac, 121, 147, 203n3. See also *administrativos*; *conserjes*; De León Méndez, Epifanio; *encargados*; González González, Modesto; Juárez González, Onésimo; *nuevos*; Pérez Bautista, Pedro; *viejos trabajadores*

Cuyuxquihui, 11, 19, 126, 202n1

Dancey, William, 31

Dawson, Alexander, 14, 204n28, 208n30

Decuir Lathiolait, Luciano, 92–94, 196n74

DeGolyer Library, 18–19

Dehesa, Teodoro, 93

De la Barra, Luis, 57

De la Luz Enríquez, Juan, 26

De la Madrid Hurtado, Miguel, 14, 150

De la Mota y Escobar, Alonso, 9, 177nn55–56

Del Cueto Decuir, Raúl, 83, 94–95, 198n92

De León Méndez, Epifanio, 114

Deloria, Philip J., 18

Del Palacio Langer, Ana Julia, 66, 193n7

Departamento de Monumentos Prehispánicos, 34, 59, 104, 127, 179n88

deregulation, 14–15, 150

De Tapia Sosa, Andrés, 10, 177n58

Díaz, Porfirio, 7, 11–12, 25–26, 54, 93, 182n39

Dirty War, 13

disentailment, 24, 26, 28–29, 40–41, 48; aftermath of, 57; El Tajín and, 33; patrimony and, 35; space and, 31, 36, 48–49

dispossession, 20, 23–25, 29, 42, 44, 47–48; land, 19–20, 24, 48, 87, 103, 110, 113–14, 167, 170; violent, 104

Dos Bocas fire (1908), 55, 58

Doyon, Wendy, 98

drilling, 59–60, 63, 67, 69, 71–72; in El Tajín, 61, 126; of Ojital-1, 55, 71; in Ojital y Potrero, 188n58; permissions, 48; in Poza Rica, 110; unauthorized, 27

Duarte de Ochoa, Javier, 158, 160, 210n72, 210n74

Ducey, Michael, 6

Dunnell, Robert, 31

Dupaix, Guillermo, 100–101

Echeverría Álvarez, Luis, 132, 150

Ecuador, 3, 15

ejidos, 24, 36–37, 40, 63, 74, 184n68; communities of, 169; solicitation for, 184n60; Totonac, 72. *See also* disentailment

Emiliano Zapata, 63, 66, 71–72

encargados, 113, 135, 137, 145, 149–50, 152–55, 160; site, 115–17, 123, 128, 130–31, 152. *See also* García Payón, José; González González, Modesto; González Méndez, Teódulo; Pérez Bautista, Pedro

Escallón, María Fernanda, 186n99

Escolin, 29, 66, 190n93

ethnography, 18, 19, 106, 176n49

Everill, Paul, 98

excavation, 53, 91, 104, 136, 152, 166; Agustín García Vega and, 60–61, 86–87; Arturo Pascual Soto and, 48;

excavation (*cont.*)
custodios and, 127; edge of, 15; Erasmo Rodríguez and, 87, 126; illicit, 7; informal, 7; José García Payón and, 41, 130; large-scale, 34; as masculine labor, 109; salvage, 47; scholarly interpretation and, 98; state-sponsored, 61, 149
experts, 19, 21, 112, 141, 145, 147, 158, 163
export economies, 4, 11
expropriation, 38, 43, 48, 53, 54, 61–63, 186n13
extractive industry, 20, 48, 53, 71

Ferral, Francisco, 110
Ferral, María Elena, 169
Ferry, Elizabeth Emma, 35
Fontecilla Agustina, Agapito, 92, 196n66
Fontecilla y Fontecilla, Agapito Guillermo, 92–94, 96, 125, 128
Fontecilla y Vidal, Agapito, 91–94, 96, 125, 128, 196n74
Foster, George, 82
Fox Quesada, Vicente, 15, 46
France, 79–80, 194n29
Frederick, Jake, 177n55
Furber, Percy Norman, 57
Furbero, 55, 57–58, 68
Furbero–Presidente Miguel Alemán–Remolino Project, 69

Gándara, Manuel, 174n10, 205n42
García, Francisco, 33–34, 44, 183n52
García, José María, 34, 183n52
García, Rosalía, 34
García Payón, José, 36–37, 40–41, 43–44, 64–66, 71, 99, 106–8, 114–16, 141, 204n35; death of, 133; excavations of, 41; *Exploraciones en El Tajín*, 97–98, 103; field house of, 51, 52, 62; INAH and, 36, 40, 149; Pedro Pérez Bautista and, 113, 130–31, 137, 150, 154; projects

of, 127–28, 130, 149; Raúl del Cueto and, 94–95; S. Jeffrey K. Wilkerson and, 112; *viejos trabajadores* and, 123, 130, 135; violence and, 87
García Vega, Agustín, 34–37, 44, 97, 141; Compañía Stanford and, 60, 71; excavations of, 60–61, 86–87, 99, 104, 107, 115, 149; masons and, 112; Pedro Pérez Bautista and, 113, 130, 154; surveys by, 40, 61; topographic expertise of, 66
Gazeta de México, 10, 99–101
gender, 109, 200n42
Gillingham, Paul, 12
González González, Modesto, 31, 33, 37, 110–11, 113, 115–16, 127–28, 129, 149, 202n85, 203n3
González Méndez, Faustino, 111–13, 115–16, 198n3
González Méndez, Rosalino, 111, 128, 204n35
González Méndez, Teódulo, 113, 115, 128, 154, 204n35, 205nn36–37
González Méndez, Tirso, 86, 110–11, 113
Guardia Nacional, 163
Guatemala, 3, 162, 176n46, 210n74

Hale, Charles R., 203n10
Hall, Raymond A., 177n64
Hamilton, Charles, 58
Hayes, Katherine, 8
heritage, 16, 94; archaeological, 150, 157; conservation of, 47; cultural, 2, 6, 16, 24, 135, 141, 145, 155, 158, 166; Indigenous, 13; industrial, 57; law, 119; legislation, 5; local politics of, 75; managers, 6, 148, 162; of Mexico, 2–3, 150, 156–57; natural, 53; practices of, 160; studies, 174n18; trekking, 18
heritage management, 4, 95, 117, 150, 153, 174n10; cultural, 148, 150; INAH and, 64, 148, 163; legal objectives of, 15; local, 21; Mexican, 166; neoliberal,

labor (*cont.*)

145; collective, 97, 126; communal, 29, 38, 103, *109*; contracts, 160; division of, 26, 75, 77, 108–9, 122, 126, 131, 136, 138, 141, 149; of enslaved Africans, 10, 79, 195n42; Indigenous, 20, 121; intercommunal, 81; mobility, 161; opportunities, 72; organized, 107, 119, 132; reciprocal, 116; state and, 108, 132; Totonac, 20, 96, 101, 167; vanilla and, 84–85, 88–89; wage, 99, 103, 106, 113–16, 130, 134, 136

land, 3, 23–26, 29, 31, 35–38, 41–44, 46–48, 59, 62, 82, 92, 106, 110–11, 139; ancestral, 16; conflicts, 37; dispossession, 19–20, 24, 48, 87, 103, 110, 113–14, 167, 170; donation of, 51; Indigenous, 110; labor and, 10; loss, 37, 185n82; ownership, 28, 33, 41, 117, 134, 151, 154; as private property, 1, 103, 166; reform, 11, 14, 19, 24, 37, 53, 136, 179n97, 184n68; Totonac, 38, 110; use, 3, 37, 41, 48, 66, 154. *See also* landowners

landowners, 40–43, 46, 49, 93, 166, 182n35; conflicts with archaeologists and, 34, 40–41, 75, 86; Totonac, 24–25, 36, 103, 109, 117

land tenure, 11, 25–26, 38, 41, 49, 185n95; archaeology and, 19; communal, 26, 40, 103; transformations in, 4–5, 8

language of lots and parcels, 24–25, 34, 41, 43, 48

La Riviere, Juan B., 61, 66

La Venta, 48

Law of Archaeological Monuments, 53, 182n40

Leighton, Mary, 98

Lemke, Thomas, 151

Ley Federal de Monumentos y Zonas Arqueológicas, 119

liberalization, 14–15

LIDAR mapping, 71, 191n114, 192n136

listas de raya, 105, 199n41, 201n68, 204n35

looting, 6–7

López Hernández, Haydeé, 6

López Luján, Leonardo, 101

López Mata, Carlos, 38, 40, 66

López Obrador, Andrés Manuel, 2

López Vallejo, Francisco Javier, 199n37

Lorenzo, José Luis, 7, 18, 33

Lucas, Gavin, 97

Lurtz, Casey Marina, 11

Madagascar, 79–80, 95, 110, 194n29

Management Plan (El Tajín), 69, 119, 153, 155, 158, 160

Marié, Isidoro O., 93–94, 194n78

Marin, Fernando, 92–93

Márquez, Pedro José, 10, 99

Marquina, Ignacio, 86, 97

Martínez de la Torre, 144, 194n26

masons, 96–97, 99, 107, 111–12, 116, 120, 198n3

Mayas, 3, 5, 12, 175n35, 175n37

Medellín Zenil, Alfonso, 41, 151, 176n46

Méndez, Agustín, 86

Méndez, Albino, 86

Méndez, Honorato, 94, 126

Merino, Jaime J., 75, 193n7

Meskell, Lynn, 6

Mesoamerica, 4, 13, 130, 174n12

mestizos, 77, 79

Mexican Miracle, 13, 75

Mexican Revolution, 6, 11–12, 28, 34, 103, 124, 127; aftermath of, 54, 107, 127; archaeological monuments and, 35; land reform and, 24; violence of, 59

Mexico City, 18, 38, 92, 110, 133, 136, 149, 161–62; 1985 earthquake and, 14; INAH in, 3–4, 152, 163; Olympics in, 13

Mickel, Allison, 98

milpas, 9, 101, 103, 111, 113, 200n55; and *acahual*, 83, 87, 106; clearing, 106, 116; pasturelands and, 38; planting, 106; preparation of, 108

To order or obtain more information on these or other University
of Nebraska Press titles, visit nebraskapress.unl.edu.

www.ingramcontent.com/pod-product-compliance
Lightning Source LLC
Chambersburg PA
CBHW030344270326
41926CB00009B/950